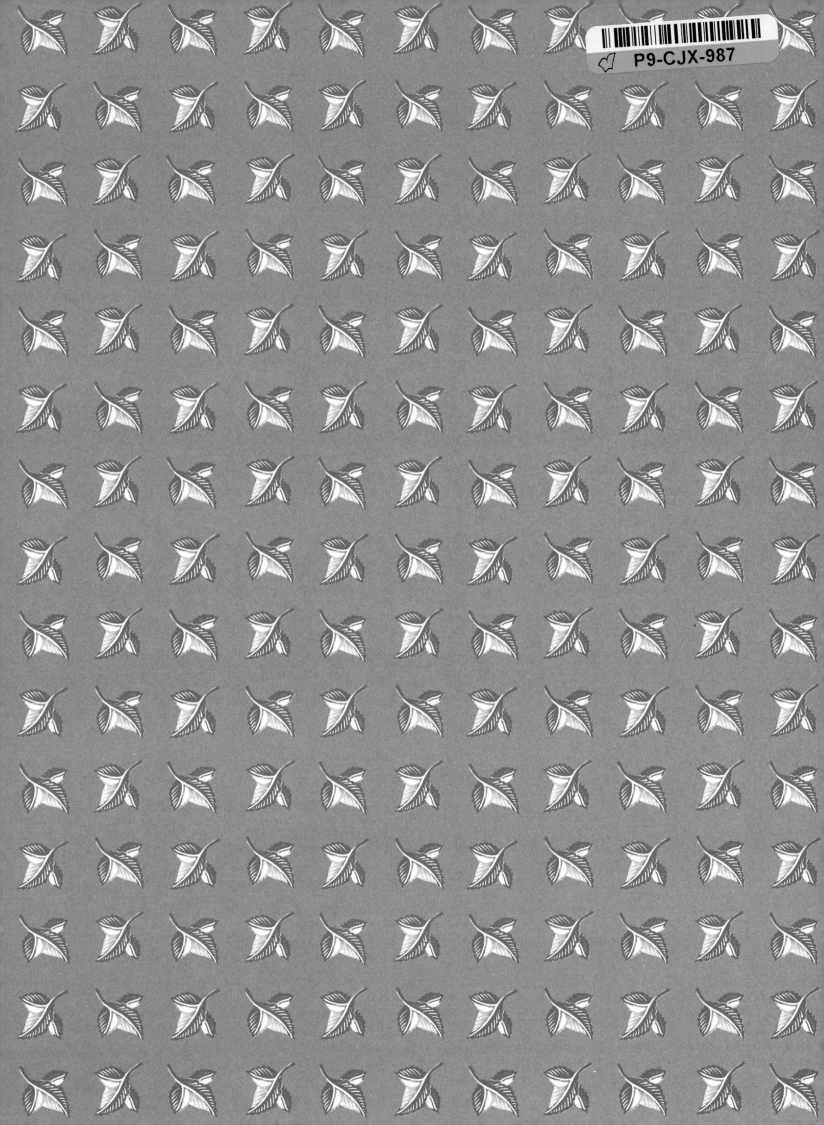

The Complete Encyclopedia of

VEGETABLES <u>AND</u>
VEGETARIAN
COOKING

The Complete Encyclopedia of

VEGETABLES AND VEGETARIAN COOKING

CHRISTINE INGRAM
WITH
ROZ DENNY AND KATHERINE RICHMOND

HERMES HOUSE

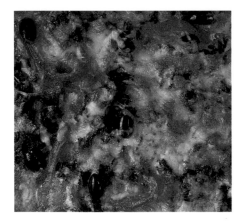

This edition published by Hermes House
27 West 20th Street, New York, NY 10011

HERMES HOUSE books are available for bulk purchase for sales promotion
and for premium use. For details, write or call the sales director,
Hermes House, 27 West 20th Street, New York, NY 10011;
(800) 354-9657

Hermes House is an imprint of
Anness Publishing Inc.

ISBN 1 901289 03 6

Publisher: Joanna Lorenz
Editors: Christopher Fagg and Lydia Darbyshire
Guide to Vegetables by: Christine Ingram
Recipes by: Christine Ingram, Roz Denny and Katherine Richmond
Photographs by: Patrick McLeavey, Michael Michaels and Michelle Garrett
Home Economists: Jane Stevenson, Wendy Lee and Liz Trigg
Design Styling by: Patrick McLeavey
Setting by: SX Composing DTP
Index by: Lydia Darbyshire

Printed and bound in Germany

© Anness Publishing Limited 1997
Updated © 1999

1 3 5 7 9 10 8 6 4 2

NOTES

....

For all recipes, quantities are given in both metric and imperial
measures and, where appropriate, measures are also given in standard
cups and spoons. Follow one set, but not a mixture, because they are
not interchangeable.

Size 3 (standard) eggs should be used unless otherwise stated.

CONTENTS

INTRODUCTION

VEGETABLES CAN PLAY A STARRING ROLE in a recipe or they may be combined with other ingredients in a harmony of flavors. Some of the best-known vegetable soups are examples of well-tuned mixtures – minestrone, for instance, is a blend of carrots, tomatoes and beans with pasta; or a good old-fashioned vegetable soup brings together simple ingredients such as carrots, turnips and leeks with a grain, such as barley. These, and many other dishes, are loved for the sum of their parts, rather than for the taste of the different vegetables from which they have been made. In general, however, in this book you will find recipes that make the most of an individual vegetable, so that the particular virtues of each one may be appreciated to the full.

The recipes in the second half of this book are an eclectic mix of classic dishes from around the world, together with others that have been devised to make the most of individual ingredients or combinations of ingredients. By far the majority of recipes in this book are designed with vegetarians in mind, and most of them are

vegetables that can delight the palate. So this book has been written not just for those converted to the virtues of vegetarianism; it is also intended to tempt "omnivores" to the vegetarian way of eating and to show that it is possible to produce a delicious and attractive meal, free from the tyranny of the "meat and two vegetables" way of menu planning.

THE VEGETARIAN DIET

The golden rule that nutritionists and doctors ask us to practice is to eat all foods in moderation and to eat a great variety of foods. This variety is especially important for vegetarians.

Because vegetarians eat more grains, vegetables, legumes and fruit in their diet than meat eaters, they seem to obtain a greater amount of dietary fiber. However, they have to be careful not to increase

particular problem for vegetarians if they are not aware of the sources from which it can be obtained. In addition, iron from vegetable sources cannot be utilized by the body unless there is vitamin C present in the same meal to act as a catalyst. But a small piece of fruit, fresh salad or even a good squeeze of lemon juice will soon redress that problem.

Vegans (those who exclude dairy products from their diet) need to make sure they take in sufficient calcium, either in the form of calcium tablets or calcium-enriched soy milk. They may also need to supplement their diet with other vitamins and minerals. A vegan diet can be just as healthy as a well-balanced omnivorous diet, as long as followers are well informed about suitable foods.

THE VEGETARIAN PANTRY

The basis of the vegetarian diet is, of course, formed by vegetables of all kinds, and on pages 14–139 we look at the enormous variety of vegetables that is available today and assess their nutritional value

suitable for vegans. There is, however, a small section of "virtually vegetarian" recipes that include seafood and fish.

The great thing about cooking with vegetables is that, once you have the hang of using them, recipes become more or less unnecessary. As you experiment, perhaps substituting seasonal produce for the ingredients listed, you will discover how to enjoy carrots, asparagus or any of the less often seen and used

their intake of high-fat dairy products such as cheese, butter and cream. Just like meat eaters, they should watch their intake of these potentially high-cholesterol products. Whenever possible, choose lower-fat versions, which are usually well labeled. Changing from whole milk to low-fat or skim milk helps, as does eating plenty of low-fat yogurt, cottage cheese and skim-milk soft cheeses.

Lack of iron can also be a

and ways of preparing them. First, however, we will review in nutritional terms the main ingredients that are used in the recipes in the second half of this book.

THE STARCHY FOODS

The total contribution of carbohydrate (starchy) foods and vegetables in a well-balanced diet may not be entirely understood, but the benefits and protective role they play in ensuring good health is widely recognized. Experts agree that we should eat a high proportion of vegetables and complex carbohydrates in our everyday diets. This is great news for vegetarians and all creative cooks, as these foodstuffs are versatile, nourishing and, best of all, cheap. They also store well without refrigeration and can be cooked with a minimum of preparation. Starchy foods have reasonable amounts of protein plus vitamins from the B group and minerals such as phosphorus, zinc, iron, potassium and, in the case of bread, added calcium. The other main advantage is that they are good sources of dietary fiber.

FLOURS

A selection of different flours is a necessity for versatile baking. Often it is a good idea to mix two types together for added flavor and texture. Use half whole-wheat and half all-purpose flour for a lighter brown pastry crust or bread loaf. Mix buckwheat flour with all-purpose flour for pancakes, and so on. Flour is a good source of protein as well as complex carbohydrate, and it is indispensable in cooking. Whole-grain flours have a shorter shelf life than the more refined types of white flours. Remember, too, that self-rising flours, with their added rising agent, lose their lightening ability after about six months.

RICE

Top of the rice range is basmati, an elegant, fragrant, long-grain rice, grown in the foothills of the Himalayas. Traditionally eaten with curries, basmati is marvelous in almost all dishes, sweet and savory,

especially pilafs. Brown basmati is a lighter whole-grain rice with higher levels of dietary fiber. Thai rices are delicate and lightly sticky, and they are particularly good in stir-fries and wonderful in milk puddings. Wild rice (which is not a true rice but an aquatic grass) has good levels of proteins. Pre-soaking shortens the cooking time.

PASTA

The mainstay of many a cook in a hurry, pasta is a good source of starchy complex carbohydrates, and it is available in a multitude of shapes, colors and flavors. Good pasta should be cooked to a tender texture but retain a firm bite, which the Italians call *al dente* ("to the tooth"). For this, choose pasta that is made with durum wheat or semolina. Cook pasta in plenty of

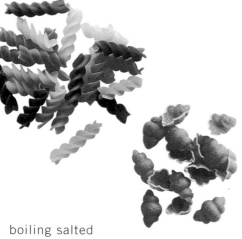

boiling salted water according to the instructions on the package, then drain, rinse in cold water and shake lightly. Italians serve pasta slightly wet. Return it to the pan with some olive oil, seasoning and a grating of fresh nutmeg.

FATS AND OILS

For general frying, choose oils high in polyunsaturates. Sunflower, canola and peanut oils have the lightest flavors, and these are the ones preferred by gourmet cooks.

Corn oil and blended vegetable oils are stronger in flavor. Olive oil is increasingly popular. Not only highly prized for flavor, it also has properties beneficial to health. Olive oil is high in monosaturates, which are thought to help reduce blood cholesterol levels. Two main qualities

are available – pure olive oil, which is excellent for general cooking, and extra-virgin oil, which is made from the first cold pressing of the olives, producing a full-flavored, almost peppery taste. It is excellent for dressing salads and as a healthier substitute for butter. Aromatic seed and nut oils, such as sesame, walnut and hazelnut, are too heavy and expensive for general use, but they are excellent for trickling on hot vegetables, legumes or pasta.

All fats, unless specifically labeled "lower" or "reduced fat," contain approximately the same amount of calories. It is the type of fat within them that counts when it comes to our health. Sunflower and olive oil spreads are lower in harmful saturates and higher in healthier polyunsaturates and monosaturates. Spreads labeled "low fat" or "reduced fat" will have more added water, which helps to reduce the calories but makes them less than ideal for frying and baking.

Fats and oils are important in our diets, contributing vital vitamins, such as A, D and E, so do not cut them out altogether. Include them in moderate amounts. Check labels for full nutritional details, and remember to restrict your fat intake to no more than one-third of your total daily intake of calories.

CHEESE

A popular high-protein food with vegetarians, cheese is also high in calories, having twice the number of many carbohydrate and protein foods. For fuller flavor, choose aged varieties of cheese such as aged farmhouse Cheddar or fresh Parmesan – you will then not need to use as much.

For cooking, choose aged, hard cheeses. As these full-flavored cheeses age, the moisture evaporates; this concentrates the flavor and makes them go further when they are finely grated. Well wrapped in foil and stored in the bottom of the refrigerator, they will keep for months. Among the most useful cheeses are fully mature Cheddar, fresh Parmesan, mature Gruyère and Pecorino (an Italian sheep's cheese). Lower-fat soft cheeses and goat cheeses are ideal for stirring into hot food to make an instant, tasty, creamy sauce.

DAIRY PRODUCTS

Supermarkets carry a wide range of cultured dairy goods, which present many exciting opportunities for the home cook. Crème fraîche is a French-style sour cream that does not curdle when boiled, so it is ideal stirred into hot dishes. It will also whip, adding a light piquancy to desserts. However, like heavy cream, it is quite high in fat (40 percent), so use it sparingly.

Fromage blanc is a smooth, lightly tangy, lower-fat to virtually fat-free "cream," ideal for use in dressings, baked potatoes and desserts. Ricotta cheese is a soft cheese made with skim milk and is, therefore, very low in fat. It is a traditional cheese for

using in cheese-cakes, but it is ideal for savory dishes, too. Cream and cottage cheeses are long-time favorites, the latter now available in very low-fat versions for even healthier eating.

DAIRY-FREE PRODUCTS

The unassuming soybean is one of the best sources of high vegetable-protein foods. As such, it is ideal as a base for dairy-free milks, creams, spreads, ice creams and cheeses, making it perfect for vegans and those with dairy-product allergies. Use these products in the same way as their dairy counterparts, although those

changing over will find that the soy products taste slightly sweeter.

Tofu, or bean curd, is made with soy milk and is particularly versatile in vegetarian cooking, both as a main ingredient in recipes or to add creamy, firm texture. On its own, tofu has little flavor, making it ideal to use as an absorber of other flavors, which is why it is so popular in Asian cooking. Firm tofu or bean curd can be cut into cubes, marinated or smoked. It is very good fried in oil or grilled to a crisp, golden crust. A softer-set tofu,

called silken tofu, is a good substitute for cream in cooking, and as such can be stirred into hot soups or used as a base for baked tarts. Indeed, at any time that cream or milk is called for in a recipe, tofu can be used. Not only high in protein, tofu is a good source of vitamins of the B group and of iron, although, since it is a vegetable source of iron, you will need to serve some vitamin C at the same meal to utilize it.

Mycoprotein (sold under the brand name Quorn) is a new man-made food which is not widely available in the United States. Low in fat and calories, it is high in protein, with as much fiber as green vegetables. It cooks quickly, absorbing flavors as easily as soy-bean curd, and it has a firmer texture. It is good for stir-frys, stews and casseroles.

NUTS AND SEEDS

Not only are they full of flavor, texture and color, but nuts and seeds are great nutritional power packs. Like cheese, however, they can be high in fat as well as protein.

Cheapest and most versatile are peanuts, which are best bought unsalted or, even better, roasted unsalted. Almonds (blanched or flaked) are also very useful, as are walnuts, pine nuts, hazelnuts and the more expensive cashews. Often it is nice to mix two or three together. But nuts can go rancid if they are stored for too long (over about six months), so if you are not a regular user, buy in small quantities.

For maximum flavor, lightly roast nuts before chopping or crushing. Use them as crisp coatings, too, but watch that they don't burn.

There is an increasing range of colorful and exciting seeds available in health-food stores. Most useful are sunflower and sesame seeds, while pumpkin and melon seeds are delicious scattered into salads or simply nibbled as a snack. Seeds for attractive garnish as well as flavor include poppy seeds, black mustard, fenugreek and caraway seeds. Most of all, nuts and seeds look simply stunning lined up in clean storage jars on kitchen shelves, tempting you to toss them into a variety of dishes, hot and cold.

HERBS

Wherever possible, try to use fresh herbs. There are many that will grow easily and obligingly in pots and small backyard gardens, as well as surviving winter cold. Good candidates include shrubby rosemary, thyme, bay and sage. Even chives and marjoram can survive well into late autumn and return obligingly in early spring. However, more and more food stores sell packages and bunches of fresh herbs that are grown commercially.

Specialty stores are good sources of a wide variety of unusual and good-flavored herbs. Most useful are flat-leaf parsley, cilantro, dill, basil, chives and mint. Do not use one herb per dish: mix and match, experimenting with different combinations. Although you should not skimp on herbs, the more

pungent ones, such as tarragon, rosemary and sage, still need a cautious touch.

Handfuls of fresh, leafy herbs are wonderfully exciting additions to green salads. There is no need to finely chop them. Fill a mug with washed sprigs of herbs, then snip them roughly with scissors. Store leafy herbs loosely in plastic food bags in the fridge, spraying them lightly with water if they look limp. They spring back almost magically.

If you use dried herbs, buy small amounts and store them in a dry,

cool cupboard so that they retain their flavor. Replace dried herbs regularly, as they soon lose their color and flavor, and end up tasting like dried grass.

SPICES

The vegetarian's best friend! Warm, aromatic, colorful and easy to use, spices can make the simplest dish

supreme. It is a misconception to think that spices are pungently hot. Most are not; it is really only those of the chili family, including cayenne, that are. Some spices, such as nutmeg, cinnamon, mace, cloves, cardamom and ginger, are useful for both sweet and savory dishes. Others, such as fenugreek, turmeric, paprika, cumin, coriander berries and chili, are used mainly

for savory dishes.

Spices are made for experimenting. Gradually you will learn which are the most pungent and to your liking. Some have glorious colors, like turmeric and paprika; others have a distinctive flavor. Add them in cautious pinches at first, until you decide what you enjoy most.

Spices are best roasted first, to bring out the aromatic oils. This can be done either in a hot oven or a frying pan. Where possible, use the seeds or grains of spices first, and grind them down in a small electric spice mill or a mortar and pestle. Saffron (a most expensive spice) is best soaked briefly in a little warm water or milk to bring out its true flavor and pretty color.

And don't keep spices just for ethnic and exotic dishes. Add them to home-cooked favorites – try macaroni and cheese with paprika and cumin or fried eggs sprinkled with black mustard seeds.

THE VEGETABLES

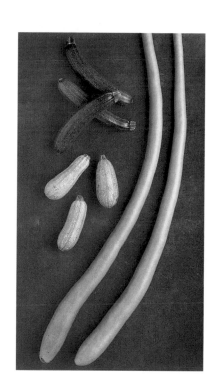

Plants have formed an essential part of man's diet since the earliest times. Archaeological evidence indicates that forms of wheat and barley, believed to be the first crops, were farmed in the Middle East as early as 8000 BC. Many edible plants are native to this area, so it can be assumed that vegetables were also eaten, if only to relieve what must have been a fairly monotonous diet.

Beans and peas were among the first vegetables to be farmed in Thessaly and Macedonia, and these legumes would have been enormously important to early societies because they grew easily, dried well for long storage and provided a starchy food, high in protein.

Many of our familiar vegetables werc cultivated in historic times: the Egyptians grew onions, garlic,

radishes, lettuce and fava beans; the Greeks and Romans farmed produce that was native to their own countries. They also discovered a wide range of plants through their contacts with other cultures. Not only did the Romans discover the fruits of other lands, but their expansion introduced ingredients to the countries they conquered. At the beginning of the first century AD, for example, beans, peas, leeks, parsnips and turnips were widely grown in Britain. By the Middle Ages a wealth of vegetables was available, and recipes for them were recorded in the first cookbooks.

Early explorers displayed exotic ingredients, the spoils of their travels, in their native countries

Left: Italian Roast Peppers.
Above: Roast Asparagus Crêpes.

Left: Shallots.

a luxury we have come to expect, and we are generally ready to pay for international variety all year round. Gluts of vegetables, once common seasonal occurrences when food was cultivated and marketed on a local scale, are not features of modern food stores, although the availability of home-grown produce, of course, is still subject to the seasons. Therefore, in addition to taking advantage of the fantastic multinational displays available in most large stores, we should also seek local growers and try to buy freshly harvested produce.

We should learn to enjoy summer vegetables during the season to which they traditionally belong and to savor winter produce in dishes like wholesome stews and broths, which are well suited to cooler weather.

Although the nutritional value of vegetables varies according to type, freshness, preparation and cooking method, they are a main source of many vitamins, especially vitamin C. Some of the B-group vitamins are also found in vegetables, particularly in green vegetables and legumes. Carrots and dark green vegetables also contain carotene, which is used by the body to manufacture vitamin A. Vegetable oils are a useful source of vitamin E. Vegetables also contain calcium, iron, potassium and magnesium, as well as some trace elements, which we all need in small quantities.

Starchy vegetables are an important source of energy-giving carbohydrate, and they may include useful quantities of fiber. Potatoes are beginning to enjoy something of a culinary

and created a huge appetite for new flavors among the wealthy classes of Europe. Marco Polo traveled to China and carried aromatic spices on his return to Europe. Christopher Columbus and subsequent explorers found potatoes, tomatoes, peppers, squashes and corn in the New World. Such produce received a somewhat lukewarm reception when it first appeared – potatoes

and tomatoes, for example, were viewed with grave suspicion – but today there is great interest in vegetables cultivated all over the world.

In contrast to many ingredients, the great characteristic of many vegetables is that they still have natural seasons. When we go into supermarkets we have the opportunity to buy almost anything we want, when we want it. This is

Above: Spinach.

renaissance as more cooks realize
that choosing the right variety for
a dish is one secret of success.
Also, more potatoes are being
grown for flavor and are often
delicious served simply boiled in
their skins and lightly dressed with
a little olive oil or butter. Choose
small, waxy, firm potatoes for
salads, larger firm ones for baking
and floury varieties for mashing.
More and more producers are
printing suitable uses on the bags,
so check these first.

In a vegetarian diet, ingredients
such as legumes, beans and
sprouting seeds make a valuable
contribution to the overall intake
of protein. It has been estimated
that over half the world's main

source of protein comes from
legumes in one form or another.
However, although they are high in
protein, legumes are not complete
in all amino acids. In particular,
they lack one of the amino acids
called methionine. Grain foods, on
the other hand, lack lysine and
tryptophan, which legumes do
have. But put them together, and
you have completed the usual
protein circle. So, when you eat
any of the legumes, try to include
starches in the same meal, for
example lentils with rice, hummus
with bread, beans with pasta, and
so on. In addition, include some
fresh vitamin C in the meal (from
fruits or leafy vegetables) so that
your body can utilize the iron in
the grains and legumes.

The variety of legumes is
exciting and seemingly endless.

Dried legumes benefit from
soaking, preferably overnight.
Older legumes may need longer. To
shorten soaking time, cover with
boiling water and leave for two
hours. Drain and boil in fresh
water. Boil legumes fast for the
first ten minutes of cooking to
destroy any potential mild toxins
present. Then lower the heat and
gently simmer. Do not add salt or
lemon juice during cooking,
because this toughens the skins,
although fresh herbs and onion
slices add flavor. As with pasta,
don't overdrain. Leave wet, season
and perhaps dress with extra-virgin
olive oil.

Certain lentils can be
cooked without pre-soaking.
The small split red lentils
(or masoor dal) are marvelous
thickeners for soups and stews,

and they take just 20 minutes to cook. Beans with a good creamy texture, perfect for soups, pâtés and purées, are lima beans, kidney beans (red or black), cannellini, navy beans, pinto beans and flageolets. Split peas and red lentils make marvelous dips. Chickpeas and aduki beans hold their texture well and make a good base for burgers and stews.

Vegetables have the highest nutritional content when they are freshly picked. The vitamin content diminishes with age and exposure to sunlight. Use fresh vegetables as soon as possible after purchase, and always avoid stale, limp specimens. The peel and the layer directly beneath it contain a high concentration of nutrients, so it is best to avoid peeling vegetables or, when this is necessary, to remove the thinnest possible layer for maximum nutrient retention.

Above: Tomato and Basil Tart.
Left: Red, orange and green peppers.

Minerals and vitamins C and B are water soluble, and they are lost by seepage into cooking water or the liquid over which vegetables are steamed. To minimize loss of nutrients, do not cut up vegetables finely, because this creates a greater surface area for seepage. Vitamin C is also destroyed by long cooking and exposure to alkalines.

Raw and lightly cooked vegetables provide the best nutritional value and source of fiber. Any cooking liquid should, whenever possible, be used in stocks, gravies or sauces.

ONE

ONIONS
AND
LEEKS

Onions

Shallots

Chives

Garlic

Leeks

ONIONS

There are bound to be vegetables you like better than others but a cook would be lost without onions. There are many classic recipes specifically for onion dishes so they can be appreciated in their own right. Onion tarts or French onion soup, for instance, have a sublime flavor, and only onions are appropriate. But also, there is hardly a recipe where onions, or their cousins – garlic, leeks or shallots – are not used. Gently fried until soft, or fried more fiercely until golden brown, they add a unique, savory flavor to dishes.

History

Onions, along with shallots, leeks, chives and garlic, belong to the *Allium* family which, including wild varieties, has some 325 members. All have the characteristic onion smell which is caused by volatile acids beneath the skin.

Archaeological and historical records show that onions have been eaten for thousands of years. They are believed to have originally come from the Middle East and their easy cultivation suggests that their use spread quickly. There are references to the onion in the Bible and it was widely eaten in Egypt. There was, we are told, an inscription on the Great Pyramid stating that the slaves who built the tomb ate their way through 1,600 talents worth of onions, radishes and garlic – presumably a lot, given that the Great Pyramid was made using more than two million 2½-ton blocks of stone.

By the Middle Ages, onions were a common vegetable throughout Europe and would have been used in soups, stews and sauces when strong flavoring was preferred.

Varieties

As they keep well in a cool place, most people keep a handy stock of onions, usually a general purpose type that can be sautéed or browned. However, onions come in a variety of different colors and strengths, and for certain recipes particular onions are needed.

Right: Spanish onions.
Far right top: Yellow onions.
Far right below: Red onions.

Spanish Onions: Onions raised in warm areas are milder in taste than onions from cooler regions, and Spanish onions are among the mildest cultivated onions. They are a beautiful pale copper color and are noticeably larger than yellow onions. They have a delicate, sweet flavor which makes them ideal for serving raw in salads, thinly sliced, while their size makes them suitable for stuffing and baking whole.

Yellow Onions: These are the widely available onions you find everywhere and, though called yellow onions, their skins are more golden brown. They are the most pungent of all the onions and are a good, all-purpose variety. The smallest ones, referred to as baby, button or pickling onions, are excellent for pickling but can also be added whole to a casserole or sautéed in butter to make a delicious vegetable accompaniment.

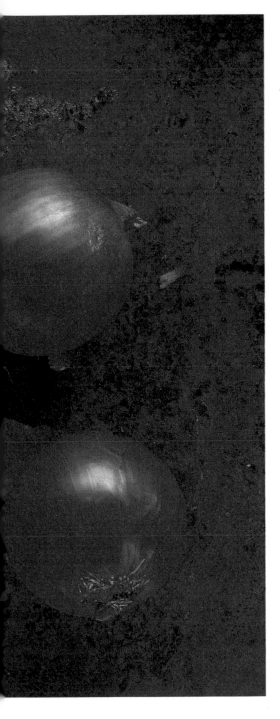

Red Onions: Sometimes called Italian onions, these mild onions have an attractive appearance and are now widely available from most good grocers and supermarkets. Below their ruby red skins the flesh is blushed with red. They have a mild, sweet flavor and are excellent thinly sliced and used raw in salads and *antipasti* dishes.

White Onions: These come in all sorts of interesting shapes and sizes – squat, round and oval, big and small. The very small white onions, with shimmery silver skins, are mild and best added whole to stews or served in a creamy sauce. Larger white onions can be mild or strong – there is no way of telling. Like yellow onions, white onions are extremely versatile whether used raw or cooked. The very small white onions, called Paris Silverskin, are the ones used for dry martinis and for commercial pickling.

Vidalia Onions: These popular American onions are a specialty of and named after a town in Georgia. They are a large, pale yellow onion and are deliciously sweet and juicy. Used in salads, or roasted with meat or with other vegetables, they are superb.

Bermuda Onions: These are similar in size to Spanish onions but are more squat. They have a mild flavor and are good thinly sliced, fried until golden and served with steaks or burgers.

remove the next layer of onion, as it is often dry or damaged. Unless slicing onions for stir-fries, for which it is customary to slice the onion into wedges, always slice the onion through the rings, widthwise. Make whole rings, or for half-rings, cut in half lengthwise through the root before slicing (*below*). For finely chopped onion, slice again lengthwise.

Scallions or Spring Onions: These are also true onions but harvested very young while their shoots are still green and fresh. They have a mild, delicate taste and both the small white bulb and the green tops can be used in salads, omelets and stir-fries, or indeed any dish which requires a mild onion flavor.

Nutrition

As well as tasting good, onions are good for you. They contain vitamins B and C together with calcium, iron and potassium. Like garlic, they also contain cycloallin, an anticoagulant which helps protect against heart disease.

Buying and Storing

It used to be a common sight in Europe to see an onion seller traveling around the streets on a bicycle with strings of onions hanging from every available support, including his own neck.

Strings of onions are hard to come by although, if you do find them in stores, they are a good way of buying and storing the vegetable.

Onions, more than almost any other vegetable, keep well provided they are stored in a cool, dry place, such as a larder or an outhouse. Do not store them in the fridge as they will go soft, and never keep cut onions in the fridge – or anywhere else – unless you want onion-flavored milk and an onion-scented home. Onions do not keep well once cut and it is worth buying onions in assorted sizes so that you do not end up having bits left over. Unused bits of onion can be added to stocks; otherwise throw them away.

Preparing

Onions contain a substance which is released when they are cut and causes the eyes to water, quite painfully sometimes. There are all sorts of ways which are supposed to prevent this, including cutting onions under running water, holding a piece of bread between your teeth or wearing goggles!

As well as the outer brown leaves,

Cooking

The volatile acids in onions are driven off during cooking, which is why cooked onion is never as strong as raw onion. The method of cooking, even the way of frying an onion, affects its eventual taste. Boiled onion or chopped onion added neat to soups or casseroles has a stronger, more raw taste. Frying or sautéing briefly, or sweating (frying in a little fat with the lid on) until soft and translucent gives a mild flavor. When fried until golden brown, onions develop a distinct flavor, both sweet and savory, that is superb with grilled meats and is essential for French onion soup.

Above far left: Vidalia onions.
Left: White onions.
Above left: Large and small scallions.

SHALLOTS

Shallots are not baby onions but a separate member of the onion family. They have a delicate flavor, less intense than most onions and they also dissolve easily into liquids, which is why they are favored for sauces. Shallots grow in small, tight clusters so that when you break one open there may be two or three bunched together at the root.

Their size makes them convenient for a recipe where only a little onion is required. Use shallots when only a small amount of onion is needed or when only a fine onion flavor is required. Shallots are a pleasant, if maybe extravagant, alternative to onions, but where recipes specify shallots (especially sauce recipes), they should be used if possible.

Although classic cooking frequently calls for particular ingredients, the art of improvisation should not be ignored. For instance, Coq au Vin is traditionally made with walnut-size white onions, but when substituted with shallots, the result is delightful.

History

Shallots are probably as ancient as onions. Roman commentators wrote eloquently about the excellence of shallots in sauces.

Varieties

Shallots are small slender onions with long necks and golden, copper-colored skins. There are a number of varieties, although there is unlikely to be a choice in the supermarkets. In any case, differences are more in size and color of skin than in flavor.

Buying and Storing

Like onions, shallots should be firm without any green shoots. They will keep well for several months in a cool dry place.

Preparing and Cooking

Skin shallots in the same way as onions, i.e. top and tail them and then peel off the outer skin. Pull apart the bulbs. Slice them carefully and thinly using a sharp knife – shallots are so small, it is easy to slip and cut yourself. When cooking them whole, fry over very low heat without browning too much.

CHIVES

Chives: In culinary terms, chives are really classed as a herb, but as members of the onion family they are worth mentioning here. As anyone who has grown them knows, chives are tufts of aromatic grass with pretty pale lilac flowers, which are also edible.

Preparing and Serving

Chives are often snipped with scissors and added to egg dishes, or used as a garnish for salads and soups, adding a pleasant but faint onion flavor. Along with parsley, tarragon and chervil, they are an essential ingredient of *fines herbes*.

Chives are also a delicious addition to soft cheeses – far nicer than commercially bought cheeses, where the flavor of chives virtually disappears. Stir also

into soft butter for an alternative to garlic butter. This can then be spread onto bread and baked like garlic bread.

If adding to cooked dishes, cook only very briefly, otherwise their flavor will be lost.

Garlic Chives: Garlic chives, sometimes called Chinese chives, have a delicate garlic flavor, and if you see them for sale in your local Chinese supermarket, they are worth buying as they add a delicate onion flavor to stir-fries and other oriental dishes.

Preparing and Serving

Use them as you would chives – both the green and white parts are edible. They are also delicious served on their own as a vegetable accompaniment.

Buying and Storing

For both types of chives, look for plump, uniformly green specimens with no brown spots or signs of wilting. They can be stored for up to a week in the fridge. Unopened flowers on garlic chives are an indication that the plant is young and therefore more tender than one with fully opened flowers.

Above left: Chives.
Above right: Garlic chives.

GARLIC

Garlic is an ingredient that almost anyone who does any cooking at all, and
absolutely everyone who enjoys cooking,
would not be without.

History

Garlic is known to have been first grown
in around 3200 BC. Inscriptions and
models of garlic found in the pyramids of
ancient Egypt testify to the fact that garlic was not only an important foodstuff
but that it had ceremonial significance
as well. The Greeks and Romans likewise
believed garlic to have magical qualities.
Warriors would eat it for strength before
going into battle, gods were appeased
with gifts of garlic, and cloves of garlic
were fastened round the necks of babies
to ward off evil. Hence, vampire myth-
ology has ancient precedents.

The Greeks and Romans also used
garlic for its therapeutic qualities. Not
only was it thought to be an aphrodisiac
but also it was believed to be good for
eczema, toothache and snake bites.

Although garlic found its way all over
Europe – vats of butter, strongly flavored
with garlic, have been found by archae-
ologists working in Ireland which date
back 200-300 years – fundamentally, its
popularity today derives from our liking
for Mediterranean, Indian and Asian
food, in which garlic plays a very important part.

Nutrition

As is often the case, what was once dis-
missed as an old wives' tale is, after thor-
ough scientific inquiry, found to be true.
Garlic is a case in point; most authorities
accept that it has many therapeutic
properties. The most significant of these
is that it lowers blood cholesterol, thus
helping prevent heart disease. Also, raw
garlic contains a powerful antibiotic and
there is evidence that it has a beneficial
effect against cancer and strokes, and
increases the absorption of vitamins.
Many garlic enthusiasts take their garlic
in tablet form, but true devotees prefer to
take it as it comes.

Right: A string of pink-skinned garlic.

Varieties

There are numerous varieties of garlic, from the large "elephant" garlic, to small tight bulbs. Their papery skin can be white, pink or purple. Color makes no difference to taste but the particular attraction of the large purple bulbs is that they make a beautiful display in the kitchen.

As a general rule, the smaller the garlic bulb, the stronger it is likely to be. However, most garlic sold in stores is not classified in either shape or form (unless it is elephant garlic) and in practice you will simply pick up whatever you need, either loose, in bunches or on strings.

Garlic grown in a hot climate is likely to be the most pungent, and fresh new season's garlic has a subtle, mild flavor that is particularly good if it is to be used raw, for example, in salads and for dressings.

Above: Elephant garlic beside normal-size bulbs.

Buying and Storing

Garlic bulbs should be firm and round with clear, papery skins. Avoid any that are beginning to sprout. Garlic bulbs keep well stored in a cool, dry place; if the air is damp they will sprout and if it is too warm the cloves will eventually turn to gray powder.

Preparing and Cooking

First break the garlic bulb into cloves and then remove the papery skin. You can blanch this off with hot water but using a fingernail or knife is just as effective. When a garlic clove is split lengthwise a shoot is revealed in the center, which is occasionally green, and some people remove this whatever the color. Cloves are the little segments which make up the bulb and most recipes call for one or more cloves of garlic. (Don't use a bulb when you just need a clove!)

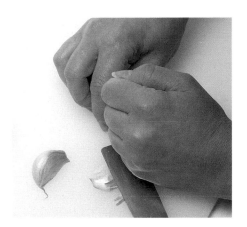

Crush cloves either with the blade of a knife or use a garlic crusher. Crushed garlic cooks more evenly and distributes its flavor in food better than when it is used sliced or finely chopped (stir-fries are the exception). Prepare garlic according to the strength of flavor required: thinly sliced garlic is milder than chopped, which in turn is milder than crushed garlic and, of course, cooking mutes the pungency.

Garlic Breath

The taste and smell of garlic tends to linger on the breath and can be a problem to get rid of. Chewing parsley is a well-known remedy but is only moderately successful. Chewing the seeds of cardamom pods is also said to work but is rather unpleasant. The best suggestion is to eat garlic with your friends so that nobody notices!

L E E K S

Leeks are very versatile, having their own distinct, subtle flavor. They are excellent in pies and casseroles with other ingredients, braised in cream and served by themselves, or simmered in butter as an accompanying vegetable.

Leeks are also wonderful in soups and broths and have rightly earned the title, "king of the soup onions." Cock-a-leekie from Scotland and *Crème Vichyssoise*, invented by the chef of New York's Ritz-Carlton, are two classic leek soups, but many other soups call for leeks.

History

Leeks, like onions and garlic, have a long history. They were grown widely in ancient Egypt and were also eaten and enjoyed throughout the Greek and Roman period. In England, there is evidence that leeks were enjoyed during the Dark Ages. There is little mention of them during the Middle Ages, and history suggests that between the sixteenth and eighteenth centuries eating leeks was not considered fashionable.

However, while they may not have enjoyed a good reputation among the notoriously fickle aristocracy, the rural communities probably continued to eat leeks. They grow in all sorts of climates and are substantial enough to make a reasonable meal for a poor family. It was probably during this time that they were dubbed "poor man's asparagus" – a name which says more about people's snobbishness about food than it does about leeks.

Many place names in England, such as Leckhampstead and Leighton Buzzard, are derived from the word leek and, of course, the leek has been a national emblem of Wales for hundreds of years.

Varieties

There are many different varieties of leeks but among them there is little difference in flavor. Commercially grown leeks tend to be about 10 inches long and about 3/4 inch in diameter. Leeks nurtured in home gardens can be left to grow to an enormous size, but these may develop a woody center.

the first layer of white; then cut a slit from one end to the other through to the center of the leek *(below)*. Wash under cold running water, pulling the sections apart so that the water rinses out any stubborn pieces of earth. If you slice the leeks – either slice thickly or thinly – place them in a colander and rinse thoroughly under cold water.

Cooking

Leeks can be steamed or boiled and then added to your recipe, or you can fry sliced leeks gently in butter for a minute or so and then cover with a lid to sweat so they cook without browning. Unlike onions, leeks shouldn't be allowed to brown; they become tough and unappetizing. They can be stir-fried, however, with a little garlic and ginger. If they begin to cook too fiercely, splash in a little stock and soy sauce and simmer until tender.

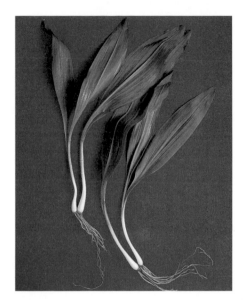

RAMP

Among the many wild onions and leeks, the Canadian ramp is perhaps the best known. Also called the wild leek, it looks a little like a scallion, but has a stronger and more assertive garlic-onion flavor. Choose unblemished, clear white specimens with bright, fresh leaves and keep in a cool place, wrapped in a plastic bag to store.

Prepare and cook as you would scallions, by trimming the root end and then slicing thinly. Use in cooking or in salads but remember the onion flavor is stronger, so use sparingly.

Buying and Storing

Buy leeks which look fresh and healthy. The white part should be firm and unblemished and the leaves green and lively. As leeks do not keep particularly well, it is best to buy them as and when you need them. If you need to store them, trim away the top of the leaves and keep them in the salad drawer of the fridge or in a cool place. After several days they will begin to shrivel.

Preparing

It is important to wash leeks thoroughly before cooking as earth and grit lodges itself between the white sections at the base. To prepare leeks, cut away the flags (leaves) and trim the base. Unless the leek is extremely fresh or home-grown, you will probably have to remove

Left: Leeks.
Above: Ramp.

TWO

SHOOTS
AND
STEMS

Asparagus

Artichokes

Celery

Celery Root

Fiddlehead Fern

Oriental Shoots

Fennel

Samphire

ASPARAGUS

Asparagus is definitely a luxury vegetable. Its price, even in season, sets it apart from cabbages and cauliflowers, and it has a taste of luxury too. The spears, especially the thick, green spears, at their best in early summer, have an intense, rich flavor that is impossible to describe but easy to remember. If the gods eat, they will eat asparagus – served simply with a good hollandaise!

History

The ancient Greeks enjoyed wild asparagus, but it was not until the Roman period that we know it was cultivated. Even then asparagus was highly thought of: it is recorded that Julius Caesar liked to eat it with melted butter. There is little mention of asparagus being eaten in England until the seventeenth century. Mrs Beeton has 14 recipes for asparagus and from the prices quoted in her cookbook it is apparent that it was expensive even in Victorian times.

Nutrition

Asparagus provides vitamins A, B2 and C and is also a good source of potassium, iron and calcium. It is a well-known diuretic.

Varieties

There are many varieties of asparagus and many different ways of raising it too. Spanish and some Dutch asparagus is white with ivory tips; it is grown under mounds of soil and cut just as the tips begin to show. The purple variety is mostly grown in France, where the spears are cut once the tips are about 1 1/2 inches above the ground. Consequently, the stalks are white and the tops tinged with green or purple. In contrast, American and English asparagus grows above the ground and the spears are entirely green. Arguments continue over which has the better flavor, most growers expressing a preference for their own asparagus!

Thin, short asparagus are excellent when briefly steamed or stir-fried and added to salads. In Italy, they are served by themselves, scattered with grated Parmesan cheese.

Preparing

Unless the asparagus comes straight from the garden, cut off the bottom of the stalk as it is usually hard and woody. If the bottom parts of the stem also feel hard, pare this away with a potato peeler *(below)*. However, if the asparagus is very fresh, this is not necessary, and thin asparagus rarely needs trimming at all.

Buying and Storing

Asparagus has a relatively short growing season, from late spring to early summer. Nowadays, it is available in stores almost all year through, but outside the season it will have been imported. It is still good, but it is expensive and will not have the flavor of home-produced asparagus, since it starts to lose its flavor once it is cut.

When buying asparagus, the tips should be tightly furled and fresh looking, and the stalks fresh and straight. If the stalks are badly scarred or droopy, it indicates that they have been hanging around for too long and it is not worth buying. Asparagus will keep for several days if necessary. Untie the bundles and store in the salad drawer of the fridge.

Cooking

The problem with cooking asparagus is that the stalks take longer to cook than the tender tips, which need to be only briefly steamed. Ideally, use an asparagus steamer. Place the asparagus spears with the tips upward in the wire basket and then lower into a little boiling salted water in the steamer. Cover and cook until the stems are tender.

Alternately, if you don't have an asparagus steamer, place the bundle upright in a deep saucepan of boiling salted water. (The bundle can be wedged into place with potatoes.) Cover with a dome of foil and cook for 5-10 minutes or until the spears are tender. The cooking time depends largely on the thickness of the spears, but it is important not to over-cook; the spears should still have a "bite" to them.

Asparagus can also be roasted in a little olive oil. This cooking method intensifies the flavor and is gratifyingly simple. Serve with just a sprinkling of sea salt – it's quite delicious! If steaming asparagus, serve simply with melted butter, which perfectly complements the luxury of the vegetable.

Left: Asparagus.
Above: White asparagus.

ARTICHOKES

Artichokes have an exquisite flavor and are a very sociable food to eat. They grow in abundance in Brittany, and during July and August farmers can frequently be seen selling them by the roadside. The globes are huge hearty specimens and are extremely fresh, so they make a good buy.

History

It is not known for certain whether artichokes were eaten in antiquity. Although they are mentioned by writers, they could have been referring to the cardoon, which is the uncultivated form of artichoke. Cardoons grew wild in many southern European countries, and, as far as we know, cultivated artichokes first became a popular food in Italy. However, Goethe did not share the Italians' liking for the vegetable and remarks in his book, *Travels Through Italy*, that "the peasants eat thistles," something he didn't care for at all.

Nowadays, artichokes are grown all over southern Europe and in California. People in Italy, France and Spain eat artichokes while the vegetable is still young, before the choke has formed and the entire artichoke is edible. Unfortunately, such young delicacies are not exported, but look out for them if you are in these countries.

Buying and Storing

It is only worth buying artichokes when they are in season, although they are available in supermarkets almost all year through. In winter, however, they are sad looking specimens, small and rather dry, and are really not worth the bother of cooking. At their best, artichokes should be lively looking with a good bloom on their leaves, the inner leaves wrapped tightly round the choke and heart inside. Artichokes will keep for 2-3 days in the salad drawer of the fridge but are best eaten as soon as possible.

Preparing and Cooking

First twist off the stalk which should also remove some of the fibers at the base and then cut the base flat and pull away any small base leaves. If the leaves are very spiky, trim them with a pair of scissors if liked *(above)*, then rinse under running water. Cook in boiling water, acidulated with the juice of half a lemon. Large artichokes need to be simmered for 30-40 minutes until tender. To test if they are done, pull off one of the outer leaves. It should come away easily and the base of the leaf should be tender.

heart. Eat the heart with a knife and fork, dipping it in the garlic butter or vinaigrette.

CARDOONS

This impressively large vegetable is closely related to the globe artichoke and has a superb flavor, a cross between artichokes and asparagus. Cultivated plants frequently grow to 6 feet in height, and once mature, cardoons, like celery, are blanched as they grow. This process involves wrapping the stalks with newspaper and black bags for several weeks, so that when harvested, in late fall, before the frosts, the stalks are a pale green.

The cardoon is a popular vegetable in southern Europe but less commonly available elsewhere. In Spain, for instance, it is much appreciated and often appears on the table, poached and served with chestnuts or walnuts. Only the inner ribs and heart are used.

Artichokes and Drink

Artichokes contain a chemical called cynarin, which in many people (although surprisingly not all) affects the taste buds by enhancing sweet flavors. Among other things, this will spoil the taste of wine. Consequently, don't waste good wine with artichokes but drink ice water instead, which should taste pleasantly sweet.

Eating Artichokes

Artichokes are fun to eat. They have to be eaten with fingers, which does away with any pomp and ceremony, always a handicap for a good dinner party. Serve one artichoke between two, so that people can share the fun of pulling off the leaves and dipping them into garlic butter or vinaigrette. If you want to serve one each, serve them in succession. The dipping sauces are an essential part of eating artichokes; people can either spoon a little onto their plates or have a little bowl each. After dipping, draw the leaf through your teeth, eating the fleshy part.

When most of the leaves have been eaten, a few thin pointed leaves remain in the center, which can be pulled off altogether. Then pull or cut away the fine prickly choke and discard, leaving the

Far left: Artichokes.
Top: Baby artichokes.
Above: Cardoons.

CELERY

Some people say that the very act of eating celery has a slimming effect because chewing it uses up more calories than the vegetable itself contains! Although it may be insubstantial, celery nevertheless has a distinct and individual flavor, sharp and savory, which makes it an excellent flavoring for soups and stuffings, as well as good on its own or in salads. The astringent flavor and crunchy texture of celery contrasts well with the other ingredients in salads such as Waldorf salad or Walnut and avocado salad.

History

Celery is known to have been commonly eaten in salads in Italy for hundreds of years.

Nutrition

Celery is very low in calories but contains potassium and calcium.

Varieties

Most grocers and supermarkets, depending on the time of year, sell both green and white celery. When celery is allowed to grow naturally, the stalks are green. However, by banking up earth against the shoots celery is blanched: the stalks are protected from sunlight and remain pale and white. Consequently, white celery is often "dirty" – covered loosely in soil – while green celery will always be clean. White celery, which is frost hardy, is only available in winter. It is more tender and less bitter than green celery and is generally considered superior. Celery is therefore thought of as a winter vegetable and is traditionally used at Christmas time, for stuffing and as a sauce to go with turkey or ham.

Buying and Storing

White celery is in season during the winter months. If possible, buy "dirty" celery which hasn't been washed. It has a better flavor than the pristine but rather bland supermarket variety. Look for celery with green fresh-looking leaves and straight stems. If the leaves or any outer stalks are missing, it is likely to be old, so worth avoiding.

Celery will keep for several days in the salad drawer of the refrigerator. Limp celery can be revived by wrapping it in absorbent paper and standing it in a jar of water.

Preparing

Wash if necessary and pull the stalks apart, trimming the base with a sharp knife. Cut into thick or thin slices according to the recipe. When served raw and whole, the coarse outer "strings" should be removed from each stalk by pulling them up from the base.

Cooking and Serving

Serve celery raw and finely sliced in salads, mixed with cream cheese or sour cream. Braised celery is tasty, either whole or sliced. Celery has a distinctive, savory, astringent flavor so is excellent in soups or stuffings.

CELERY ROOT

Strictly speaking, celery root is classified as a root vegetable rather than a shoot or stem. It is knobbly with a patchy brown/white skin and has a similar but less pronounced flavor than celery. Grated and eaten raw, it has a crunchy texture, but when cooked it is more akin to potatoes. Thin slices of potato and celery root cooked *au gratin* with cream is a popular way of serving this vegetable.

Buying and Preparing

If possible, buy smallish bulbs of celery root. The flesh discolors when exposed to light, so as soon as you have peeled, sliced, diced or grated the celery root, plunge it into a bowl of acidulated water (water with lemon juice added).

Cooking

Celery root can be used in soups and broths, or can be diced and boiled and eaten in potato salads.

Left: Green celery.
Above: White celery.
Right: Celery root.

FIDDLEHEAD FERN

Sometimes called the ostrich fern, these shoots are a rich green color and are normally about 2 inches long. They have an unusual flavor, something like a cross between asparagus and okra, and have a slightly chewy texture, which makes them a popular choice for oriental dishes.

Preparing and Cooking

To prepare and cook, trim the ends and then steam or simmer in a little water or sauté in butter until tender. Use in salads or serve as a first course with a hollandaise sauce.

Right: Fiddlehead ferns.
Below left: Alfalfa sprouts.
Below right: Mung bean sprouts.

ORIENTAL SHOOTS

BAMBOO SHOOTS

In the Far East, edible bamboo shoots are sold fresh in the market. The young shoots are stripped of their brown outer skins and the insides are then eaten. Although fresh bamboo shoots can occasionally be found in oriental stores, the most readily available variety is sold in cans. The flavor is undoubtedly spoiled. Fresh bamboo shoots have a mild but distinct taste, faintly reminiscent of artichokes, while canned ones really taste of nothing at all. However, the texture, which, in Chinese cuisine particularly, is as important as the flavor, is not so impaired, and bamboo shoots have a pleasantly crunchy bite.

Preparing and Cooking

Peel away the outer skin and then cook in boiling water for about half an hour. They should feel firm, but not "rock" hard. Once cooked, slice thinly and serve by themselves as a side dish, with garlic butter or a sauce, or add to stir-fries, spring rolls or any oriental dish

where you need a contrast of textures. Since canned bamboo shoots have been preserved in brine, always rinse well before using.

BEAN SPROUTS

Bean sprouts are a neglected vegetable, used almost carelessly for oriental dishes but otherwise passed by as being insipid and not very interesting. It's a reputation they don't deserve: not only do they have a lovely fresh flavor, but they are also good for you.

All sorts of seeds can be sprouted, but the bean family are favorites among the sprouted vegetables. The bean sprouts most commonly available in the shops are sprouted mung beans, but aduki beans, alfalfa, lentils and soy beans can all be sprouted and taste delicious.

Nutrition

Beans sprouts contain a significant amount of protein, Vitamin C and many of the B vitamins. They have an excellent flavor too, best appreciated eaten raw in salads or sandwiches, and for slimmers they are an ideal food, low in calories, yet with sufficient substance to be filling, and with a flavor and texture that can be enjoyed without a dressing.

Buying and Storing

Bean sprouts should only be bought when absolutely fresh. They don't keep for long and they will taste sour if past their best. The sprouts should be firm, not limp, and and the tips should be green or yellow; avoid any that are beginning to turn brown.

Cooking

If stir-frying, add the bean sprouts at the last minute so they cook for the minimum period to keep plenty of crunch and retain their nutritional value. Most health food shops will have instructions on sprouting your own beans. Only buy seeds intended for sprouting.

PALM HEARTS

Fresh palm hearts are the buds of cabbage palm trees and are considered a delicacy in many parts of the world. They are available canned from oriental stores, but are most prized when fresh. These should be blanched before being cooked to eliminate any bitterness. They can be braised or sautéed and then served hot with a hollandaise sauce, or cold with a simple vinaigrette.

WATER CHESTNUTS

Water chestnut is the common name for a number of aquatic herbs and their nut-like fruit, the best known and most popular variety being the Chinese water chestnut, sometimes known as the Chinese sedge. In China they are grown in exactly the same way as rice, the plants needing the same conditions of

high temperatures, shallow water and good soil. In spring, the corms are planted in paddy fields which are then flooded to a depth of some 4 inches. These are drained in fall, and the corms are harvested and stored over the winter. Water chestnuts are much used in Chinese cooking and have a sweet crunchy flavor with nutty overtones.

They are edible cooked or raw and are excellent in all sorts of Chinese dishes.

Above: Sprouting mung beans.
Below: Clockwise from top left: Canned Water chestnuts, canned Bamboo shoots, fresh Water chestnuts, canned Palm hearts.

FENNEL

The vegetable fennel is closely related to the herb and spice of the same name. It is called variously bulb fennel, Florence fennel, sweet fennel, *finocchio dulce* or Italian fennel.

Like the herb, Florence fennel has the distinct flavor of anise, a taste that seems to go particularly well with fish, so the vegetable is often served with fish dishes while the herb or spice is commonly used in fish stocks, sauces or soups. The leaves are edible and can be used in soups and stocks as well as for garnishing.

History

Bulb fennel has only been popular for the last ten or so years, although it has a long history of cultivation, having been eaten by the ancient Egyptians, Greeks and Romans. In Italy, fennel has been eaten for several centuries: many of the best fennel recipes come from Italy and other parts of the Mediterranean.

Buying and Storing

If possible, buy small tender bulbs. The bulbs should be clean and white with no bruises or blemishes and the feathery leaves should be green and lively. Fennel will keep for a day or two in the salad drawer of the fridge.

Preparing

Unless the bulbs are very young and tender, remove the first layer of skin, as it is likely to be tough (this can be used for a stock). Fennel can then be sliced into slivers by cutting downward or into rings by cutting across the bulb. When used raw in salads, it must be cut into smaller pieces.

Cooking and Serving

Fennel can be served raw if it is thinly sliced and dressed with a light vinaigrette. In salads, its flavor contrasts well with apple, celery and other crunchy ingredients. Fennel is also excellent braised with onions, tomatoes and garlic.

Right: Bulb fennel.
Far right: Marsh samphire.

SAMPHIRE

There are two types of samphire. Marsh samphire grows in estuaries and salt marshes while rock samphire, sometimes called sea fennel, grows on rocky shores. The two are understandably confused since they are both connected with the sea, yet they are completely different plants.

The type likely to be sold by a fish dealer is marsh samphire. It is also known as glasswort and is sometimes called sea asparagus, as its shoots are similar to small asparagus shoots.

Although marsh samphire grows easily and is commonly found all over North America and Europe, it is not cultivated and is only available for a short time while it is in season, normally in late summer and early autumn.

Samphire has a distinctly salty, iodine flavor and a pleasant crisp texture. The flavor is reminiscent of the sea and goes particularly well with fish and seafood. However, samphire can be enjoyed simply steamed and dipped into melted butter.

Buying and Storing

When in season, good fish dealers get regular stocks of marsh samphire, and it should look bright and fresh. Buy it as you need it, as it will not keep for long.

Preparing and Cooking

If necessary, wash marsh samphire under cold running water. It is best steamed over a pan of boiling water for no more than 3 minutes. Alternately, blanch it in boiling water for 3-5 minutes and then drain. Samphire can be eaten raw but blanching it removes some of the saltiness.

To eat samphire, draw the shoots through the teeth to peel the succulent part from the thin central core.

THREE
ROOTS

POTATOES

History

The potato originates from South America. Most people learned at school that Sir Walter Raleigh brought the tubers to England from Virginia, but this never convinced historians as the potato was completely unknown in North America until the eighteenth century. They now believe that Sir Francis Drake was responsible. In 1586, after battling against the Spaniards in the Caribbean, Drake stopped to pick up provisions from Cartegena in northern Colombia – and these included tobacco and potato tubers. En route home, he stopped off at Roanoke Island, off the coast of Virginia. The first group of English colonists had been sponsored to settle there by Sir Walter Raleigh, but by this time they had had enough. Drake brought them back to England, along with some of Raleigh's men and, of course, the provisions – including the potato tubers.

Potatoes apparently fascinated Queen Elizabeth and intrigued horticulturists, but they were not an overnight success among the people. The wealthy frequently reviled them as being flavorless and the food of the poor. People distrusted the fact that they reached maturity underground, believing them to be the work of

the devil. In Scotland, Presbyterian ministers darkly advised their congregations that there was no mention of potatoes in the Bible, and thus the eating of them was an ungodly act!

In spite of such a bad press, potatoes nevertheless were slowly recognized for their merit. By 1650 they were the staple food of Ireland, and elsewhere in Europe potatoes began to replace wheat as the most important crop, both for people and for livestock. In an early English cookbook, *Adam's Luxury and Eve's Cookery*, there are 20 different recipes for cooking and serving potatoes.

The first mention of potatoes in America is in 1719 in Londonderry, New Hampshire. They arrived not from the south, but via Irish settlers who brought their potatoes with them.

The current popularity of potatoes is probably thanks to a Frenchman called Antoine-Auguste Parmentier. A military pharmacist of the latter part of the eighteenth century, Parmentier recognized the virtues of the potato, both for its versatility and as an important food for the poor, and set out to improve its image. He persuaded Louis XVI to let him ostentatiously grow potatoes on royal land around the palace in Versailles to

impress the fashion-conscious Parisians. He also produced a court dinner in which each course contained potatoes. Gradually, eating potatoes became chic, first among people in the French court and then in French Society. Today, if you see *Parmentier* in a recipe or on a menu, it means "with potato."

Nutrition

Potatoes are an important source of carbohydrate. Once thought to be fattening, we now know that, on the contrary, potatoes can be an excellent part of a calorie-controlled diet – provided, of course, they are not fried in oil or mashed with too much butter. Potatoes are also a very good source of vitamin C, and during the winter potatoes are often the main source of this vitamin. They also contain potassium, iron and vitamin B.

Varieties

There are more than 400 international varieties of potato, but unless you are a gardener, you will find only some 15 varieties generally available. Thanks to labeling laws, packaged potatoes carry their names, which makes it easier to learn to differentiate between the varieties and find out which potato is good for what.

New Potatoes

Carlingford: Available as a new potato or as main crop, Carlingford has a close white flesh.

Jersey Royal: Often the first new potato of the season, Jersey Royals have been shipped from Jersey for over a hundred years and have acquired an enviable reputation among everyone who enjoys good food. Boiled or steamed and then served with butter and a sprinkling of parsley, they cannot be beaten.

Jersey Royals are kidney-shaped, with yellow firm flesh and a distinctive flavor. Don't confuse Jersey Royals with Jersey Whites, which are actually Maris Pipers, grown in Jersey.

Maris Bard: A regularly shaped, slightly waxy potato with white flesh.

Maris Peer: This variety has dry firm flesh and a waxy texture and doesn't disintegrate when cooked – consequently, it is good in salads.

Main Crop Potatoes

Desiree: A potato with a pink skin and yellow soft-textured flesh. It is good for baking, frying, roasting and mashing.

Yukon Gold: A good masher with yellow flesh and pale skin.

Idaho: A russet-skinned potato that was the original favorite for making chips. It has an excellent, distinctive flavor, and should you find them for sale, buy them at once for baked potatoes. They are also good boiled or roasted.

Kerr's Pink: A good cooking potato with pink skin and creamy flesh.

King Edward: Probably the best known of potatoes, although not the best in flavor. King Edwards are creamy white in color with a slightly floury texture.

Red King Edwards are virtually identical except for their red skin. Both are good roasted or baked. However, the flesh disintegrates when boiled, so while good for mashing do not use King Edwards if you want whole boiled potatoes.

Maris Piper: This is a widely grown variety of potato, popular with growers and cooks because it is good for all kinds of cooking methods – baking, frying, roasting and mashing. It has a pale, smooth skin and creamy white flesh.

Left: Maris Bard potatoes.
Above: Kerr's pink (left) and Maris Piper (right) potatoes.
Right: Romano potatoes.

Pentland Dell: A long, oval-shaped potato with a floury texture that tends to disintegrate when boiled. For this reason, it is popular for roasting as the outside becomes soft when parboiled and then crisps up with the fat during roasting.

Romano: The Romano has a distinctive red skin with creamy flesh and is a good all-rounder, similar to Desiree.

Wilja: Introduced from Holland, this is a pale, yellow-fleshed potato with a good, sweet flavor and waxy texture.

Other Varieties

Although most of these varieties are also main crop, they are less widely available than those listed above but are increasingly sold in supermarkets. They are recommended for salads but many are also excellent sautéed or simply boiled.

Cara: A large main crop potato, which is excellent baked or boiled but is a good all-rounder.

Fingerlings: Thumb-sized, long baby potatoes are sometimes called finger potatoes. Among the many varieties are the German Lady's Finger. Since they are new crop potatoes, they need simply be boiled and then served either in salads or with a little butter and a sprinkling of parsley.

La Ratte: A French potato with a smooth skin and waxy yellow flesh. It has a chestnut flavor and is good in salads.

Linzer Delikatess: These small, kidney-shaped potatoes look a little like Jersey Royals but have a pale smooth skin. They do not have much taste and are best in salads where their flavor can be enhanced with other ingredients.

Pink Fir Apple: This is an old English variety, with pink skin and a smooth yellow flesh. It is becoming increasingly popular and has a distinctive flavor.

Above left: Cara (left) and Yukon Gold (right) potatoes.
Left: Linzer Delikatess potatoes.
Above: Desiree (left) and King Edward (right) potatoes.
Right: Fingerlings.

Blue: If you want to startle your friends, serve some of these striking purple-blue potatoes. There are several varieties of blue potato, ranging from a pale lavender to a wonderful deep purple. They have a dense texture, which makes them good for boiling. They are best served simply with a little butter and do retain their color when cooked.

Truffe de Chine: Another deep purple, almost black potato, of unknown origin but now grown in France. It has a nutty, slightly mealy flavor and is best served in a salad with a simple dressing. Like the Blue Potato, it retains its color after being cooked.

Recommended Varieties for Cooking

Baking: As for roasting, use potatoes with a floury texture, such as Idaho, Pentland Dell, King Edward and Maris Piper.

Boiling: Jersey Royal, Maris Bard and Maris Peer, or any of the Egyptian or Belgian new crop varieties. In addition, Pink Fir Apple, La Ratte and Linzer Delikatess are excellent.

Frying: King Edward, Idaho, Romano, Maris Piper and Desiree.

Mashing: Idaho, Maris Piper, King Edward, Wilja, Romano and Pentland Dell and Yukon Gold.

Roasting: Pentland Dell, Idaho, Maris Piper, King Edward, Desiree and Romano are among the best roasting potatoes. Ideally, use potatoes with a floury texture.

Salads: All the small, specialist potatoes, such as La Ratte, Pink Fir Apple and Linzer Delikatess as well as Fingerlings and small new potatoes.

Sautéing: Any waxy type of potato, such as Maris Bard, Maris Peer, any of the

specialist potatoes, and Romano and Maris Piper.

Buying and Storing

Potatoes should always be stored in a dark, cool, dry place. If they are stored exposed to the light, green patches will develop which can be poisonous, and they will go moldy if kept in the damp. When buying potatoes in bulk, it is best to buy them in paper sacks rather than plastic bags as humid conditions will cause them to go rotten. Similarly, if you buy potatoes in plastic bags, remove them when you get home and place them in a vegetable rack or in a paper bag, in a dark place.

Main crop potatoes will keep for several months in the right conditions but will gradually lose their nutritional value. New potatoes should be eaten within two or three days as they will go moldy if stored for too long.

Preparing

Most of the minerals and vitamins contained in potatoes are contained in or just below the skin. It is therefore better to eat potatoes in their skins. New potatoes need only be washed under running water; older potatoes need to be scrubbed.

If you peel potatoes, use a peeler that removes only the very top surface (*below left*) or, alternately, for salads and cold dishes, boil the potatoes in their skins and peel when cool.

Cooking

Baking: Cook baked potatoes in a low oven for well-browned and crunchy skins and fluffy flesh. Baked potatoes can be cooked more quickly in a microwave oven; for a crunchy texture to the skin place them in a hot oven for 10 minutes.

Boiling: It is impossible to generalize on how long to boil as it depends so much on the variety of potato. Try to cut potatoes to an even size (new potatoes should not need to be cut), salt the water if liked, cover and cook over a moderate heat. Don't boil potatoes too fiercely; old ones especially may disintegrate and leave you with a pan of starchy water.

French fries: Home-cooked French fries are a treat worth occasionally giving the family instead of the convenient but otherwise disappointing oven fries. However, they are fatty and therefore not good for you when eaten in great quantities or too often.

To make them, cut the potatoes into even-size pieces and place in a bowl of cold water for about 10 minutes before frying. Drain and then dry in a piece of muslin or an old dish towel before frying. Fry only as many pieces as will comfortably sit in the fat. Halfway through cooking, drain them and allow the oil to come back to temperature before plunging the fries back in. This browns the fries and they don't soak up excessive amounts of oil. Be warned; the cooking smells from making fries tend to linger!

Mashing: Boil the potatoes until tender, drain thoroughly and then tip them back into the pan; mash with a little milk and

butter using a potato masher (*below right*), and season to taste with a little salt, if necessary, and pepper. Never use a food processor or blender: the potatoes will turn into an inedible thick gray paste. You may lightly whisk potatoes with a fork after mashing to fluff them up, but no more – for once modern machines have not improved on the basic utensil.

Roast Potatoes: The best roast potatoes are made using a floury textured potato such as Maris Piper or King Edward. Wash and cut them into even-size chunks and parboil them in lightly salted water until they begin to go tender and the outside looks soft. Drain them through a strainer or colander and then tip them back into the saucepan, put the lid on and shake the pan two or three times. This roughens up the surface of the potato. Place the potatoes in a dish of hot oil or fat, or around a joint of meat, and turn them over so that they are evenly coated. Roast them in the oven for 40-50 minutes until golden. Serve as soon as possible once cooked as the outsides become leathery if they are kept in a warm oven for too long.

Sautéing: There are various ways to sauté potatoes and no one way is better than another. For sautéed sliced potatoes, parboil whole potatoes for 5-10 minutes until they begin to soften. Drain them thoroughly and then slice into thick rounds. Using sunflower oil or a mixture of sunflower and olive oil (not butter as it will burn), fry them in a large frying pan. Turn the potatoes occasionally and cook until evenly browned. For sautéed, diced potatoes, cut the potatoes into small cubes, blanch for 2 minutes and then drain well. Either fry them on the stove or cook them in a little oil in the oven; turn them once or twice to brown evenly.

Steaming: New potatoes are excellent steamed. Place them on a bed of mint in a steamer or a colander over a pan of boiling water for 15-20 minutes.

Above left: Blue potatoes.
Below left: Truffe de Chine (left) and Pink Fir Apple (right) potatoes.

PARSNIPS

There's something very old-fashioned about parsnips. They conjure up images of cold winter evenings and warm comforting broths supped in front of a blazing wood fire. Nowadays parsnips are available all year through, but many people still feel they belong to winter, adding their characteristic flavor to soups and stews.

Parsnips are related to carrots, similarly sweet but with a distinct earthy flavor that blends well with other root vegetables and is also enhanced with spices and garlic.

History

Parsnips have a long history. The Romans grew and cooked them to make broths and stews. When they conquered Gaul and Britain, the Romans discovered that root vegetables grown in northerly areas had a better flavor than those grown in the south – they may have been the first to decree that parsnips should be eaten after the first frost!

Throughout the Dark Ages and early Middle Ages, parsnips were the main starchy vegetable for ordinary people (the potato had yet to be introduced). Parsnips were not only easy to grow but were a welcome food to eat during the lean winter months. They were also valued for their sugar content. Sweet parsnip dishes like jam and desserts became part of traditional English cookery, and they were also commonly used for making beer and wine. Parsnip wine is still one of the most popular of the country wines, with a beautiful golden color and a rich sherry-like flavor.

Nutrition

Parsnips contain moderate amounts of vitamins A and C, along with some of the B vitamins. They are also a source of calcium, iron and potassium.

Buying and Storing

Parsnips are really a winter crop, although nowadays they are available all year through. Tradition has it that parsnips are best after the first frost, but many people like the very young tender parsnips available in the early summer. When buying parsnips, choose small or

medium-size specimens as the large ones tend to be rather fibrous. They should feel firm and be a pale ivory color without any sprouting roots. Store parsnips in a cool place, ideally an airy larder or cool outhouse, where they will keep well for 8-10 days.

Preparing

Very small parsnips need little or no peeling; just trim the ends and cook according to your recipe. Medium-size and large parsnips must be peeled. Larger parsnips also must have the woody core removed; if it is cut out before cooking, the parsnips will cook more quickly and evenly.

Cooking

Roast parsnips are best parboiled for a few minutes before adding to the roasting dish. Very young parsnips can be roasted whole but larger ones are best halved or quartered lengthwise. Roast in butter or oil for about 40 minutes in an oven preheated to 400°F .

To boil parsnips, cut them into pieces about 2 inches long and boil for 15-20 minutes until tender. When boiled briefly like this, they keep their shape, but when added to a casserole or stew they eventually disintegrate. Don't worry if this happens; parsnips need plenty of cooking so that the flavor can blend with the other ingredients.

JERUSALEM ARTICHOKES

Jerusalem artichokes are related to the sunflower and have nothing to do with Jerusalem. One explanation for their name is that they were christened girasole, "Jerusalem," because their yellow flowers turned toward the sun. The Italian name for the Jerusalem artichoke is *girasole articocco.*

These small knobbly tubers have a lovely distinct flavor and are good in Palestine soup, a popular classic recipe. They are also delicious baked or braised.

History

Jerusalem artichokes are thought to have come from the central United States and Canada, where they were cultivated by the Native Americans as long ago as the fifteenth century. However, many writers have alluded to the fact that they cause "wind," which tempers their popularity.

Buying and Storing

Jerusalem artichokes are at their best during winter and early spring. They are invariably knobbly, but if possible buy neat ones with the minimum of knobs to save waste. The skins should be pale brown without any dark or soft patches. If they are stored in a cool dark place they will keep well for up to 10 days.

Preparing

The white flesh of artichokes turns purplish brown when exposed to light, so when peeling or slicing them raw, place them in a bowl of acidulated water (water to which the juice of about half a lemon has been added). Because artichokes are so knobbly, it is often easier to boil them in acidulated water in their skins and peel them afterward – the cooked skins should slip off easily.

Cooking

Jerusalem artichokes can be cooked in many of the ways in which you would cook potatoes or parsnips. They are excellent roasted, sautéed or dipped in batter and fried, but first parboil them for 10-15 minutes until nearly tender. For creamed artichokes, mix with potatoes in equal amounts; this slightly blunts their flavor, making a tasty side dish which is not too overpowering.

Left: Parsnips.
Below: Jerusalem artichokes.

TURNIPS AND RUTABAGAS

Turnips and rutabagas are both members of the cabbage family and are closely related to each other – so close that it is not surprising that their names are often confused. For instance, rutabagas are sometimes called Swedish turnips or swede-turnips and in Scotland, where they are thought of as turnips, they are called neeps.

Nowadays, the confusion is not so acute. Many grocers and supermarkets sell early or baby turnips or, better still, French turnips – *navets*.

Both are small and white, tinged either with green or in the case of *navets*, with pink or purple. Consequently, people are learning to tell their rutabagas from their turnips and also discovering what a delicious vegetable the turnip is.

History

Turnips have been cultivated for centuries, principally as an important livestock feed but also for humans. Although they were not considered the food of gourmets, they have been grown by

poorer families as a useful addition to the winter table.

Rutabagas were known as turnip-rooted cabbages until the 1780s, when Sweden began exporting the vegetable to Britain and the shorter name resulted.

Until recently, turnips and rutabagas have not enjoyed a very high reputation among cooks in many parts of the world. This is partly because they are perceived as cattle food and partly because few people have taken the trouble to find acceptable ways of cooking them. Many cooks

tend to boil and then mash them to a watery pulp, and for many people this is the only way they have eaten either vegetable.

The French, in contrast, have had far more respect for the turnip, at least. For centuries they have devised recipes for their delicate *navets*, roasting them, caramelizing them in sugar and butter or simply steaming and serving with butter. Young, tender turnips have also been popular all over the Mediterranean region for many years, and there are many dishes using turnips with fish, poultry, or teamed with tomatoes, onions and spinach.

Nutrition

Both turnips and rutabagas are a good source of calcium and potassium.

Varieties

French *navets*, small round, squash-shaped turnips tinged with pink or purple, are increasingly available in grocers and supermarkets in the spring. Less common, but even more prized by the French, are the long carrot-shaped turnips, called *vertus*. English turnips are generally larger and are mainly green and white. Both have the characteristic peppery flavor, but this is less pronounced in *navets* which are generally sweeter.

Rutabagas generally have a more substantial, fuller-bodied flavor than turnips but at their best have a subtle, pleasant taste. The Marian is a yellow fleshed variety with a distinct "rutabaga" flavor. White-fleshed swedes, like Merrick, have a more watery, turnip-like flavor.

Buying and Storing

Turnips: If possible, buy French *navets* or failing that, the smallest and youngest turnips, available in stores from spring. They should be firm, smooth and unblemished, ideally with fresh green tops. Store in a cool dry place.

Rutabagas: Unlike turnips, rutabagas generally seem to come large. However, if possible, choose small rutabagas with smooth and unblemished skins as large ones are likely to be tough and fibrous. Store as for turnips.

Preparing and Cooking

Turnips: Young turnips should not require peeling; simply trim, then simmer or steam until tender. They are delicious raw, thinly sliced or grated into salads.

Peel older turnips (*below*) and then slice or dice before cooking. Remember, turnips are members of the cabbage family and older specimens particularly can show signs of that unpleasant cabbage rankness if overcooked. To avoid this, blanch turnips if they are to be served as a vegetable dish, or add sparingly to soups and casseroles, so that the rank flavor is dispersed.

Rutabagas: Peel to remove the skin and then cut into chunks (*below*). Rutabagas will disintegrate if overcooked, and they are unpleasantly raw tasting if not cooked sufficiently. The only answer is to check frequently while they are cooking. Rutabagas are particularly good when teamed with other root vegetables in soups and casseroles, adding a pleasant, slightly nutty flavor.

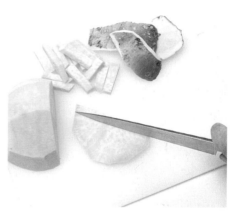

Far left: Navets and Turnips.
Below: Rutabagas.

CARROTS

After potatoes, carrots are without doubt our best-known and best-loved root vegetable. In the days when vegetables were served merely as an accessory to meat, carrots always made an appearance – often overcooked but still eaten up because, we were told, they helped you to see in the dark.

Carrots have many different flavors, depending on how they are cooked. Young, new season carrots braised in butter and a splash of water are intensely flavored and sweet; when steamed, they are tender and melting. Carrots grated into salads are fresh and clean tasting, while in casseroles they are savory with the characteristic carrot flavor. In soups they are fragrant and mild, and in cakes their flavor can hardly be detected, yet their sweetness adds richness.

History

Until the Middle Ages, carrots were purple. The orange carrots came from Holland, from where they were exported in the seventeenth and eighteenth centuries. Although purple and white carrots continued to be eaten in France, nowadays they are something of a rarity.

Nutrition

Carrots contain large amounts of carotene and vitamin A, along with useful amounts of vitamins B3, C and E. When eaten raw, they also provide good quantities of potassium, calcium, iron and zinc, but these are reduced when carrots are boiled.

The idea that carrots are good for your night sight originated in the Second World War. Early radar stations were established along the south and east coasts of England in 1939 to detect aggressors in the air or at sea. The Germans attributed this sudden remarkable night vision to the British habit of eating carrots. Indeed, the vitamin A in carrots forms retinal, a lack of which brings on night blindness.

Buying and Storing

Home-grown carrots are so much nicer than shop bought ones. Almost all vegetables have a better flavor if grown organically, but this is particularly true of carrots.

When buying carrots, look out for the very young, pencil-thin ones, which are beautifully tender either eaten raw or steamed for just a few minutes. Young carrots are commonly sold with their feathery tops intact, which should be fresh and green. Older carrots should be firm and unblemished. Avoid tired looking carrots as they will have little nutritional value.

Carrots should not be stored for too long. They will keep for several days if stored in a cool, airy place or in the salad drawer of the fridge.

Preparing

Preparation depends on the age of the carrots. The valuable nutrients lie either in or just beneath the skin, so if the carrots are young, simply wash them under cold running water. Medium-size carrots may need to be scraped and large carrots will need either scraping or peeling.

Cooking

Carrots are excellent cooked or raw. Children often like raw carrots as they have a very sweet flavor. They can be cut into julienne strips, with a dressing added, or grated into salads and coleslaw – their juices run and blend wonderfully with the dressing. Carrots can be cooked in almost any way you choose. As an accompaniment, cut them into julienne strips and braise in butter and cider, or cook in the minimum of stock and toss in butter and a sprinkling of caraway seeds.

Roasted carrots are delicious, with a melt-in-the-mouth sweetness. Parboil large ones first, but younger carrots can be quickly blanched or added directly to the pan with a joint of meat.

HORSERADISH

Horseradish is grown for its pungent root, which is normally grated and mixed with cream or oil and vinegar and served with roast beef. Fresh horseradish is available in many supermarkets in the spring, and you can make your own horseradish sauce by simply peeling the root and then mixing 3 tablespoons of grated horseradish with $2/3$ cup heavy or whipping cream and adding a little Dijon mustard, vinegar and sugar to taste. As well as being excellent with hot or cold beef, horseradish sauce is delicious with smoked trout or mackerel or spread thinly on sandwiches with a fine pâté.

Left: Carrots.
Right: Horseradish.

BEETS

Experience of vinegar-sodden beets has doubtlessly put many people off them. Those who love them know to buy their beets fresh, so that they can cook them themselves. They can be served in a number of different ways: baked and served with sour cream, braised in a creamy sauce, grated in a salad or used for the classic soup *borscht*.

History

Beets are closely related to sugar beets and mangelwurzels. As the demand for sugar increased over the centuries, when sugar could successfully be extracted from beets, sugar production became a big industry in Britain and Europe.

Mangelwurzels were eaten in parts of Europe and in England in times of famine, although they were primarily grown as cattle fodder.

Beets, however, have probably been eaten since Roman times. By the mid-nineteenth century they were clearly a popular vegetable, and Mrs Beeton in her famous cookbook has 11 recipes for them, including a beet and carrot jam and beet fritters.

Nutrition

Beets are an excellent provider of potassium. The leaves, which have the flavor of spinach, are high in vitamin A, iron and calcium.

Buying and Storing

If possible, buy small beets which have their whiskers intact and have at least 2 inches of stalk at the top; if they are too closely cropped they will bleed during cooking. Beets will keep for several weeks if stored in a cool place.

Preparing

To cook beets whole, first rinse under cold running water. Cut the stalks to about 1 inch above the root and don't cut away the root or peel it – or the glorious deep red color will bleed away. When serving cold in salads, or where the recipe calls for chopped or grated beets, peel away the skin with a potato peeler or sharp knife.

Cooking

To bake in the oven, place the cleaned beet in a dish with a tight-fitting lid, and add 4-5 tablespoons of water. Lay a double layer of foil over the dish before covering with the lid, then bake in a low oven for 2-3 hours or until the beets are tender. Check occasionally to ensure the pan doesn't dry out and to see whether the beets are cooked. They are ready when the skin begins to wrinkle and can be easily rubbed away with your fingers. Alternately, simply wrap the beets in a double layer of foil and cook as above. To boil beets, prepare as above and simmer for about 1½ hours.

BEET GREENS

The tops of several root vegetables are not only edible, but are also extremely nutritious. Beet greens are particularly good, being very high in vitamins A and C, and indeed have more iron and calcium than spinach itself. They are delicious, but not easily available unless you grow your own. If you are lucky enough to get some, boil the greens for a few minutes, then drain well and serve with butter or olive oil.

Left: Beets.
Above right: Scorzonera.
Below right: Salsify.

SALSIFY <u>AND</u> SCORZONERA

These two root vegetables are closely related to each other as well as to members of the same family as dandelion and lettuce. All have long tapering roots.

Salsify has a white or pale brownish skin and scorzonera, sometimes called black salsify, has a black skin. They both have a pale creamy flesh and a fairly similar flavor reminiscent of artichokes and asparagus. Salsify is said to have the superior flavor and has been likened to oysters (it is sometimes referred to as the oyster plant), although many people fail to detect this.

Both salsify and scorzonera make an unusual and pleasant accompaniment, either creamed or fried in butter. They can also be also used in soups.

History

Salsify is native to the Mediterranean but now grows in most areas of North America and Europe. Scorzonera is a southern European plant.

Both roots are classified as herbs and, like many wild plants and herbs, their history is bound up with their use in medicines. The roots, together with their leaves and flowers, were used for the treatment of heartburn, loss of appetite and various liver diseases.

Buying and Storing

Choose specimens that are firm and smooth and, if possible, still with their tops on, which should look fresh and lively. Salsify will keep for several days stored in a cool dark place.

Preparing

Salsify and scorzonera are difficult to clean and peel. Either scrub the root under cold running water and then peel after cooking, or peel with a sharp stainless steel knife (*below*). As the flesh discolors quickly, place the trimmed pieces into acidulated water (water to which lemon juice has been added).

Cooking

Cut into short lengths and simmer for 20–30 minutes until tender. Drain well and sauté in butter, or serve with lemon juice, melted butter or chopped parsley.

Alternately, they can be puréed for soups or mashed. Cooked and cooled salsify and scorzonera can be served in a mustard or garlic vinaigrette with a simple salad.

EXOTIC ROOTS

Throughout the tropical regions of the world all sorts of tubers are grown and used for a fabulous variety of dishes. Yams, sweet potatoes, cassava and taro, to name but a few, are for many people a staple food, not only cooked whole as a vegetable accompaniment, but ground or pounded for bread and cakes. There is an enormous variety of these tropical and subtropical tubers, and while they cannot be cultivated in a moderate climate, the more common tubers are now widely available in specialist shops and in most supermarkets.

SWEET POTATOES

Sweet potatoes are another one of those vegetables that once tasted, are never forgotten. They are, as the name suggests, sweet, but they also have a slightly spicy taste. It's this distinct sweet and savory flavor which makes them such an excellent foil to many savory dishes and

they are fittingly paired with meat dishes that need a touch of sweetness, like turkey or pork.

History

Sweet potatoes are native to tropical America, but today they are grown all over the tropical world. They have been grown in South America from before the Inca civilizations and were introduced into Spain before the ordinary potato. They also have a long history of cultivation in Asia spreading from Polynesia to New Zealand in the fourteenth century.

They are an important staple food in the Caribbean and southern United States, and many famous recipes feature these vegetables. Candied sweet potatoes, for instance, are traditionally served with ham or turkey at Thanksgiving all over the United States, while Jamaica and the West Indies abound with sweet potato dishes, from the simple baked

potato to Caribbean pudding, a typically sweet and spicy dish with sweet potatoes, coconut, limes and cinnamon.

Sweet potatoes appear to have been introduced to England even earlier than regular potatoes. Henry VIII was said to have been very partial to them baked in a pie, believing they would improve his love life! If Henry VIII was eating sweet potatoes in the early/mid-sixteenth century, then it's likely he received them via the Spanish, who, thanks to Christopher Columbus, were busy conquering the New World, thus experiencing a whole range of tropical vegetables and fruit.

Varieties

The skin color ranges from white to pink to reddish brown. The red-skinned variety, which has a whitish flesh, is the one most commonly used in African and Caribbean cooking.

Buying and Storing

Choose small or medium-size ones if possible as larger specimens tend to be rather fibrous. They should be firm and evenly shaped; avoid those that seem withered, have damp patches or are sprouting. They will keep for several days in a cool place.

Preparing and Cooking

If baking, scrub the potatoes well and cook exactly as you would for ordinary potatoes. To boil, either cook in their skins and remove these after cooking, or peel and place in acidulated water (water to which lemon juice has been added). This prevents them turning brown and it's worth boiling them in lightly acidulated water for the same reason. Sweet potatoes can be cooked in any of the ways you would cook ordinary potatoes - roast, boiled, mashed or baked. However, avoid using them in creamy or gratin-type dishes. They are both too sweet and too spicy for that.

It is preferable to roast or sauté them with onions and other savory ingredients to bring out their flavor, or mash them and serve them over chunks of chicken for a crusted chicken pie.

YAMS

Yams have been a staple food for many cultures for thousands of years. There are today almost countless varieties, of different shapes, sizes and colors and called different names by different people. Most varieties are thought to have been native to China, although they found their way to Africa during a very early period and became a basic food, being easy to grow in tropical and subtropical conditions, and containing the essential carbohydrate of all staple foods.

Although cush-cush or Indian yam was indigenous to America, most yams were introduced to the New World as a result of the slave trade in the sixteenth century. Today with such a huge variety of this popular vegetable available, there are innumerable recipes for yam, many probably not printed and published, but handed down by word of mouth from mother to daughter and making their appearance at mealtimes all over the hot regions of the world.

Varieties

The greater yam, as the name suggests, can grow to a huge size. A weight of 137 pounds has been recorded. The varieties you are likely to find in stores will be about the size of a small marrow, although smaller yams are also available such as the sweet yam, which looks like a large potato and is normally covered with whiskery roots. All sizes have a coarse brown skin and can be white or red-fleshed.

In Chinese stores, you may find the Chinese yam, which is a more elongated, club-like shape and is covered with fine whiskers.

Buying

Look out for firm specimens with unbroken skins. The flesh inside should be creamy and moist and if you buy from a grocery, the storekeeper may well cut open a yam so you can check that it is fresh. They can be stored for several weeks in a cool, dark place.

Preparing

Peel away the skin thickly to remove the outer skin and the layer underneath that contains the poison dioscorine. This in fact is destroyed during cooking, but discard the peel carefully. Place the peeled yam in salted water as it discolors easily.

Cooking

Yams, like potatoes, are used as the main starchy element in a meal, boiled and mashed, fried, sautéed or roasted. They tend to have an affinity with spicy sauces and are delicious cut into discs, fried and sprinkled with a little salt and cayenne pepper. African cooks frequently pound boiled yam to make a dough which is then served with spicy stews and soups.

TARO/EDDO

Like yams, taro is another hugely important tuber in tropical areas, and for thousands of years it has been a staple food for many people. It goes under many different names; in South-east Asia, South and Central America, all over Africa and in the Caribbean it is called variously eddo and dasheen.

There are two basic varieties of taro – a large barrel-shaped tuber and a smaller variety, which is often called eddo or dasheen. They are all a dark mahogany brown with a rather shaggy skin, looking like a cross between a beet and a rutabaga.

Although they look very similar, taro belongs to a completely different family from yam and in flavor and texture is noticeably different. Boiled, it has a completely unique flavor, something like a floury water chestnut.

Buying and Storing

Try to buy small specimens; the really small smooth bulbs are tiny attachments to the larger taro and are either called eddoes, or rather sweetly, "sons of taro." Stored in a cool, dark place, they should keep for several weeks.

Left: Sweet potatoes.
Above: Yams.

Preparing

Taros, like yams, contain a poison just under the skin which produces an allergic reaction. Consequently, either peel taros thickly, wearing rubber gloves, or cook in their skins. The toxins are completely eliminated by boiling, and the skins peel off easily.

Cooking

Taros soak up large quantities of liquid during cooking, and this can be turned to advantage by cooking in well-flavored stock or with tomatoes and other vegetables. For this reason, they are excellent in soups and casseroles, adding bulk and flavor in a similar way to potatoes. They can also be steamed or boiled, deep-fried or puréed for fritters, but must be served hot as they become sticky if allowed to cool.

CALLALOO

Callaloo are the leaves of the taro plant, poisonous if eaten raw, but used widely in Asian and Caribbean recipes. They are cooked thoroughly, then used for wrapping meat and vegetables. Callaloo can also be shredded and cooked together with pork, bacon, crab, shrimp, okra, chili, onions and garlic, together with lime and coconut milk to make one of the Caribbean's most famous dishes, named after the leaves themselves, Callaloo.

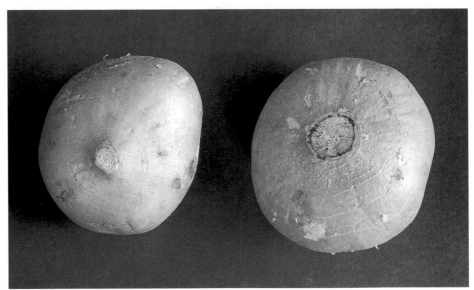

JICAMA

Also known as the Mexican potato, this large root vegetable is a native of central America. It has a thin brown skin and white, crunchy flesh which has a sweet, nutty taste. It can be eaten cooked in the same way as potatoes or sliced and added raw to salads.

Buy specimens that are firm to the touch. Jicama in good condition will keep for about two weeks if stored in a plastic bag in the refrigerator.

Top: Taros (Eddoes).
Above: Jicama.
Left: Callaloo.

CASSAVA

This is another very popular West Indian root, used in numerous Caribbean dishes. It is native to Brazil, and found its way to the West Indies surprisingly via Africa, where it also became a popular vegetable. Known as cassava in the West Indies, it is called manioc or mandioc in Brazil, and juca or yucca is used in other parts of South America.

Cassava is used to make tapioca, and in South America a sauce and an intoxicating beverage are prepared from the juice. However, in Africa and the West Indies it is eaten as a vegetable either boiled, baked or fried, or cooked and pounded to a dough to make *fufu,* a traditional savory African pudding.

Right: Cassava.
Below left: Ginger.
Below right: Galangal.

GINGER AND GALANGAL

GINGER

This is probably the world's most important and popular spice and is associated with a number of different cuisines - Chinese, Indian and Caribbean, to name but a few. It was known in Europe during the Roman period, but was still fairly rare until the spice routes opened up trade in the sixteenth and seventeenth centuries. Like many spices, ginger has the quality of enhancing and complementing both sweet and savory food, adding a fragrant spiciness to all sorts of dishes. However, while ground ginger is best in recipes which will be baked, and preserved ginger, where the ginger is preserved in syrup, tastes wonderful in desserts, for savory dishes, always use fresh ginger.

Nowadays, the pale, knobbly roots of fresh ginger are widely available in supermarkets and whenever possible, buy just a small quantity, as you will not need a great deal and fresh ginger will not keep indefinitely.

To prepare, simply peel away the skin with a sharp knife and grate or thinly slice according to the recipe.

GREATER GALANGAL

Galangal looks similar to ginger except that the rhizome is thinner and the young shoots are bright pink. The roots should be prepared in the same way as ginger and can be used in curries and satay sauces.

FOUR

GREENS

SPINACH

For many people, spinach is inextricably linked with Popeye, the cartoon character who used to eat huge amounts of spinach. It is a wonderfully versatile vegetable, popular worldwide, with nearly every cuisine featuring spinach somewhere in its repertoire. The Italians are particularly partial to spinach and have hundreds of dishes using the vegetable. The words *à la florentine* mean the dish contains spinach.

As well as being delicious on its own, chopped or puréed spinach can be mixed with a range of other ingredients with superb results. It has a particular affinity with dairy products and in the Middle East, feta or helim cheese is used to make boreks or other spinach pies. The Italians mix spinach with ricotta or Parmesan cheese for a huge range of recipes, and the English use eggs and sometimes Cheddar for a spinach soufflé.

History

Spinach was first cultivated in Persia several thousands of years ago. It came to Europe via the Arab world; the Moors introduced it to Spain, and Arabs in the Middle East took it to Greece. It first appeared in England in the fourteenth century, probably via Spain. It is mentioned in the first known English cookbook, where it is referred to as *spynoches*, which echoes the Spanish word for spinach, *espinacas*. It quickly became a popular vegetable, probably because it is quick and easy to grow and similarly easy and quick to cook.

Nutrition

Spinach is an excellent source of vitamin C if eaten raw, as well as vitamins A and B, calcium, potassium and iron. Spinach was originally thought to provide far more iron than it actually does, but the iron is "bound" up by oxalic acid in cooked spinach, which prevents the body absorbing anything but the smallest amounts. Even so, it is still an extremely healthy vegetable whether eaten cooked or raw.

Buying and Storing

Spinach grows all year through, so you should have no difficulty in buying it fresh. Frozen spinach is a poor substitute, mainly because it has so little flavor, so it is worth the effort to use the fresh product.

Spinach leaves should be green and lively; if they look tired and the stalks are floppy, shop round until you find something in better condition. Spinach reduces significantly when cooked: about 1 pound will serve two people. Store it in the salad drawer of the fridge, where it will keep for 1-2 days.

Preparing

Wash well in a bowl of cold water and remove any tough or large stalks.

Cooking

Throw the leaves into a large pan with just the water that clings to the leaves and place over a low heat with a sprinkling of salt. Cover the pan so the spinach steams in its own liquid and shake the pan occasionally to prevent the spinach sticking to the bottom. It cooks in 4-6 minutes, wilting down to about an eighth of its former volume. Drain and press out the remaining liquid with the back of a spoon.

Spinach can be used in a variety of ways. It can be chopped and served with lots of butter, or similarly served with other spring vegetables such as

BRUSSELS SPROUTS

baby carrots or young fava beans. For frittatas, chop the spinach finely, stir in a little Parmesan cheese, a good sprinkling of salt and pepper and a dash of cream, if liked, and stir into the omelet before cooking. Alternately, purée it for sauces or blend it for soups. Spinach is also delicious raw, served with chopped bacon or croûtons. A fresh spinach salad is delicious as the leaves have just the right balance of flavor – sharp but not overpowering.

Below: Spinach.
Below right: Brussels sprouts.

Brussels sprouts have a pronounced and sweet nutty flavor, quite unlike cabbage, although the two are closely related. They are traditionally served at Christmas with chestnuts and indeed have a definite affinity for certain nuts – particularly the sweet flavored nuts, e.g. almonds, pair well rather than hazelnuts or walnuts.

History

Brussels sprouts were cultivated in Flanders (now Belgium) during the Middle Ages. They are basically miniature cabbages which grow in a knobbly row on a long tough stalk. The Germans call sprouts *rosenkohl* – rose cabbage – a pretty and descriptive name as they look like small rosebuds.

Buying and Storing

Buy Brussels sprouts as fresh as possible as older ones are more likely to have that strong unpleasant "cabbage" flavor. They should be small and hard with tightly wrapped leaves. Avoid any that are turning yellow or brown or have loose leaves.

Brussels sprouts will keep for several days in a cool place such as a larder or salad drawer of a fridge, but it is far better to buy them as you need them.

Preparing

Cut away the bottom of the stalk and remove the outer leaves. Some people cut a cross through the bottom of the stalk although this is not really necessary. If you haven't been able to avoid buying big Brussels sprouts, cut them in half or into quarters, or slice them thinly for stir-frying.

Cooking

As with cabbage, either cook Brussels sprouts very briefly or braise slowly in the oven. Cook in small amounts of fast boiling water for about 3 minutes until just tender. To stir-fry Brussels sprouts, slice into three or four pieces and then fry in a little oil and butter – they taste great with onions and ginger.

CAULIFLOWER

Cauliflower is a member of the cabbage family, *Brassica oleracea*. Like all cabbages, cauliflower suffers terribly from overcooking. A properly cooked cauliflower has a pleasant fresh flavor but when overcooked it turns grey and becomes unpalatably soft, taking on a nasty rank flavor with an unpleasant aftertaste. Children often like raw cauliflower even though they may not connect it with the same vegetable served up as boiled.

History

Cauliflower is thought to have come originally from China and thence to the Middle East. The Moors introduced it to Spain in the twelfth century and from there it found its way to England via established trading routes. The early cauliflower was the size of a tennis ball but is has gradually been cultivated to the enormous sizes we see today. Ironically, baby cauliflowers are now fashionable.

Varieties

Green and occasionally purple cauliflowers are available in the stores. The purple variety was originally grown in Sardinia and Italy but is increasingly grown by other market gardeners. They look pretty and unusual but are otherwise similar to white cauliflower. Dwarf varieties of cauliflower are now commonly available in stores.

Broccoli Romanescoes: As well as baby white cauliflowers, broccoli romanescoes are also avaliable.These pretty green or white vegetables look like a cross between broccoli and cauliflower, but are more closely related to cauliflower. They taste very much like cauliflower, but since they are quite small, they are less likely to be overcooked and consequently retain their excellent flavor.

Broccoflower: A cross between broccoli and cauliflower, this looks like a pale green cauliflower. It has a mild flavor and should be cooked in the same way as you would cauliflower.

Right: Baby cauliflowers.
Far right top: Broccoli romanescoes.
Far right bottom: Green cauliflowers.

Nutrition

Cauliflower contains potassium, iron and zinc, although cooking reduces the amounts. It is also a good source of vitamins A and C.

Buying and Storing

In top condition, a cauliflower is a creamy white color with the outer leaves curled round the flower. The head should be unblemished with no black or discolored areas and the outer leaves should look fresh and crisp. Keep cauliflower in a cool place for no longer than 1-2 days; after that it will deteriorate and valuable nutrients will be lost.

Preparing

To cook a cauliflower whole, first trim away the coarse bottom leaves (leave the inner ones on, if liked). Very large cauliflowers are best halved or broken into florets, as the outside will overcook before the inside is tender. Some people trim away the stalk, but others like this part and only trim off the very thick stalk at the bottom of the plant.

Cooking

Cauliflowers are excellent steamed, either whole or in florets. Place in a steamer or colander over a pan of boiling water, cover and steam until just tender and immediately remove from the heat. The florets can then be fried in olive oil or butter for a few minutes to give a lightly browned finish.

When cooking a cauliflower whole, start testing it after 10 minutes; it should feel tender but still have plenty of "bite" left in it. Cauliflower is a popular vegetable accompaniment, either served with just a little butter, or with a tomato or cheese sauce. It is also good stir-fried with onions and garlic together with a few tomatoes and capers.

Cauliflower is excellent in salads or used for crudités. Either use it raw or blanch it in boiling water for 1-2 minutes, then refresh under cold running water.

Small cauliflowers and broccoli romanescoes are intended to be cooked whole, and can be steamed or boiled, covered with a lid, in the minimum of water for 4-5 minutes until just tender.

SPROUTING BROCCOLI AND CALABRESE

Varieties

Calabrese Broccoli: This is the vegetable we today commonly call broccoli, with large beautiful, blue-green heads on succulent stalks. It is named after the Italian province of Calabria where this variety was first developed.

Purple Sprouting Broccoli: The original variety – it has long thin stalks with small flowerheads that are normally purple but can be white or green. Heads, stalks and tender leaves are all edible. The purple heads turn green when cooked but the others keep their color. Purple sprouting broccoli is more seasonal than the easily available calabrese; it is usually available from late winter onward.

Buying and Storing

If possible, buy loose broccoli rather than the pre-wrapped bundles, because it is easier to check that it is fresh and also because wrapped vegetables tend to deteriorate more quickly.

Purple sprouting broccoli can also be sold loose or prepacked. Check that the stalk, flower head and leaves all look fresh and that the florets are tightly closed and bright green. Neither type will keep for long.

Broccoli or calabrese is a relatively modern vegetable and is one of the most popular. It is quick and easy to prepare with little or no waste and similarly easy to cook. It is attractive, whether served raw or cooked, and you can buy it in the quantity you require, unlike cauliflower or cabbage.

History

Before calabrese came into our stores, people bought and ate purple sprouting broccoli. This is basically an "untidy" version of calabrese, with long shoots and clusters of flowerheads at the end – the broccoli we know today has neat tidy heads. The stalks of purple sprouting broccoli have a faint asparagus flavor.

The Romans cooked purple sprouting broccoli in wine or served it with sauces and it is still a popular vegetable today in Italy, cooked in the oven with anchovies and onions or served with pasta in a garlic and tomato sauce.

Preparing and Cooking

Trim the ends and remove any discolored leaves.

Calabrese Broccoli: Break into even-size pieces, dividing the stem and floret lengthwise if they are thick. Cook in a little boiling water for 4-5 minutes until just tender and then drain. Do not steam this variety of broccoli as its vibrant green color tends to turn gray.

Purple Sprouting Broccoli: Either steam in long, even-size lengths in a steamer or, if you have an asparagus steamer, cook as you would asparagus. Alternately, tie the stems loosely together and stand in a little water – if necessary, wedge it in with a potato or rolled up piece of foil. Cover with a dome of foil and steam for 4-5 minutes until tender.

Serving

Serve both varieties simply with butter and lemon juice or with a hollandaise or béarnaise sauce as an accompaniment. They are also excellent stir-fried.

Above far left: Purple cauliflower.
Below far left: Purple sprouting broccoli.
Above: Calabrese broccoli.
Below: Turnip tops.

TURNIP TOPS

Turnip tops, like beet greens, are both delicious and nutritious. They are not widely available but if you are able to buy some or if you grow your own, slice them *(below)* and boil or steam for a few minutes, then drain and serve with butter.

CABBAGE

Cabbage, sliced and cooked, can be one of two things: deliciously crisp, with a mild pleasant flavor – or overcooked and horrible! Cabbage and other brassicas contain the chemical hydrogen sulphide, which is activated during cooking at about the point the vegetable starts to soften. It eventually disappears, but during the in-between time, cabbage acquires its characteristic rank smell and flavor. So, either cook cabbage briefly, or cook it long and slow, preferably with other ingredients so that flavors can mingle.

History

Cabbage has a long and varied history. However, because there are many varieties of cabbage under the general heading of "brassica", it is difficult to be sure whether the variety the Greeks and Romans enjoyed is the same as today's round cabbage, or something more akin to kale or even Chinese cabbage.

The round cabbages we know today were an important food during the Dark Ages, and by the Middle Ages they were in abundance, as you will see if you study the paintings of that period. These commonly show kitchen tables or baskets at market positively groaning with fruit and vegetables, and cabbages in all their shapes and sizes were often featured.

Medieval recipes suggest cooking cabbages with leeks, onions and herbs. In the days when all except the very wealthy cooked everything in one pot, it is fair to assume that cabbages were cooked long and slow.

Varieties

Savoy Cabbage: This is a variety of green cabbage with crimped or curly leaves. It has a mild flavor and is particularly tender, thus needing less cooking than other varieties.
Spring Greens: These have fresh loose heads with a pale yellow-green heart. They are available in spring and are delicious simply sliced, steamed and served with butter.

Right: Savoy cabbage.
Above far right: Green cabbage.
Below far right: Spring greens.

Green Cabbage: The early green, or spring, cabbages are dark green, loose-leafed and have a slightly pointed head. They have little or no heart as they are picked before this has had time to develop. Nevertheless, they are a very good cabbage and all but the very outside leaves should be tender. As the season progresses, larger, firmer and more pale green cabbages are available. These are a little tougher than the spring cabbages and need longer cooking.

Red Cabbage: A beautifully colored cabbage with smooth firm leaves. The color fades during cooking unless a little vinegar is added to the water. Red cabbage can be pickled or stewed with spices and flavorings.

White Cabbage: Sometimes called Dutch cabbages, white cabbages have smooth firm pale green leaves. They are available throughout the winter. They are good cooked or raw. To cook, slice them thinly, then boil or steam and serve with butter. To serve raw, slice thinly and use in a coleslaw.

Buying and Storing

Cabbages should be fresh looking and unblemished. When buying, avoid any with wilted leaves or those that look or feel puffy. Savoys and collard greens will keep in a cool place for several days; firmer cabbages will keep happily for much longer.

Preparing

Remove the outer leaves, if necessary, and then cut into quarters. Remove the stalk and then slice or shred according to your recipe or to taste.

Cooking

For green or white cabbages, place the shredded leaves in a pan with a pat of butter and a couple of tablespoons of water to prevent burning. Cover and cook over a medium heat until the leaves are tender, occasionally shaking the pan or stirring.

Red cabbage is cooked quite differently and is commonly sautéed in oil or butter and then braised in a low oven for up to 1½ hours with apples, currants, onions, vinegar, wine, sugar and spices.

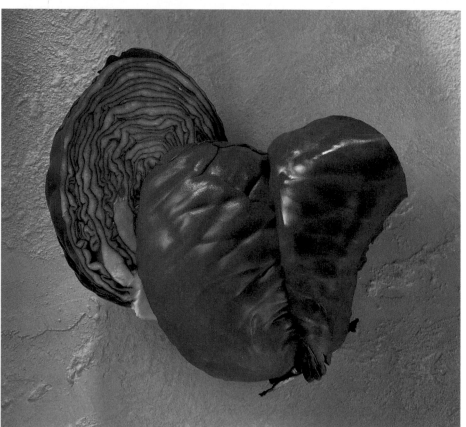

KALE AND CURLY KALE

Kale is the name used for a variety of green-leafed vegetables of the brassica family. Most kales have thick stems and robust leaves that do not form a head. Many kales have curly leaves, which are the variety most commonly eaten. Large coarse-leafed kales are grown for cattle and sheep feeds.

History

Kale is thought to be one of the first cultivated brassicas. Colewort, the wild ancestor, still grows along the coasts of western Europe.

Varieties

Collards: Collards, or collard greens, are a popular green vegetable in the southern United States. They are grown in summer and autumn for harvesting in the spring and are a good source of vitamin A.

Curly Kale: With its crimped, curly leaves, this is the most commonly available kale, although even this can be quite hard to come by. If you are a big fan and don't grow your own, try farm stores in early spring.

Purple or Silver Kale: This is an ornamental variety, and is grown almost exclusively for display.

Preparing and Cooking

Kale is probably the strongest tasting of the brassicas and is best cooked simply, paired with a bland-flavored vegetable, such as potatoes. To prepare, break the leaves from the stalk and then cut out any thick stalk from the leaf. This can then be rolled and sliced or cooked whole. Boil the leaves in a little salted water for 3-5 minutes until tender. Owing to its robust nature, kale is frequently teamed with fairly hot spices and is consequently popular in many Indian dishes.

Above far left: White cabbage.
Below far left: Red cabbage.
Left: Collards.
Above: Curly kale.

GARDEN <u>AND</u> WILD LEAVES

VINE LEAVES

All leaves from vines that produce grapes can be eaten when young. They make an ideal wrapping for various meats and vegetables as they are surprisingly strong and of course edible. Most countries that produce wine will have dishes where vine leaves appear. *Dolmades*, commonly eaten in Greece and the Middle East is perhaps the best known dish, but in France, Spain and Italy, there are recipes using vine leaves to wrap small birds, like quail or snipe.

Vine leaves have a faintly lemon/cabbage flavor which can be detected at its best in a good *dolmades*. The leaves must be cooked briefly before using, so that they are pliable and don't crack or break as you wrap the food. Bring to the boil and simmer for about 1 minute. The leaves should then be drained and separated until you are ready to use them.

DANDELION

Any child who has picked dandelions for his or her rabbits or guinea pigs and has watched them gobble them up greedily will know that this weed, though hated by the gardener in the family, has something going for it. Some gardeners, of course, are very partial to dandelion and raise the plant carefully so that the leaves are fresh and tender for the salad, and in France dandelions can often be seen for sale at market.

Look in any book of herbal remedies, and dandelions will feature prominently.

They are a well-known diuretic, their French name – *pissenlits* (piss-a-bed) – attesting to this in no uncertain terms.

Although it's gratifying to pick your own vegetables for free, it is generally recommended, if you like dandelions, that you buy the domestic seeds and grow your own. These are likely to be the juiciest and least bitter plants. If you do pick your own, do so well away from the roadside and wash the leaves carefully.

Dandelion leaves can be added to salads or used in *pissenlits au lard*, where whole young dandelion plants are dressed in vinaigrette and then covered in finely chopped pieces of salt pork or bacon and bacon fat.

SORREL

Sorrel is not always available commercially, although it is in France and is greatly prized. However, it grows wild in cool soils, or can be grown in your own garden. Young leaves are delicious in salads, or, later in the year, can be used in soups or sauces to accompany fish. It has a sharp, distinct, lemon flavor and is commonly teamed with eggs and cream.

ORACHE

Although not related to spinach, this beautiful red or golden-leafed plant is called mountain spinach and its large leaves can be treated like spinach.

GOOD KING HENRY AND FAT HEN

These are both members of the goose-foot family and were popular vegetables in Europe in the sixteenth century. Today, Good King Henry has all but disappeared, and Fat Hen only grows wild as a weed. Both were superseded by spinach, which they are said to resemble in taste, although Fat Hen is milder.

NETTLES

Wild food enthusiasts get very excited about nettles as food, perhaps because they are plentiful and free and maybe because they take pleasure in eating something that everyone else avoids. Of course, once cooked, the sting completely disappears. They should be picked when they are very young and are good used in soups.

Above far left: Fresh vine leaves.
Above left: Dandelion.
Below left: Sorrel.
Right: Good King Henry.
Below: Nettles.

CHINESE GREENS

CHINESE CABBAGE/LEAVES (PE-TSAI)

Chinese cabbage, also called Napa cabbage, has pale green, crinkly leaves with long, wide, white ribs. Its shape is a little like a very fat head of celery, which gives rise to another of its alternative names, celery cabbage. It is pleasantly crunchy with a faint cabbage flavor, and, since it is available all year through, it makes a useful winter salad component. Chinese cabbage is also very good stir-fried with a tasty sauce. It is an essential ingredient of many oriental recipes.

Buying and Storing

For some reason, Chinese leaves almost always look fresh and perky when on sale in the supermarket, which probably indicates that they travel well and are transported quickly. Avoid any with discoloured or damaged stems. The leaves should be pale green and straight without blemishes or bruises. They will keep for up to six days in the salad drawer of the fridge.

Preparing

Remove the outside leaves and slice as much as you need.

Many Chinese greens are members of the brassica family. If you go into a popular and reasonably large Chinese supermarket, you'll be astonished at the varieties of green vegetables for sale. Discovering the names of these vegetables, on the other hand, can be a bit of a hit-and-miss undertaking, as the storekeepers, although always well intentioned, rarely know the English name, if indeed there is one.

CHINESE MUSTARD GREENS

Mustard greens are worth buying if you can, as they are very good to eat. The plant is a member of the cabbage family, but is grown in Europe solely for its mustard seed. In India and Asia it has long been grown for its oil seed, but the Chinese developed the plant for its leaves as well. These are deep green and slightly puckered-looking and have a definite mustard flavor, which can be quite fiery.

If you grow your own, then you'll be able to enjoy the young leaves which can be added to lettuce to spice up salads. Older leaves are best stir-fried and then dressed with a light Chinese sauce. They are also good cooked with onion and garlic and served as a side dish to accompany pork or bacon.

Preparing and Cooking

Break apart the stalks, rinse, then cut both stalks and leaves into thick or thin slices. These can then be stir-fried with garlic and onions, or cooked and served as you would chard. It has a pleasant flavor, milder than mustard greens, yet with more bite than the bland Chinese cabbage.

CHINESE BROCCOLI

This is another leafy vegetable, but with slender heads of flowers that look a little like our own broccoli, except that the flowers are usually white or yellow. Once the thicker stalks are trimmed, the greens can be sliced and cooked and served in the same way as Chinese mustard greens.

Far left: Chinese mustard greens.
Left: Chinese leaves.
Above: Chinese broccoli.
Below: Pak-choi.

Cooking and Serving

If adding to salads, combine Chinese cabbage with something fairly forceful, like Belgian endive or arugula, and add a well-flavored dressing. If adding to a stir-fry, cook with garlic, ginger and other fairly strong flavors. While the faint cabbage flavor will be lost, you will still get the pleasant crunchy "bite" of the stalk, and the leaves will carry the sauce.

PAK-CHOI

If you frequent your local Chinese supermarket, you will almost certainly have come across *Pak-Choi*. In English it should correctly be called Chinese celery cabbage and its thick stalks, joined at the end in a small root, are vaguely celery-like. Its leaves, on the other hand, are generally large and spoon shaped. There are many different species of this vegetable, and smaller specimens look more like the tops of radishes and have small slim stalks. Consequently the vegetable can be known by all sorts of picturesque names, like "horse's ear" and "horse's tail." There's no rule for discovering exactly what you are buying, but the important thing is to choose a fresh plant whatever its size: look for fresh green leaves and crisp stalks.

KOHLRABI

Kohlrabi looks like a cross between a cabbage and a turnip and is often classified as a root vegetable, even though it grows above ground. It is a member of the brassica family, but, unlike cabbages, it is the bulbous stalk that is edible rather than the flowering heads.

There are two varieties of kohlrabi: one is purple and the other pale green. They both have the same mild and fresh tasting flavor, not dissimilar to water chestnuts. Kohlrabi is neither as peppery as turnip nor as distinctive as cabbage, but it is easy to see why people think it a little like both. It can be served as an alternative to carrots or turnips.

History

Although kohlrabi is not a very popular vegetable in North America, it is commonly eaten in Europe, as well as in China, India and Asia. In Kashmir, where it is grown, there are many recipes – the bulbs are often finely sliced and eaten in salads and the greens are cooked in mustard oil with garlic and chilies.

Buying and Storing

Kohlrabi is best when small and young, since larger specimens tend to be coarse and fibrous. It keeps well for 7-10 days if stored in a cool place.

Preparing

Peel the skin with a knife and then cook whole or slice.

Cooking

Very small kohlrabies are tender and can be cooked whole. However, if they are any bigger than 2 inches in diameter, they can be stuffed. To do this, hollow out a little before cooking and then stuff with fried onions and tomatoes, for instance. For sliced kohlrabi, cook until just tender and serve with butter or a creamy sauce. They can also be cooked long and slow in gratin dishes, with, for instance, potatoes as a variation of *gratin Dauphinois*. Alternately, parboil them and bake in the oven covered with a cheese sauce.

CHARD

Chard is one of those vegetables that needs plenty of water when growing, which explains why it is a popular garden vegetable in many places which have a high rainfall. Gardeners are very fond of chard, not only because it is delicious to eat but also because it is so very striking.

Chard is often likened to spinach. The leaves have similarities, although they are not related and chard is on an altogether larger scale. Chard leaves are large and fleshy with distinctive white ribs, and the flavor is stronger and more robust than spinach. It is popular in France where it is baked with rice, eggs and milk in *tians*, and cooked in a celebrated pastry from Nice – *tourte de blettes* – which is a sweet tart filled with raisins, pine nuts, apples and chard bound together with eggs. It is also often combined with eggs in frittatas and tortillas.

Chard is a member of the beet family and is called by several names on this theme, including sea kale beet and spinach beet.

Ruby or rhubarb chard has striking red ribs and leaf beet is often cultivated as a decorative plant, but they both have the same flavor, and unlike sugar beet and beets, they are cultivated only for their leaves.

Buying and Storing

Heads of chard should be fresh and bright green; avoid those with withered leaves or flabby stems. It keeps better than spinach but should be eaten within a couple of days.

Preparing

Some people buy or grow chard for the white stems alone and discard the leaves (or give them to pet guinea pigs), but this is a waste of a delicious vegetable. The leaf needs to be separated from the ribs, and this can be done roughly with a sharp knife (*right*) or more precisely using scissors. The ribs can then be sliced. Either shred the leaves, or blanch them and use them to wrap little parcels of fragrant rice or other food. If the chard is young and small, the ribs do not need to be removed.

Cooking

For pies, frittatas and gratins, the leaves and ribs can be cooked together. Gently sauté the ribs in butter and oil and then add the leaves a minute or so later. Alternately, the ribs can be simmered in a little water until tender and the leaves added a few minutes later or steamed over the top.

Above far left: Kohlrabi.
Left: Purple kohlrabi.
Above: Chard.

FIVE

BEANS, PEAS AND SEEDS

Fava Beans

Wax Beans

Peas

Green Beans

Corn

Okra

Dried Beans and Peas

FAVA BEANS

One of the delights of having a garden is discovering how truly delicious some vegetables are when garden fresh. This seems particularly true of fava beans, which have a superb sweet flavor that sadly can never be reproduced in the frozen product. If you're lucky enough to grow or be given fresh fava beans, don't worry about recipes; just cook them until tender and serve with butter. It will be a revelation! However, if you're not one of those lucky few, don't dismiss fava beans, as they are still a wonderfully versatile vegetable. They can be used in soups or casseroles, and, since they have a mealy texture, they also purée well.

History

People have been eating fava beans almost since time began. A variety of wild fava bean grew all over southern Europe, North Africa and Asia, and it would have been a useful food for early man. There is archaeological evidence that by Neolithic times fava beans were being farmed, making them one of the first foods to be cultivated.

Fava beans will grow in most climates and most soils. They were a staple food for people throughout the Dark Ages and the Middle Ages, grown for feeding people and livestock until being replaced by the potato in the seventeenth and eighteenth centuries. Fava beans were an important source of protein for the poor, and because they dry well, they would have provided nourishing meals for families until the next growing season.

Nutrition

Beans are high in protein and carbohydrates and are also a good source of vitamins A, B1 and B2. They also provide potassium and iron as well as several other minerals.

Buying and Storing

Buy beans as fresh as possible. The pods should preferably be small and tender. Use as soon as possible.

Preparing

Very young beans in tender pods, no more than 3 inches in length, can be eaten pod and all; top and tail, and then

slice roughly. Usually, however, you will need to shell the beans. Elderly beans are often better skinned after they are cooked to rid them of the strong, bitter flavor that puts many people off this vegetable.

Cooking

Plunge shelled beans (or in their pods if very young) into rapidly boiling water and cook until just tender. They can also be parboiled and then finished off braised in butter. For a simple broad bean purée, blend the cooked beans with garlic cooked in butter, cream and a pinch of fresh herbs, such as savory or thyme.

LIMA BEANS

These are popular in the US, named after the capital of Peru, and are sold mainly shelled. They are an essential ingredient in the Native American dish *succotash*. Lima beans should be cooked in a little boiling water until tender. Elderly beans need skinning after they are cooked. The dried bean, also known as the butter bean, can be large or small. These large beans tend to become mushy when cooked so are best used in soups or purées.

Above: Fava beans.
Below: Lima beans.
Right: Wax beans.

WAX BEANS

The wax bean is native to South America, where it has been cultivated for more than 2000 years, and there is archaeological evidence of its existence much earlier than that.

It is a popular vegetable to grow. Most home vegetable gardeners have a patch of wax beans – they are easy to grow and, like all legumes, their roots contain bacteria that help renew nitrogen supplies in the soil.

They have a more robust flavor and texture than French beans and are distinct from green beans in several ways: they are generally much larger with long, flattened pods; their skin is rough textured, although in young beans this softens during cooking; and they contain purple beans within the pods, unlike green beans whose beans are mostly white or pale green. Nevertheless, runner beans belong to the same family as all the green beans.

Buying and Storing

Always buy young beans as the pods of larger beans are likely to be tough. The pods should feel firm and fresh; if you can see the outline of the bean inside the pod it is likely to be fibrous – although you could leave the beans to dry out and use the dried beans later in the season. Ideally, the beans inside should be no larger than your small fingernail.

Use as soon as possible after buying; they do not store well.

Preparing

Wax beans need to be topped and tailed and may also need stringing. Carefully put your knife through the top of the bean without cutting right through, and then pull downward; if a thick thread comes away, the beans need stringing, so do the same on the other side. The beans can then be sliced either using a sharp knife or a slicer.

Slice through lengthwise, not diagonally, so that you will be able to serve the beans with just a little skin and lots of succulent flesh.

Cooking

Plunge the beans into boiling salted water and cook until *al dente*.

PEAS

Fresh peas are wonderful – try tasting them raw, straight from the pod. Unfortunately, the season for garden peas is short, and frozen peas, which are the next best thing, never quite come up to the mark. If you grow your own peas, for three or four weeks in early summer, you can eat like a king; otherwise you can buy them from a good grocer, who may be able to keep you supplied all through the early summer.

History

Peas have an even longer history than fava beans, with archaeological evidence showing they were cultivated as long ago as 5700 BC. High in protein and carbohydrates, they would have been another important staple food and were eaten fresh or dried for soups or potage.

"Pease" porridge is mentioned in a Greek play written in 5 BC. "Pease pudding," probably something similar, made with split peas with onion and herbs, is an old-fashioned but still very popular dish, especially in the north of England, traditionally eaten with ham and pork.

One of the first recipes for peas, however, comes from *Le Cuisinier Français*, which was translated into English in the middle of the seventeenth century and gives a recipe for *petits pois à la française* (peas cooked with small-hearted lettuces) – still a popular recipe today.

Varieties

Snow Peas: These are eaten whole and have a delicate flavor, providing they are not overcooked. Unfortunately, they are easy to overcook and the texture then becomes rather slippery. Alternately, blanch or stir-fry them. They are also good served raw in salads.

Petits Pois: These are not, as you might expect, immature peas but are a dwarf variety. Gardeners grow their own, but they are not available fresh in the stores as they are mainly grown commercially for canning or freezing.

Sugar Peas, Sugar Snaps: These have the distinct fresh flavor of raw peas and are more plump and have more snap than snow peas.

Buying and Storing

Only buy fresh peas; if they are old they are bound to be disappointing and you would be better off buying them frozen. In top condition, the pods are bright green and lively looking; the more withered the pod, the longer they have been hanging around. It is possible to surreptitiously sample peas on occasion, to check if they are fresh (grocers don't seem to mind if you buy some). Use fresh peas as soon as possible.

Preparing

Shelling peas can be very relaxing. Press open the pods and use your thumb to push out the peas *(below)*. Snow peas and sugar snaps just need to be topped and tailed *(below right)*.

Left: Peas.
Above right: Sugar snap peas.

Cooking

Cook peas with a sprig of mint in a pan of rapidly boiling water or in a covered steamer until tender. Alternately, melt butter in a flameproof casserole, add the peas and then cover and sweat over low heat for 4–5 minutes. Cook snow peas and sugar snaps in any of these ways but for a shorter time.

GREEN BEANS

Whether you call beans French beans, haricots or green beans, they all belong to a large and varied family.

History

The bean is a New World vegetable that had been cultivated for thousands of years by native peoples in both the north and south of the continent, which accounts for its wide diversity.

Varieties

One variety or another is available all year through and so they are one of the most convenient fresh green vegetables.
French Beans: This name encompasses a range of green beans, including the snap bean and bobby bean. They are mostly fat and fleshy, and when fresh, should be firm so that they break in half with a satisfying snapping sound.

Haricots Verts: These are considered the best French beans and are delicate and

slim in shape. They should be eaten when very young, no more than 2¹/₂-3 inches in length.
Thai Beans: These long beans are similar to French beans and can be prepared and cooked in the same way.
Yellow Wax Beans: This is also a French bean and has a mild, slightly buttery taste.

Buying and Storing

Whatever variety, beans should be bright and crisp. Avoid wilted ones, or those with overly mature pods which feel spongy when lightly squeezed. They do not keep well, so use as soon as possible after buying or picking.

Preparing

To remove the ends of the beans: gather them together in one hand and then slice away the top ¹/4 inch *(below)*, then do the same at the other end. If necessary, pull off any stringy bits.

Cooking

Plunge beans into rapidly boiling salted water and cook until *al dente*. When overcooked, beans have a flabby texture and also lose much of their flavor. Drain and toss them in butter or serve in a sauce with shallots and bacon. For salads, cook until just tender and then refresh under cold water. They are excellent with a garlicky vinaigrette. Serve with carrots or other root vegetables and savor the contrast in flavors.

Above left: Bobby beans.
Below left: Yellow wax beans.
Right: Haricots verts.
Below: Thai beans.

CORN

Fresh corn, eaten on the cob with salt and a little butter, is deliciously sweet. Some gardeners who grow it have a pan ready on the boil, so that when they cut the corn it goes into the pan in only the time it takes to race up from the garden to the kitchen. Buying it from the supermarket is inevitably a bit hit-or-miss, although if purchased in season, corn can be very good indeed.

History

In 1492, as Christopher Columbus disembarked on the island now called Cuba, he was met by Native Americans offering two gifts of hospitality – one was tobacco and the other something the Native Americans called *maïs*. The English word for staple food was then corn, so that when Columbus and his crew saw that maize was the staple food for the Native Americans, it was dubbed "Indian corn."

Corn originated in South America and had enormous significance to the Native Americans of the whole continent, who were said to have lived and died by corn. They referred to it as their "first mother and father, the source of life." By far their most important food, corn was used in many other ways as well. They used the plant for their shelters and for fences, and they wore it and decorated their bodies with it.

The Aztecs had corn planting ceremonies that included human sacrifices, and other tribes had similar customs to appease the god "corn." Countless myths and legends have been woven around corn, each tribe telling a slightly different story, but each on the same theme of planting and harvesting corn. For anthropologists and historians, they make compelling study.

Nutrition

Corn is a good carbohydrate food and is rich in vitamins A, B and C. It contains protein, but less so than most other cereals. It is also a good source of potassium, magnesium, phosphorus and iron.

Varieties

There are five main varieties of corn – popcorn, sweet corn, dent corn, flint corn and flour corn. Dent corn is the

most commonly grown worldwide, for animal feeds and oil, and the corn we eat on the cobs is sweet corn. Baby corn cobs are picked when immature and are cooked and eaten whole.

Buying and Storing

As soon as corn is picked, its sugar begins to turn to starch and therefore the sooner it goes into the pot, the better. Wherever possible, buy locally grown corn.

Look for husks that are clean and green and tassels which are golden, with no sign of matting. The corn itself should look plump and yellow. Avoid cobs with pale or white kernels or those with older shriveled kernels which will undoubtedly be disappointing.

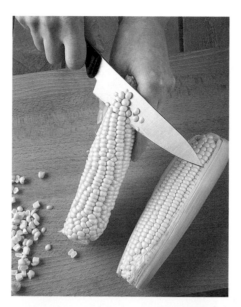

Preparing

Strip away the husks. To use the kernels for recipes, cut downward using a sharp knife from top to bottom *(left)*.

Cooking

Cook corn on the cob in plenty of boiling salted water until tender. Timing depends on the size of the cobs but 10-15 minutes will normally be enough. Serve them with sea salt and butter, but if the cobs are really sweet, leave out the butter. Stir-fry baby corn cobs briefly and serve in oriental dishes.

Far left: Corn cobs.
Below: Baby corn cobs.

OKRA

History

Okra originated in Africa. In the sixteenth century, when African people were enslaved by the Spanish and shipped to the New World, they took with them the few things they could, including the plants and seeds from home – dried peas, yams, ackee – and okra. This lantern-shaped pod containing rows of seeds oozes a sticky mucilaginous liquid when cooked, and it was popular not only for its subtle flavor but also for thickening soups and stews.

The plant thrived in the tropical climate and by the early nineteenth century, when the slave trade was finally abolished, okra was an important part of the cuisine of the Caribbean and the southern United States. In and around New Orleans, the Creoles, the American-born descendants of European-born settlers, adopted a popular Native American dish called *gumbo*. An essential quality of this famous dish was its thick gluey consistency. The Native Americans used filé powder (the dry pounded leaves of the sassafras tree), but okra was welcomed as a more satisfactory alternative.

Gumbos are now the hallmark of Creole cooking, and in some parts of America, the word "gumbo" is an alternative word for okra itself.

Buying and Storing

Choose young, small pods as older ones are likely to be fibrous. They should be bright green, firm and slightly springy when squeezed. Avoid any that are shriveled or bruised. They will keep for a few days in the salad drawer of the fridge.

Preparing

When cooking whole, trim the top but don't expose the seeds inside or the viscous liquid will ooze into the rest of the dish. If, however, this is what you want, slice thickly or thinly according to the recipe *(right)*. If you want to eliminate some of this liquid, first soak the whole pods in acidulated water (water to which lemon juice has been added) for about an hour.

Cooking

The pods can be steamed, boiled or lightly fried, and then added to or used with other ingredients. If cooked whole, okra is not mucilaginous but is pleasantly tender. Whether cooked whole or sliced, use garlic, ginger or chili to perk up the flavor, or cook Native American-style, with onions, tomatoes and spices.

Above: Okra.

DRIED BEANS AND PEAS

Dried beans feature in traditional cuisines all over the world, from Mexican refried beans to Italy's *pasta e fagioli*. They are nutritious, providing a good source of protein when combined with rice, and are a marvelous store cupboard standby.

Black-eyed Peas: Sometimes called black-eyed beans, these small cream-colored beans have a black spot or eye. When cooked, they have a tender, creamy texture and a mildly smoky flavor. Black-eyed beans are widely used in Indian cooking.

Chana Dhal: Chana dhal is very similar to yellow split peas but smaller in size and with a slightly sweeter taste. It is used in a variety of vegetable dishes.

Chickpeas: These round beige-colored pulses have a strong, nutty flavor when cooked. As well as being used for curries, chickpeas are also ground into a flour which is widely used in many Indian dishes such as *pakoras* and *bhajees*.

Flageolet Beans: Small oval beans which are either white or pale green in color. They have a very mild, refreshing flavor and feature in classic French dishes.

Green Lentils: Also known as continental lentils, these have quite a strong flavor and retain their shape during cooking. They are very versatile and are used in a number of dishes.

Haricot Beans: Small, white oval beans which come in different varieties. Haricot beans are ideal for Indian cooking because not only do they retain their shape but they also absorb the flavors of the spices.

Kidney Beans: Kidney beans are one of the most popular pulses. They are dark red/brown, kidney-shaped beans with a strong flavor.

Mung Beans: These are small, round green beans with a slightly sweet flavor and creamy texture. When sprouted they produce the familiar bean sprouts.

Red Split Lentils: A readily available lentil that can be used for making dhal. Use instead of toovar dhal.

Toovar Dhal: A dull orange-colored split pea with a very distinctive earthy flavor. Toovar dhal is available plain and in an oily variety.

Soaking and Cooking Tips

Most dried pulses, except lentils, need to be soaked overnight before cooking. Wash the beans thoroughly and remove any small stones and damaged beans. Put into a large bowl and cover with plenty of cold water. When cooking, allow double the volume of water to beans and boil for 10 minutes. This initial boiling period is essential to remove any harmful toxins. Drain, rinse and cook in fresh water. The cooking time for all pulses varies depending on the type and their freshness. Pulses can be cooked in a pressure cooker to save time. Lentils, on the whole, do not need soaking. They should be washed in several changes of cold water before being cooked.

Left: Clockwise from bottom right: Mung beans, Flageolet beans, Chickpeas, Haricot beans, Black-eyed peas, Kidney beans.
Above: Clockwise from top: Red split lentils, Green lentils, Toovar dhal, Chana dhal.

SIX

SQUASHES

Zucchini
....
Marrows and Summer Squashes
....
Pumpkins and Winter Squashes
....
Exotic Gourds
....
Cucumbers

ZUCCHINI

Zucchini are the best loved of all the squashes as they are so versatile. They are quick and easy to cook and are succulent and tender with a delicate, un-assuming flavor. Unlike other squashes, they are available all year through.

Vegetables taste best when eaten immediately after they have been picked, and this particularly applies to zucchini. They have a long season and are good to grow since the more you cut, the more the plants produce. Left unchecked, they turn into marrows.

Varieties

The zucchini is classified as a summer squash, *cucurbita pepo*, along with marrows and pattypan squashes.

Zucchini: Sometimes called courgettes, zucchini are basically immature marrows. The word is a diminutive of the Italian *zucca*, meaning gourd, and similarly courgette means miniature *courge*, French for marrow. Zucchini have a deep green skin, with firm pale flesh. The seeds and pith found in marrows have yet to form but are visible in more mature zucchini. Conversely, the prized baby zucchini have no suggestion of seeds or pith and the flesh is completely firm.

Yellow Zucchini: These are bright yellow and somewhat straighter than green zucchini. They have a slightly firmer flesh than green zucchini but are otherwise similar.

Pattypan Squashes: These little squashes look like tiny custard squashes. They can be pale green, yellow or white and have a slightly firmer texture than zucchini, but a similar flavor. They can be sliced and broiled in the same way as zucchini but, to make the most of their size and shape, steam them whole until tender.

Summer Crooknecks: Pale yellow with curves at the neck and a bumpy skin, crooknecks are prepared and cooked in the same way as zucchini.

Italian Zucchini: These very long, thin zucchini are grown in Italy. They are treated liked ordinary zucchini but are strictly a bottle gourd.

Buying and Storing

Zucchini should be firm with a glossy, healthy looking skin. Avoid any that feel soft or generally look limp, as they will be dry and not worth using. Choose small zucchini whenever possible and buy in small quantities as needed.

Preparing

The tiny young zucchini need no preparation at all, and if they still have their flowers, so much the better. Other zucchini should be topped and tailed and then prepared according to the recipe, either sliced or slit for stuffing.

Cooking

Baby zucchini need little or no cooking. Steam them whole or just blanch them. Sliced larger zucchini can be steamed or boiled but take care that they do not overcook as they go soggy very quickly. Alternately, grill, roast or fry them. Try dipping slices in a light batter and then shallow frying in a blend of olive and sunflower oil. To roast, place them in a ovenproof dish, scatter with crushed garlic and a few torn basil leaves and sprinkle with olive oil; then bake in a very hot oven until tender, turning the slices occasionally.

Top left: Pattypan squashes.
Far left: Baby zucchini.
Left: Yellow zucchini.
Right: Italian zucchini beside white and green zucchini.

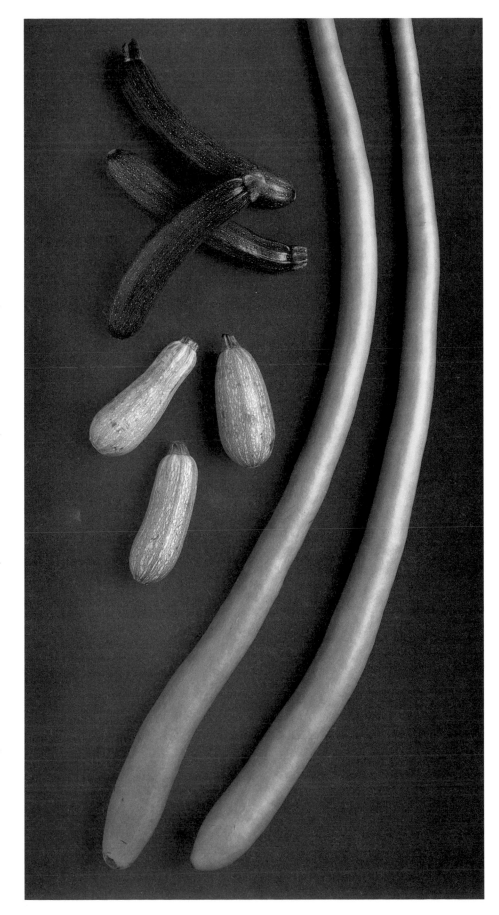

MARROWS AND SUMMER SQUASHES

Vegetable marrow is classified as a summer squash yet it is rather the poor relation of squashes. Most of the edible flesh is water and at best it is a rather bland vegetable, with a slightly sweet flavor. At worst, it is insipid and if cooked to a mush (which isn't unheard of), it is completely tasteless.

Marrows can be stuffed, although it involves a lot of energy expended for very little reward; but marrow cooked over low heat in butter with no added water (so that it steams in its own juice) brings out the best in it.

History

Marrows, like all the summer and winter squashes, are native to America. Squashes were eaten by Native Americans, traditionally with corn and beans, and in an Iroquois myth the three vegetables are represented as three inseparable sisters. Although the early explorers would almost certainly have come into contact with them, they were not brought back home, and vegetable marrow was not known in England until the nineteenth century. Once introduced, however, it quickly became very popular. Mrs Beeton gives eight recipes for vegetable marrow and observes that "it is now extensively used." No mention at all is made of zucchini, which of course are simply immature marrows, as any gardener will know.

Varieties

The word "marrow" as a general term tends to refer to the summer squashes. At the end of summer and in the early fall a good variety of the large summer squashes is available.

Vegetable Marrows: This is the proper name for the large prize marrows, beloved of harvest festivals and country fairs. Buy small specimens whenever possible.

Spaghetti Squashes/Marrows: Long and pale yellow, like all marrows these squashes can grow to enormous sizes, but buy small specimens for convenience as well as flavor. They earned their name from the resemblance of the cooked flesh to spaghetti.

To boil a spaghetti squash, first pierce the end, so that the heat can reach the middle, then cook for about 25 minutes or until the skin feels tender. Cut the squash in half lengthwise, remove the seeds, and then fork the strands of flesh out onto a plate. It has a fragrant, almost honey and lemon flavor and tastes good with garlic butter or pesto.

Custard Marrows: These are pretty, pale green squashes with scalloped edges and a similar flavor to zucchini. If possible, buy small specimens, about 4 inches across. Boil these whole until tender, then cut a slice off the tops, scoop out the seeds and serve with a pat of butter.

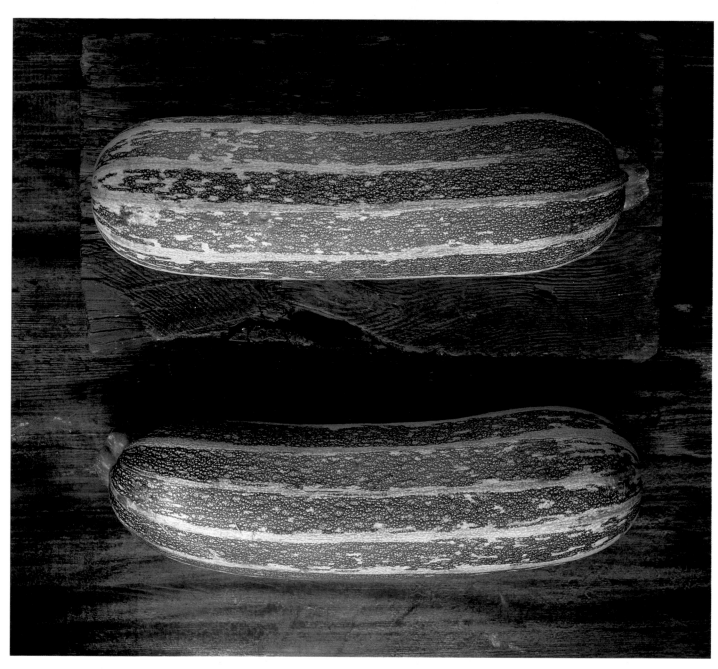

Buying and Storing

Buy vegetables that have clear, unblemished flesh and avoid any with soft or brown patches. Vegetable marrows and spaghetti squashes will keep for several months provided they are kept in a cool, dark place. Custard marrows will keep up to a week.

Preparing

Wash the skin. For sautéing or steaming, or if the skin is tough, peel it away. For braised marrow, cut into chunks and discard the seeds and pith (*right*). For

stuffing, cut into thick slices or cut lengthwise and discard the seeds and pith.

Cooking

Place chunks of marrow in a heavy-based pan with a little butter, cover and cook until tender. It can then be livened up with garlic, herbs or tomatoes. For stuffed marrow, blanch first, stuff, then cover or wrap it in foil to cook.

Above: Vegetable marrows.
Far left: Spaghetti squashes.
Left: Custard marrows.

PUMPKINS AND WINTER SQUASHES

Pumpkins are the most famous of the winter squashes; aesthetically they are one of nature's most pleasing vegetables for their huge size, their color and the smoothness of their skin. They originated in America and, from a culinary point of view, they have their home here.

The name squash comes from America and as well as pumpkins, the family includes acorn, butternut and turban squashes to name but a few. There are simply hundreds of different squashes, including Sweet Dumpling, Queensland Blue (from Australia), Calabaza, Cushaw and Golden Nugget.

History

The tradition of eating pumpkin at Thanksgiving came from when the Pilgrim Fathers, who had settled in New England and proclaimed a day of thanks-giving and prayer for the harvest. The early tradition was to serve the pumpkin with its head and seeds removed, the cavity filled with milk, honey and spices, and baked until tender. The custom of eating pumpkin at Thanksgiving has remained, but it is now served in a dif-ferent way: puréed pumpkin, either fresh or canned, is used to make golden tarts.

Varieties

There are a huge number of varieties of winter squashes and, confusingly, many are known by several different names. However, from a cooking point of view, most are interchangeable, although it is best to taste dishes as you cook them, as seasoning may differ from one to the other. In general, they all have a floury and slightly fibrous flesh and a mild, almost bland flavor tinged with sweet-ness. Because of this blandness, they harmonize well with other ingredients.
Acorn Squashes: These are small and heart-shaped with a beautiful deep green or orange skin, or a mixture of the two. Peel, then use as for pumpkins or bake whole, then split and serve with butter.
Butternut Squashes: Perfectly pear-shaped, these are a buttery color. Use in soups or in any pumpkin recipe.
Delicata Squashes: This pretty pale yellow squash has a succulent yellow

flesh, tasting like a cross between sweet potato and butternut squash.
English Pumpkins: These have a softer flesh than the American variety and are good for soups or, if puréed, combined with potatoes or other root vegetables.
Hubbard Squashes: These large winter squashes have a thick, bumpy, hard shell which can range in color from bright orange to dark green. If they are exceptionally large, they are sometimes sold in halves or large wedges. They have a grainy texture and are best mashed with butter and seasoning.
Kabocha Squashes: Attractive bright green squashes with a pale orange flesh.

They are similar in flavor and texture to acorn squashes and can be prepared and cooked in the same way.
Onion Squashes: Round, yellow or pale orange, onion squashes have a mild flavor, less sweet than pumpkin but still with a slightly fruity or honey taste. They are good in risottos or in most pumpkin recipes, but taste for flavor – you may need to add extra seasoning or sugar.

Above: Clockwise from right: A pumpkin hybrid, Kabocha squash, Acorn squash. Right: Clockwise from top right: Hybrid squash, two Golden Acorn squashes, two small and one large pumpkin.

Buying and Storing

All winter squashes may be stored for long periods. Buy firm, unblemished vegetables with clear smooth skins.

Preparing

For larger squashes, or for those being used for soups or purées, peel and cut into pieces, removing the seeds (*left*).

Cooking

Boil in a little water for about 20 minutes until tender, then mash and serve with butter and plenty of salt and pepper. Smaller squashes can be baked whole in their skins, then halved, seeded and served with butter and maple syrup. Pumpkin and other squashes can also be lightly sautéed in butter before adding stock, cream or chopped tomatoes.

Pumpkins: Large, bright yellow or orange squashes, with a deep orange flesh. They have a sweet, slightly honeyed, flavor and are very much a taste North Americans and Australians grow up with. However, they are not to everyone's liking and some people find them rather cloying. Pumpkin soup, pumpkin bread and pumpkin pie are part of the American tradition, as are faces carved from the shell at Halloween.

EXOTIC GOURDS

While the squashes are native to America, most gourds originated in the Old World – from Africa, India and the Far East. However, over the millennia, seeds crossed water and, over the centuries, people crossed continents so that squashes and gourds are now common all over the world. Both belong to the family *Cucurbitacea,* and both are characterised by their rapid-growing vines.

Bottle Gourds: Bottle gourds are still a familiar sight in Africa, where they are principally grown not for their fruit, but for their dried shells. The gourds can grow to enormous sizes and the shells are used for water bottles, cups and musical instruments. The young fruit can be eaten, but it is extremely bitter and is normally only added to highly flavored stews, like curries.

Chayotes: The chayote (pronounced chow-chow) is a popular gourd in all sorts of regions of the world and can be found in just about any ethnic supermarket, be it Chinese, African, Indian or Caribbean. In each it is known by a different name, christophine being the Caribbean term, but choko, shu-shu and chinchayote among its many other names used elsewhere. Unlike most gourds, it originated in Mexico but was widely grown throughout the tropics after the invasions of the Spanish.

It is a pear-shaped fruit with a large central pit and has a cream-colored or green skin. It has a bland flavor, similar to marrow, and a slightly firmer texture something like pumpkin. It is commonly used in Caribbean cooking, primarily as a side dish or in soufflés. Alternately it can be used raw in salads.

Chinese Bitter Melons: These are a common vegetable in all parts of Asia and go by a myriad of names – bitter gourd and bitter cucumber to name but two. They are popular throughout Asia, eaten when very young, but are extremely bitter and rarely eaten in the West. They are easily recognized as they have warty, spiny skins, looking like a toy dinosaur. The skins are white when young but will probably have ripened to a dark green by the time they appear in the shops.

Most recipes from China suggest halving the gourd, removing the pulp and then slicing before boiling for several minutes to remove their bitterness. They can then be added to stir-fries or other oriental dishes.

Far left: Sweet dumpling.
Left: Pumpkin.
Top right: Chinese bitter melon.
Middle right: Loofah.
Below: Chayote.

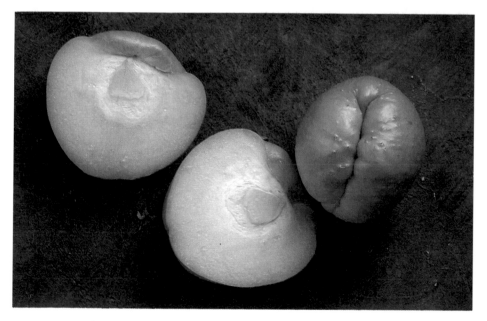

Smooth and Angled Loofahs: The smooth loofah must be one of the strangest plants. When young it can be eaten, although it is not much valued. However, the plant is grown almost exclusively for sponges, used everywhere as a back rub in the bath. The ripe loofahs are picked and, once the skin has been stripped off and the seeds shaken out, allowed to dry. The plant then gradually dries to a fibrous skeleton and thence to bathrooms everywhere - so now you know!

Angled or ribbed loofahs are more commonly eaten but again are only edible when young as they become unpleasantly bitter when mature. They taste something like zucchini and are best cooked in a similar way, either fried in butter or cooked with tomatoes, garlic and oil.

CUCUMBERS

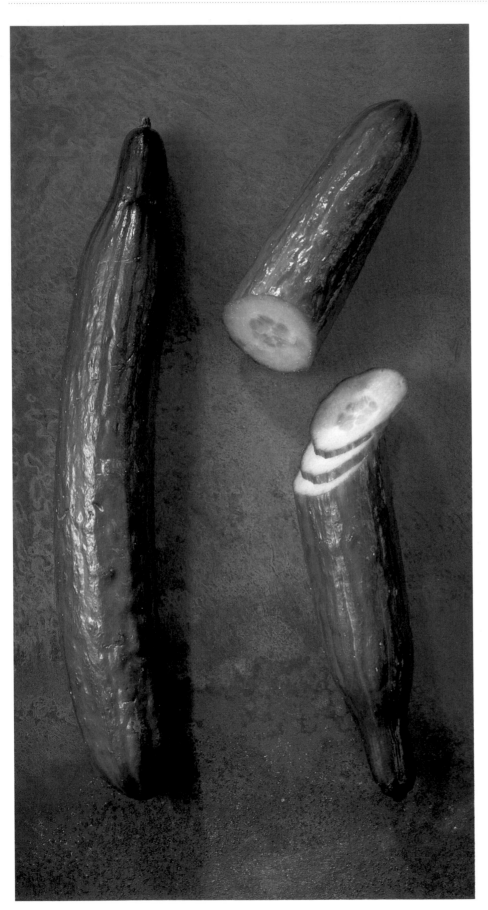

The Chinese say food should be enjoyed for its texture as well as flavor; cucumbers have a unique texture and refreshing cool taste. An afternoon tea with cucumber sandwiches, thinly sliced cucumber between wafer thin brown buttered bread, provides a delight of contrasts – the soft bread, the smooth butter and the cool crisp cucumber.

Varieties

English Cucumbers: These are the cucumbers the English are most familiar with. They have fewer seeds and thinner skin than the ridged cucumber.
Gherkins: These are tiny cucumbers with bumpy, almost warty skins and are mostly pickled in vinegar and eaten with cold meats or chopped into mayonnaise.
Kirbys: Small cucumbers, available in the United States and used for pickling.
Ridged Cucumbers: These are smaller than most cucumbers with more seeds and a thick, bumpy skin. The waxed ones need to be peeled before eating but most ridged cucumbers on the European Continent are unwaxed and good without peeling.

Buying and Storing

Cucumbers should be firm from top to bottom. They are often sold prewrapped in plastic and can be stored in the salad drawer of the fridge for up to a week. Remove the plastic packaging once you've "started" a cucumber. Discard once it begins to go soggy.

Preparing

Whether you peel a cucumber or not is a matter of personal preference, but wash it if you don't intend to peel it. Some producers use wax coatings to give a glossy finish and these cucumbers must be peeled. If you are in doubt, buy organic cucumbers. Special citrus peelers can remove strips of peel to give an attractive striped effect when sliced.

Left: Cucumbers.
Above right: Ridged cucumbers.
Above far right: Baby cucumbers.
Below right: Kirbys.

Serving

Thinly sliced cucumber is most frequently served with a light dressing or sour cream. In Greece cucumber is an essential part of a Greek country salad, *horiatiki salata*, cut into thick chunks and served with tomatoes, peppers and feta and dressed simply with olive oil and a little wine vinegar.

Iced cucumber soup is delicious, and cucumber can also be puréed with yogurt, garlic and herbs and served with sour cream stirred in.

Cooking

Cucumbers are normally served raw, but are surprisingly good cooked. Cut the cucumber into wedges, remove the seeds and then simmer for a few minutes until tender. Once drained, return the cucumber to the pan and stir in a little cream and seasoning.

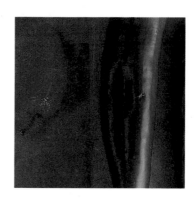

SEVEN

FRUIT

Tomatoes

Eggplant

Peppers

Chilies

Plantains and Green Bananas

Ackee

Avocados

Breadfruit

TOMATOES

Next to onions, tomatoes are one of the most important fresh ingredients in the kitchen. In Mediterranean cooking, they are fundamental. Along with garlic and olive oil, they form the basis of so many Italian, Spanish and Provençal recipes that it is hard to find many dishes in which they are not included.

History

Tomatoes are related to potatoes, eggplant and sweet and chili peppers, and all are members of the nightshade family. Some very poisonous members of this family may well have deterred our ancestors from taking to tomatoes. Indeed, the leaves of tomatoes are toxic and can result in a very bad stomach ache.

Tomatoes are native to western South America. By the time of the Spanish invasions in the sixteenth century, they were widely cultivated throughout the whole of South America and Mexico. Hernán Cortés, conqueror of the Aztecs, sent the first tomato plants, a yellow variety, to Spain (no doubt along with the plundered Aztec gold).

However, people did not instinctively take to this "golden apple." English horticulturists mostly grew them as ornamental plants to adorn their gardens and had little positive to say about them as food. Spain is recorded as the first country to use tomatoes in cooking, stewing them with oil and seasoning. Italy followed suit, but elsewhere they were treated with suspicion.

The first red tomatoes arrived in Europe in the eighteenth century, brought to Italy by two Jesuit priests. They were gradually accepted in northern Europe where, by the mid-nineteenth century, they were grown extensively, eaten raw, cooked or used for pickles.

Above right: Red and yellow cherry tomatoes.
Below right: Yellow pear tomatoes.
Opposite above: Round or salad tomatoes on the vine.
Opposite below: Beefsteak tomatoes.

Varieties

There are countless varieties of tomatoes, ranging from the huge beef tomatoes that measure 4 inches across, to tiny cherry tomatoes, not much bigger than a thumb nail. They come in all shapes, too – elongated, plum-shaped or slightly squarish and even pear-shaped.

Beefsteak Tomatoes: Large, ridged and deep red or orange in color, these have a good flavor so are good in salads.

Canned Tomatoes: Keep a store of canned tomatoes, especially in the winter when fresh ones tend to taste insipid. Tomatoes are one of the few vegetables that take well to canning, but steer clear of any that are flavored with garlic or herbs. It is far better to add flavoring yourself.

Cherry Tomatoes: These small, dainty tomatoes were once the prized treasures of gardeners but are now widely available. Although more expensive than round tomatoes, they have a delightful

sweet flavor and are worth paying the extra money for serving in salads or for cooking whole.

Plum Tomatoes: Richly flavored with fewer seeds than regular tomatoes, these Italian-grown tomatoes are usually recommended for cooking, although they can be used in salads.

Round or Salad Tomatoes: These are the common tomatoes found in grocers and supermarkets. They vary in size according to the exact type and season. Sun-ripened tomatoes have the best flavor, however; for through-the-year availability the fruit is often picked and ripened off the plant. These tomatoes are versatile in everyday cooking. Adding a pinch of sugar and taking care to season the dish well helps to overcome any weakness in flavor.

Sun-dried Tomatoes: This is one of the fashionable foods of the late Eighties and early Nineties. They add an evocative flavor to many Mediterranean dishes, but don't use them too indiscriminately.

Tomato Paste: This is good for adding an intense tomato flavor, but use carefully or the flavor will be overpowering. Tubes have screw tops and are better than cans

as, once opened, they can be kept for up to 4–6 weeks in the fridge.

Yellow Tomatoes: These are exactly like red tomatoes - they may be round, plum or cherry-sized - except they are yellow.

Buying and Storing

Ideally, tomatoes should be allowed to ripen slowly on the plant so that their flavor can develop. Consequently, home-grown tomatoes are best, followed by those grown and sold locally. When buying from a supermarket or grocer, look at the leafy green tops; the fresher they look the better. Buy locally grown beefsteak or cherry tomatoes for salads and plum tomatoes for rich sauces. Paler tomatoes or those tinged with green will redden if kept in a brown paper bag or the salad drawer of the fridge, but if you intend to use tomatoes right away, buy bright red specimens. Overripe tomatoes, where the skin has split and they seem to be bursting with juice, are excellent in soups. However, check for any sign of mold or decay, as this will spoil all your good efforts.

Preparing

Slice tomatoes across rather than downward for salads and pizza toppings. For wedges, cut downward; halve or quarter and cut into two or three depending on the size of the tomato.

Cooking

Among the many classic tomato dishes is tomato soup, cooked to a delicate orange color with stock or milk, or simmered with vegetables, garlic and basil. Recipes *à la provençale* indicate that tomatoes are in the dish; in Provençal cooking and Italian dishes, tomatoes are used with fish, meat and vegetables, in sauces and stuffings, with pasta and in superb salads. The Italian *tri colore salata* is a combination of large tomatoes, mozzarella and basil (the three colors of the Italian flag). The natural astringency of tomatoes means that, in salads, they need only be sprinkled with a fruity olive oil.

Chopped Tomatoes

Chopped tomatoes add a depth of flavor to all sorts of meat and vegetarian dishes. Ideally, even in fairly rustic meals, the tomatoes should be peeled, since the skin can be irritating to eat once cooked. Some sauces also recommend seeding tomatoes, in which case cut the tomato into halves and scoop out the seeds before chopping (above).

Skinning Tomatoes

Cut a cross in the tops of the tomatoes, then place in a bowl and pour over boiling water. Leave for a minute (*above*), then use a sharp knife to peel away the skin, which should come away easily. Do a few at a time (five at most) otherwise they will begin to cook while soaking; boil water for the next batch when you have finished peeling. The water must be boiling.

EGGPLANT

Many varieties of eggplants are cultivated and cooked all over the world. In Europe, Asia or America, they feature in a multitude of different dishes.

History

Although eggplant is a member of the nightshade family and thus related to potatoes, tomatoes and peppers, it was not discovered in the New World. The first mention of its cultivation is in China in 5 BC, and it is thought to have been eaten in India long before that. The Moors introduced the eggplant to Spain some 1200 years ago and it was grown in Andalucia. It is likely that they also introduced it to Italy, and possibly from there to other southern and eastern parts of Europe.

In spite of their popularity in Europe, eggplants did not become popular in the United States or Britain until very recently; although previous generations of food writers knew about them, they gave only the occasional recipe for cooking with them.

Above left: Plum tomatoes.
Top: Eggplants.
Above: Baby eggplants.
Left: Japanese eggplants.

Meanwhile, in the southern and eastern parts of Europe, eggplant had become extremely well liked, and today it is one of the most popular vegetables in the Mediterranean. Indeed, Italy, Greece and Turkey claim to have 100 ways of cooking it. In the Middle East, eggplant is also a central part of their cuisine.

Varieties

There are many different varieties of eggplants, differing in color, size and shape according to their country of origin. Small ivory-white and plump eggplants look like large eggs (hence their name in the States; they are called aubergines in the UK). Pretty striped eggplants may be either purple or pink and flecked with white irregular stripes. The Japanese or Asian eggplant is straight and very narrow, ranging in color from a pretty variegated purple and white to a solid purple. It has a tender, slightly sweet flesh. Most eggplants, however, are either glossy purple or almost black and can be long and slim or fat like zeppelins. All eggplants have a similar

flavor and texture; they taste bland yet slightly smoky when cooked, and the flesh is spongy to touch when raw, but soft after cooking.

Buying and Storing

Eggplants should feel heavy and firm to the touch, with glossy, unblemished skins. They will keep well in the salad drawer of the fridge for up to two weeks.

Preparing

When frying eggplants for any dish where they need slicing (e.g. ratatouille), it is a good idea to salt the slices first in order to draw out some of their moisture, otherwise, they absorb enormous quantities of oil during cooking (they absorb copious amounts anyway, but

salting reduces this slightly). Salting also used to be advised to reduce their bitterness but today's varieties are rarely bitter.

To salt eggplants, cut into slices, about ¹/₂ inch thick for fried slices, *(top right)* or segments *(above right)* and sprinkle generously with salt. Leave them to drain in a colander for about one hour, then rinse well and gently squeeze out the moisture from each slice or carefully pat dry with a piece of cheesecloth.

Cooking

Eggplant slices can be fried in olive oil, as they are or first coated in batter – both popular Italian and Greek starters.

For moussaka, *parmigiana* and other dishes where eggplant is layered with

other ingredients, fry the slices briefly in olive oil. This gives them a tasty crust, while the inside stays soft.

To make a purée, such as for Poor Man's Caviar, first prick the eggplant all over with a fork and then roast in a moderately hot oven for about 30 minutes until tender. Scoop out the flesh and mix with scallions, lemon juice and olive oil. One of the most famous eggplant dishes is *Imam Bayaldi* – "the Iman fainted" – fried eggplant stuffed with onions, garlic, tomato, spices and lots of olive oil.

Above left: White eggplants.
Below left: Striped eggplants.
Above: Thai eggplants, including white, yellow and Pea eggplants.

PEPPERS

In spite of their name, peppers have nothing to do with the spice pepper used as a seasoning, although early explorers may have been mistaken in thinking the fruit of the shrubby plant looked like the spice they were seeking. It is thanks to this 400-year-old mistake that the name "pepper" has stuck.

History

The journeys Christopher Columbus and the conquistadors made were partly to find the spices Marco Polo had found a hundred years earlier in the Far East. Instead of the Orient, however, Columbus discovered the Americas, and instead of spices, he found maize, potatoes and tomatoes. He would have noted, though, that the Native Americans flavored their food with ground peppers, and since it was hot, like pepper, perhaps wishful thinking colored his objectivity. In any case, he returned with the new vegetables, describing them as peppers and advertising them as more pungent than those from Caucasus.

Varieties

Peppers and chilies are both members of the capsicum family. To distinguish between them, peppers are called sweet peppers, bell peppers and even bullnose peppers and come in a variety of colors – red, green, yellow, white, orange and a dark purple-black.

The color of the pepper tells you something about its flavor. Green peppers are the least mature and have a fresh "raw" flavor. Red peppers are ripened green peppers and are distinctly sweeter. Yellow/orange peppers taste more or less like red peppers, although perhaps slightly less sweet and if you have a fine palate you may be able to detect a difference. Black peppers have a similar flavor to green peppers but when cooked are a bit disappointing as they turn green; so if you buy them for their dramatic color, they are best used in salads.

In Greece and other parts of southern Europe, longer, slimmer peppers are often available which have a more pronounced sweet and pungent flavor than the bell-shaped peppers in the US – although this may be because they are locally picked and therefore absolutely fresh. Whichever is the case, they are quite delicious.

Buying and Storing

Peppers should look glossy and sprightly and feel hard and crisp; avoid any that look wrinkled or have damp soft patches. They will keep for a few days at the bottom of the fridge.

Preparing

To prepare stuffed peppers, cut off the top and then cut away the inner core and pith, and shake out the seeds. The seeds and core are easily removed when halving, quartering or slicing.

Cooking

There are countless ways of cooking peppers. Sliced, they can be fried with onions and garlic in olive oil and then braised with tomatoes and herbs. This is the basic ratatouille; other vegetables, such as zucchini and eggplant, can of course be added.

Peppers can be roasted, either with ratatouille ingredients or with only onions and garlic. Cut into large pieces, place in a roasting pan and sprinkle with olive oil, torn basil and seasoning. Roast in a very hot oven (425°F) for about 30 minutes, turning occasionally. Broiled peppers are another superb dish. Once broiled they can be skinned to reveal a soft, luxurious texture and added to salads.

Above far left: Red, green and orange bell peppers.
Below far left: Yellow bell peppers.
Above left: White bell peppers.
Above right: Purple bell peppers.

Skinning Peppers

Cut the pepper into quarters lengthwise and broil, skin side up (*above*), until the skin is charred and evenly blistered. Place the pieces immediately into a plastic bag (you will need tongs or a fork as they will be hot) and close the top of the bag with a tie or a loose knot. Leave for a few minutes and then remove from the bag and the skin will peel off easily.

CHILIES

Some people apparently become so addicted to the taste of hot food that they carry little jars of chopped dried chilies around with them and scatter them over every meal. Although this is a bit extreme, it is chilies more than any other ingredient that spice up our mealtimes.

Varieties

Chilies are the most important seasoning in the world after salt. Unlike peppers, to which they are closely related, the different varieties of chili can have widely different heat values – from the "just about bearable" to the "knock your head off" variety.

Anaheim Chili: A long, thin chili with a blunt end, named after the Californian city. It can be red or green and has a mild, sweet taste.

Ancho Chili/Pepper: These look like tiny peppers. They are mild enough to taste their underlying sweetness.

Birdseye or Bird Chili: These small red chilies are fiery hot. Also known as pequin chilies.

Cayenne Pepper: This is made from the dried, ground seeds and pods of chilies. The name comes from the capital of French Guiana, north of Brazil, although the cayenne chili does not grow there any longer and the pepper is made from chilies grown all over the world.

Early Jalapeño: A popular American chili, which starts dark green and gradually turns to red.

Habañero: Often called Scotch Bonnet, this is the hottest of all chilies and is small and can be green, red or yellow. Color is no real guide to its heat properties, so don't be fooled into thinking that green ones are mild. They are all *very* hot. The habañero comes from Mexico and is frequently used in Mexican and Caribbean dishes.

Hot Gold Spike: A large, pale, yellow-green fruit grown in the southwestern United States: it is very hot.

Above: Birdseye chilies.
Left: Habañero chilies (in and below bowl) and Yellow wax peppers.

Preparing

The capsaicin in chilies is most concentrated in the pith inside the pod and this, together with the seeds, should be cut away (*below*) unless you want maximum heat. Capsaicin irritates the skin and especially the eyes, so take care when preparing chilies. Either wear gloves or wash your hands thoroughly after handling chilies.If you rub your eyes, even if you have washed your hands carefully, it will be painful.

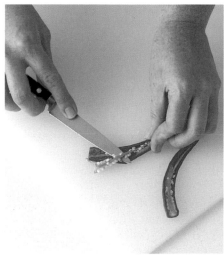

Poblano: A small, dark green chili, served whole in Spain either roasted or broiled. They are mostly mild but you can get the rogue fiery one, so beware if eating them whole.

Red Chili: These are long, rather wrinkled chilies which are green at first and then gradually ripen to red. They are of variable hotness and, because they are so long and thin, are rather difficult to prepare.

Serrano Chili: A long, red and extremely hot chili.

Tabasco: A sauce made with chilies, salt and vinegar and first made in New Orleans. It is a fiery sauce, popular in Creole, Caribbean and Mexican cookery – or indeed in any dish requiring last minute heat.

Yellow Wax Pepper: Pale yellow to green, these can vary from mild to hot.

Buying and Storing

Some fresh chilies look wrinkled even in their prime and therefore this is not a good guide to their freshness. They should, however, be unblemished, and avoid any which are soft or bruised.

The substance which makes the chili hot is a volatile oil called capsaicin. This differs not only from one type to another but also from plant to plant, depending on growing conditions; the more the plant has to struggle to survive in terms of light, water, soil, etc, the more capsaicin will be produced. It is therefore impossible to tell how hot a chili will be before tasting, although some types are naturally hotter than others. The belief that green chilies are milder than red ones does not necessarily follow; generally red chilies will have ripened for longer in the sun with the result that they will only be sweeter for all that sunshine. Chilies can be stored in a plastic bag in the fridge for a few days.

Cooking

In Mexican cooking chilies play a vital, and almost central role. It is difficult to think of any savory Mexican dish that does not contain either fresh chilies or some form of processed chili, whether canned, dried or ground. Other cuisines, however, are equally enthusiastic about chilies. They are essential in curries and similar dishes from India and the Far East, and in Caribbean and Creole food they are also used extensively.

If you have developed a tolerance for really hot food, then there is no reason why you shouldn't add as many as you wish. In general, however, use chilies discreetly, if for no better reason than you can't take the heat away if you make a mistake.

Above: Ancho chilies (left) and Anaheim chilies (on board).

PLANTAINS <u>AND</u> GREEN BANANAS

While bananas are well and truly fruit, eaten almost exclusively as a dessert or by themselves as fruit, plantains can reasonably be considered among the vegetable fraternity as they have a definite savory flavor, are normally eaten as a first or main course and can only be eaten once cooked.

Varieties

Plantains: Also known as cooking bananas, these have a coarser flesh and more savory flavor than sweet bananas. While superficially they look exactly like our own bananas, they are, on closer inspection, altogether larger and heavier looking. They can vary in color from the unripe fruit, which is green, through yellow to a mottled black color, which is when the fruit is completely ripe.
Green Bananas: Only certain types of green bananas are used in African and Caribbean cooking, and the "greenish" bananas you find in most western supermarkets are normally eating bananas, just waiting to ripen. If you need green bananas for a recipe, look out for them in West Indian or African stores.

Preparing

Plantains: These are inedible raw and must be cooked before eating. Unless very ripe, the skin can be tricky to remove. With yellow and green plantains, cut the fruit into short lengths, then slit the skin along the natural ridge of each piece of plantain. Gently ease the skin away from the flesh and pull the skin until it peels off completely (*below*).

Once peeled, plantains can be sliced horizontally or into lengths and then roasted or fried. Like bananas, plantains will discolor if exposed to the air so, if not using immediately, sprinkle with lemon juice or place in a bowl of salted water.

Green Bananas: These should be prepared in a similar way. As with plantains, green bananas should not be eaten raw and are usually boiled, either in their skins or not, according to the recipe.

If making green banana crisps, use a potato peeler to produce the thinnest slices (*left*).

If cooking plantains or green bananas in their skins, slit the skin lengthwise along the sides and place in a saucepan of salted water. Bring to the boil, simmer gently for about 20 minutes until tender and then cool. The peel can then easily be removed before slicing.

Cooking and Serving

Plantains and green bananas both have an excellent flavor. In many African and Caribbean recipes they are roasted or fried and then served simply with salt. However, if boiled, they can be sliced and served in a simple salad with a few sliced onions, or added to something far more elaborate like a gado gado salad, with mango, avocado, lettuce and shrimp.

Plantains also make a delicious soup, where they are often teamed with corn. After frying an onion and a little garlic, add two sliced and peeled plaintains, together with tomatoes, if liked. Fry gently for a few minutes and then add vegetable stock to cover and one or two sliced chilies, together with about 6 ounces of corn. Simmer gently together until the plantain is tender.

Above left: Plantains.
Below left: Green bananas.
Below: Canned ackee.

ACKEE

Ackee is a tropical fruit which is used in a variety of savory dishes, mainly of Caribbean origin, where the fruit is very popular. The fruit itself is bright red and, when ripe, bursts open to reveal three large black seeds and a soft, creamy flesh resembling scrambled eggs. It has a slightly lemony flavor and is traditionally served with saltfish to make one of Jamaica's national dishes. Only buy ripe fruit as, when under-ripe, certain parts of the fruit are toxic.

However, unless you are visiting the Caribbean you are probably only likely to find ackee in cans, and indeed most recipes call for canned ackee which is a good substitute for the fresh fruit.

Jamaican cooks also use ackee to add a subtle flavor to a variety of vegetable and bean dishes. The canned ackee needs very little cooking, and should be added to dishes in the last few minutes of cooking. Take care when stirring into a dish as it breaks up very easily.

AVOCADOS

The avocado has been known by many names – butter pear and alligator pear to name but two. It earned the title butter pear clearly because of its consistency, but alligator pear was the original Spanish name. Although you would be forgiven for thinking this was due to its knobbly skin (among some varieties anyway), the name in fact derives from the Spanish which was based on the Aztec word, the basically unpronounceable *ahuacatl*. From this to the easily-said alligator and thence to avocado was but a short step.

History

The avocado is a New World fruit, native to Mexico, but while it would have been "discovered" by the Old World explorers, it didn't become a popular food in Europe until the middle of this century, when modern transport meant that growers in California, who started farming avocados in the middle of the nineteenth century, could market this fruit worldwide. Avocados are now also exported by South Africa and Australia.

Nutrition

The avocado is high in protein and carbohydrate. It is one of the few fruits that contains fat, and it is also rich in potassium, Vitamin C, some B vitamins and Vitamin E. Its rich oils, particularly its Vitamin E content, mean that it is not only useful as food, but for skin and hair care too, something the Aztecs and Incas were aware of a thousand years ago. The cosmetic industry may have been in its infancy, but it still knew a good thing when it saw it.

Because of their valuable protein and vitamin content, avocados are a popular food for babies. They are easily blended, and small children generally enjoy their creamy texture and pleasant flavor.

Varieties

There are four varieties: Hass, the purple-black small knobbly avocado, the Ettinger and Fuerte, which are pear-shaped and have smooth green skin, and the Nabal, which is rounder in shape. The black-colored Hass has golden-yellow flesh, while green avocados have pale green to yellow flesh.

Buying and Storing

The big problem in buying avocados is that they're never ripe when you want them to be. How often do you see shoppers standing by the avocado shelves, feeling around for that rare creature, the perfectly ripe avocado? Most times they all feel as hard as rocks; that or else they're hopelessly soft and squashy and clearly past their best. The proper and sensible thing to do is buy fruit a few days before you need it. An unripe avocado will ripen in between 4-7 days at room temperature. Once it is ripe, it will keep well in the fridge for a few days, but you still need to plan well in advance if you want to be sure of the perfect avocado.

The alternative is to hope for the best and keep feeling around until you find a ripe fruit. A perfect avocado should have a clean, unblemished skin without any brown or black patches. If ripe, it should

"give" slightly if squeezed gently in the hand, but not so much that it actually feels soft. Over-ripe avocados are really not worth bothering with, however persuasive and generous the offer from the man on the market. The flesh will be unattractively brown and stringy and the bits of good flesh you do manage to salvage will be soft and pulpy. Good for a dip, but nothing much else.

Preparing

Although they are simple fruits, avocados can be the devil to prepare. Once peeled, you are left with a slippery object which is then almost impossible to remove from the stone.

If you intend to eat the avocados in halves, it's fairly simple to just prise out the pit once halved. If you want to slice the fruit, use this tip. The only thing you need is a very sharp knife. Cut the avocado in half, remove the stone and then, with the skin still on, cut through the flesh and the skin to make slices. It is then relatively simple to strip off the peel.

Remember to sprinkle the slices with lemon juice as the flesh discolors once exposed to the air.

Cooking

Most popular raw, avocados can also be baked, broiled or used in sautéed and sauced dishes.

Serving Ideas

As well as shrimp or vinaigrette, a half avocado can hold a mixture of chopped tomatoes and cucumber, a mild garlic cheese dip or a sour cream potato salad. Slices of avocado are delicious served with sliced tomatoes and mozzarella, sprinkled simply with olive oil, lemon juice and plenty of black pepper. Avocado can be chopped and added to a salad, or puréed for a rich dressing.

In Mexico, where avocados grow in abundance, there are countless avocado recipes. Guacamole is perhaps the best known, but they are also eaten in soups and stews and commonly used to garnish tacos and enchiladas.

BREADFRUIT

Breadfruit is the name for a tropical tree that grows on the islands of the South Pacific ocean. The fruit of the tree is about the size of a small melon with a rough rind and a pale, mealy flesh.

Preparing

The fruit should be peeled and the core removed.

Cooking

Breadfruit can be treated like potatoes: the flesh may be boiled, baked or fried. It is a staple food for the people of the Pacific islands who bake the flesh, or dry and grind it for biscuits, bread and puddings. It has a sweet flavor and soft texture when ripe.

Left: Clockwise from the right: Fuerte, Hass and Nabal avocados.
Right: Breadfruit.

EIGHT

SALAD VEGETABLES

Lettuce

Arugula

Chicory and Radicchio

Radishes

Watercress

Mustard and Cress

LETTUCE

One aspect of lettuce that sets it apart from any other vegetable is that you can only buy it in one form – fresh.

History

Lettuce has been cultivated for thousands of years. In Egyptian times it was sacred to the god Min, and tubs of lettuce were ceremoniously carried before this fertility god. It was then considered a powerful aphrodisiac, yet for the Greeks and the Romans lettuce was thought to have quite the opposite effect, making one sleepy and generally soporific. Chemists today confirm that lettuce contains a hypnotic similar to opium, and in herbal remedies lettuce is recommended for insomniacs.

Varieties

There are hundreds of different varieties of lettuce. Today, an increasing variety is available in stores so that the salad bowl can contain a wealth of color and texture.

Round Lettuces

Sometimes called head or cabbage lettuces, round lettuces have cabbage-like heads and include:

Butterheads: These are the classic lettuces seen in kitchen gardens. They have a pale heart and floppy, loosely packed leaves. They have a pleasant flavor as long as they are fresh.

Crispheads: Crisp lettuces, such as Iceberg, have an excellent crunchy texture and will keep their vitality long after butterheads have faded and died.

Looseheads: These are non-hearting lettuce with loose leaves and include *lollo rosso* and *lollo biondo*, oakleaf lettuce and Red Salad Bowl. Although they are not particularly remarkable for their flavor, they look superb.

Cos Lettuces

The romaine is the only lettuce that would have been known in antiquity. It is known

Above: Butterhead lettuce.
Right: Lollo rosso lettuce.
Above far right: Romaine lettuce.
Below far right: Lamb's lettuce.
Below extreme right: Bibb lettuce.

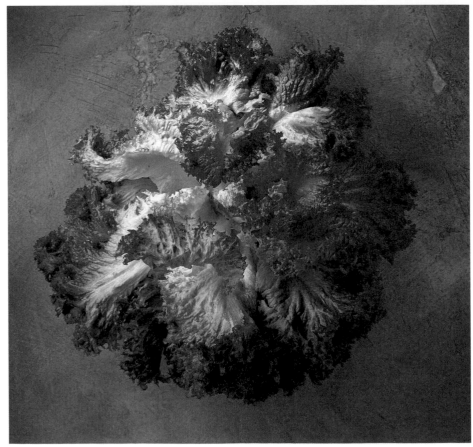

by two names: cos, derived from the Greek island where it was found by the Romans; and romaine, the name used by the French after it was introduced to France from Rome. There are two romaine lettuces, both with long, erect heads.

Romaine: Considered the most delicious lettuce, this has a firm texture and a faintly nutty taste. It is the correct lettuce for Caesar Salad, one of the classic salads.

Bibb: In appearance Bibbs look like something between a baby romaine and a tightly furled butterhead. They have firm hearts and are enjoyed for their distinct flavor. Like other lettuce hearts, they cope well with being cooked.

LAMB'S LETTUCE OR CORN SALAD

This popular winter leaf does not actually belong to the lettuce family (it is related to Fuller's teasel), but as it makes a lovely addition to salads, this seems a good place to include it. Called *mâche* in France, it has spoon-shaped leaves and an excellent nutty flavor.

Nutrition

As well as containing vitamins A, C and E, lettuce provides potassium, iron and calcium and traces of other minerals.

Buying and Storing

The best lettuce is that fresh from the garden. The next best thing is to buy lettuce from a farm store or pick-your-own (although if fertilizers and pesticides are used, their flavor will be disappointing compared to the organic product).

Nowadays, lettuce is frequently sold ready shredded and packed with herbs etc, an acceptable and convenient form of buying lettuce. Whether you buy lettuce prepacked or from the shelf, it must be fresh. Soil and bugs can be washed off but those with limp or yellow leaves are of no use. Eat lettuce as soon as possible after purchasing; in the meantime keep it in a cool dark place, such as the salad drawer of the fridge.

Making Salads

Salads can be made using only one lettuce or a mixture of many. There are no rules but, when mixing salads, choose leaves to give contrast in texture and color as well as flavor. Fresh herbs, such as parsley, cilantro and basil also add an interesting dimension.

Tear rather than cut the leaves of loose-leafed lettuce; icebergs and other large lettuces are commonly sliced or shredded. Eat as soon as possible after preparing.

Dressings should be well-flavored with a hint of sharpness, but never too astringent. Make them in a blender, a screw-top jar or in a large bowl so that the ingredients can be thoroughly blended. Always use the best possible oils and vinegars, in roughly the proportion of five oil to one vinegar or lemon juice. Use half good olive oil and half sunflower oil, or for a more fragrant dressing, a combination of walnut oil and sunflower oil. A pinch of salt and pepper is essential, French mustard is optional and the addition of a little sugar will blunt the flavor.

Add the dressing to the salad when you're ready to serve – never before.

ARUGULA

Arugula, also called rocket, has a wonderful peppery flavor and is excellent in a mixed green salad. It has small, bright green dandelion-shaped leaves. The Greeks and Romans commonly ate *arugula* in mixed salads, apparently to help counterbalance the dampening effect lettuce had on the libido – arugula's aphrodisiac properties in antiquity are well cataloged. It used to be sown around the statues of Priapus, the mythological Greek god of fertility and protector of gardens and herbs and son of Aphrodite and Dionysus.

Buying and Storing

Arugula is to be found either among the salads or fresh herbs in supermarkets. Buy fresh green leaves and use soon after purchasing. If necessary, the leaves can be kept immersed in cold water.

Preparing and Serving

Discard any discolored leaves. Add arugula to plain green salads, or grind with garlic, pine nuts and olive oil for a dressing for pasta.

Since it has such a striking flavor, a little arugula goes a long way, making it an excellent leaf for garnishing. It tastes superb contrasted with grilled goat cheese, or one or two leaves can be added to sandwiches, or loosely packed into pita bread pockets along with tomatoes, avocado, peanuts and bean sprouts.

Above left: Oak Leaf lettuce.
Below left: Frisée.
Below: Arugula.

CHICORY AND RADICCHIO

Chicory, radicchio, endive and escarole are all related to each other and when they are tasted together you can easily detect their family resemblance. Their names are occasionally interchanged: chicory is often referred to as Belgian or French endive, and French and Belgian *chicorée* as the English curly endive and the American frisée.

CHICORY

During the late eighteenth century, chicory was grown in Europe for its root, which was added to coffee. A Belgian, M. Brezier, discovered that the white leaves could be eaten, a fact he kept secret during his lifetime; but after his death chicory became a popular vegetable, first in Belgium and later elsewhere in Europe. Its Flemish name is *witloof*, meaning "white leaf," and its characteristic pale leaf is due to its being grown in darkness; the paler it is, the less bitter its flavor.

Chicory can be eaten raw but is commonly cooked, either baked, stir-fried or poached. To eat raw, separate the leaves and serve with fruit, such as oranges or grapefruit, which counteract chicory's slight bitterness.

RADICCHIO

This is one of many varieties developed from wild chicory. It looks like a small lettuce with deep wine-red leaves and striking cream ribs and owes its splendid foliage to careful shading. If it is grown completely in the dark the leaves are marbled pink, and those that have been exposed to some light can be patched with a green or copper color. Its flavor tends to be bitter but contrasts well with green salads. Radicchio can be stir-fried or poached, although the leaves turn dark green when cooked.

FRISÉE AND ESCAROLE

These are robust salad ingredients in both flavor and texture. The curly-leaved frisée looks like a green frizzy mop and the escarole is broad-leaved, but both have a distinct bitter flavor. Serve mixed with each other and a well-flavored dressing. This dampens down the bitter flavor but gives the salad a pleasant "bite."

Preparing

To prepare chicory, take out the core at the base with a sharp knife (*left*) and discard any wilted or damaged leaves. Rinse thoroughly, then dry the leaves.

Above: Chicory.
Above right: Radicchio.
Below right: Escarole.

Preparing Salad Leaves

Pull the leaves away from the stalk, discarding any wilted or damaged leaves.

Wash the leaves in plenty of cold water, swirling gently to make sure all dirt and any insects are washed away.

Place the washed leaves in a soft dish towel and then gently pat dry.

Place in a dry dish towel in a large plastic bag. Chill in the fridge for about 1 hour.

RADISHES

Radishes have a peppery flavor that can almost be felt in the nostrils as you bite into one. Their pungency depends not only on the varieties but also on the soil in which they are grown. Freshly harvested radishes have the most pronounced flavor and crisp texture.

Varieties

Radishes were loved throughout antiquity and consequently there are many varieties worldwide. Both the small red types and the large white radishes are internationally popular.

Red Radishes: These small red orbs have many pretty names, but are mostly sold simply as radishes. They are available all year round, have a deep pink skin, sometimes paler or white at the roots and a firm white flesh. Their peppery flavor is milder in the spring and they are almost always eaten raw. Finely sliced and sandwiched in bread and butter, they make an interesting *hors d'oeuvre*.

French Breakfast Radishes: These are red and white and slightly more elongated than the red radish. They tend to be milder than the red radishes and are popular in France either eaten on their own or served with other raw vegetables as *crudités*.

Daikon or Mooli Radishes: Sometimes known as the oriental radish, the daikon is a smooth-skinned, long, white radish. Those bought in stores have a mild flavor, less peppery than the red radish – perhaps because they lose their flavor after long storage (daikons straight from the garden are hot and peppery). They can be eaten raw or pickled, or added to stir-fries.

Buying and Storing

Buy red radishes that are firm with crisp leaves. If at all possible, buy daikons or moolis which still have their leaves; this is a good indication of their freshness as they wilt quickly. The leaves should be green and lively and the skins clear with no bruises or blemishes. They can be stored in the fridge for a few days.

Preparing and Serving

Red radishes need only to be washed. They can then be sliced or eaten whole by themselves or in salads. You can make a feature of them by slicing into a salad of, say, oranges and walnuts, perhaps with a scattering of arugula and dressed with a walnut oil vinaigrette. To use daikon in a stir-fry, cut into slices and add to the dish for the last few minutes of cooking. It adds not only flavor but also a wonderfully juicy and crunchy texture.

Left: Red radishes.
Above: French breakfast radishes.
Right: Daikon, or Mooli, radishes.

WATERCRESS

Watercress is perhaps the most robustly flavored of all the salad ingredients and a handful of watercress is all you need to perk up a rather dull green salad. It has a distinctive "raw" flavor, both peppery and slightly pungent and this, together with its bright green leaves, make it a popular garnish.

Watercress, as the name suggests, grows in water. It needs fast flowing clean water to thrive and is really only successful around freshwater springs on chalk hills. The first watercress beds were cultivated in Europe, but watercress is now grown worldwide.

WINTER CRESS

Winter cress or land cress is often grown as an alternative to watercress, when flowing water is not available. It looks like a robust form of watercress and indeed has a similar if even more assertive flavor, with a distinct peppery taste. Use as you would use watercress, either in salads or in soups.

Nutrition

Watercress is extremely rich in vitamins A, B2, C, D and E. It is also rich in calcium, potassium and iron and provides significant quantities of sulphur and chloride.

Buying and Storing

Only buy fresh-looking watercress – the darker and larger the leaves the better. Avoid any with wilted or yellow leaves. It will keep for several days in the fridge or better still, submerged in a bowl, or arranged in a jar of cold water, and kept in a cool place.

Preparing and Cooking

Discard any yellow leaves and remove thick stalks which will be too coarse for salads or soups. Small sprigs can be added to salads.

For soups and purées, either blend watercress raw or cook briefly in stock, milk or water. Cooking inevitably destroys some of the nutrients but cooked watercress has a less harsh flavor, while still retaining its characteristic peppery taste.

MUSTARD AND CRESS

Mustard and cress are often grown together, to provide spicy greenery as a garnish or for salads. They are available all year through.

Mustard seedlings germinate 3-4 days sooner than the cress, so if you buy mustard and cress from the supermarket, or grow your own on the windowsill, initially the punnets will only show mustard seedlings.

History

Cress has been grown for thousands of years, known first to the Persians. There is a story that the Persians would always eat cress before they baked bread, and there are other references in antiquity to people eating cress with bread.

Serving

Today mustard and cress are often enjoyed in sandwiches, either served simply on buttered bread, or with avocado or cucumber added. Cress probably wouldn't be substantial enough as a salad in itself, but, with its faint spicy flavor, it can perk up a plain green salad, and it is also excellent in a tomato salad, dressed simply with olive oil and tarragon vinegar.

Above left: Watercress.
Below left: Winter cress.
Above right: Mustard seedlings.
Right: Cress seedlings.

NINE

MUSHROOMS

White Mushrooms

Field Mushrooms

Woodland Mushrooms

*Wild Mushrooms
and Other Fungi*

WHITE MUSHROOMS

Mushrooms are generally cooked, although some white mushrooms are served raw in salads. Eat them quickly; after frying they can go soft and flabby.

History

In the past, mushrooms have had a firm association with the supernatural and even today their connection with the mysterious side of life hasn't completely disappeared. Fairy rings – circles of mushrooms – inexplicably appear overnight in woods and fields and thunder is still thought to bring forth fresh crops of mushrooms.

Many types of mushrooms and fungi are either poisonous or hallucinogenic, and in the past their poisons have been distilled for various murderous reasons.

The use of the term mushroom to mean edible species, and toadstool to mean those considered poisonous, has no scientific basis, and there is no simple rule for distinguishing between the two. Picking wild mushrooms is not safe unless you are confident about identifying edible types. In France during the autumn, people take the wild mushrooms they have gathered to the local pharmacy, where safe mushrooms are identified.

Varieties

White/Button Mushrooms: Cultivated mushrooms are widely available in stores and are sold when very young and tiny. The slightly larger ones are known as closed cap, while larger ones still are open capped, or open cup, mushrooms. They have ivory or white caps with pinky/beige gills that darken as they mature. All have a pleasant flavor.

Cremini Mushrooms: These have a thicker stem and a darker, pale brown cap. They have a more pronounced "mushroomy" flavor and a meatier texture than white mushrooms.

Buying and Storing

It is easy to see whether or not white mushrooms are fresh – their caps will be clean and white, without bruises or blemishes. The longer they stay on the shelves, the darker and more discolored the caps become, while the gills underneath turn from pink to brown.

If possible, use the paper bags provided in many supermarkets nowadays when buying mushrooms. Mushrooms in plastic bags sweat in their own heat, eventually turning slippery and unappetizing. If you have no choice or you buy mushrooms in cellophane-wrapped cartons, transfer loose to the bottom of the fridge as soon as possible. They will keep only for a day or two.

Preparing

Mushrooms should not be washed but wiped with a damp cloth or a piece of paper towel (*below*). This is partly because you don't want to increase their water content, and also because they should be fried as dry as possible.

Unless the skins are very discolored, it should not be necessary to peel them, although you probably will need to trim the very base of the stem.

Cooking

Mushrooms are largely composed of water and shrink noticeably during cooking. They also take up a lot of fat as they cook so it is best to use butter or a good olive oil for frying. Fry mushrooms briskly over a moderately high heat so that as they shrink the water evaporates and they don't stew in their own juice. For the same reason do not fry too many mushrooms at once in the same pan.

Most of the recipes in this book use fried mushrooms as their base and they are completely interchangeable – so if you can't get wild mushrooms or cremini mushrooms for instance, white mushrooms can be used instead.

Above: White mushrooms.
Top right: Flat mushrooms.
Far right: Field mushrooms.
Right: Cremini mushrooms (top) and open capped or cup mushrooms.

FIELD MUSHROOMS

Field mushrooms are the wild relatives of the cultivated mushroom and when cooked have a wonderful aroma. Flat mushrooms, although indistinguishable from field mushrooms in appearance, have probably been cultivated and are also excellent. Connoisseurs say that only wild mushrooms have any flavor but many would argue against this. However, if you know where to find field mushrooms, keep the secret to yourself (most mushroom devotees seem to know this) and count yourself lucky!

Buying and Storing

Field mushrooms are sometimes available during the autumn in farm stores. Since they are likely to have been picked recently, they should be fresh unless obviously wilting. Unless you intend to stuff them, don't worry if they are broken in places as you will be slicing them anyway. Use as soon as possible after purchase.

Preparing

Trim the stalk bottoms if necessary and wipe the caps with a damp cloth. Slice according to the recipe.

Cooking

For true field mushrooms, you need do nothing more complicated than simply fry them in butter or olive oil with a suggestion of garlic if liked. However, like flat mushrooms, field mushrooms can be used for stuffing, in soups or indeed any mushroom recipe. They are darker than white mushrooms and will color soups and sauces brown, but the flavor will be extremely good.

When stuffing mushrooms, gently fry the caps on both sides for a few minutes. The stalks can be chopped and added to the stuffing or can be used for soups or stocks.

WOODLAND MUSHROOMS

Varieties

Ceps: Popular in France, where they are known as *cèpes* and in Italy where they are called *porcini*, these meaty, bun-shaped mushrooms have a fine almost suede-like texture and a good flavor. Instead of gills they have a spongy texture beneath the cap and unless they are very young it is best to scrape this away as it goes soggy when cooked. Ceps are excellent fried in oil or butter over a brisk heat to evaporate the liquid and then added to omelets.

Alternately, an Italian way of cooking is to remove the stalk and the spongy tubes, and brush the tops with olive oil. Broil for about 10 minutes under a moderate broiler and then turn them over and pour olive oil and a sprinkling of garlic into the center. Broil for a further 5 minutes and then serve sprinkled with seasoning and parsley.

Chanterelles: Frilly, trumpet-shaped chanterelles are delicate mushrooms which range in color from cream to a vivid yellow. Later, winter chanterelles have grayish-lilac gills on the underside of their dark caps. Chanterelles have a delicate, slightly fruity flavor and a firm, almost rubbery texture. They are difficult to clean as their tiny gills tend to trap grit and earth. Rinse them gently under cold running water and then shake dry. Fry in butter over a gentle heat to start with so they exude their liquid and then increase the heat to boil it off. They are delicious with scrambled eggs, or served by themselves with finely cut toast.

Horn of Plenty/Black Trumpets: Taking its name from its shape, this mushroom ranges in color from mid-brown to black. As it is hollow, it will need to be brushed well to clean or, if a large specimen, sliced in half. It is very versatile, but goes particularly well with fish.

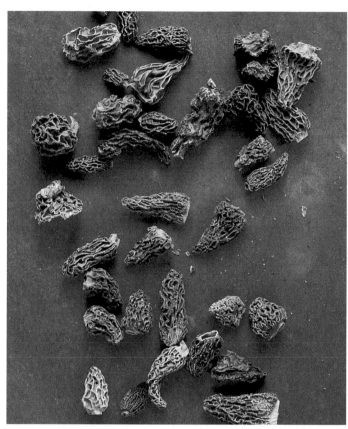

Morels: These are the first mushroom of the year, appearing not in autumn but in spring. In Scandinavia they are called the "truffles of the north" and are considered among the great edible fungi. They are cone-shaped with a crinkled spongy cap but are hollow inside. You will need to wash them well under running water as insects tend to creep into their dark crevices. Morels need longer cooking than most mushrooms: sauté them in butter, add a squeeze of lemon and then cover and simmer for up to an hour until tender. The juices can then be thickened with cream or egg yolks.

Dried Mushrooms: Most wild mushrooms are available dried. To reconstitute, soak in warm water for about 20-30 minutes; in the case of morels when they are added to stews, soak for about 10 minutes. Dried wild mushrooms, particularly ceps, have an intense flavor.

Left: Clockwise from the top: Ceps, Horn of Plenty, Chanterelles.
Above right: Dried mushrooms.
Above left: Morels.
Right: Winter chanterelles.

WILD MUSHROOMS <u>AND</u> OTHER FUNGI

Mushroom gathering, a seasonal event throughout Eastern Europe, Italy and France, is increasingly popular. The French are particularly enthusiastic: in autumn whole families drive to secret locations to comb the ground for prizes like shaggy ink caps or ceps. Wild mushrooms are sold in supermarkets.

OYSTER MUSHROOMS

These ear-shaped fungi grow on rotting wood. Cap, gills and stem are all the same color, which can be grayish brown, pink or yellow. They are now widely cultivated, although they are generally thought of as wild mushrooms. Delicious both in flavor and texture, they are softer than the white mushroom when cooked but seem more substantial, having more "bite" to them.

Buying and Storing

Fresh specimens are erect and lively looking with clear gills and smooth caps. They are often sold packed in plastic boxes under cellophane wrappings and

will wilt and go soggy if left on the shelf for too long. Once purchased, remove them from the plastic packaging and use as soon as possible.

Preparing

Oyster mushrooms rarely need trimming at all but if they are large, tear rather than cut them into pieces. In very large specimens the stems can be tough and should be discarded.

Cooking

Fry in butter until tender – they take less time to cook than white mushrooms. Do not overcook oyster mushrooms as the flavor will be lost and the soft texture will become more rubbery.

Left: Pink and yellow oyster mushrooms.
Above: Gray oyster mushrooms.

ENOKITAKI MUSHROOMS

This is another Japanese mushroom. The wild variety is orangy-brown with shiny caps but outside Japan, you will probably only be able to find the cultivated variety, which are similarly fine, with pin-size heads, but are pale colored with snowy white caps. They have a fine, sweet and almost fruity flavor. In Japanese cookery they are added to salads or used as a garnish for soups or hot dishes. Since they become tough if overcooked, add enokitaki mushrooms at the very last minute of cooking.

SHIITAKE MUSHROOMS

These Japanese fungi are now commonly available in supermarkets. They are among a variety of tree mushrooms (called *take* in Japan, the *shii* being the hardwood tree from which they are harvested). They have a meaty, slightly acid flavor and a distinct slippery texture. Shiitake mushrooms, though once only available in oriental stores, are now widely available in most supermarkets. Unlike white mushrooms that can be flash-fried, shiitake need to be cooked through, although even this only takes 3–5 minutes. Add them to stir-fries for a delicious flavor and texture. Alternatively, fry them in oil until tender. Sprinkle with sesame oil and then serve with a little soy sauce.

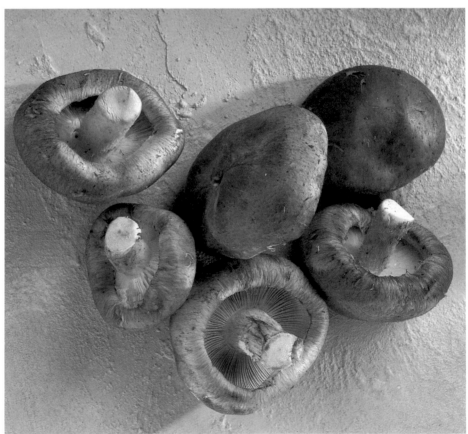

Above: Enokitaki mushrooms.
Right: Shiitake mushrooms.

SOUPS
AND
APPETIZERS

Tantalizing appetizers, ranging from traditional favorites to more exotic dishes for elegant dinners. There are soups that could be served either before a main course or on their own as light, wholesome meals, in addition to dozens of ideas for tempting starters.

VEGETABLE STOCK

USE THIS VERSATILE STOCK AS THE BASIS FOR ALL GOOD SOUPS AND SAUCES. IF YOU HAVE AN EXTRA-LARGE SAUCEPAN OR A STOCKPOT, WHY NOT DOUBLE THE RECIPE AND FREEZE SEVERAL BATCHES?

MAKES 10 CUPS

INGREDIENTS

   2 leeks, coarsely chopped
   3 stalks celery, coarsely chopped
   1 large onion, with skin, chopped
   2 pieces fresh ginger, chopped
   3 garlic cloves, unpeeled
   1 yellow bell pepper, chopped
   1 parsnip, chopped
   mushroom stalks
   tomato peelings
   3 tablespoons light soy sauce
   3 bay leaves
   bundle of parsley stalks

   3 sprigs of fresh thyme
   1 sprig of fresh rosemary
   2 teaspoons salt
   freshly ground black pepper
   15 cups cold water

1 Put all the ingredients into a very large saucepan or a stockpot.

2 Bring slowly to the boil, then lower the heat and simmer for 30 minutes, stirring occasionally.

3 Let the liquid and vegetables cool. Strain and discard the vegetables and the stock is ready to use. Alternatively, chill or freeze the stock and keep it to use as required.

CRISP CROUTONS

Easy to make and simple to store, these croutons add a delightful touch to fresh homemade soups. They are also an ideal way of using up stale bread. Specialty bread such as ciabatta or baguettes can be thinly sliced to make the nicest, crunchiest croutons, but everyday sliced loaves can be cut into interesting shapes for fun entertaining. Use a good quality, flavorless oil such as sunflower or peanut, or for a fuller flavor brush with extra-virgin olive oil. Alternatively, you could use a flavored oil, such as one with garlic and herbs or chili.

   Preheat the oven to 400°F. Place the croutons on a baking sheet, brush with your chosen oil, then bake for about 15 minutes, until golden and crisp. They crisp up further as they cool. Store them in an airtight container for up to a week. Reheat in a warm oven, if desired, before serving.

SPICED INDIAN CAULIFLOWER SOUP

THIS MILDLY SPICY SOUP MAKES A WARMING FIRST COURSE, AN APPETIZING QUICK MEAL OR A DELICIOUS SUMMER APPETIZER.

SERVES FOUR TO SIX

INGREDIENTS

   1 large potato, peeled and diced
   1 small cauliflower, chopped
   1 onion, chopped
   1 tablespoon sunflower oil
   1 garlic clove, crushed
   1 tablespoon grated fresh ginger
   2 teaspoons ground turmeric
   1 teaspoon cumin seeds
   1 teaspoon black mustard seeds
   2 teaspoons ground coriander
   4 cups vegetable stock
   1¼ cups plain yogurt
   salt and freshly ground black pepper
   fresh cilantro or parsley, to garnish

1 Put the potato, cauliflower and onion in a large saucepan with the oil and 3 tablespoons water. Heat until hot and bubbling, then cover and turn the heat down. Continue cooking the mixture for about 10 minutes.

2 Add the garlic, ginger and spices. Stir well and cook for another 2 minutes, stirring occasionally. Pour in the stock and season well. Bring to a boil, then cover and simmer for about 20 minutes. Stir in the yogurt, season well and garnish with cilantro or parsley.

WINTER WARMER SOUP

SIMMER A VARIETY OF WINTER ROOT VEGETABLES TOGETHER FOR A WARMING AND SATISFYING SOUP.

SERVES SIX

INGREDIENTS

3 medium carrots, chopped
1 large potato, chopped
1 large parsnip, chopped
1 large turnip or small rutabaga, chopped
1 onion, chopped
2 tablespoons sunflower oil
2 tablespoons butter
6 cups water
salt and freshly ground black pepper
1 piece fresh ginger, grated
1¼ cups milk
3 tablespoons sour cream or plain yogurt
2 tablespoons chopped fresh dill
fresh lemon juice

1 Put the carrots, potato, parsnip, turnip or rutabaga and onion into a large saucepan with the oil and butter. Fry lightly, then cover and sweat the vegetables over very low heat for 15 minutes, shaking the pan occasionally.

2 Pour in the water, bring to a boil and season well. Cover and simmer for 20 minutes, until the vegetables are soft.

3 Strain the vegetables, reserving the stock, add the ginger and purée in a food processor or blender until smooth.

4 Return the purée and stock to the pan. Add the milk and stir while the soup gently reheats.

5 Remove from the heat, stir in the sour cream or yogurt plus the dill, lemon juice and extra seasoning, if necessary. Reheat the soup, if desired, but do not allow it to boil as you do so, or it may curdle.

EGG FLOWER SOUP

FOR THE BEST FLAVOR, YOU DO NEED TO USE A HOMEMADE STOCK FOR THIS SOUP. THE EGG SETS INTO PRETTY STRANDS, GIVING THE SOUP A FLOWERY LOOK, HENCE THE NAME.

SERVES SIX

INGREDIENTS

    4 cups stock
    3 tablespoons light soy sauce
    2 tablespoons dry sherry or vermouth
    3 scallions, diagonally sliced
    small piece fresh ginger, shredded
    4 large lettuce leaves, shredded
    1 teaspoon sesame seed oil
    2 eggs, beaten
    salt and freshly ground black pepper
    sesame seeds, to garnish

1 Pour the stock into a large saucepan. Add all the ingredients except the eggs, seasoning and seeds. Bring to the boil and then cook for about 2 minutes.

2 Very carefully, pour the eggs in a thin, steady stream into the center of the boiling liquid.

3 Count to three, then quickly stir the soup. The egg will begin to cook and form long threads. Season to taste, ladle the soup into warm bowls and serve immediately, sprinkled with sesame seeds.

BROCCOLI AND BLUE BRIE SOUP

A POPULAR VEGETABLE, BROCCOLI MAKES A DELICIOUS SOUP WITH AN APPETIZING DEEP GREEN COLOR. FOR A TASTY TANG, STIR IN SOME CUBES OF BLUE BRIE CHEESE JUST BEFORE SERVING.

SERVES SIX

INGREDIENTS

    1 onion, chopped
    1 pound broccoli spears, chopped
    1 large zucchini, chopped
    1 large carrot, chopped
    1 medium potato, chopped
    2 tablespoons butter
    2 tablespoons sunflower oil
    8 cups stock or water
    3 ounces blue Brie (or Dolcellate)
      cheese, cubed
    salt sand ground black pepper
    almond flakes, to garnish (optional)

1 Put all the vegetables in a large saucepan with the butter and oil, plus about 3 tablespoons stock or water.

2 Heat the ingredients until sizzling and stir well. Cover and cook gently for 15 minutes, shaking the pan occasionally, until all the vegetables soften.

3 Add the rest of the stock or water, season and bring to a boil, then cover and simmer gently for 25–30 minutes.

4 Strain the vegetables and reserve the liquid. Purée the vegetables in a food processor or blender, then return them to the pan with the reserved liquid.

5 Bring the soup back to a gentle boil and stir in the cheese until it melts. (Don't let the soup boil too hard or the cheese will become stringy.) Season to taste and garnish with a scattering of almond slices.

HOMEMADE MUSHROOM SOUP

HOMEMADE MUSHROOM SOUP IS QUITE, QUITE DIFFERENT FROM CANNED OR PACKAGED SOUPS.

SERVES FOUR TO SIX

INGREDIENTS
1 pound white mushrooms, sliced
½ cup sliced shiitake mushrooms
3 tablespoons sunflower oil
1 onion, chopped
1 stalk celery, chopped
5 cups vegetable stock or water
2 tablespoons soy sauce
¼ cup long grain rice
salt and freshly ground black pepper
1¼ cups milk
chopped fresh parsley, and sliced
   almonds, to garnish

1 Put all the mushrooms in a large saucepan with the oil, onion and celery. Heat until sizzling, then cover and simmer for about 10 minutes, shaking the pan occasionally.

2 Add the stock or water, soy sauce, rice and seasoning. Bring to a boil, then cover and simmer gently for 20 minutes, until the vegetables and rice are soft.

3 Strain the vegetables, reserving the stock, and purée in a food processor or blender until smooth. Return the vegetables and reserved stock to the pan.

4 Stir in the milk, reheat until boiling and taste for seasoning. Serve hot, sprinkled with a little chopped parsley and a few sliced almond flakes.

CLASSIC MINESTRONE

THE HOMEMADE VERSION OF THIS
FAMOUS SOUP IS A DELICIOUS
REVELATION AND MOUTH-
WATERINGLY HEALTHY.

SERVES FOUR

INGREDIENTS

1 large leek, thinly sliced
2 carrots, chopped
1 zucchini, thinly sliced
4 ounces whole green beans, halved
2 stalks celery, thinly sliced
3 tablespoons olive oil
6 cups vegetable stock
1 can (14 ounces) tomatoes, chopped
1 tablespoon fresh basil, chopped
1 teaspoon chopped fresh thyme
   leaves, or ½ teaspoon dried thyme
salt and freshly ground black pepper
1 can (14 ounces) cannellini
   or kidney beans
⅓ cup small pasta shapes or macaroni
fresh Parmesan cheese, finely grated
   (optional) and fresh parsley, chopped,
   to garnish

1 Put all the fresh vegetables in a large saucepan with the olive oil. Heat until sizzling, then cover, lower the heat and sweat the vegetables for 15 minutes, shaking the pan occasionally.

2 Add the stock (use water if desired), tomatoes, herbs and seasoning. Bring to a boil, replace the lid and simmer gently for about 30 minutes.

3 Add the beans and their liquor together with the pasta, and simmer for another 10 minutes. Check the seasoning and serve hot, sprinkled with the Parmesan cheese (if using) and parsley.

COOK'S TIP
Minestrone is also delicious served cold on a hot summer's day. In fact, the flavor improves if it is made a day or two ahead and stored in the refrigerator. It can also be frozen and reheated.

CLASSIC FRENCH ONION SOUP

*WHEN FRENCH ONION SOUP IS MADE SLOWLY AND CAREFULLY, THE ONIONS ALMOST CARAMELIZE TO A
DEEP MAHOGANY COLOR. THE SOUP HAS A SUPERB FLAVOR AND IS A PERFECT WINTER DISH.*

SERVES FOUR

INGREDIENTS

    4 large onions
    2 tablespoons sunflower or olive oil, or
     1 tablespoon of each
    2 tablespoons butter
    4 cups vegetable stock
    salt and freshly ground black pepper
    4 slices French bread
    1½–2 ounces Gruyère or Cheddar
     cheese, grated

1 Peel and quarter the onions and slice
or chop them into ¼-inch pieces. Heat
the oil and butter together in a deep,
heavy-bottomed saucepan, preferably
with a medium-size base, so that the
onions form a thick layer.

3 When the onions are a rich mahogany
brown, add the stock and a little
seasoning. Simmer, partially covered, for
30 minutes, then taste and adjust the
seasoning according to taste.

4 Preheat the broiler and toast the
bread. Spoon the soup into four ovenproof serving dishes and place a piece of
bread in each. Sprinkle with cheese and
broil for a few minutes until golden.

2 Fry the onions briskly for a few
minutes, stirring constantly, and then
reduce the heat and cook gently for
45–60 minutes. At first the onions
need to be stirred only occasionally, but
as they begin to color, stir frequently.
The color of the onions gradually turns
golden and then more rapidly to brown,
so take care to stir constantly at this
stage so they do not burn.

ASPARAGUS SOUP

HOMEMADE ASPARAGUS SOUP HAS A DELICATE FLAVOR, QUITE UNLIKE THAT FROM A CAN. THIS SOUP IS BEST MADE WITH YOUNG ASPARAGUS, WHICH IS TENDER AND BLENDS WELL. SERVE IT WITH WAFER-THIN SLICES OF BREAD.

SERVES FOUR

INGREDIENTS
    1 pound young asparagus
    3 tablespoons butter
    6 shallots, sliced
    1 tablespoon all-purpose flour
    2½ cups vegetable stock
      or water
    1 tablespoon lemon juice
    salt and freshly ground black pepper
    1 cup milk
    ½ cup light cream or half-and-half
    2 teaspoons chopped fresh chervil

1 Trim the stalks of the asparagus if necessary. Cut 1½ inches off the tops of half the asparagus and set aside for a garnish. Slice the remaining asparagus.

2 Melt 2 tablespoons of the butter in a large saucepan and gently fry the sliced shallots for 2–3 minutes, stirring occasionally, until soft but not brown.

3 Add the asparagus and fry over a low heat for about 1 minute. Stir in the flour, and cook for 1 minute. Stir in the stock or water and lemon juice, and season to taste. Bring to a boil and then simmer, partially covered, for 15–20 minutes, until the asparagus is very tender.

4 Cool slightly and then process the soup in a food processor or blender until smooth. Then press the puréed asparagus through a sieve placed over a clean saucepan. Add the milk by pouring and stirring it through the sieve with the asparagus so as to extract the maximum amount of asparagus purée.

5 Melt the remaining butter and fry the reserved asparagus tips over low heat for about 3–4 minutes to soften.

6 Heat the soup over low heat for 3–4 minutes. Stir in the cream and the asparagus tips. Heat gently and serve sprinkled with the chopped fresh chervil.

CARROT AND CORIANDER SOUP

NEARLY ALL ROOT VEGETABLES MAKE EXCELLENT SOUPS, AS THEY PURÉE WELL AND HAVE AN EARTHY FLAVOR THAT COMPLEMENTS THE SHARPER FLAVORS OF HERBS AND SPICES. CARROTS ARE PARTICULARLY VERSATILE, AND THIS SIMPLE SOUP IS ELEGANT IN BOTH FLAVOR AND APPEARANCE.

SERVES FOUR TO SIX

INGREDIENTS
   1 pound carrots, preferably young and
      tender
   1 tablespoon sunflower oil
   3 tablespoons butter
   1 onion, chopped
   1 celery stalk, sliced, plus 2–3 pale
      leafy celery tops
   2 small potatoes, chopped
   4 cups vegetable stock
   2–3 teaspoons ground coriander
   1 tablespoon chopped fresh cilantro
   1 cup milk
   salt and freshly ground black pepper

1 Trim the carrots, peel if necessary and cut into chunks. Heat the oil and 2 tablespoons of the butter in a large flameproof casserole or heavy-bottomed saucepan and fry the onion over low heat for 3–4 minutes, until slightly softened but not browned.

2 Cut the celery stalk into slices. Add the celery and potato to the onion in the pan, cook for a few minutes and then add the carrots. Fry over low heat for 3–4 minutes, stirring frequently, and then cover. Reduce the heat even further and sweat for about 10 minutes. Shake the pan or stir occasionally so the vegetables do not stick to the bottom.

3 Add the stock, bring to the boil and then partially cover and simmer for another 8–10 minutes, until the carrots and potato are tender.

4 Remove 6–8 tiny celery leaves for garnish and finely chop the remaining celery tops (about 1 tablespoon once chopped). Melt the remaining butter in a small saucepan and fry the ground coriander for about 1 minute, stirring constantly.

5 Reduce the heat, add the chopped celery tops and fresh cilantro and fry for about 1 minute. Set aside.

6 Process the soup in a food processor or blender and pour into a clean saucepan. Stir in the milk, coriander mixture and seasoning. Heat gently, taste and adjust the seasoning. Serve garnished with the reserved celery leaves.

COOK'S TIP
For a more piquant flavor, add a little lemon juice just before serving.

BORSCHT

This classic soup was the staple diet of prerevolution Russian peasants for hundreds of years. There are many variations, and it is rare to find two recipes the same.

SERVES SIX

INGREDIENTS

12 ounces whole uncooked beets
1 tablespoon sunflower oil
1 large onion, thinly sliced
1 large carrot, cut into julienne strips
3 celery stalks, thinly sliced
6 cups vegetable stock
8 ounces tomatoes, peeled, seeded and sliced
2 tablespoons lemon juice or wine vinegar
2 tablespoons chopped dill
salt and freshly ground black pepper
4 ounces white cabbage, thinly sliced
⅔ cup sour cream

1 Peel the beets, slice and then cut into very thin strips.

2 Heat the oil in a large, heavy-bottomed saucepan and fry the thinly sliced onion for 2–3 minutes, then add the carrots, celery and beets. Cook for 4–5 minutes, stirring frequently, until the oil has been absorbed.

3 Add the stock, tomatoes, lemon juice or wine vinegar, half of the dill and seasoning. Bring to a boil and simmer for about 30–40 minutes, until the vegetables are completely tender.

4 Add the cabbage and simmer for 5 minutes, until tender. Adjust the seasoning and serve sprinkled with remaining dill and the sour cream.

SPICY BORSCHT

THE FLAVOR MATURES AND
IMPROVES IF THE SOUP IS MADE
THE DAY BEFORE IT IS NEEDED.

SERVES SIX

INGREDIENTS

   1 onion, chopped
   1 pound raw beets, peeled and
     chopped
   1 large cooking apple, chopped
   2 celery stalks, chopped
   ½ red bell pepper, chopped
   ½ cup chopped mushrooms
   2 tablespoons butter
   2 tablespoons sunflower oil
   8 cups stock or water
   1 teaspoon cumin seeds
   pinch dried thyme
   1 large bay leaf
   fresh lemon juice
   salt and ground black pepper
   ⅔ cup sour cream
   few sprigs fresh dill, to garnish

1 Place all the chopped vegetables into a large saucepan with the butter, oil and 3 tablespoons of the stock or water. Cover and cook gently for about 15 minutes, shaking the pan occasionally.

2 Stir in the cumin seeds and cook for a minute, then add the remaining stock or water, dried thyme, bay leaf, lemon juice and seasoning.

3 Bring to a boil, then cover and turn down to a gentle simmer. Cook for about 30 minutes.

4 Strain the vegetables and reserve the liquid. Process the vegetables in a food processor or blender until they are smooth and creamy.

5 Return the vegetables to the pan, stir in the reserved stock and reheat. Check the seasoning.

6 Serve the borscht with swirls of sour cream and topped with a few sprigs of fresh dill.

VARIATION
This soup can be served fairly thick, as long as the vegetables are finely chopped first.
   The beet is something of an under-valued vegetable, although popular in many European countries. For example, it is delicious served as a hot vegetable accompaniment with a creamy béchamel sauce and topped with crisp bread crumbs. Alternatively, try it raw and coarsely grated, then tossed in dressing for a side salad.

SUMMER SQUASH RISOTTO

SUMMER SQUASHES ARE NOT AS SWEET AS PUMPKINS, BUT THEY HAVE A DELICATE FRUITY TASTE THAT IS IDEAL IN A RISOTTO. SERVE THIS AS A TASTY APPETIZER OR LIGHT LUNCH.

SERVES FOUR

INGREDIENTS

   1 summer squash or pumpkin,
     about 2 pounds
   2 tablespoons olive oil
   1 onion, chopped
   1–2 garlic cloves, crushed
   ½ cup arborio rice
   2½–3 cups vegetable stock
   salt and freshly ground black pepper
   3 tablespoons grated Parmesan
     cheese
   1 tablespoon chopped fresh parsley

1 Halve or quarter the squash or pumpkin, remove the seeds and skin, and then cut into ¾-inch chunks.

2 Heat the oil in a flameproof casserole and fry the onion and garlic for about 3–4 minutes, stirring frequently. Continue frying until both the onion and garlic are lightly golden.

3 Add the squash or pumpkin and stir-fry for a few minutes. Add the rice and cook for about 2 minutes, stirring all the time.

4 Pour in about half of the stock and season. Stir well and then half-cover and simmer gently for about 20 minutes, stirring occasionally. As the liquid is absorbed, add more stock and stir to prevent the mixture from sticking to the base.

5 When the squash and rice are nearly tender, add a little more stock. Cook, uncovered, for 5–10 minutes. Stir in the Parmesan cheese and parsley and serve.

PUMPKIN SOUP

THE SWEET FLAVOR OF PUMPKIN IS GOOD IN SOUPS, TEAMING WELL WITH OTHER MORE SAVORY INGREDIENTS SUCH AS ONIONS AND POTATOES TO MAKE A WARM AND COMFORTING DISH.

SERVES FOUR TO SIX

INGREDIENTS

   1 tablespoon sunflower oil
   2 tablespoons butter
   1 large onion, sliced
   1½ pounds pumpkin, cut into
     large chunks
   1 pound potatoes, sliced
   2½ cups vegetable stock
   generous pinch of nutmeg
   1 teaspoon chopped fresh tarragon
   salt and freshly ground black pepper
   2½ cups milk
   1–2 teaspoons lemon juice

1 Heat the oil and butter in a heavy saucepan and fry the onion for 4–5 minutes over low heat, stirring frequently, until soft but not browned.

2 Add the pumpkin and potato, stir well and then cover and sweat over low heat for about 10 minutes, until the vegetables are almost tender, stirring occasionally to prevent them from sticking to the pan.

3 Stir in the stock, nutmeg, tarragon and seasoning. Bring to a boil and then simmer for about 10 minutes, until the vegetables are completely tender.

4 Allow to cool slightly, then pour into a food processor or blender and process until smooth. Pour back into a clean saucepan and add the milk. Heat gently and then taste, adding the lemon juice and extra seasoning if necessary. Serve piping hot with crusty brown bread.

CREAM OF MUSHROOM SOUP

A GOOD MUSHROOM SOUP MAKES THE MOST OF THE SUBTLE AND SOMETIMES ELUSIVE FLAVOR OF MUSHROOMS. WHITE MUSHROOMS ARE USED HERE FOR THEIR PALE COLOR; CRIMINI OR, BETTER STILL, WILD MUSHROOMS GIVE A FULLER FLAVOR BUT TURN THE SOUP BROWN.

SERVES FOUR

INGREDIENTS
    10 ounces white mushrooms
    1 tablespoon sunflower oil
    3 tablespoons butter
    1 small onion, finely chopped
    1 tablespoon all-purpose flour
    1¾ cups vegetable stock
    1¾ cups milk
    pinch of dried basil
    salt and freshly ground black pepper
    2–3 tablespoons light cream or
        half-and-half (optional)
    fresh basil leaves, to garnish

1 Separate the mushroom caps from the stalks. Finely slice the caps and finely chop the stalks.

2 Heat the oil and half the butter in a heavy-bottomed saucepan and add the onion, mushroom stalks and half the sliced mushroom caps. Fry for 1–2 minutes, stirring frequently, and then cover and sweat over low heat for 6–7 minutes, stirring occasionally.

3 Stir in the flour and cook for about 1 minute. Gradually add the stock and milk to make a smooth thin sauce. Add the basil and season with salt and pepper. Bring to a boil and then simmer, partly covered, for 15 minutes.

4 Cool slightly and then pour the soup into a food processor or blender and process until smooth. Melt the rest of the butter in a frying pan and fry the remaining mushrooms gently for 3–4 minutes, until they are just tender.

5 Pour the soup into a clean saucepan and stir in the sliced mushrooms. Heat until very hot and adjust the seasoning. Add a little cream, if using. Serve sprinkled with fresh basil leaves.

SOUFFLÉ OMELET WITH MUSHROOM SAUCE

A SOUFFLÉ OMELET INVOLVES A LITTLE MORE PREPARATION THAN AN ORDINARY OMELET BUT THE RESULT IS LIGHT AND SPRINGY TO TOUCH. THIS DISH MAKES A DELICIOUS LIGHT LUNCH.

SERVES ONE

INGREDIENTS
    2 eggs, separated
    1 tablespoon butter
    sprig of parsley or cilantro
For the mushroom sauce
    1 tablespoon butter
    3 ounces white mushrooms,
        thinly sliced
    1 tablespoon all-purpose flour
    ½ cup milk
    1 teaspoon chopped fresh parsley
        (optional)
    salt and freshly ground black pepper

1 To make the mushroom sauce, melt the butter in a saucepan or frying pan and fry the sliced mushrooms for 4–5 minutes, until tender.

2 Stir in the flour and then gradually add the milk, stirring all the time, to make a smooth sauce. Add the parsley, if using, and season with salt and pepper. Set aside and keep warm.

3 Beat the egg yolks with 1 tablespoon water and season with a little salt and pepper. Whisk the egg whites until stiff and then fold into the egg yolks using a metal spoon. Preheat the broiler.

4 Melt the butter in a large frying pan and pour the egg mixture into the pan. Cook over low heat for 2–4 minutes. Place the frying pan under the broiler and cook for another 3–4 minutes, until the top is golden brown.

5 Slide the omelet onto a warmed serving plate, top with the mushroom sauce and fold the omelet in half. Serve garnished with a sprig of parsley or cilantro leaves.

GAZPACHO

GAZPACHO IS A CLASSIC SPANISH SOUP. IT IS POPULAR ALL OVER SPAIN BUT NOWHERE MORE SO THAN IN ANDALUCIA, WHERE THERE ARE HUNDREDS OF VARIATIONS. IT IS A COLD SOUP OF TOMATOES, TOMATO JUICE, GREEN BELL PEPPER AND GARLIC, WHICH IS SERVED WITH A SELECTION OF GARNISHES.

SERVES FOUR

INGREDIENTS
 3–3½ pounds ripe tomatoes
 1 green bell pepper, seeded and
  roughly chopped
 2 garlic cloves, crushed
 2 slices white bread, crusts removed
 4 tablespoons olive oil
 4 tablespoons tarragon wine vinegar
 ⅔ cup tomato juice
 good pinch of sugar
 salt and freshly ground black pepper
 ice cubes, to serve
For the garnishes
 2 tablespoons sunflower oil
 2–3 slices white bread, diced
 1 small cucumber, peeled and
  finely diced
 1 small onion, finely chopped
 1 red bell pepper, seeded and finely diced
 1 green bell pepper, seeded and finely
  diced
 2 hard-boiled eggs, chopped

1 Skin the tomatoes, then quarter them and remove the cores.

2 Place the pepper in a food processor and process for a few seconds. Add the tomatoes, garlic, bread, olive oil and vinegar and process again. Add the tomato juice, sugar, seasoning and a little extra tomato juice or cold water and process. The consistency should be thick but not too stodgy.

3 Pour into a bowl and chill for at least 2 hours but no more than 12 hours, otherwise the textures deteriorate.

4 To prepare the bread cubes to use as a garnish, heat the oil in a frying pan and fry them until golden brown. Drain well.

5 Place each garnish in a separate small dish, or alternately arrange them in rows on a large plate.

6 Just before serving, stir a few ice cubes into the soup and then spoon into serving bowls. Serve with the garnishes.

PEAR AND WATERCRESS SOUP WITH STILTON CROUTONS

PEARS AND STILTON TASTE VERY GOOD WHEN EATEN TOGETHER AFTER THE MAIN COURSE. HERE, FOR A CHANGE, THEY ARE COMBINED IN AN APPETIZER.

SERVES SIX

INGREDIENTS
   1 bunch watercress
   4 medium pears, sliced
   3¾ cups vegetable stock
   salt and pepper
   ½ cup heavy cream
   juice of 1 lime
For the croutons
   2 tablespoons butter
   1 tablespoon olive oil
   3 cups stale bread, cubed
   1 cup chopped Stilton cheese

1 Set aside about one-third of the watercress leaves. Place all the rest of the leaves and the stalks in a pan with the pears, stock and a little seasoning. Simmer for about 15–20 minutes. Reserving a few watercress leaves for garnish, add the rest and immediately blend in a food processor until smooth.

2 Put the mixture in a bowl and stir in the cream and lime juice to mix the flavors thoroughly. Season again to taste. Pour all the soup back into a pan and reheat, stirring until warmed through.

3 To make the croutons, melt the butter and oil in a pan and fry the bread cubes until golden brown. Drain on paper towels. Put the cheese on top, then heat under a hot broiler until bubbling.

4 Pour the reheated soup into bowls. Use the croutons and remaining watercress leaves to garnish the soup before serving.

GARLIC MUSHROOMS

GARLIC AND MUSHROOMS MAKE A WONDERFUL COMBINATION. THEY MUST BE SERVED PIPING HOT, SO IF POSSIBLE USE A CAST-IRON FRYING PAN AND SERVE STRAIGHT FROM THE PAN.

SERVES FOUR (as an appetizer)

INGREDIENTS
    2 tablespoons sunflower oil
    2 tablespoons butter
    5 scallions, thinly sliced
    3 garlic cloves, crushed
    1 pound white mushrooms
    3 tablespoons white bread crumbs
    1 tablespoon chopped fresh parsley
    2 tablespoons lemon juice
    salt and freshly ground black pepper

1 Heat the oil and butter in a wok or cast-iron skillet. Add the scallions and garlic and stir-fry over medium heat for 1–2 minutes.

2 Add the whole white mushrooms and fry over high heat for 4–5 minutes, stirring and tossing with a large wide spatula or wooden spoon.

3 Stir in the bread crumbs, parsley, lemon juice and seasoning. Stir-fry for a few minutes, until the lemon juice has nearly evaporated, and then serve.

ROAST GARLIC WITH CROUTONS

YOUR GUESTS WILL BE ASTONISHED TO BE SERVED A WHOLE ROAST GARLIC AS AN APPETIZER. ROAST GARLIC HAS A HEAVENLY FLAVOR AND IS SO IRRESISTIBLE THAT THEY WILL EVEN FORGIVE YOU THE NEXT DAY!

SERVES FOUR

INGREDIENTS
    2 garlic bulbs
    3 tablespoons olive oil
    3 tablespoons water
    sprig of rosemary
    sprig of thyme
    1 bay leaf
    sea salt and freshly ground
      black pepper
To serve
    slices of French bread
    olive or sunflower oil, for frying
    6 ounces young goat cheese or soft
      cream cheese
    2 teaspoons chopped fresh herbs
      (marjoram, parsley and chives)

3 Heat a little oil in a frying pan and fry the French bread on both sides until golden. Blend the cheese with the mixed herbs and place in a serving dish.

1 Preheat the oven to 375°F. Place the garlic bulbs in a small ovenproof dish and drizzle with the oil and water. Add the rosemary, thyme and bay leaf and sprinkle with sea salt and pepper. Cover with foil and bake for 30 minutes.

2 Remove the foil, baste the garlic heads with the juices from the dish and bake for another 15–20 minutes, until they feel soft when pressed.

4 Cut each garlic bulb in half and open out slightly. Serve the garlic on small plates with the croutons and soft cheese. Each garlic clove should be squeezed out of its papery shell, spread over a crouton and eaten with the cheese.

MUSHROOMS ON TOAST

SERVE THESE ON TOAST FOR A QUICK, TASTY STARTER OR POP THEM INTO SMALL RAMEKINS AND SERVE WITH SLICES OF WARM CRUSTY BREAD. USE SOME SHITAKE MUSHROOMS, IF YOU CAN FIND THEM, FOR A RICHER FLAVOR.

SERVES FOUR

INGREDIENTS

   1 pound white mushrooms, sliced if
     large
   3 tablespoons olive oil
   3 tablespoons vegetable stock or water
   2 tablespoons dry sherry (optional)
   3 garlic cloves, crushed
   4 ounces low-fat cream cheese
   2 tablespoons chopped fresh parsley
   1 tablespoon chopped fresh chives
   salt and freshly ground black pepper

1 Put the mushrooms into a large saucepan with the olive oil, stock or water and sherry, if using. Heat until bubbling then cover and simmer for 5 minutes.

2 Add the garlic and stir well. Cook for another 2 minutes. Remove the mushrooms with a slotted spoon and set them aside. Cook the liquor until it reduces down to 2 tablespoons. Remove from the heat and stir in the cheese and herbs.

3 Stir the mixture well until the cheese melts, then return the mushrooms to the pan so that they become coated with the cheese mixture. Season to taste.

4 Pile the mushrooms onto thick slabs of hot toast. Alternatively, spoon them into four ramekins and serve accompanied by slices of crusty bread.

RICOTTA AND PINTO BEAN PÂTÉ

FOR AN ATTRACTIVE PRESENTATION, SPOON THE PÂTÉ INTO SMALL, OILED RING MOLDS, TURN OUT AND FILL WITH WHOLE BORLOTTI BEANS, DRESSED WITH LEMON JUICE, OLIVE OIL AND FRESH HERBS.

SERVES FOUR

INGREDIENTS

   1 can (14 ounces) pinto beans, drained
   1 garlic clove, crushed
   1 cup ricotta cheese,
     or cream cheese
   ¼ cup butter, melted
   juice of ½ lemon
   salt and freshly ground black pepper
   2 tablespoons chopped fresh parsley
   1 tablespoon chopped fresh thyme
     or dill
To serve
   extra canned beans (optional)
   fresh lemon juice, olive oil and
     chopped herbs (optional)
   lettuce leaves, radish slices and a few
     sprigs fresh dill, to garnish

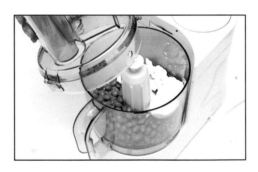

1 Blend the beans, garlic, cheese, butter, lemon juice and seasoning in a food processor until smooth.

2 Add the chopped herbs and continue to blend. Spoon into one serving dish or four lightly oiled ramekins, the bottoms lined with discs of waxed paper. Chill the pâté so that it sets firm.

3 If serving with extra beans, dress them with lemon juice, olive oil and herbs, season well and spoon on top. Garnish with lettuce leaves and serve with warm crusty bread or toast.

4 If serving individually, turn each pâté out of its ramekin onto a small plate and remove the disc of paper. Top with radish slices and sprigs of dill.

VARIATION
You could try other canned pulses for this recipe, although the softer lentils would not be suitable. Lima beans are surprisingly good. For an attractive presentation, fill the center with dark red kidney beans and chopped fresh green beans.

MEDITERRANEAN VEGETABLES WITH TAHINI

WONDERFULLY COLORFUL, THIS
APPETIZER IS EASILY PREPARED IN
ADVANCE. TAHINI IS A PASTE
MADE FROM SESAME SEEDS.

SERVES FOUR

INGREDIENTS
    2 bell peppers, seeded and quartered
    2 zucchini, halved lengthwise
    2 small eggplants, halved lengthwise,
       and degorged (see Cook's Tip)
    1 fennel bulb, quartered
    olive oil
    salt and freshly ground black pepper
    4 ounces Greek Halloumi cheese, sliced
For the tahini cream
    1 cup tahini paste
    1 garlic cloves, crushed
    2 tablespoons olive oil
    2 tablespoons fresh lemon juice
    ½ cup cold water

1 Preheat the broiler or barbecue until hot. Brush the vegetables with the oil and broil until just browned, turning once. (If the peppers blacken, don't worry. The skins can be peeled off.) Cook the vegetables until just softened.

2 Place the vegetables in a shallow dish and season. Let cool. Meanwhile, brush the cheese slices with oil and broil or grill on both sides until just charred. Remove them with a spatula.

3 To make the tahini cream, place all the ingredients, except the water, in a food processor or blender. Pulse for a few seconds to mix, then, with the motor still running, pour in the water and blend until smooth.

4 Serve the vegetables and cheese on a platter and drizzle the cream on top of them. Delicious served with warm pita pockets or naan.

COOK'S TIP
To degorge eggplants, sprinkle cut slices with salt and let the juices that form drain away in a colander. After 30 minutes or so, rinse well and pat dry. Degorged eggplants are less bitter and easier to cook.

IMAM BAYILDI

LEGEND HAS IT THAT A MUSLIM HOLY MAN — THE IMAM — WAS SO OVERWHELMED BY THIS DISH THAT HE FAINTED IN SHEER DELIGHT! TRANSLATED, IMAM BAYILDI MEANS "THE IMAM FAINTED."

SERVES FOUR

INGREDIENTS

  2 medium eggplants, halved
    lengthwise
salt
¼ cup olive oil
  2 large onions, sliced thinly
  2 garlic cloves, crushed
  1 green bell pepper, seeded and sliced
  1 can (14 ounces) tomatoes, chopped
  3 tablespoons sugar
  1 teaspoon ground coriander
freshly ground black pepper
  2 tablespoons chopped fresh cilantro or
    parsley

1 Gently fry the eggplants, cut side down, in the oil for 5 minutes, then drain and place in a shallow ovenproof dish.

2 In the same pan gently fry the onions, garlic and green pepper, adding extra oil if necessary. Cook for about 10 minutes, until the vegetables have softened.

3 Add the tomatoes, sugar, ground coriander and seasoning and cook for about 5 minutes, until the mixture is reduced. Stir in the cilantro or parsley.

4 Spoon this mixture on top of the eggplants. Preheat the oven to 375°F, cover and bake for 30–35 minutes. When cooked, cool, then chill. Serve cold, with crusty bread.

COOK'S TIP
Before cooking, slash the eggplant flesh a few times, sprinkle with salt and place in a colander for about half an hour. Rinse and pat dry.

TWICE-BAKED GOAT CHEESE SOUFFLÉS

A GOOD CHEF'S TRICK IS TO REHEAT SMALL BAKED SOUFFLÉS OUT OF THEIR RAMEKINS TO SERVE WITH A SALAD. THEY PUFF UP AGAIN AND THE OUTSIDES BECOME NICE AND CRISPY.

SERVES SIX

INGREDIENTS

   2 tablespoons butter
   3 tablespoons flour
   1¼ cups hot milk
   pinch cayenne pepper
   squeeze of lemon juice
   salt and freshly ground black pepper
   3½ ounces semi-hard goat cheese
   2 eggs, separated
   melted butter, for brushing
   3 tablespoons dried bread crumbs
   3 tablespoons ground hazelnuts or
    walnuts
   2 egg whites
   salad for garnish (optional)

1 Melt the butter and stir in the flour. Cook to a roux for a minute, then gradually whisk in the hot milk to make a thick white sauce.

VARIATION

There is another good chef's trick – making soufflés in advance and chiling them unbaked. It helps to add an extra egg white or two when whisking, depending on the mixture. It is also possible to freeze unbaked soufflés in small ramekins and then to bake them from frozen, allowing an extra 5 or 10 minutes' baking time.

2 Simmer for a minute, then season with cayenne, lemon juice, salt and pepper. Remove the pan from the heat and stir in the crumbled cheese until it melts. Cool slightly, then beat in the egg yolks.

3 Brush the insides of six ramekins with the melted butter and coat them with the bread crumbs and nuts. Shake out any excess.

4 Preheat the oven to 375°F and prepare a bain marie – a roasting pan with boiling water.

5 Whisk the four egg whites to the soft peak stage and carefully fold them into the mixture using a figure-eight motion. Spoon into the ramekins.

6 Place the soufflés in the bain marie and bake for 12–15 minutes, until risen and golden brown. You can, of course, serve them at this stage; otherwise, let them cool then chill.

7 To serve twice-baked, reheat the oven to the same temperature. Run a knife round the inside of each ramekin and turn out each soufflé onto a baking tray.

8 Bake the soufflés for about 12 minutes. Serve on prepared plates with a dressed salad garnish.

TRICOLOR SALAD

*THIS CAN BE A SIMPLE APPETIZER
OR PART OF A LIGHT BUFFET.
LIGHTLY SALTED TOMATOES MAKE
A TASTY DRESSING WITH THEIR
OWN NATURAL JUICES.*

SERVES FOUR TO SIX

INGREDIENTS
    1 small red onion, sliced thinly
    6 large full-flavored tomatoes
    extra-virgin olive oil, to sprinkle
    1 small bunch arugula, watercress,
      coarsely chopped
    salt and freshly ground black pepper
    6 ounces mozzarella cheese, thinly
      sliced or grated
    2 tablespoons pine nuts (optional)

1 Soak the onion slices in a bowl of cold water for 30 minutes, then drain and pat dry. Peel the tomatoes by slashing and dipping briefly in boiling water. Remove the core and slice the flesh.

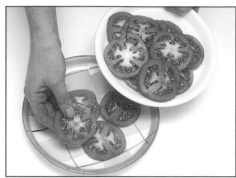

2 Slice the tomatoes and arrange half on a large platter or divide them among small plates.

3 Sprinkle liberally with olive oil then layer with the chopped arugula, and soaked onion slices, seasoning well. Add the cheese, sprinkling with more oil and seasoning as you go.

4 Repeat with the remaining tomato slices, greens, cheese and oil.

5 Season well and finish with some oil and a good scattering of pine nuts. Cover the salad and chill for at least 2 hours before serving.

GUACAMOLE SALSA IN RED LEAVES

SERVE THIS LOVELY DIP WITH CHUNKS OF WARM GARLIC BREAD.

SERVES FOUR

INGREDIENTS

2 tomatoes, skinned and chopped
1 tablespoon grated onion
1 garlic clove, crushed
1 green chili, halved, seeded and chopped
2 ripe avocados
2 tablespoons olive oil
½ teaspoons ground cumin
2 tablespoons chopped fresh cilantro or parsley
juice of 1 lime
salt and freshly ground black pepper
leaves from radicchio lettuce

1 Using a sharp knife, slash a small cross on the top of the tomatoes, then dip them briefly in a bowl of boiling water. The skins will slip off easily. Remove the core and chop the flesh.

2 Put the tomato flesh in a bowl together with the onion, garlic and chopped chili. Halve the avocados, remove the pits, then scoop the flesh into the bowl, mashing it with a fork.

3 Add the remaining ingredients, except for the radicchio leaves, and combine well, seasoning to taste.

4 Lay the radicchio leaves on a platter and spoon in the salsa. Serve immediately, as avocados turn black when exposed to the air.

COOK'S TIP
Take care when cutting chilies. The juice can sting, so be careful not to rub your eyes until you have washed your hands.

EXTRA-HOT GUACAMOLE

THIS IS QUITE A FIERY VERSION OF A POPULAR MEXICAN DISH, ALTHOUGH PROBABLY NOWHERE NEAR AS HOT AS YOU WOULD BE SERVED IN MEXICO, WHERE IT SEEMS HEAT KNOWS NO BOUNDS!

SERVES FOUR

INGREDIENTS

2 ripe avocados, peeled and pitted
2 tomatoes, peeled, seeded and finely
 chopped
6 scallions, finely chopped
1–2 chilies, seeded and finely
 chopped
2 tablespoons fresh lime or lemon juice
1 tablespoon chopped fresh cilantro
salt and freshly ground black pepper
cilantro sprig, to garnish

1 Put the avocado halves in a large bowl and mash them roughly with a large fork.

2 Add the remaining ingredients. Mix well and season according to taste. Serve garnished with fresh cilantro.

PLANTAIN APPETIZER

PLANTAINS ARE A TYPE OF COOKING BANANA WITH A LOWER SUGAR CONTENT THAN DESSERT BANANAS. THEY ARE UNSUITABLE FOR EATING RAW AND CAN BE USED IN A WIDE RANGE OF DISHES. THIS DELICIOUS ASSORTMENT OF SWEET AND SAVORY PLANTAINS IS A POPULAR DISH IN AFRICA.

SERVES FOUR

INGREDIENTS
  2 green plantains
  3 tablespoons vegetable oil
  1 small onion, very thinly sliced
  1 yellow plantain
  ½ garlic clove, crushed
  salt and cayenne pepper
  vegetable oil, for frying

1 Peel one of the green plantains and cut into wafer-thin rounds, preferably using a swivel-headed potato peeler.

2 Heat about 1 tablespoon of the oil in a large frying pan and fry the plantain slices for 2–3 minutes until golden, turning occasionally. Transfer to a plate lined with paper towels and keep warm.

3 Coarsely grate the other green plantain and mix with the onion.

4 Heat 1 tablespoon of the remaining oil in the pan and fry the plantain and onion mixture for 2–3 minutes until golden, turning occasionally. Transfer to the plate with the plantain slices.

5 Peel the yellow plantain, cut into small chunks. Sprinkle with cayenne pepper. Heat the remaining oil and fry the yellow plantain and garlic for 4–5 minutes until brown. Drain and sprinkle with salt.

ROAST ASPARAGUS CRÊPES

ROAST ASPARAGUS IS DELICIOUS AND GOOD ENOUGH TO EAT JUST AS IT COMES. HOWEVER, FOR A REALLY SPLENDID APPETIZER, TRY THIS SIMPLE RECIPE. EITHER MAKE SIX LARGE OR TWICE AS MANY COCKTAIL-SIZE CRÊPES TO USE WITH SMALLER STEMS OF ASPARAGUS.

SERVES SIX (as an appetizer)

INGREDIENTS
   1 pound fresh asparagus
   6–8 tablespoons olive oil
   6 ounces mascarpone cheese
   4 tablespoons light cream
   2 tablespoons grated Parmesan cheese
   sea salt
For the crêpes
   ¾ cup all-purpose flour
   pinch of salt
   2 eggs
   1½ cups milk
   vegetable oil, for frying

1 To make the crêpe batter, mix the flour with the salt in a large bowl, food processor or blender, then add the eggs and milk and beat or process to make a smooth, fairly thin batter.

2 Heat a little oil in a large frying pan and add a small amount of batter, swirling the pan to coat the base evenly. Cook over medium heat for about 1 minute, then flip over and cook the other side until golden. Set aside and cook the rest of the crêpes in the same way. The mixture makes about 6 large or 12 smaller crêpes.

3 Preheat the oven to 350° and lightly grease a large shallow ovenproof dish or roasting pan with some of the olive oil.

4 Trim the asparagus by placing on a board and cutting off the bases. Using a small sharp knife, peel away the woody ends, if necessary.

5 Arrange the asparagus in a single layer in the dish and drizzle with the remaining olive oil, rolling the asparagus to coat each one thoroughly. Sprinkle with a little salt and then roast in the oven for about 8–12 minutes, until tender (the cooking time depends on the stem thickness).

6 Blend the mascarpone cheese with the cream and Parmesan cheese and spread a generous tablespoonful over each of the crêpes, leaving a little extra for the topping. Preheat the broiler.

7 Divide the asparagus spears among the crêpes, roll up and arrange in a single layer in an ovenproof dish. Spoon the remaining cheese mixture on top and then place under a medium-hot broiler for 4–5 minutes, until heated through and golden brown. Serve immediately.

ARTICHOKES WITH GARLIC AND HERB BUTTER

IT IS FUN EATING ARTICHOKES AND EVEN MORE FUN TO SHARE ONE BETWEEN TWO PEOPLE. YOU CAN ALWAYS HAVE A SECOND ONE TO FOLLOW SO THAT YOU GET YOUR FAIR SHARE!

SERVES FOUR

INGREDIENTS
   2 artichokes
   salt
For the garlic and herb butter
   3 ounces butter
   1 garlic clove, crushed
   1 tablespoon mixed chopped fresh
     tarragon, marjoram and parsley

1 Wash the artichokes well in cold water. Using a sharp knife cut off the stalks level with the bases. Cut off the top ½ inch of leaves. Snip off the pointed ends of the remaining leaves with scissors.

2 Put the prepared artichokes in a large saucepan of lightly salted water. Bring to a boil, cover and cook for about 40–45 minutes or until a lower leaf comes away easily when gently pulled.

3 Drain upside down for a couple of minutes while making the sauce. Melt the butter over low heat, add the garlic and cook for 30 seconds. Remove from the heat, stir in the herbs and then pour into one or two small serving bowls.

4 Place the artichokes on serving plates and serve with the garlic and herb butter.

COOK'S TIP
To eat an artichoke, pull off each leaf and dip into the garlic and herb butter. Scrape off the soft fleshy base with your teeth. When the center is reached, pull out the hairy choke and discard it, as it is inedible. The base can be cut up and eaten with the remaining garlic butter.

STUFFED ARTICHOKES

ARTICHOKES ARE TRICKY TO PREPARE, BUT THEIR DELICIOUS TASTE MAKES IT WORTHWHILE. THIS DISH CAN BE MADE IN ADVANCE AND REHEATED BEFORE SERVING.

<u>SERVES FOUR</u>

INGREDIENTS
   4 medium artichokes
   salt
   lemon slices
For the stuffing
   1 medium onion, chopped
   1 garlic clove, crushed
   3 tablespoons olive oil
   ½ cup chopped mushrooms, chopped
   1 medium carrot, grated
   3 tablespoons sun-dried tomatoes in
      oil, drained and sliced
   leaves from a sprig of thyme
   3–4 tablespoons water
   freshly ground black pepper
   2 cups fresh bread crumbs
   extra olive oil, to cook
   fresh parsley, chopped, to garnish

1 Boil the artichokes in plenty of salted water with a few slices of lemon for about 30 minutes or until a leaf pulls easily from the base. Drain in a colander and cool the artichokes, laying them upside down.

2 To make the stuffing for the artichokes, gently fry the onion and garlic in the oil for 5 minutes, then add the mushrooms, carrot, sun-dried tomatoes and thyme.

3 Stir in the water, season well and cook for another 5 minutes, then mix in the bread crumbs.

VARIATION
For a lighter meal, rather than stuffing the artichokes, you could simply fill the centers with homemade mayonnaise or serve with a dish of vinaigrette or melted butter for dipping the leaves.

4 Pull the artichoke leaves apart and pull out the purple-tipped central leaves. Using a small teaspoon, scrape out the hairy choke, making sure that you remove it all. Discard it.

5 Spoon the stuffing into the center of the artichoke and push the leaves back into shape. Put the artichokes in an ovenproof dish and pour a little oil into the center of each one.

6 Half an hour before serving, heat the oven to 375°F and bake the artichokes for 20–25 minutes, until heated through. Serve garnished with a little chopped fresh parsley on top.

BRUSCHETTA WITH GOAT'S CHEESE AND TAPENADE

Simple to prepare in advance, this appealing dish can be served as an appetizer or at finger buffets.

SERVES FOUR TO SIX

INGREDIENTS
For the tapenade
  1 can (14 ounces) pitted black olives, finely chopped
  ¼ cup chopped sun-dried tomatoes in oil
  2 tablespoons capers, chopped
  1 tablespoon green peppercorns in brine, crushed
  3–4 tablespoons olive oil
  2 garlic cloves, crushed
  3 tablespoons chopped, fresh basil, or 1 teaspoon dried basil
  salt and freshly ground black pepper
For the bases
  12 slices ciabatta or other crusty bread
  olive oil, for brushing
  2 garlic cloves, halved
  4 ounces soft goat cheese
  fresh herb sprigs, to garnish

1 Mix all the tapenade ingredients together and check the seasoning. It should not need too much. Let marinate overnight, if possible.

2 To make the bruschetta, broil both sides of the bread lightly until golden. Brush one side with oil and then rub with a cut clove of garlic. Set aside until ready to serve.

3 Spread the bruschetta with the cheese, roughing it up with a fork, and spoon the tapenade on top. Garnish with sprigs of herbs.

COOK'S TIP
The bruschetta is best grilled over an open flame, if possible. Failing that, a broiler will do, but avoid using a toaster – it gives too even a color and the bruschetta is supposed to look rustic.

WARM AVOCADOS WITH TANGY TOPPING

Lightly broiled with a tasty topping of red onions and cheese, this makes a delightful alternative to the rather humdrum avocado vinaigrette.

SERVES FOUR

INGREDIENTS
  1 small red onion, sliced
  1 garlic clove, crushed
  1 tablespoon sunflower oil
  Worcestershire sauce
  2 ripe avocados, halved and pitted
  2 small tomatoes, sliced
  1 tablespoon fresh chopped basil, marjoram or parsley
  2 ounces Lancashire or mozzarella cheese, sliced
  salt and ground black pepper

1 Gently fry the onion and garlic in the oil for about 5 minutes, until just softened. Shake in a little Worcestershire sauce.

2 Preheat the broiler. Place the avocado halves on the broiler and spoon the onions into the center.

3 Divide the tomato slices and fresh herbs between the four halves and top each one with the cheese.

4 Season well and broil until the cheese melts and starts to brown.

VARIATION
Avocados are wonderful served in other hot dishes too. Try them chopped and tossed with hot pasta or sliced and layered in a lasagne.

TEMPURA VEGETABLES <u>WITH</u> DIPPING SAUCE

*A JAPANESE FAVORITE, THINLY
SLICED, FRESH VEGETABLES ARE
FRIED IN A LIGHT CRISPY BATTER
AND SERVED WITH FLAVORED SOY
SAUCE.*

<u>SERVES FOUR TO SIX</u>

INGREDIENTS
   1 medium zucchini, julienned
   1 bell pepper, seeded and cut in
   wedges
   3 large mushrooms, quartered
   1 fennel bulb, cut in wedges
   ½ medium eggplant, thinly sliced
   oil, for deep-frying
For the sauce
   3 tablespoons soy sauce
   1 tablespoon medium dry sherry
   1 teaspoon sesame seed oil
   few shreds fresh ginger or scallion
For the batter
   1 egg
   1 cup all-purpose flour
   ¾ cup cold water
   salt and freshly ground black pepper

1 Prepare all the vegetables and lay them out on a tray. Have sheets of paper towels for draining the vegetables after cooking.

2 Combine the sauce ingredients by whisking them in a bowl or shaking them together in a sealed jar. Pour into a bowl.

3 Half fill a deep-frying pan with oil and preheat to a temperature of about 375°F. Quickly whisk the batter ingredients together, but don't overbeat them. It doesn't matter if the batter is a little lumpy.

4 Fry the vegetables in stages by dipping a few quickly into the batter and lowering into the hot oil in a wire basket. Fry for just a minute, until golden brown and crisp. Drain on the paper towels.

5 Repeat until all the vegetables are fried. Keep those you have cooked, uncovered, in a warm oven while you fry the rest. Serve the vegetables on a large platter alongside the dipping sauce.

COOK'S TIP
Successful deep-frying can be quite tricky and a bit hazardous. Never leave the pan of oil unattended while the heat is turned on. If you have to leave the stove, turn off the oil. The oil will drop in temperature during cooking, so keep reheating it between batches.

CORN BLINIS WITH DILL CREAM

A MOUTHWATERING APPETIZER, THESE BLINIS ARE ALSO SUITABLE FOR COCKTAIL BUFFETS. IDEALLY, MAKE THEM AN HOUR OR TWO BEFORE SERVING, ALTHOUGH THE BATTER WILL STAND FOR LONGER.

SERVES SIX TO EIGHT

INGREDIENTS
- ¾ cup all-purpose flour
- ⅔ cup whole-wheat flour
- 1 cup buttermilk
- 4 small eggs, beaten
- ½ teaspoon salt
- ½ teaspoon baking powder
- 2 tablespoons butter, melted
- generous pinch of baking soda
- 1 tablespoon hot water
- 1 can (7 ounces) corn kernels, drained
- oil, for the griddle

For the dill cream
- 1 cup crème fraîche
- 2 tablespoons chopped fresh dill
- 2 tablespoons chopped fresh chives
- salt and freshly ground black pepper

1 Mix the two flours and buttermilk together until completely smooth. Cover and leave to chill for about 8 hours in the refrigerator.

2 Beat in the eggs, salt, baking powder and butter. Mix the baking soda with the hot water and add this too, along with the corn kernels.

3 Heat a griddle or heavy-bottomed frying pan until quite hot. Brush with a little oil and drop spoonfuls of the blinis mixture onto it. The mixture should start to sizzle immediately.

4 Cook until holes appear on the top and the mixture looks almost set. Using a spatula, flip the blinis over and cook briefly. Stack the blinis under a clean dish towel while you make the rest.

5 To make the cream, simply blend the crème fraîche with the herbs and seasoning. Serve the blinis with a few spoonfuls of cream and garnished with sliced radishes and herbs.

CORN AND CHEESE PURSES

THESE TASTY PURSES ARE SO SIMPLE TO MAKE, WHY NOT MAKE DOUBLE THE AMOUNT, AS THEY'LL GO LIKE HOTCAKES.

MAKES 18–20

INGREDIENTS

   9 ounces corn
   4 ounces feta cheese
   1 egg, beaten
   2 tablespoons heavy cream
   1 tablespoon grated Parmesan cheese,
   3 scallions, chopped
   freshly ground black pepper
   8–10 small sheets filo pastry
   1 cup butter, melted

1 Preheat the oven to 375°F and butter two cookie sheets.

2 If using fresh corn, strip the kernels from the cob using a sharp knife and simmer in a little salted water for 3–5 minutes, until tender. For canned corn, drain and rinse well under cold running water.

3 Crumble the feta cheese into a bowl and stir in the corn. Add the egg, cream, Parmesan cheese, scallions and ground black pepper and stir well.

4 Take one sheet of pastry and cut it in half to make a square. (Keep the remaining pastry covered with a damp cloth to prevent it from drying out.) Brush with melted butter and then fold in fourths to make a smaller square (about 3 inches).

5 Place a heaping teaspoon of the corn mixture in the center of each pastry square and then squeeze the pastry around the filling to make a "money bag" casing.

6 Continue making purses until all the mixture is used up. Brush the outside of each "bag" with any remaining butter and then bake in the oven for about 15 minutes, until golden. Serve hot.

HOT BROCCOLI TARTLETS

APART FROM THE UBIQUITOUS QUICHE, VEGETABLE TARTS ARE NOT VERY COMMON IN NORTH AMERICA. HOWEVER, IN FRANCE YOU CAN FIND A WHOLE VARIETY OF SAVORY TARTLETS, FILLED WITH ONIONS, LEEKS, MUSHROOMS AND BROCCOLI.

MAKES EIGHT TO TEN

INGREDIENTS
    1 tablespoon oil
    1 leek, finely sliced
    6 ounces broccoli, broken into florets
    ½ ounce butter
    ½ ounce all-purpose flour
    ⅔ cup milk
    2 ounces Cheddar cheese, grated
    fresh chervil, to garnish
For the pastry
    6 ounces all-purpose flour
    3 ounces butter
    1 egg
    pinch of salt

1 To make the pastry, place the flour and salt in a large bowl and rub in the butter and egg to make a dough. Add a little cold water if necessary, knead lightly, then cover with plastic wrap and leave to rest in the fridge for 1 hour.

2 Preheat the oven to 375°F. Let the dough return to room temperature for 10 minutes and then roll out on a lightly floured surface and line 8–10 deep muffin pans. Prick the bases with a fork and bake in the oven for about 10–15 minutes until the pastry is firm and lightly golden. Increase the oven temperature to 400°F.

3 Heat the oil in a small saucepan and sauté the leek for 4–5 minutes until soft. Add the broccoli, stir-fry for about 1 minute and then add a little water. Cover and steam for 3–4 minutes until the broccoli is just tender.

4 Melt the butter in a separate saucepan, stir in the flour and cook for a minute, stirring all the time. Slowly add the milk and stir to make a smooth sauce. Add half of the cheese and season with salt and pepper.

5 Spoon a little broccoli and leek into each tartlet case and then spoon over the sauce. Sprinkle each tartlet with the remaining cheese and then bake in the oven for about 10 minutes until golden.

6 Serve the tartlets as part of a buffet or as a starter, garnished with chervil.

LIGHT LUNCHES
AND
SUPPERS

*Experiment with these delicious recipes for
mouthwatering lunches that are not too filling as
well as for a sparkling selection of tasty snacks and
suppers. Ingredients range from protein-rich tofu
to irresistible cheeses and healthy pasta.*

MEXICAN BRUNCH EGGS

INSTEAD OF EGGS ON TOAST, WHY NOT TRY THEM ON FRIED CORN TORTILLAS WITH CHILIES AND CREAMY AVOCADO?

SERVES FOUR

INGREDIENTS
oil, for frying
8 corn tortillas
1 avocado
1 large tomato
4 tablespoons butter
8 eggs
4 jalapeño chilies, sliced
salt and freshly ground black pepper
1 tablespoon fresh cilantro, chopped,
  to garnish

1 Heat the oil and fry the tortillas for a few seconds on each side. Remove and drain. Keep the tortillas warm.

2 Halve, pit and peel the avocado, then cut into slices. Dip the tomato in boiling water, then skin and chop coarsely.

3 Melt the butter in a frying pan and fry the eggs, in batches, sunny side up.

4 Place two tortillas on four plates, slip an egg on each and top with sliced chilies, avocado and tomato. Season and serve garnished with cilantro.

FRIED TOMATOES WITH POLENTA CRUST

IF YOU SAW THE FILM FRIED GREEN TOMATOES *YOU SHOULD ENJOY THIS DISH! NO NEED TO SEARCH FOR HOMEGROWN GREEN TOMATOES — ANY SLIGHTLY UNDERRIPE ONES WILL DO.*

SERVES FOUR

INGREDIENTS
4 large firm underripe tomatoes
1 cup polenta or coarse cornmeal
1 teaspoon dried oregano
½ teaspoon garlic powder
flour, for dredging
1 egg, beaten with seasoning
oil, for deep-frying

1 Cut the tomatoes into thick slices. Mix the polenta or cornmeal with the oregano and garlic powder.

2 Put the flour, egg and polenta in different bowls. Dip the tomato slices into the flour, then into the egg and finally into the polenta.

3 Fill a shallow frying pan about one-third full of oil, and heat steadily until it is quite hot.

4 Slip the tomato slices into the oil carefully, a few at a time, and fry on each side until crisp. Remove and drain. Repeat with the remaining tomatoes, reheating the oil in between. Serve with salad.

PISSALADIÈRE

A French Mediterranean classic, this is a delicious and colorful tart full of flavor.

SERVES SIX

INGREDIENTS
For the pastry
   2 cups all-purpose flour
   8 tablespoons butter or sunflower
      margarine
   1 teaspoon Italian herbs
   pinch of salt
For the filling
   2 large onions, thinly sliced
   2 garlic cloves, crushed
   3 tablespoons olive oil
   grated, fresh nutmeg, to taste
   1 can (14 ounces) tomatoes, chopped
   1 teaspoon sugar
   leaves from small sprig of thyme
   salt and freshly ground black pepper
   ⅔ cup pitted black olives, sliced
   2 tablespoons capers
   chopped fresh parsley, to garnish

1 Rub the flour and butter or margarine together until it forms fine crumbs, then mix in the herbs and salt. Mix to a firm dough with cold water. Preheat the oven to 375°F.

2 Roll out dough and use to line a 9-inch tart pan. Line with waxed paper and weight with dried beans. Bake blind. removing the beans and paper for the last 5 minutes.

3 Gently fry the onions and garlic in the oil for about 10 minutes, until soft, and mix in the nutmeg.

4 Stir in the tomatoes, sugar, thyme and seasoning and simmer gently for about 10 minutes, until the mixture is reduced and slightly syrupy.

5 Remove from the heat and let cool. Mix in the olives and capers.

6 When ready to serve, spoon into the pastry, sprinkle with some fresh chopped parsley and serve at room temperature. Ideally, put the base and fillings together just before serving so that the base remains crisp.

VARIATION
To serve Pissaladière hot, top with grated cheese and broil until the cheese is golden and bubbling. The crisp-baked pastry shell can be used as a base for a number of other vegetable mixtures. Try filling it with a Russian Salad – chopped, cooked root vegetables, including potato and carrot, mixed with peas, beans and onions, blended with mayonnaise and sour cream. Top with slices of hard-boiled egg and garnish with chopped fresh herbs.

TOMATO AND BASIL TART

IN FRANCE, PÂTISSERIES DISPLAY MOUTHWATERING SAVORY TARTS IN THEIR WINDOWS. THIS IS A VERY SIMPLE YET EXTREMELY TASTY TART MADE WITH RICH PASTRY FILLED WITH SLICES OF MOZZARELLA CHEESE AND TOMATOES AND TOPPED WITH OLIVE OIL AND BASIL LEAVES.

SERVES FOUR

INGREDIENTS
    5 ounces fresh mozzarella, thinly
      sliced
    4 large tomatoes, thickly sliced
    about 10 basil leaves
    2 tablespoons olive oil
    2 garlic cloves, thinly sliced
    sea salt and freshly ground
      black pepper
For the pastry
    ½ cup all-purpose flour
    pinch salt
    ½ cup butter or margarine
    1 egg yolk

1 To prepare the pastry, combine the flour and salt, then rub in the butter and egg yolk. Add enough cold water to make a smooth dough and knead lightly on a floured surface. Place in a plastic bag and chill for 1 hour.

2 Preheat the oven to 375°. Remove the pastry from the fridge and allow about 10 minutes for it to return to room temperature, then roll out into an 8-inch round. Press into the base of an 8-inch pie dish or pan. Prick all over with a fork and then bake in the oven for about 10 minutes, until firm but not brown. Let cool slightly. Reduce the oven temperature to 350°F.

3 Arrange the mozzarella slices over the pastry shell. On top, arrange a single layer of the sliced tomatoes, overlapping them slightly. Dip the basil leaves in olive oil and arrange them on the tomatoes.

4 Scatter the garlic on top, drizzle with the remaining olive oil and season with a little salt and a good sprinkling of black pepper. Bake for 40–45 minutes, until the tomatoes are well cooked. Serve hot.

HOT SOUR CHICKPEAS

THIS DISH, KHATTE CHOLE, IS EATEN AS A SNACK ALL OVER INDIA, SOLD BY ITINERANT STREET
VENDORS. THE HEAT OF THE CHILIES IS DAMPENED PARTLY BY THE CILANTRO, WHILE THE LEMON JUICE
ADDS A WONDERFUL SOURNESS.

SERVES FOUR

INGREDIENTS
   12 ounces chickpeas, soaked
      overnight
   4 tablespoons vegetable oil
   2 medium onions, very finely chopped
   8 ounces tomatoes, peeled and finely
      chopped
   1 tablespoon ground coriander
   1 tablespoon ground cumin
   1 teaspoon ground fenugreek
   1 teaspoon ground cinnamon
   1–2 hot green chilies, seeded
      and finely sliced
   about 1-inch piece fresh ginger,
      grated
   4 tablespoons lemon juice
   1 tablespoon chopped fresh cilantro
   salt

1 Drain the chickpeas and place them in a large saucepan, cover with water and bring to a boil. Cover and simmer for 1–1¼ hours until tender, making sure the chick-peas do not boil dry. Drain, reserving the cooking liquid.

2 Heat the oil in a large flameproof casserole. Reserve about 2 tablespoons of the chopped onions and fry the remainder in the casserole over moderate heat for 4–5 minutes, stirring frequently, until tinged with brown.

3 Add the tomatoes and continue cooking over moderately low heat for 5–6 minutes until soft. Stir frequently, mashing the tomatoes to a pulp.

4 Stir in the coriander, cumin, fenugreek and cinnamon. Cook for 30 seconds and then add the chickpeas and 12 fluid ounces of the reserved cooking liquid. Season with salt, cover and simmer very gently for about 15–20 minutes, stirring occasionally and adding more cooking liquid if the mixture becomes too dry.

5 Meanwhile, mix the reserved onion with the chili, ginger and lemon juice.

6 Just before serving, stir the onion and chili mixture and the cilantro into the chickpeas, and adjust the seasoning.

LEEKS IN EGG AND LEMON SAUCE

THE COMBINATION OF EGGS AND LEMON IN SAUCES AND SOUPS IS COMMONLY FOUND IN RECIPES FROM GREECE, TURKEY AND THE MIDDLE EAST. THIS SAUCE HAS A DELICIOUS FRESH TASTE AND BRINGS OUT THE BEST IN THE LEEKS. BE SURE TO USE TENDER BABY LEEKS FOR THIS RECIPE.

SERVES FOUR

INGREDIENTS
   1½ pounds baby leeks
   1 tablespoon cornstarch
   2 teaspoons sugar
   2 egg yolks
   juice of 1½ lemons
   salt

1 Trim the leeks, slit them from top to bottom and rinse very well under cold water to remove any dirt.

2 Place the leeks in a large saucepan, preferably so they lie flat on the bottom, cover with water and add a little salt. Bring to boil, cover and simmer for 4–5 minutes until just tender.

3 Carefully remove the leeks using a slotted spoon, drain well and arrange in a shallow serving dish. Reserve 7 fluid ounces of the cooking liquid.

4 Blend the cornstarch with the cooled cooking liquid and place in a small saucepan. Bring to boil, stirring all the time, and cook over low heat until the sauce thickens slightly. Stir in the sugar and then remove the saucepan from the heat and allow to cool slightly.

5 Beat the egg yolks thoroughly with the lemon juice and stir gradually into the cooled sauce. Cook over very low heat, stirring all the time, until the sauce is fairly thick. Be careful not to overheat the sauce or it may curdle. As soon as the sauce has thickened remove the pan from the heat and continue stirring for a minute. Taste and add salt or sugar as necessary. Cool slightly.

6 Stir the cooled sauce with a wooden spoon. Pour the sauce over the leeks and then cover and chill well for at least 2 hours before serving.

LEEK SOUFFLÉ

SOME PEOPLE THINK OF A SOUFFLÉ AS A DINNER PARTY DISH, AND A RATHER TRICKY ONE AT THAT. HOWEVER, OTHERS FREQUENTLY SERVE THEM FOR FAMILY MEALS BECAUSE THEY ARE QUICK AND EASY TO MAKE, AND PROVE TO BE VERY POPULAR AND SATISFYING.

SERVES TWO TO THREE

INGREDIENTS
- 1 tablespoon sunflower oil
- 3 tablespoons butter
- 2 leeks, thinly sliced
- 1¼ cups milk
- 2 tablespoons all-purpose flour
- 4 eggs, separated
- 3 ounces Gruyère or Emmenthal cheese, grated
- salt and freshly ground black pepper

1 Preheat the oven to 350°F and butter a large soufflé dish. Heat the oil and 1 tablespoon of the butter in a small saucepan or flameproof casserole and fry the leeks over low heat for 4–5 minutes, stirring occasionally, until soft but not brown.

2 Stir in the milk and bring to a boil. Cover and simmer for 4–5 minutes, until the leeks are tender. Strain the liquid through a sieve into a measuring cup.

3 Melt the remaining butter in a saucepan, stir in the flour and cook for 1 minute. Remove pan from the heat. Add milk to the reserved liquid to make 1¼ cups. Gradually stir the milk into the pan to make a smooth sauce. Return to the heat and bring to the boil, stirring. When thickened, remove from the heat. Cool slightly and then beat in the egg yolks, cheese and the leeks.

4 Whisk the egg whites until stiff and, using a large metal spoon, fold into the leek and egg mixture. Pour into the prepared soufflé dish and bake for about 30 minutes, until golden and puffy. Serve immediately.

ASPARAGUS TART <u>WITH</u> RICOTTA

RICOTTA GIVES THE FILLING A DELIGHTFULLY SMOOTH, CREAMY TEXTURE, WHILE THE PARMESAN ADDS THE NECESSARY ZING.

SERVES FOUR

INGREDIENTS
For the pastry
   6 tablespoons butter or margarine
   ¾ cup all-purpose flour
   pinch of salt
For the filling
   8 ounces asparagus
   2 eggs, beaten
   8 ounces ricotta cheese
   2 tablespoons plain yogurt
   3 tablespoons grated Parmesan cheese
   salt and freshly ground black pepper

1 Preheat the oven to 400°F. Rub the butter or margarine into the flour and salt until the mixture resembles fine bread crumbs. Stir in enough cold water to form a smooth dough and knead lightly on a floured surface.

2 Roll out the pastry and line a 9-inch tart pan. Press firmly into the tin and prick all over with a fork. Bake for about 10 minutes, until the pastry is pale but firm. Remove from the oven and reduce the temperature to 350°F.

3 To make the filling, trim the asparagus, cut 2 inches from the top and chop the remaining stalks into 1-inch pieces. Add the stalks to a saucepan of boiling water, and after 1 minute add the tops. Simmer for 4–5 minutes, until almost tender, then drain and refresh under cold water.

4 Beat together the eggs, ricotta, yogurt, Parmesan cheese and seasoning. Stir in the asparagus stalks and pour the mixture into the pastry shell. Arrange the asparagus tips on top, pressing them down slightly into the ricotta mixture.

5 Bake in the oven for 35–40 minutes, until golden. Serve warm or cold.

ASPARAGUS <u>WITH</u> TARRAGON HOLLANDAISE

THIS IS THE IDEAL APPETIZER FOR AN EARLY SUMMER DINNER PARTY WHEN THE NEW SEASON'S ASPARA-GUS IS JUST IN AND AT ITS BEST. MAKING HOLLANDAISE SAUCE IN A BLENDER OR FOOD PROCESSOR IS INCREDIBLY EASY AND VIRTUALLY FOOLPROOF.

SERVES FOUR

INGREDIENTS
   1 pound fresh asparagus
For the Hollandaise sauce
   2 eggs yolks
   1 tablespoon lemon juice
   salt and ground black pepper
   1 cup butter
   2 teaspoons chopped fresh tarragon

1 Trim the asparagus, lay it in a steamer or in an asparagus kettle and place over a saucepan of rapidly boiling water. Cover and steam for 6–10 minutes, until tender (the cooking time will depend on the thickness of the asparagus stems).

2 To make the Hollandaise sauce, place the egg yolks, lemon juice and seasoning in a blender or food processor and process briefly. Melt the butter in a small pan until foaming and then, with the blender running, pour it into the egg mixture in a slow, steady stream.

3 Stir in the tarragon by hand or process it (for a sauce speckled with green or a pale green sauce, respectively).

4 Arrange the asparagus on plates and top with some of the Hollandaise sauce. Serve remaining sauce on the side.

ARTICHOKE RÖSTI

SERVES FOUR TO SIX

INGREDIENTS
1 pound Jerusalem artichokes
juice of 1 lemon
salt
1 pound potatoes
about 6 tablespoons butter

1 Peel the Jerusalem artichokes and place in a saucepan of water together with the lemon juice and a pinch of salt. Bring to a boil and cook for about 5 minutes, until barely tender.

2 Peel the potatoes and place in a separate pan of salted water. Bring to a boil and cook until barely tender – they will take slightly longer than the artichokes.

3 Drain and cool both the artichokes and potatoes, and then grate them into a bowl. Mix them with your fingers, without breaking them up too much.

4 Melt the butter in a large, heavy frying pan. Add the artichoke mixture, spreading it out with the back of a spoon. Cook gently for about 10 minutes.

5 Turn out the "cake" onto a plate and return to the pan. Cook for about 10 minutes, until golden. Serve immediately.

ARTICHOKE TIMBALES WITH SPINACH SAUCE

SERVES SIX

INGREDIENTS
2 pounds Jerusalem artichokes
juice of 1 lemon
2 tablespoons butter
1 tablespoon oil
1 onion, finely chopped
1 garlic clove, crushed
¼ cup fresh white bread crumbs
1 egg
4–5 tablespoons vegetable stock
  or milk
1 tablespoon chopped fresh parsley
1 teaspoon finely chopped sage
salt and freshly ground black pepper
For the sauce
8 ounces fresh spinach
1 tablespoon butter
2 shallots, finely chopped
⅔ cup light cream
¾ cup vegetable stock
salt and freshly ground black pepper

1 Preheat the oven to 350°F. Grease six ⅔-cup ramekins, and then place a circle of waxed paper in each base.

2 Peel the artichokes and put in a saucepan with the lemon juice and water to cover. Bring to a boil and simmer for about 10 minutes, until tender. Drain and mash with the butter.

3 Heat the oil in a small frying pan and fry the onion and garlic until soft. Place in a food processor with the bread crumbs, egg, stock or milk, parsley, sage and seasoning. Process to a smooth purée, add the artichokes and process again briefly. Do not overprocess.

4 Put the mixture in the prepared dishes and smooth the tops. Cover with waxed paper, place in a roasting pan half filled with boiling water and bake for 35–40 minutes, until firm.

5 To make the sauce, rinse and cook the spinach without water in a large covered saucepan for 2–3 minutes. Shake the pan occasionally. Strain and press out the excess liquid.

6 Melt the butter in a small saucepan and fry the shallots gently, until slightly softened but not browned. Place in a food processor or blender and process to make a smooth purée. Pour back into the pan, add the cream, stock and seasoning and keep warm over a very low heat. Do not allow the mixture to boil.

7 Allow the timbales to stand for a few minutes after cooking and then turn out onto warmed serving plates. Spoon the warm sauce over them and serve.

COOK'S TIP
When puréeing the artichokes in a food processor or blender, use the pulse button and process for a very short time. The mixture will become cloying if it is overprocessed.

YAM FRITTERS

YAMS HAVE A SLIGHTLY DRIER FLAVOR THAN POTATOES AND ARE PARTICULARLY GOOD WHEN MIXED WITH SPICES AND THEN FRIED. THE FRITTERS CAN ALSO BE MOLDED INTO SMALL BALLS AND DEEP-FRIED. THIS IS A FAVORITE AFRICAN WAY OF SERVING YAMS.

MAKES ABOUT 18–20

INGREDIENTS
  1½ pounds yams
  milk, for mashing
  2 small eggs, beaten
  3 tablespoons chopped tomato
  3 tablespoons finely chopped scallions
  1 green chili, seeded and finely sliced
  salt and freshly ground black pepper
  flour, for shaping
  3 tablespoons white bread crumbs
  vegetable oil, for shallow frying

1 Peel the yams and cut into chunks. Place in a saucepan of salted water and boil for 20–30 minutes, until tender. Drain and mash with a little milk and about 3 tablespoons of the beaten eggs.

2 Add the chopped tomato, scallions, chili and seasoning and stir well to mix thoroughly.

3 Using floured hands, shape the yam and vegetable mixture into round fritters, about 3 inches in diameter.

4 Dip each in the remaining beaten egg and then coat evenly with the bread crumbs. Heat a little oil in a large frying pan and fry the yam fritters for about 4–5 minutes, until golden brown. Turn the fritters once during cooking. Drain well on paper towels and serve.

TARO, CARROT AND PARSNIP MEDLEY

TARO, LIKE YAMS, IS WIDELY EATEN IN AFRICA AND THE CARIBBEAN, OFTEN AS A PURÉE. HERE, IT IS ROASTED AND COMBINED WITH MORE COMMON ROOT VEGETABLES TO MAKE A COLORFUL DISPLAY.

SERVES FOUR TO SIX

INGREDIENTS
  1 pound taro
  12 ounces parsnips
  1 pound carrots
  2 tablespoons butter
  3 tablespoons sunflower oil
For the dressing
  2 tablespoons fresh orange juice
  2 tablespoons light brown sugar
  2 teaspoons soft green peppercorns
  salt
  fresh parsley, to garnish

1 Preheat the oven to 400°F. Peel the taros, cut them into pieces about 2 x ¾ inches and place in a large bowl.

2 Peel the parsnips, halve lengthwise and remove the inner core if necessary. Cut into the same size pieces as the taro and add to the bowl. Blanch in boiling water for 2 minutes and then drain. Peel or scrub the carrots and halve or quarter them according to their size.

3 Place the butter and sunflower oil in a roasting pan and heat in the oven for 3–4 minutes. Add the vegetables, turning them in the oil to coat evenly. Roast for 30 minutes.

4 Meanwhile, blend the orange juice, sugar and soft green peppercorns in a small bowl. Remove the roasting pan from the oven and allow to cool for a minute or so, then carefully pour the mixture over the vegetables, stirring to coat them all. (If the liquid is poured on immediately, the hot oil will spit.)

5 Return the pan to the oven and cook for another 20 minutes, until the vegetables are crisp and golden. Transfer to a warmed serving plate and sprinkle with salt. Garnish with parsley and serve.

SPINACH RAVIOLI

HOME-MADE RAVIOLI IS TIME-CONSUMING, YET IT IS WORTH THE EFFORT AS EVEN THE BEST SHOP-BOUGHT PASTA NEVER TASTES QUITE AS FRESH. TO COMPLEMENT THIS EFFORT, MAKE THE FILLING EXACTLY TO YOUR LIKING, TASTING IT FOR THE RIGHT BALANCE OF SPINACH AND CHEESE.

SERVES FOUR

INGREDIENTS
   8 ounces fresh spinach
   1½ ounces butter
   1 small onion, finely chopped
   1 ounce Parmesan cheese, grated
   1½ ounces Dolcellate cheese,
     crumbled
   1 tablespoon chopped fresh parsley
   salt and freshly ground black pepper
For the pasta dough
   12 ounces unbleached all-purpose
     flour
   ¾ teaspoon salt
   2 eggs
   1 tablespoon olive oil
   shavings of Parmesan cheese, to serve

1 To make the pasta dough, mix together the flour and salt in a large bowl or food processor. Add the eggs, olive oil and about 3 tablespoons of cold water or enough to make a pliable dough. If working by hand, mix the ingredients together and then knead the dough for about 15 minutes until very smooth. Or, process for about 1½ minutes in a food processor. Place the dough in a plastic bag and chill for at least 1 hour (or overnight if more convenient).

2 Cook the spinach in a large, covered saucepan for 3–4 minutes, until the leaves have wilted. Strain and press out the excess liquid. Set aside to cool a little and then chop finely.

3 Melt half the butter in a small saucepan and fry the onion over low heat for about 5–6 minutes until soft. Place in a bowl with the chopped spinach, the Parmesan and Dolcellate cheeses, and seasoning. Mix well.

4 Grease a ravioli sheet. Roll out half or a quarter of the pasta dough to a thickness of about ⅛ inch. Lay the dough over the ravioli sheet, pressing it well into each of the squares.

5 Spoon a little spinach mixture into each cavity, then roll out a second piece of dough and lay it on top. Press a rolling pin evenly over the top of the sheet to seal the edges and then cut the ravioli into squares using a pastry cutter.

6 Place the ravioli in a large saucepan of boiling water and simmer for about 4–5 minutes until cooked through but *al dente*. Drain well and then toss with the remaining butter and the parsley.

7 Divide between four serving plates and serve scattered with shavings of Parmesan cheese.

COOK'S TIP
For a small ravioli sheet of 32 holes, divide the dough into quarters. Roll the dough out until it covers the sheet comfortably – it takes some time but the pasta needs to be thin otherwise the ravioli will be too stodgy. For a large ravioli sheet of 64 holes, divide the dough in half.

THAI NOODLES ᵂᴵᵀᴴ GARLIC CHIVES

THIS RECIPE REQUIRES A LITTLE TIME FOR PREPARATION, BUT THE COOKING TIME IS VERY FAST.
EVERYTHING IS COOKED SPEEDILY IN A HOT WOK AND SHOULD BE EATEN AT ONCE.

SERVES FOUR

INGREDIENTS

    12 ounces dried rice noodles
    ½-inch piece fresh ginger, grated
    2 tablespoons light soy sauce
    3 tablespoons vegetable oil
    2 garlic cloves, crushed
    1 large onion, cut into thin wedges
    4 ounces fried bean curd,
      thinly sliced
    1 green chili, seeded
      and finely sliced
    6 ounces bean sprouts
    4 ounces garlic chives, cut into
      2-inch lengths
    2 ounces roasted peanuts, ground
    2 tablespoons dark soy sauce
    2 tablespoons chopped fresh
      cilantro
    1 lemon, cut into wedges

1 Place the noodles in a large bowl, cover with warm water and soak for 20–30 minutes, then drain. Blend together the ginger, light soy sauce and 1 tablespoon of the oil in a bowl. Set aside for 10 minutes. Drain, reserving the marinade.

2 Heat 1 tablespoon of the oil in a wok or large frying pan. Fry the garlic for a few seconds, then remove from pan and discard.

5 When hot, spoon onto serving plates and garnish with the remaining ground peanuts, cilantro and lemon wedges.

COOK'S TIP
This a vegetarian meal, however, thinly sliced pork or chicken could be used instead. Stir-fry it initially for 4–5 minutes.

3 Heat the remaining oil in the wok or frying pan and stir-fry the onion for 3–4 minutes until softened and tinged with brown. Add the bean curd and chili, stir-fry briefly and then add the noodles. Stir-fry for 4–5 minutes.

4 Stir in the bean sprouts, garlic chives and most of the ground peanuts, reserving a little for the garnish. Stir well, then add the dark soy sauce and the reserved marinade.

CAULIFLOWER AND MUSHROOM GOUGÈRE

THIS IS AN ALL-ROUND FAVORITE VEGETARIAN DISH. WHEN COOKING THIS DISH FOR MEAT LOVERS, CHOPPED ROAST HAM OR FRIED BACON CAN BE ADDED.

SERVES FOUR TO SIX

INGREDIENTS

1¼ cups water
4 ounces butter or margarine
5 ounces all-purpose flour
4 eggs
4 ounces Gruyère or Cheddar cheese, finely diced
1 teaspoon French mustard
salt and freshly ground black pepper
For the filling
14-ounce can tomatoes
1 tablespoon sunflower oil
½ ounce butter or margarine
1 onion, chopped
4 ounces white mushrooms, halved if large
1 small cauliflower, broken into small florets
sprig of thyme
salt and freshly ground black pepper

1 Preheat the oven to 400°F and butter a large oval ovenproof dish. Place the water and butter together in a large saucepan and heat until the butter has melted. Remove from the heat and add all the flour at once. Beat well with a wooden spoon for about 30 seconds until smooth. Allow to cool slightly.

2 Beat in the eggs, one at a time, and continue beating until the mixture is thick and glossy. Stir in the cheese and mustard and season with salt and pepper. Spread the mixture around the sides of the ovenproof dish, leaving a hollow in the center for the filling.

3 To make the filling, purée the tomatoes in a blender or food processor and then pour into a measuring jug. Add enough water to make up to 1¼ cups of liquid.

4 Heat the oil and butter in a flameproof casserole and fry the onion for about 3–4 minutes until softened but not browned. Add the mushrooms and cook for 2–3 minutes until they begin to be flecked with brown. Add the cauliflower florets and stir-fry for 1 minute.

5 Add the tomato liquid, thyme and seasoning. Cook, uncovered, over low heat for about 5 minutes until the cauliflower is only just tender.

6 Spoon the mixture into the hollow in the ovenproof dish, adding all the liquid. Bake in the oven for about 35–40 minutes, until the outer pastry is well risen and golden brown.

COOK'S TIP
For a variation, ham or bacon can be added. Use about 4–5 ounces thickly sliced roast ham and add to the sauce at the end of step 5.

DOLMADES

DOLMADES ARE STUFFED VINE LEAVES, A TRADITIONAL GREEK DISH. IF YOU CAN'T OBTAIN FRESH VINE LEAVES, USE A PACKET OF BRINED VINE LEAVES. SOAK THE LEAVES IN HOT WATER FOR 20 MINUTES THEN RINSE AND DRY WELL ON PAPER TOWELS BEFORE USE.

MAKES 20–24

INGREDIENTS
  20–30 fresh young vine leaves
  2 tablespoons olive oil
  1 large onion, finely chopped
  1 garlic clove, crushed
  8 ounces cooked long grain rice,
    or mixed white and wild rice
  about 3 tablespoons pine nuts
  1 tablespoon slivered almonds
  1½ ounces golden raisins
  15ml/ 1 tablespoon snipped chives
  1 tablespoon finely chopped
    fresh mint
  juice of ½ lemon
  ⅔ cup white wine
  hot vegetable stock
  salt and freshly ground black pepper
  sprig of mint, to garnish
  Greek yogurt, to serve

1 Bring a large pan of water to a boil and cook the vine leaves for about 2–3 minutes. They will darken and go limp after about 1 minute and simmering for a further minute or so ensures they are pliable. If using leaves from a packet, place them in a large bowl, cover with boiling water and leave for a few minutes until the leaves can be easily separated. Rinse them under cold water and drain on paper towels.

2 Heat the oil in a small frying pan and fry the onion and garlic for 3–4 minutes over low heat until soft.

3 Spoon the onion and garlic mixture into a bowl and add the cooked rice.

4 Stir in 2 tablespoons of the pine nuts, the almonds, golden raisins, chives, mint, lemon juice and seasoning and mix well.

5 Lay a vine leaf on a clean work surface, veined side uppermost. Place a spoonful of filling near the stem, fold the lower part of the leaf over it and roll up, folding in the sides as you go. Continue stuffing the vine leaves in the same way.

6 Line the bottom of a deep frying pan with four large vine leaves. Place the stuffed vine leaves close together in the pan, seam side down, in a single layer.

7 Add the wine and enough stock to just cover the vine leaves. Place a plate directly over the leaves, then cover and simmer gently for 30 minutes, checking to make sure the pan does not boil dry.

8 Chill the vine leaves garnished with the remaining pine nuts and a sprig of mint and serve with a little yogurt.

MUSHROOM AND CHILI CARBONARA

DRIED PORCINI MUSHROOMS GIVE THIS QUICK EGGY SAUCE A RICHER MUSHROOM FLAVOR.

<u>SERVES FOUR</u>

INGREDIENTS

  1 package (½ ounce) dried porcini
    mushrooms
  1¼ cups hot water
  8 ounces spaghetti
  1 garlic clove, crushed
  2 tablespoons butter
  1 tablespoon olive oil
  8 ounces white or crimini mushrooms,
    sliced
  1 teaspoon dried red pepper flakes
  2 eggs
1¼ cups light cream or half-and-half
salt and freshly ground black pepper
grated fresh Parmesan cheese, and
  chopped fresh parsley, to serve

1 Soak the dried mushrooms in the hot water for 15 minutes, drain and reserve the liquid.

2 Boil the spaghetti according to the instructions on the package in salted water. Drain and rinse in cold water.

3 In a large saucepan, lightly sauté the garlic with the butter and oil for half a minute, then add the mushrooms, including the soaked porcini, and the dried red pepper flakes, and stir well. Cook for about 2 minutes, stirring a few times.

4 Pour in the reserved mushroom stock and boil to reduce slightly.

5 Beat the eggs with the cream and season well. Return the cooked spaghetti to the pan and toss in the eggs and cream. Reheat, without boiling, and serve hot sprinkled with Parmesan cheese and chopped parsley.

VARIATION
Instead of mushrooms, try using either finely sliced and sautéed leeks or perhaps coarsely shredded lettuce with peas. If red pepper flakes are too hot and spicy for you, then try the delicious alternative of skinned and chopped tomatoes with torn fresh basil leaves.

TAGLIATELLE <u>WITH</u> "HIT-THE-PAN" SALSA

*IT IS POSSIBLE TO MAKE A HOT,
FILLING MEAL IN JUST
15 MINUTES WITH THIS
QUICK SALSA.*

<u>SERVES TWO</u>

INGREDIENTS
   4 ounces tagliatelle
   3 tablespoons olive oil, preferably
     extra-virgin
   3 large tomatoes
   1 garlic clove, crushed
   4 scallions, sliced
   1 green chili, seeded and sliced
   juice of 1 orange (optional)
   2 tablespoons chopped fresh parsley
   salt and freshly ground black pepper
   grated cheese, to garnish (optional)

1 Boil the tagliatelle in plenty of salted water until it is al dente. Drain and toss in a little of the oil. Season well.

2 Skin the tomatoes by dipping them briefly in a bowl of boiling water. The skins should slip off easily. Chop the tomatoes coarsely. If you don't have time to peel the tomatoes, don't bother.

3 Heat the remaining oil until it is quite hot and stir-fry the garlic, onions and chili for a minute. The pan should sizzle.

4 Add the tomatoes, orange juice (if using) and parsley. Season well and stir in the tagliatelle to reheat. Serve with the grated cheese (if used).

COOK'S TIP
You could use any pasta shape for this recipe. It would be particularly good with large rigatoni or linguini, or as a sauce for fresh ravioli or tortellini.

CHEESY BUBBLE AND SQUEAK

THIS POPULAR LONDON BREAKFAST DISH IS ENJOYING A REVIVAL. ORIGINALLY MADE ON MONDAYS WITH LEFTOVER POTATOES AND CABBAGE FROM SUNDAY LUNCH, IT IS SUITABLE FOR ANY LIGHT MEAL. FOR BREAKFAST, SERVE THE BUBBLE AND SQUEAK WITH EGGS, GRILLED TOMATOES AND MUSHROOMS.

SERVES FOUR

INGREDIENTS
    3 cups mashed potatoes
    8 ounces cooked cabbage or kale, shredded
    1 egg, beaten
    ½ cup grated Cheddar cheese
    fresh nutmeg, grated
    salt and freshly ground black pepper
    flour, for coating
    oil, for frying

1 Mix the potatoes with the cabbage or kale, egg, cheese, nutmeg and seasoning. Divide and shape into eight patties.

2 Chill for an hour or so, if possible, as this enables the mixture to become firm and makes it easier to fry. Toss the patties in the flour. Heat about ½ inch of oil in a frying pan until it is quite hot.

3 Carefully slide the patties into the oil and fry on each side for about 3 minutes, until golden and crisp. Drain on paper towels and serve hot and crisp.

CHEESE AND CHUTNEY TOASTIES

QUICK CHEESE ON TOAST CAN BE MADE QUITE MEMORABLE WITH A FEW TASTY ADDITIONS. SERVE THESE SCRUMPTIOUS TOASTIES WITH A SIMPLE SALAD.

SERVES FOUR

INGREDIENTS
    4 slices whole-wheat bread, thickly sliced
    butter or low-fat spread
    ½ cup grated Cheddar cheese
    1 teaspoon dried thyme
    freshly ground black pepper
    2 tablespoons chutney or relish

1 Toast the bread slices lightly on each side, then spread sparingly with butter or low-fat margarine.

2 Mix the cheese and thyme together and season with pepper.

3 Spread the chutney or relish on the toast and divide the cheese among the four slices.

4 Return to the broiler and cook until browned and bubbling. Cut into halves, diagonally, and serve with salad.

RISOTTO PRIMAVERA

REAL RISOTTO SHOULD BE CREAMY AND FULL OF FLAVOR. FOR BEST RESULTS USE A HIGH QUALITY ARBORIO RICE, WHICH HAS A GOOD BITE.

SERVES FOUR

INGREDIENTS

    4 cups hot vegetable stock, preferably homemade
    1 red onion, chopped
    2 garlic cloves, crushed
    2 tablespoons olive oil
    2 tablespoons butter
    1 cup Arborio rice
    (do not rinse)
    3 tablespoons dry white wine
    4 ounces asparagus spears or green beans, sliced and blanched
    2 young carrots, sliced and blanched
    2 ounces baby white mushrooms
    salt and freshly ground black pepper
    ¼ cup freshly grated Pecorino or Parmesan cheese

1 It is important to follow the steps for making real risotto so that you achieve the right texture. First, heat the stock in a saucepan to simmering.

2 Next to it, in a large saucepan, sauté the onion and garlic in the oil and butter for 3 minutes.

3 Stir in the rice, making sure each grain is coated well in the oil, then stir in the wine. Allow to reduce and spoon in two ladles of hot stock, stirring continuously.

4 Allow this to bubble down, then add more stock and stir again. Continue like this, ladling in the stock and stirring frequently, for up to 20 minutes, by which time the rice will have swelled greatly.

5 Mix in the asparagus or beans, carrots and mushrooms, seasoning well, and cook for a minute or two more. Serve immediately in bowls with a sprinkling of grated cheese.

VARIATION

If you have any leftover risotto, shape it into small balls and then coat in beaten egg and dried bread crumbs. Chill for 30 minutes before deep-frying in hot oil until golden and crisp.

KITCHIRI

*THIS IS THE INDIAN ORIGINAL
THAT INSPIRED THE CLASSIC
BREAKFAST DISH KNOWN AS
KEDGEREE. MADE WITH BASMATI
RICE AND SMALL, TASTY LENTILS,
THIS WILL MAKE AN AMPLE
SUPPER OR BRUNCH DISH.*

SERVES FOUR

INGREDIENTS

   1 cup Indian masoor
     dal or green lentils
   1 onion, chopped
   1 garlic clove, crushed
   ¼ cup vegetarian ghee or butter
   2 tablespoons sunflower oil
   1¼ cups basmati rice
   2 teaspoons ground coriander
   2 teaspoons cumin seeds
   2 cloves
   3 cardamom pods
   2 bay leaves
   1 stick cinnamon
   4 cups vegetable stock
   2 tablespoons tomato paste
salt and freshly ground black pepper
   3 tablespoons chopped fresh cilantro or
     parsley, to garnish

1 Cover the dal or lentils with boiling water and soak for 30 minutes. Drain and boil in fresh water for 10 minutes. Drain once more and set aside.

2 Fry the onion and garlic in the ghee or butter and oil in a large saucepan for about 5 minutes.

3 Add the rice, stir well to coat the grains in the ghee or butter and oil, then stir in the spices. Cook gently for a minute or so.

4 Add the lentils, stock, tomato paste and seasoning. Bring to a boil, then cover and simmer for 20 minutes, until the stock is absorbed and the lentils and rice are just soft. Stir in the cilantro or parsley and check the seasoning. Remove the cinnamon stick and bay leaf.

MULTI-MUSHROOM STROGANOFF

*A PAN-FRY OF SLICED
MUSHROOMS SWIRLED WITH SOUR
CREAM IS MADE ESPECIALLY
INTERESTING IF TWO OR THREE
VARIETIES OF MUSHROOM ARE
USED.*

SERVES THREE TO FOUR

INGREDIENTS
    3 tablespoons olive oil
    1 pound mushrooms (such as porcini,
       shiitakes or oysters), sliced
    3 scallions, sliced
    2 garlic cloves, crushed
    2 tablespoons dry sherry or vermouth
    salt and ground black pepper
    1¼ cups sour cream or crème fraîche
    1 tablespoon fresh marjoram or thyme
       leaves, chopped
    fresh parsley, chopped

1 Heat the oil in a large frying pan and
fry the mushrooms gently, stirring them
occasionally until they are softened and
just cooked.

2 Add the scallions, garlic and sherry or
vermouth and cook for a minute more.
Season well.

3 Stir in the sour cream or crème fraîche
and heat to just below boiling. Stir in the
marjoram or thyme, then scatter the
parsley on top. Serve with rice, pasta or
boiled new potatoes.

LIMA BEAN AND PESTO PASTA

*BUY GOOD-QUALITY, READY-MADE PESTO, RATHER THAN MAKING YOUR OWN. PESTO FORMS THE BASIS OF
SEVERAL VERY TASTY SAUCES, AND IT IS ESPECIALLY GOOD WITH LIMA BEANS.*

SERVES FOUR

INGREDIENTS
    8 ounces pasta shapes
    salt and freshly ground black pepper
    fresh nutmeg, grated
    2 tablespoons extra-virgin olive oil
    1 can (14 ounces) lima beans, drained
    3 tablespoons pesto sauce
    ⅔ cup light cream or half-and-half
To serve
    3 tablespoons pine nuts
    grated Parmesan cheese,
       (optional)
    sprigs of fresh basil, to garnish
       (optional)

1 Boil the pasta until al dente, then
drain, leaving it a little wet. Return the
pasta to the pan, season, and stir in the
nutmeg and oil.

2 Heat the beans in a saucepan with the
pesto and cream, stirring the mixture until
it begins to simmer. Toss the beans and
pesto into the pasta and mix well. Serve in
bowls, topped with pine nuts. Add a little
grated cheese and a few basil sprigs if
desired.

BAKED POTATOES AND THREE FILLINGS

POTATOES BAKED IN THEIR JACKETS AND PACKED WITH A VARIETY OF FILLINGS MAKE A TASTY AND NOURISHING MEAL.

INGREDIENTS
    4 medium-size baking potatoes
    olive oil, for greasing
    sea salt, to serve

1 Preheat the oven to 400°F. Score the potatoes with a cross and rub all over with the olive oil.

2 Place on a baking sheet and cook for 45 minutes to 1 hour until a knife inserted into the centers indicates they are cooked.

3 Cut the potatoes open along the score lines and push up the flesh from the base with your fingers. Season with salt and fill with your chosen filling.

EACH FILLING IS FOR FOUR POTATOES

Red bean filling
    1 can (15 ounces) red
      kidney beans
    7 ounces low-fat cream cheese
    2 tablespoons mild chili sauce
    1 teaspoon ground cumin
Drain the beans, heat in a pan or microwave and stir in the cream cheese, chili sauce and cumin.

Soy-vegetable filling
    2 leeks, thinly sliced
    2 carrots, cut in sticks
    1 zucchini, thinly sliced
    ½ cup baby corn, halved
    3 tablespoons peanut or sunflower oil
    4 ounces white mushrooms, sliced
    3 tablespoons soy sauce
    2 tablespoons dry sherry or vermouth
    1 tablespoon sesame oil
    sesame seeds, to sprinkle
Stir-fry the leeks, carrots, zucchini and baby corn in the oil for about 2 minutes, then add the mushrooms and cook for another minute. Mix together the soy sauce, sherry and sesame oil and pour over the vegetables. Heat until bubbling, then scatter the sesame seeds on top.

Cheesy creamed-corn filling
    1 can (15 ounces) creamed corn
    ½ cup grated cheese
    1 teaspoon dried mixed herbs
Heat the corn, then add the cheese and mixed herbs.

PEANUT BUTTER FINGERS

CHILDREN LOVE THESE CRISPY CROQUETTES. FREEZE SOME READY TO FILL YOUNG TUMMIES!

MAKES 12

INGREDIENTS
2 pounds potatoes
1 large onion, chopped
2 bell peppers, red or green, chopped
3 carrots, coarsely grated
3 tablespoons sunflower oil
2 zucchini, coarsely grated
4 ounces mushrooms, chopped
1 tablespoon dried Italian herbs
½ cup grated Cheddar cheese
½ cup crunchy peanut butter
salt and freshly ground black pepper
2 eggs
½ cup dried bread crumbs
3 tablespoons grated Parmesan cheese
oil, for deep-frying

1 Boil the potatoes until tender, then drain well and mash. Set aside.

2 Fry the onion, peppers and carrot in the oil for about 5 minutes. Add the zucchini and mushrooms and cook for 5 minutes.

3 Mix the potatoes with the dried mixed herbs, grated cheese and peanut butter. Season, allow to cool for 30 minutes, then beat and stir in one of the eggs.

4 Spread the mixture out on a large plate, cool and chill, then divide into 12 portions and shape into fingers. Dip your hands in cold water if the mixture sticks.

5 Beat the second egg in a bowl. Dip the potato fingers into the egg first, then into the crumbs and Parmesan cheese, until coated evenly. Put in fridge to set.

6 Heat oil in a deep-fat frier to 375°F, then fry the fingers in batches for 3 minutes, until golden. Drain well on paper towels. Serve hot.

COOK'S TIP
To reheat, thaw for about 1 hour, then broil or oven bake at 375°F for 15 minutes.

EGGPLANT AND ZUCCHINI CASSEROLE

EGGPLANT AND ZUCCHINI ALWAYS GO WELL TOGETHER, AND THEY FORM THE BASIS OF MANY DELICIOUS RECIPES.

SERVES FOUR TO SIX

INGREDIENTS
  1 large eggplant
  2 tablespoons olive oil
  1 large onion, chopped
  1–2 garlic cloves, crushed
  2 pounds tomatoes, peeled and chopped
  1 handful basil leaves, shredded,
    or 1 teaspoon dried basil
  1 tablespoon chopped fresh parsley
  salt and freshly ground black pepper
  2 zucchini, sliced lengthwise
  plain flour, for coating
  5–6 tablespoons sunflower oil
  12 ounces mozzarella, sliced
  2 tablespoons grated Parmesan cheese

1 Slice the eggplant, sprinkle with salt and set aside for 45 minutes to 1 hour.

2 Heat the olive oil in a large frying pan. Fry the onion and garlic for 3–4 minutes, until soft. Stir in the tomatoes, half the basil, the parsley and seasoning. Bring to a boil. Reduce the heat and cook, stirring, for 25–35 minutes, until thickened. Mash the tomatoes to a pulp.

3 Rinse and dry the eggplant. Dust the eggplant and zucchini with flour.

4 Heat the sunflower oil in another frying pan and fry the eggplant and zucchini until golden brown. Set aside.

5 Preheat the oven to 350°F. Butter an ovenproof dish. Put a layer of eggplant and then zucchini in the dish, top with half the sauce and scatter with half the mozzarella. Sprinkle most of the remaining basil and a little parsley on top. Repeat the layers, ending with mozzarella. Sprinkle the Parmesan cheese and remaining herbs on top and bake for 30–35 minutes. Serve at once.

EGGPLANT WITH TZATZIKI

SERVES FOUR

INGREDIENTS
  2 medium-size eggplants
  oil, for deep frying
  salt
For the batter
  ¾ cup all-purpose flour
  pinch salt
  1 egg
  ½–⅔ cup milk,
    or half milk, half water
For the tzatziki
  ½ cucumber, peeled and diced
  ⅔ cup plain yogurt
  1 garlic clove, crushed
  1 tablespoon chopped fresh mint

1 To make the tzatziki, place the cucumber in a colander, sprinkle with salt and leave for 30 minutes. Rinse, drain well and pat dry with paper towels. Mix the yogurt, garlic, mint and cucumber in a bowl. Cover and chill. Slice the eggplants lengthwise. Sprinkle with salt. Let sit 1 hour.

2 To make the batter, sift the flour and salt into a large bowl, add the egg and milk and beat until smooth.

3 Rinse the eggplant slices and pat dry. Heat ½ inch oil in a large frying pan. Dip the eggplant slices in the batter and fry them for 3–4 minutes, until golden, turning once. Drain on paper towels and serve with the tzatziki.

EGGS FLAMENCO

*A VARIATION OF THE POPULAR BASQUE DISH PIPERADE, THE EGGS ARE COOKED WHOLE INSTEAD OF
BEATING THEM BEFORE ADDING TO THE PEPPER MIXTURE. THE RECIPE IS KNOWN AS CHAKCHOUKA IN
NORTH AFRICA AND MAKES A GOOD LUNCH OR SUPPER DISH.*

SERVES FOUR

INGREDIENTS

   2 red bell peppers, seeded
   1 green bell pepper, seeded
   2 tablespoons olive oil
   1 large onion, finely sliced
   2 garlic cloves, crushed
   5–6 tomatoes, peeled and chopped
   ½ cup puréed canned tomatoes or
     tomato juice
   good pinch of dried basil
   4 eggs
   8 teaspoons light cream
   pinch of cayenne pepper (optional)
   salt and freshly ground black pepper

1 Preheat the oven to 350°F. Thinly slice
the red and green peppers. Heat the
olive oil in a large frying pan. Fry the
onion and garlic gently for about 5
minutes, stirring, until softened.

2 Add the peppers to the onions and fry
for 10 minutes. Stir in the tomatoes and
tomato purée or juice, the basil and
seasoning. Cook gently for a further
10 minutes until the peppers are soft.

3 Spoon the mixture into four ovenproof
dishes, preferably earthenware. Make a
hole in the centre and break an egg into
each. Spoon 2 teaspoons cream over the
yolk of each egg and sprinkle with a little
black pepper or cayenne, as preferred.

4 Bake in the oven for 12–15 minutes
until the white of the egg is lightly set.
Serve at once with chunks of crusty
warm Italian bread.

SPINACH AND PEPPER PIZZA

MAKES TWO 12-inch PIZZAS

INGREDIENTS

- 1 pound fresh spinach
- 4 tablespoons light cream
- 1 ounce Parmesan cheese, grated
- 1 tablespoon olive oil
- 1 large onion, chopped
- 1 garlic clove, crushed
- ½ green bell pepper, seeded and thinly sliced
- ½ red bell pepper, seeded and thinly sliced
- 6–8 fluid ounces passata sauce or puréed tomatoes
- 2 ounces black olives, pitted and chopped
- 1 tablespoon chopped fresh basil
- 6 ounces mozzarella cheese, grated
- 6 ounces Cheddar cheese, grated
- salt

For the dough

- 1 ounce fresh yeast or 1 tablespoon dried yeast and 1 teaspoon sugar
- 12 ounces unbleached all-purpose flour
- 2 tablespoons olive oil
- 1 teaspoon salt
- about ⅞ cup warm water

1 To make the dough, cream together the fresh yeast and ⅔ cup of the water and set aside until frothy. If using dried yeast, stir the sugar into ⅔ cup water, sprinkle over the yeast and leave until frothy.

2 Place the flour and salt in a large bowl, make a well in the center and pour in the olive oil and yeast mixture. Add the remaining water, mix to make a stiff but pliable dough. Knead on a lightly floured surface for about 10 minutes until smooth and elastic.

3 Shape the dough into a ball and place in a lightly oiled bowl, cover with plastic wrap and leave in a warm place for about 1 hour until it has doubled in size.

4 To prepare the topping, cook the spinach over moderate heat for 4–5 minutes until the leaves have wilted. Strain and press out the excess liquid. Place in a bowl and mix with the cream, Parmesan cheese and salt to taste.

5 Heat the oil in a frying pan and fry the onion and garlic over moderate heat for 3–4 minutes until the onion has slightly softened. Add the peppers and continue cooking until the onion is lightly golden, stirring regularly.

6 Preheat the oven to 425°F. Knead the dough briefly on a lightly floured surface. Divide the dough and roll out into two 12-inch rounds.

7 Spread each base with the passata sauce or puréed tomatoes. Add the onions and peppers and then spread over the spinach mixture. Scatter the olives and basil leaves and sprinkle with the mozzarella and Cheddar cheeses.

8 Bake in the oven for 15–20 minutes, or until the crust is lightly browned and the top is beginning to turn golden. Allow to cool slightly before serving.

RADICCHIO PIZZA

This unusual pizza topping consists of chopped radicchio with leeks, tomatoes and Parmesan and mozzarella cheeses. The base is a scone dough, making this a quick and easy supper dish to prepare. Serve with a crisp green salad.

SERVES TWO

INGREDIENTS
    14-ounce can chopped tomatoes
    2 garlic cloves, crushed
    pinch of dried basil
    1½ tablespoons olive oil, plus extra
        for dipping
    2 leeks, sliced
    3½ ounces radicchio, roughly chopped
    ¾ ounces Parmesan cheese, grated
    4 ounces mozzarella cheese, sliced
    10–12 black olives, pitted
    basil leaves, to garnish
    salt and freshly ground black pepper
    For the dough
    8 ounces self-rising flour
    ½ teaspoon salt
    2 ounces butter or margarine
    about ½ cup milk

1 Preheat the oven to 425°F and grease a baking sheet. Mix the flour and salt in a bowl, rub in the butter or margarine and gradually stir in the milk and water and mix to a soft dough.

4 Heat the olive oil in a large frying pan and fry the leeks and remaining garlic for 4–5 minutes until slightly softened. Add the radicchio and cook, stirring continuously for a few minutes, and then cover and simmer gently for about 5–10 minutes. Stir in the Parmesan cheese and season with salt and pepper.

5 Cover the dough base with the tomato mixture and then spoon the leek and radicchio mixture on top. Arrange the mozzarella slices on top and scatter over the black olives. Dip a few basil leaves in olive oil, arrange on top and then bake the pizza for 15–20 minutes until the scone base and top are golden brown.

2 Roll the dough out on a lightly floured surface to make a 10–11-inch round. Place on the baking sheet.

3 Purée the tomatoes and then pour into a small saucepan. Stir in one of the crushed garlic cloves, together with the dried basil and seasoning, and simmer over moderate heat until the mixture is thick and reduced by about half.

ITALIAN ROAST PEPPERS

SIMPLE AND EFFECTIVE, THIS DISH WILL DELIGHT ANYONE WHO LIKES PEPPERS. IT CAN BE EATEN EITHER AS A STARTER SERVED WITH ITALIAN BREAD, OR AS A LIGHT LUNCH WITH COUSCOUS OR RICE.

SERVES FOUR

INGREDIENTS

4 small red bell peppers, halved,
  cored and seeded
2–3 tablespoons capers, chopped
10–12 black olives, pitted
  and chopped
2 garlic cloves, finely chopped
2–3 ounces mozzarella, grated
1–1½ ounces fresh white bread
  crumbs
½ cup white wine
3 tablespoons olive oil
1 teaspoon finely chopped fresh mint
1 teaspoon chopped fresh parsley
freshly ground black pepper

1 Preheat the oven to 350°F and butter a shallow ovenproof dish. Place the peppers tightly together in the dish and sprinkle over the chopped capers, black olives, garlic, mozzarella and bread crumbs.

2 Pour over the wine and olive oil and then sprinkle with the mint, parsley and freshly ground black pepper.

3 Bake for 30–40 minutes until the topping is crisp and golden brown.

STUFFED MUSHROOMS

THIS IS A CLASSIC MUSHROOM DISH, STRONGLY FLAVORED WITH GARLIC. IF YOU PREFER A MORE
SUBTLE GARLIC FLAVOR, BRIEFLY FRY THE GARLIC FIRST.

SERVES FOUR

INGREDIENTS
    1 pound large flat mushrooms
    butter, for greasing
    3 tablespoons finely chopped fresh
        parsley
    1½–2 ounces fresh white bread crumbs
    2 garlic cloves, minced or very
        finely chopped
    about 5 tablespoons olive oil
    salt and freshly ground black pepper
    sprig Italian parsley, to garnish

1 Preheat the oven to 350°F. Cut off the mushroom stalks and reserve on one side.

2 Arrange the mushroom caps in a buttered shallow dish, gill sides upward.

3 Finely chop the mushroom stalks and mix with the parsley, bread crumbs, garlic, 2 tablespoons of the olive oil and seasoning to taste, and then pile a little of the mixture into each mushroom.

4 Add the remaining oil to the dish and cover the mushrooms with buttered wax paper. Bake for about   15–20 minutes, removing the paper for the last 5 minutes to brown the tops. Garnish with a sprig of Italian parsley.

COOK'S TIP
The cooking time for the mushrooms depends on their size and thickness. If they are fairly thin, cook for slightly less time. They should be tender but not too soft when cooked. If preferred, the garlic may be cooked before adding to the bread crumb mixture. Heat about 1 tablespoon of oil in a frying pan and fry the garlic very briefly and then stir into the breadcrumb mixture.

TAGLIATELLE FUNGHI

THE MUSHROOM SAUCE IS QUICK TO MAKE AND THE PASTA COOKS VERY QUICKLY; BOTH NEED TO BE COOKED AS CLOSE TO SERVING TIME AS POSSIBLE, SO CAREFUL COORDINATION IS REQUIRED. PUT THE PASTA IN TO COOK WHEN THE MASCARPONE CHEESE IS ADDED TO THE SAUCE.

<u>SERVES FOUR</u> (as a snack or appetizer)

INGREDIENTS
   4 tablespoons butter
   8–12 ounces chanterelles
      or other wild mushrooms
   1 tablespoon all-purpose flour
   ⅔ cup milk
   ¾ cup sour cream
   1 tablespoon chopped fresh parsley
   10 ounces fresh tagliatelle,
      preferably multicolored
   olive oil
   salt and freshly ground black pepper

3 Add the sour cream, parsley, mushrooms and seasoning and stir well. Cook very gently to heat through and then keep warm while cooking the pasta.

4 Cook the pasta in a large saucepan of boiling water for 4–5 minutes (or according to the instructions on the package). Drain well, toss with a little olive oil and turn onto a warmed serving plate. Pour the mushroom sauce on top and serve immediately.

COOK'S TIP
Chanterelles are a little tricky to wash because they are so delicate. However, since these are woodland mushrooms, it's important to clean them thoroughly. Hold each one by the stalk and let cold water run under the gills to dislodge hidden dirt. Shake gently to dry.

1 Melt 3 tablespoons of the butter in a frying pan and fry the mushrooms for about 2–3 minutes over low heat until the juices begin to run, then increase the heat and cook until the liquid has almost evaporated. Transfer the mushrooms to a bowl using a slotted spoon.

2 Stir in the flour, adding a little more butter if necessary, and cook for about 1 minute, then gradually stir in the milk to make a smooth sauce.

WILD MUSHROOMS IN BRIOCHE

SERVES FOUR

INGREDIENTS
    4 small brioches
    olive oil, for glazing
    4 teaspoons lemon juice
    sprigs of parsley, to garnish
For the mushroom filling
    1 ounce butter
    2 shallots
    1 garlic clove, crushed
    6–8 ounces assorted wild mushrooms,
        halved if large
    3 tablespoons white wine
    3 tablespoons double cream
    1 teaspoon chopped fresh basil
    1 teaspoon chopped fresh parsley
    salt and freshly ground black pepper

1 Preheat the oven to 350°F. Using a serrated or grapefruit knife, cut a circle out of the top of the brioche and reserve. Scoop out the bread inside to make a small cavity.

2 Place the brioches and the tops on a baking sheet and brush inside and out with olive oil. Bake for 7–10 minutes until golden and crisp. Squeeze 1 teaspoon of lemon juice inside each brioche.

3 To make the filling, melt the butter in a frying pan and fry the shallots and garlic for 2–3 minutes until softened.

4 Add the mushrooms and cook gently for about 4–5 minutes, stirring.

5 When the juices begin to run, reduce the heat and continue cooking for about 3–4 minutes, stirring occasionally, until the pan is fairly dry.

6 Stir in the wine. Cook for a few more minutes and then stir in the cream, basil, parsley and seasoning to taste.

7 Pile the mushroom mixture into the brioche shells and return to the oven and reheat for about 5–6 minutes. Serve as a starter, garnished with a sprig of parsley.

WILD MUSHROOMS WITH PANCAKES

SERVES SIX (as a starter)

INGREDIENTS
    8–10 ounces assorted wild
        mushrooms
    2 ounces butter
    1–2 garlic cloves
    splash of brandy (optional)
    freshly ground black pepper
    sour cream, to serve
For the pancakes
    4 ounces self-rising flour
    ¾ ounce buckwheat flour
    ½ teaspoon baking powder
    pinch of salt
    2 eggs
    about 1 cup milk
    oil, for frying

1 To make the pancakes, mix together the flours, baking powder and salt in a large bowl or food processor. Add the eggs and milk and beat or process to make a smooth batter, about the consistency of light cream.

2 Grease a large griddle or frying pan with a little oil and when hot, pour small amounts of batter (about 1–2 tablespoons per pancake) onto the griddle, well spaced apart.

3 Fry for a few minutes until bubbles begin to appear on the surface and the underside is golden, and then flip over. Cook for about 1 minute until golden. Keep warm, wrapped in a clean dish towel. (Makes about 18–20 pancakes.)

4 If the mushrooms are large, cut them in half. Melt the butter in a frying pan and add the garlic and mushrooms. Fry over moderate heat for a few minutes until the juices begin to run and then increase the heat and cook, stirring frequently, until nearly all the juices have evaporated. Stir in the brandy, if using, and season with a little black pepper.

5 Arrange the warm pancakes on a serving plate and spoon over a little sour cream. Top with the hot mushrooms and serve immediately.

COOK'S TIP
This makes a delicious and elegant starter for a dinner party. Alternatively, make cocktail-size pancakes and serve as part of a buffet supper.

PASTA SALADE TIÈDE

*BOIL A PAN OF PASTA SHAPES
AND TOSS WITH VINAIGRETTE
AND SOME FRESHLY PREPARED
SALAD VEGETABLES, AND YOU
HAVE THE BASIS FOR A DELICIOUS
WARM SALAD.*

SERVES TWO

INGREDIENTS

    4 ounces pasta shapes (e.g., shells)
    3 tablespoons vinaigrette dressing
    3 sun-dried tomatoes in oil, snipped
    2 scallions, sliced
    2 or 3 sprigs watercress or arugula,
      chopped
    ¼ cucumber, halved, seeded and sliced
    salt and freshly ground black pepper
    about 3 tablespoons coarsely grated
      Pecorino cheese

1 Boil the pasta according to the instructions on the package. Drain and toss in the dressing.

2 Mix in the tomatoes, onions, watercress and cucumber. Season to taste.

3 Divide between two plates and sprinkle the cheese on top. Eat at room temperature, if possible.

PENNE WITH "CAN CAN" SAUCE

*THE QUALITY OF CANNED BEANS
AND TOMATOES IS SO GOOD THAT
IT IS POSSIBLE TO TRANSFORM
THEM INTO A VERY FRESH-
TASTING PASTA SAUCE IN
MINUTES. AGAIN, CHOOSE
WHATEVER PASTA YOU LIKE.*

SERVES THREE TO FOUR

INGREDIENTS

    8 ounces penne pasta
    1 onion, sliced
    1 red bell pepper, seeded and sliced
    2 tablespoons olive oil
    1 can (14 ounces) tomatoes, chopped
    1 can (14 ounces) chickpeas
    2 tablespoons dry vermouth (optional)
    1 teaspoon dried oregano
    1 large bay leaf
    2 tablespoons capers
    salt and freshly ground black pepper

2 Add the tomatoes, chickpeas with their liquid, vermouth (if liked), herbs and capers.

1 Boil the pasta as instructed on the package, then drain. In a saucepan, gently fry the onion and pepper in the oil for about 5 minutes, stirring occasionally, until softened.

3 Season and bring to a boil, then simmer for about 10 minutes. Remove the bay leaf and mix in the pasta. Reheat and serve hot.

TOFU AND CRUNCHY VEGETABLES

TOFU IS BEST IF MARINATED
LIGHTLY BEFORE COOKING.
SMOKED TOFU IS EVEN TASTIER.

SERVES FOUR

INGREDIENTS
    2 packages (8 ounces each) smoked tofu
    3 tablespoons soy sauce
    2 tablespoons dry sherry or vermouth
    1 tablespoon sesame oil
    3 tablespoons peanut or sunflower oil
    2 leeks, thinly sliced
    2 carrots, cut in sticks
    1 large zucchini, thinly sliced
    4 ounces baby corn, halved
    4 ounces white or shiitake
        mushrooms, sliced
    1 tablespoon sesame seeds
    1 package egg noodles, cooked

1 Cut the tofu into cubes and marinate it in the soy sauce, sherry or vermouth and sesame oil for at least 30 minutes. Drain and reserve the marinade.

2 Heat the peanut or sunflower oil in a wok and stir-fry the tofu cubes until browned all over. Remove and reserve.

3 Stir-fry the leeks, carrots, zucchini and baby corn, stirring and tossing for about 2 minutes. Add the mushrooms and cook for another minute.

4 Return the tofu to the wok and pour in the marinade. Heat until bubbling, then sprinkle with the sesame seeds.

5 Serve as soon as possible with the hot cooked noodles, dressed in a little sesame oil, if desired.

VARIATION
Tofu is also excellent marinated and skewered, then lightly broiled. Push the tofu off the skewers into pockets of pita bread. Fill with lemon-dressed salad and serve with a drizzle of tahini.

EGG FOO YUNG

A GREAT WAY OF TURNING A BOWL OF LEFTOVER COOKED RICE INTO A MEAL FOR FOUR, THIS ASIAN DISH IS TASTY AND FULL OF TEXTURE. BUY BEAN SPROUTS OR GROW YOUR OWN — IT'S EASY AND FUN.

SERVES FOUR

INGREDIENTS

- salt and ground black pepper
- 3 eggs, beaten
- generous pinch five spice powder (optional)
- 3 tablespoons peanut or sunflower oil
- 4 scallions, sliced
- 1 garlic clove, crushed
- 1 small green bell pepper, seeded and chopped
- ½ cup fresh bean sprouts
- 3 cups cooked white rice
- 3 tablespoons light soy sauce
- 1 tablespoon sesame oil

1 Season the eggs and beat in the five spice powder, if using.

2 In a wok or large frying pan, heat one tablespoon of the oil and when quite hot, add the egg. Cook like an omelet, pulling the mixture away from the sides and allowing the rest to slip underneath.

3 Cook the egg until firm, then remove from the pan. Chop into small strips.

4 Heat the remaining oil and stir-fry the onion, garlic, pepper and bean sprouts for about 2 minutes, stirring and tossing continuously.

5 Stir in the rice and heat thoroughly, mixing well. Add the soy sauce and sesame oil, then return the egg and mix in well. Serve immediately, piping hot.

EGGS BENEDICT WITH QUICK HOLLANDAISE

TO MAKE TRADITIONAL
HOLLANDAISE QUICKLY, YET
STILL ACHIEVE A THICK, CREAMY
SAUCE, USE A BLENDER.

SERVES FOUR

INGREDIENTS
  2 egg yolks
  1 teaspoon dry mustard
  generous pinch each salt and freshly
    ground black pepper
  1 tablespoon wine vinegar
    or lemon juice
  ¾ cup butter
  4 English muffins, split
  butter or margarine
  4 large eggs
  2 tablespoons capers
  a little fresh parsley, chopped, to
    garnish

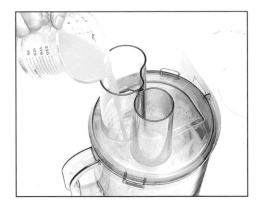

2 Heat the butter until it is almost bubbling, then, with the machine still running, slowly pour the butter onto the egg yolks.

3 The mixture should emulsify instantly and become thick and creamy. Switch off the blender and set the sauce aside.

5 Poach the eggs either in gently simmering water or in an egg poacher. Drain well and slip carefully onto the uncut muffin halves.

1 Blend the egg yolks with the mustard and seasoning in a blender or food processor for a few seconds, until well mixed. Mix in the vinegar or lemon juice.

4 Toast the split English muffins. Cut four of the halves in two and lightly butter. Place the four uncut halves on warmed plates and leave unbuttered.

6 Spoon the sauce over the muffins and then sprinkle with capers and parsley. Serve immediately with the buttered muffin quarters.

VARIATION
This classic brunch dish is said to have originated in New York, and is ideal to serve on a special occasion such as a birthday treat or New Year's Day.
  Instead of the toasted English muffin, you could make more of a main meal by serving the dish on a bed of lightly steamed or blanched spinach mixed with quick-fried sliced mushrooms and onions. The quick Hollandaise sauce is, of course, ideal as an all-purpose serving sauce for vegetables, baked potatoes, cauliflower and broccoli.

LIGHT RATATOUILLE

*THIS DELIGHTFUL MEDLEY IS
COOKED WITH SIMPLE POACHED
EGGS AND TOPPED WITH CRISP
BREAD CRUMBS.*

SERVES FOUR

INGREDIENTS

    3 tablespoons olive oil
    1 cup fresh bread crumbs
    1 green bell pepper, thinly sliced
    2 garlic cloves, crushed
    2 leeks, thinly sliced
    2 zucchini, thinly sliced
    2 tomatoes, peeled and sliced
    1 teaspoon dried rosemary, crushed
    4 eggs
    salt and freshly ground black pepper

1 Heat half the oil in a shallow flameproof dish (or frying pan with a lid) and fry the bread crumbs until they are golden and crisp. Drain on paper towels.

2 Add the remaining oil and fry the pepper, garlic and leeks in the same pan for about 10 minutes, until softened.

3 Add the zucchini, tomatoes and rosemary and cook for another 5 minutes. Season well.

4 Using the back of a spoon, make four wells in the vegetable mixture and break an egg into each one. Lightly season the eggs, then cover and cook over low heat for about 3 minutes, until they are just set.

5 Sprinkle with the crisp bread crumbs and serve immediately, piping hot.

MACARONI SOUFFLÉ

*THIS IS GENERALLY A BIG
FAVORITE WITH CHILDREN. IT IS
A LOT LIKE A LIGHT AND FLUFFY
MACARONI AND CHEESE.*

SERVES THREE TO FOUR

INGREDIENTS
    3 ounces elbow macaroni
    melted butter, to coat
    3 tablespoons dried bread crumbs
    4 tablespoons butter
    1 teaspoon ground paprika
    ⅓ cup all-purpose flour
    1¼ cups milk
    6 tablespoons grated Cheddar or
        Gruyère cheese
    4 tablespoons grated Parmesan cheese
    salt and freshly ground black pepper
    3 eggs, separated

1 Boil the macaroni according to
the instructions on the package. Drain
well and set aside. Preheat the oven
to 300°F.

2 Brush the insides of a 1-quart
soufflé dish with melted butter, then coat
evenly with the bread crumbs, shaking
out any excess.

3 Put the butter, paprika, flour and milk
in a saucepan and bring to a boil slowly,
whisking constantly until the mixture is
smooth and thick.

4 Simmer the sauce for a minute, then
remove from the heat and stir in the
cheeses until they melt. Season well and
mix with the macaroni.

5 Beat in the egg yolks. In a clean bowl,
whisk the egg whites until they form soft
peaks and spoon a quarter into the sauce
mixture, beating it gently to loosen it up.

6 Using a large metal spoon, carefully
fold in the rest of the egg whites and
transfer to the prepared soufflé dish.

7 Bake in the center of the oven for
about 40–45 minutes, until the soufflé has
risen and is golden brown. The middle
should wobble very slightly and the soufflé
should be lightly creamy inside.

COWBOY HOT POT

*A GREAT DISH TO SERVE AS A
CHILDREN'S MAIN MEAL. YOU
CAN USE ANY VEGETABLE
MIXTURE YOU LIKE — ALTHOUGH
BEANS ARE A MUST FOR EVERY
SELF-RESPECTING COWBOY!*

SERVES FOUR TO SIX

INGREDIENTS

1 onion, sliced
1 red bell pepper, sliced
1 sweet potato or 2 carrots, chopped
3 tablespoons sunflower oil
4 ounces green beans, chopped
1 can (14 ounces) baked beans
1 can (7 ounces) corn
1 tablespoon tomato paste
1 teaspoon seasoned salt
4 ounces smoked cheese, cubed
1 pound potatoes, thinly sliced
2 tablespoons butter, melted
salt and freshly ground black pepper

1 Fry the onion, pepper and sweet potato or carrots gently in the oil until softened but not browned.

2 Add the green beans, baked beans, corn with liquid, tomato paste and seasoned salt. Bring to a boil, then simmer for 5 minutes.

3 Transfer the vegetables to a shallow ovenproof dish and scatter the cubed cheese on top.

4 Cover the vegetable and cheese mixture with the sliced potatoes, brush with butter, season and bake at 375°F for 30–40 minutes, until the potatoes are cooked and golden brown on top.

STIR-FRY RICE AND VEGETABLES

*LEFTOVER COOKED RICE AND A FEW VEGETABLES FROM THE CRISPER ARE THE BASIS FOR THIS QUICK AND
TASTY MEAL.*

SERVES FOUR

INGREDIENTS

½ cucumber
2 scallions, sliced
1 garlic clove, crushed
2 carrots, thinly sliced
1 small red or yellow bell pepper,
  seeded and sliced
3 tablespoons sunflower
  or peanut oil
¼ small green cabbage, shredded
4 cups cooked long-grain rice
2 tablespoons light soy sauce
1 tablespoon sesame oil
salt and ground black pepper
fresh parsley or cilantro, chopped
  (optional)
4 ounces unsalted cashew nuts,
  almonds or peanuts

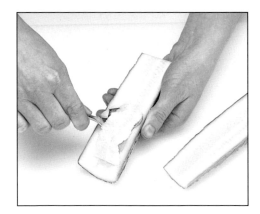

1 Halve the cucumber lengthwise and scoop out the seeds with a teaspoon. Slice the flesh diagonally. Set aside.

2 In a wok or large frying pan, stir-fry the onions, garlic, carrots and pepper in the oil for about 3 minutes, until they are just soft.

3 Add the cabbage and cucumber and fry for another minute or two, until the leaves begin to wilt. Mix in the rice, soy sauce, sesame oil and seasoning. Reheat the mixture thoroughly, stirring and tossing all the time.

4 Add the herbs, if using, and nuts. Check the seasoning and serve piping hot.

PEPPER AND POTATO TORTILLA

TRADITIONALLY A SPANISH DISH, EGG TORTILLA IS BEST EATEN COLD IN CHUNKY WEDGES. USE A HARD SPANISH CHEESE, SUCH AS MAHON, OR A GOAT CHEESE, IF YOU CAN.

SERVES FOUR

INGREDIENTS
2 medium-size potatoes
3 tablespoons olive oil
1 large onion, thinly sliced
2 garlic cloves, crushed
2 bell peppers, one green and one red, thinly sliced
6 eggs, beaten
4 ounces aged cheese, grated
salt and freshly ground black pepper

1 Do not peel the potatoes, but wash them thoroughly. Parboil them for about 10 minutes, then drain and slice them thickly. Switch on the broiler so that it has time to warm up while you prepare the tortilla.

2 In a large nonstick, ovenproof frying pan or cast-iron skillet, heat the oil and fry the onion, garlic and peppers over medium heat for 5 minutes, until softened.

3 Add the potatoes and continue frying, stirring occasionally, until the potatoes are completely cooked and the vegetables are soft. Add a little extra oil if the pan seems a little dry.

4 Pour in half the eggs, then sprinkle with half the cheese, then the rest of the egg, seasoning as you go. Finish with a layer of cheese.

5 Continue to cook over low heat, without stirring, half covering the pan with a lid to help set the eggs.

6 When the mixture is firm, run the pan under the hot broiler to just lightly seal the top. Leave the tortilla in the pan to cool. This helps it firm up further and makes it easier to turn out.

VARIATION
You can add any sliced and lightly cooked vegetables, such as mushrooms, zucchini or broccoli, to this tortilla dish instead of peppers. Cooked pasta or brown rice are excellent alternatives, too.

CAULIFLOWER AND EGG WITH CHEESE

A QUICK ALL-IN-ONE SAUCE CAN BE MADE IN MINUTES, WHILE A SMALL PACKAGE OF SOUP CROUTONS GIVES THE DISH A DELICIOUS CRUNCHY TOPPING.

SERVES FOUR

INGREDIENTS
    1 medium-size cauliflower, in florets
    1 medium onion, sliced
    2 eggs, hard-cooked, peeled and chopped
    3 tablespoons whole-wheat flour
    1 teaspoon mild curry powder
    2 tablespoons butter or margarine
    2 cups milk
    ½ teaspoon dried thyme
    salt and freshly ground black pepper
    4 ounces aged cheese, grated
    small package of soup croutons

1 Boil the cauliflower and onion in enough salted water to cover until they are just tender. Be careful not to overcook them. Drain well.

2 Arrange the cauliflower and onion in a shallow ovenproof dish and top with the chopped egg.

3 Put the flour, curry powder, butter or margarine and milk in a saucepan. Bring slowly to a boil, stirring well, until thickened and smooth. Stir in the thyme and seasoning and allow the sauce to simmer for a minute or two. Remove the pan from the heat and stir in about three-quarters of the cheese.

4 Pour the sauce over the cauliflower, and sprinkle with the croutons and the remaining cheese. Brown under a hot broiler until golden and serve. This dish is delicious with thick crusty bread.

QUICK BASMATI AND NUT PILAF

LIGHT AND FRAGRANT BASMATI RICE FROM THE FOOTHILLS OF THE HIMALAYAS COOKS PERFECTLY USING THIS SIMPLE PILAF METHOD. USE WHATEVER NUTS ARE YOUR FAVORITE — EVEN UNSALTED PEANUTS ARE GOOD, ALTHOUGH ALMONDS, CASHEWS OR PISTACHIOS ARE MORE EXOTIC.

SERVES FOUR TO SIX

INGREDIENTS

1¼ cups basmati rice
1 onion, chopped
1 garlic clove, crushed
1 large carrot, coarsely grated
1–2 tablespoons sunflower oil
1 teaspoon cumin seeds
2 teaspoons ground coriander
2 teaspoons black mustard seeds
   (optional)
4 cardamom pods
2 cups vegetable stock or water
1 bay leaf
salt and freshly ground black pepper
½ cup unsalted nuts
fresh chopped parsley or cilantro,
   to garnish

RINSING BASMATI

For light, fluffy grains, basmati rice is best rinsed before cooking to remove any surface starch. The traditional method is to put the rice in a large bowl of cold water. Swill the grains around with your hands, then pour out the cloudy water. (The rice will quickly sink to the bottom.) Ideally, leave the rice to soak for 30 minutes in the last rinsing water. This ensures a lighter, fluffier grain.

1 Wash the rice either by the traditional Indian method (see note) or in a sieve under running water. If there is time, soak the rice for 30 minutes, then drain well in a sieve.

2 In a large shallow pan, gently fry the onion, garlic and carrot in the oil for a few minutes.

3 Stir in the rice and spices and cook 1–2 more minutes, so that the grains are coated in oil.

4 Pour in the stock or water, add the bay leaf and season well. Bring to a boil, cover and simmer very gently for about 10 minutes.

5 Remove from the heat without lifting the lid – this helps the rice to firm up and cook further. Leave for about 5 minutes.

6 If the rice is cooked, there will be small steam holes in the center. Discard the bay leaf and cardamom pods.

7 Stir in the nuts and check the seasoning. Scatter the chopped parsley or cilantro over the mixture. The whole dish can be made ahead and reheated.

TOFU WITH GINGER, CHILI AND LEEKS

TOFU EASILY ABSORBS DIFFERENT FLAVORS AND RETAINS A FIRM TEXTURE, WHICH IS IDEAL FOR STIR-FRYING.

SERVES FOUR

INGREDIENTS

8 ounces tofu cubes
3 tablespoons soy sauce
2 tablespoons dry sherry or vermouth
2 teaspoons honey
⅔ cup vegetable stock
2 teaspoons cornstarch
3 tablespoons sunflower or peanut oil
3 leeks, thinly sliced
1 red chili, seeded and sliced
1-inch piece fresh ginger,
  peeled and shredded
salt and freshly ground black pepper

1 Toss the tofu in the soy sauce and sherry or vermouth until well coated and leave to marinate for about 30 minutes.

2 Strain the tofu from the marinade and reserve the juices in a measuring cup. Mix the marinade with the honey, stock and cornstarch to make a paste.

3 Heat the oil in a wok or large frying pan and when hot, stir-fry the tofu until it is crisp on the outside. Remove the tofu and set aside.

4 Reheat the oil and stir-fry the leeks, chili and ginger for about 2 minutes, until they are just soft. Season lightly.

5 Return the tofu to the pan together with the marinade and stir well until the liquid is thick and glossy. Serve hot with rice or egg noodles.

CHINESE POTATOES <u>WITH</u> CHILI BEANS

AN AMERICAN-STYLE DISH WITH A CHINESE FLAVOR. TRY IT AS A QUICK SUPPER DISH WHEN YOU FEEL LIKE A MEAL WITH ZING.

<u>SERVES FOUR</u>

INGREDIENTS

4 medium potatoes, cut into chunks
3 scallions, sliced
1 large fresh chili, seeded and sliced
2 tablespoons sunflower or peanut oil
2 garlic cloves, crushed
1 can (14 ounces) red kidney beans, drained
2 tablespoons soy sauce
1 tablespoon sesame oil

To serve

salt and freshly ground black pepper
1 tablespoon sesame seeds
chopped fresh cilantro or parsley, to garnish

1 Boil the potatoes until they are just tender. Take care not to overcook them. Drain and reserve.

2 In a large frying pan or wok, stir-fry the onions and chili in the oil for about 1 minute, then add the garlic and fry for a few seconds longer.

3 Add the potatoes, stirring well, followed by the beans and finally the soy sauce and sesame oil.

4 Season to taste and cook the vegetables until they are heated through. Sprinkle with the sesame seeds and the cilantro or parsley.

TABBOULEH

*ALMOST THE ULTIMATE QUICK
GRAIN SALAD — IT SIMPLY NEEDS
TO BE SOAKED, DRAINED AND
MIXED. BULGUR IS PARBOILED
WHEAT. MAKE THIS A DAY AHEAD,
IF POSSIBLE, SO THAT THE
FLAVORS HAVE TIME TO DEVELOP.*

SERVES FOUR

INGREDIENTS
    ¾ cup bulgur wheat
    6 tablespoons fresh lemon juice
    5 tablespoons extra-virgin olive oil
    6 tablespoons chopped fresh parsley
    ¼ cup chopped fresh mint,
    3 scallions, finely chopped
    4 firm tomatoes, peeled and chopped
    salt and freshly ground black pepper

1 Cover the bulgur with cold water and soak for 20 minutes, then drain well and squeeze out more water from it with your hands.

2 Put the bulgur into another bowl and add all the other ingredients, stirring and seasoning well.

3 Cover and chill for a few hours—overnight, if possible.

CRUDITÉS with HUMMUS

*ALWAYS A GREAT FAMILY
FAVORITE, HOMEMADE HUMMUS IS
SPEEDILY MADE WITH THE HELP
OF A BLENDER. THE TAHINI PASTE
IS THE SECRET OF HUMMUS, AND
IT IS READILY AVAILABLE IN
DELICATESSENS OR LARGER
SUPERMARKETS.*

SERVES TWO TO THREE

INGREDIENTS
    1 can (15 ounces) chickpeas, drained
    2 tablespoons tahini paste
    2 tablespoons fresh lemon juice
    1 garlic clove, crushed
    salt and ground black pepper
    olive oil and paprika, to garnish
To serve
    selection of salad vegetables (such as
        cucumber, chicory, baby carrots,
        pepper strips, radishes)
    bite-size chunks of bread (such as pita,
        walnut, naan, bruschetta or grissini
        sticks)

1 Put the chickpeas, tahini paste, lemon juice, garlic and plenty of seasoning in a food processor or blender and mix to a smooth paste.

2 Spoon the hummus into a bowl and swirl the top with the back of a spoon. Drizzle with a little olive oil and drizzle with paprika.

3 Prepare a selection of fresh salad vegetables and chunks of your favorite fresh bread or grissini sticks into finger-size pieces.

4 Set out in a colorful jumble on a large plate with the bowl of hummus in the center. Then dip and eat!

PITA PIZZAS

*PITA BREADS MAKE VERY GOOD
BASES FOR QUICK, THIN AND
CRISPY PIZZAS.*

SERVES FOUR

INGREDIENTS

Basic pizzas

    4 pita breads, preferably whole-wheat

    small jar of pasta sauce

    8 ounces mozarella cheese, sliced
      or grated

    dried oregano or thyme, to sprinkle

    salt and freshly ground black pepper

Extra toppings – choose from

    1 small red onion, thinly sliced and
      lightly fried

    mushrooms, sliced and fried

    1 can (7 ounces) corn, drained

    jalapeño chilis, sliced

    black or green olives, pitted and sliced

    capers, drained

1 Prepare two or three toppings of your choice for the pizzas.

2 Preheat the broiler and lightly toast the pita breads on each side.

3 Spread pasta sauce on each pita, right to the edge. This prevents the edges of the pita from burning.

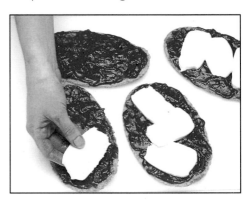

4 Arrange cheese slices or grated cheese on top of each pita and sprinkle with herbs and seasoning.

5 Add the toppings of your choice and then broil the pizzas for 5–8 minutes, until they are golden brown and bubbling. Serve immediately.

TAGLIATELLE <u>WITH</u> SPINACH <u>AND</u> SOY GARLIC CHEESE

ITALIAN PASTA AND SPINACH COMBINE WITH CHINESE SOY SAUCE AND FRENCH GARLIC CREAM CHEESE TO CREATE THIS WONDERFULLY MOUTHWATERING DISH.

SERVES FOUR

INGREDIENTS

8 ounces tagliatelle
8 ounces fresh leaf spinach
2 tablespoons light soy sauce
3 ounces garlic and herb cheese
3 tablespoons milk
salt and freshly ground black pepper

1 Boil the tagliatelle according to the instructions on the package and drain. Return the pasta to the pan.

2 Meanwhile, blanch the spinach in a tiny amount of water until just wilted, then drain very well, squeezing dry with the back of a wooden spoon. Chop roughly with kitchen scissors.

3 Return the spinach to its pan and stir in the soy sauce, garlic and herb cheese and milk. Bring slowly to a boil, stirring until smooth. Season to taste.

4 When the sauce is ready, pour it over the pasta. Toss the pasta and sauce together well and serve hot.

SPAGHETTI WITH FETA

*WE THINK OF PASTA AS BEING
ESSENTIALLY ITALIAN, BUT
THE GREEKS HAVE A GREAT
APPETITE FOR IT TOO, AND IT
BEAUTIFULLY COMPLEMENTS
THE TANGY, FULL-FLAVORED FETA
CHEESE.*

SERVES TWO OR THREE

INGREDIENTS
    4 ounces spaghetti
    1 garlic clove
    2 tablespoons extra-virgin olive oil
    8 cherry tomatoes, halved
    a little freshly grated nutmeg
    salt and freshly ground black pepper
    3 ounces feta cheese, crumbled
    1 tablespoon chopped fresh basil
    a few black olives (optional), to serve

1 Boil the spaghetti in plenty of lightly
salted water according to the instructions
on the package, then drain.

2 In the same pan, gently heat the garlic
clove in the oil for a minute or two, then
add the cherry tomatoes.

3 Increase the heat to fry the tomatoes
lightly for a minute, then remove the
garlic and discard.

4 Toss in the spaghetti, season with the
nutmeg and seasoning to taste, then stir
in the crumbled feta and basil.

5 Check the seasoning, remembering
that feta can be quite salty, and serve hot,
topped with olives.

POTATOES WITH BLUE CHEESE AND WALNUTS

*WE ARE SO USED TO EATING POTATOES AS A SIDE DISH, WE FORGET THEY CAN BE A GOOD MAIN MEAL
TOO. THIS DISH IS SO VERSATILE IT CAN BE SERVED AS EITHER. USE STILTON, DANISH BLUE, BLUE BRIE
OR ANY OTHER BLUE CHEESE.*

SERVES FOUR

INGREDIENTS
    1 pound small new potatoes
    small head of celery, sliced
    small red onion, sliced
    4 ounces blue cheese, mashed
    ⅔ cup light cream
    salt and freshly ground black pepper
    ½ cup walnut pieces
    2 tablespoons chopped fresh parsley

1 Cover the potatoes with water and boil
for about 15 minutes, adding the sliced
celery and onion to the pan for the last
5 minutes or so.

2 Drain the vegetables and put them in a
shallow serving dish.

3 In a small saucepan melt the cheese in
the cream slowly, stirring occasionally. Do
not allow the mixture to boil, but heat it
until it scalds.

4 Season the sauce to taste. Pour it over
the vegetables and top with the walnuts
and parsley. Serve hot.

ADUKI BEAN BURGERS

*ALTHOUGH NOT QUICK TO MAKE,
THESE ARE A DELICIOUS
ALTERNATIVE TO STORE-BOUGHT
BURGERS.*

<u>MAKES 12</u>

INGREDIENTS
    1 cup brown rice
    1 onion, chopped
    2 garlic cloves, crushed
    2 tablespoons sunflower oil
    4 tablespoons butter
    1 small green bell pepper, seeded and
        chopped
    1 carrot, coarsely grated
    1 can (14 ounces) aduki beans, drained
        (or 4 ounces dried weight,
        soaked and cooked)
    1 egg, beaten
    ½ cup grated aged cheese
    1 teaspoon dried thyme
    ½ cup roasted hazelnuts or toasted
        flaked almonds
    salt and freshly ground black pepper
    whole-wheat flour or cornmeal, for
        coating
    oil, for deep-frying

1 Cook the rice according to the instructions on the package, allowing it to slightly overcook so that it is softer. Strain the rice and transfer it to a large bowl.

2 Fry the onion and garlic in the oil and butter together with the green pepper and carrot for about 10 minutes, until the vegetables are softened.

3 Mix this vegetable mixture into the rice, together with the aduki beans, egg, cheese, thyme, nuts or almonds and plenty of seasoning. Chill until firm.

4 Shape into 12 patties, using wet hands if the mixture sticks. Coat the patties in flour or cornmeal and set aside.

5 Heat ½ inch oil in a large, shallow frying pan and fry the burgers in batches until browned on each side, about 5 minutes total. Remove and drain on paper towels. Eat some burgers freshly cooked, and freeze the rest for later. Serve in buns with salad and relish.

COOK'S TIP
To freeze the burgers, cool them after cooking, then open-freeze them before wrapping and bagging. Use within six weeks. Cook frozen by baking in a preheated, moderately hot oven for 20–25 minutes.

ZUCCHINI QUICHE

IF POSSIBLE, USE A HARD GOAT CHEESE FOR THIS QUICHE, AS ITS FLAVOR COMPLEMENTS THE ZUCCHINI NICELY. BAKE THE PASTRY SHELL BLIND FOR A CRISP CRUST.

SERVES SIX

INGREDIENTS

For the pastry
    scant 1 cup whole-wheat flour
    1 cup all-purpose flour
    ½ cup sunflower margarine

For the filling
    1 red onion, thinly sliced
    2 tablespoons olive oil
    2 large zucchini, sliced
    6 ounces cheese, grated
    2 tablespoons fresh basil, chopped
    3 eggs, beaten
    1¼ cups milk
    salt and freshly ground black pepper

1 Preheat the oven to 400°F. Mix the flours together and rub in the margarine until the mixture resembles crumbs, then mix to a firm dough with cold water.

2 Roll out the pastry and use it to line a 9–10 inch tart pan, ideally at least 1 inch deep. Prick the base, chill for 30 minutes, then line with paper or foil and fill with dried beans.

3 Bake the pastry shell blind on a baking sheet for 20 minutes, uncovering it for the last 5 minutes so that it can crisp up.

4 Meanwhile, sweat the onion in the oil for 5 minutes, until it is soft. Add the zucchini and fry for another 5 minutes.

5 Spoon the onions and zucchini into the pastry shell. Scatter most of the cheese and all of the basil on top.

6 Beat together the eggs, milk and seasoning and pour over the filling. Top with the remaining cheese.

7 Turn the oven down to 350°F and cook the quiche for about 40 minutes, until risen and just firm to the touch in the center. Allow to cool slightly before serving.

Spring Rolls

Bamboo shoots and bean sprouts are perfect companions in this popular snack, providing the contrast in texture that is the principle element in Chinese cooking. The bamboo shoots retain their crispness, while the bean sprouts become more chewy when cooked.

MAKES ABOUT TWENTY

INGREDIENTS
    4 tablespoons vegetable oil
    2 tablespoons dark soy sauce
    2 tablespoons medium-dry sherry
    about ½-inch piece fresh ginger,
      finely grated
    8 ounces firm tofu, chopped finely
    2 ounces rice vermicelli
    4–5 shiitake mushrooms
    4–5 scallions
    7-ounce can bamboo shoots
    1 garlic clove, crushed
    1 carrot, grated
    3 ounces bean sprouts, roughly
      chopped
    1 tablespoon cornstarch, blended
      with 2 tablespoons water
    about 20 x 6-inch spring roll wrappers
    vegetable oil, for deep frying

1   Blend together 2 tablespoons of the oil, the soy sauce, sherry and ginger in a medium-size bowl. Add the tofu, stir well and set aside for 10–15 minutes.

2   Place the rice vermicelli in a large bowl, cover with boiling water and leave to stand for 10 minutes. Drain well and then chop roughly.

3   Wipe the mushrooms, remove the stalks and slice the caps thinly, halving them if the mushrooms are large.

4   Using a sharp knife, cut the scallions into diagonal slices, including all but the tips of the green parts.

5   Drain the bamboo shoots and rinse them very well under cold running water. Cut in half if they are large.

6   Heat 1 tablespoon of the remaining oil in a wok or large frying pan and cook the garlic for a few seconds. Add the scallions and stir-fry for 2–3 minutes. Add the mushrooms and stir-fry for a further 3–4 minutes. Transfer the vegetables to a plate, using a slotted spoon.

7   Heat the remaining oil in the wok. Drain the tofu, reserving the marinade, and then stir-fry for 4–5 minutes.

8   Add the bamboo shoots to the tofu together with the carrot, vermicelli, the mushroom and onion mixture and the reserved marinade, and stir well. Add the bean sprouts, stir well and then remove from the heat and cool.

9   Place a level tablespoon of mixture at one corner of a spring roll sheet. Brush the edges of the pastry with the cornstarch mixture and roll up, folding the left and right corners inward as you roll. Continue making spring rolls in this way, until all the mixture is used up.

10   Heat the oil in a large wok or deep-fryer and fry two or three rolls at a time for 3–4 minutes until golden, turning them so that they cook evenly. Drain on paper towels and keep warm. Serve with extra soy sauce.

LOOFAH AND EGGPLANT RATATOUILLE

LOOFAHS HAVE A SIMILAR FLAVOR TO ZUCCHINI AND CONSEQUENTLY TASTE EXCELLENT WITH EGGPLANT AND TOMATOES. THE CILANTRO ADDS AN EXTRA EXOTIC TOUCH.

SERVES FOUR

INGREDIENTS

1 large or 2 medium eggplants
1 pound young loofahs or
   sponge gourds
1 large red bell pepper, cut into
   large chunks
8 ounces cherry tomatoes
8 ounces shallots, peeled
2 teaspoons ground coriander
4 tablespoons olive oil
2 garlic cloves, finely chopped
a few cilantro leaves
salt and freshly ground black pepper

1 Cut the eggplants into thick chunks and sprinkle the pieces with salt. Set aside in a colander for about 45 minutes and then rinse well under cold running water and pat dry.

2 Preheat the oven to 425°F. Slice the loofahs into ¾-inch pieces. Place the eggplant, loofah and pepper pieces, together with the tomatoes and shallots in a roasting pan which is large enough to take all the vegetables in a single layer.

3 Sprinkle with the ground coriander and olive oil and then scatter the chopped garlic and cilantro leaves on top. Season to taste.

4 Roast for about 25 minutes, stirring the vegetables occasionally, until the loofah is golden brown and the peppers are beginning to char at the edges.

MAIN
COURSES

*Create healthy and satisfying meals that make
the most of a wonderful variety of herbs and
spices as well as nutritious ingredients such as
lentils, rice and every possible type of vegetable.*

ARABIAN SPINACH

*STIR-FRY SPINACH WITH ONIONS
AND SPICES, THEN MIX IN A CAN
OF CHICKPEAS, AND YOU HAVE A
DELICIOUS MAIN-COURSE FAMILY
MEAL IN NEXT TO NO TIME.*

SERVES FOUR

INGREDIENTS
1 onion, sliced
2 tablespoons olive or sunflower oil
2 garlic cloves, crushed
1 teaspoon cumin seeds
14 ounces spinach, washed and
  shredded
1 can (15 ounces) chickpeas, drained
pat of butter
salt and freshly ground black pepper

1 In a large frying pan or wok, fry the onion in the oil for about 5 minutes, until softened. Add the garlic and cumin seeds and fry for another minute.

2 Add the spinach in stages, stirring it until the leaves begin to wilt. Fresh spinach condenses dramatically on cooking, and it will all fit into the pan.

3 Stir in the chickpeas, butter and seasoning. Reheat until just bubbling, then serve hot. Drain off any pan juices, if you like, but this dish is very good served slightly wet.

VEGETABLE MEDLEY WITH LENTIL BOLOGNESE

*INSTEAD OF A WHITE OR CHEESE
SAUCE, IT MAKES A NICE CHANGE
TO TOP A SELECTION OF LIGHTLY
STEAMED VEGETABLES WITH A
HEALTHY AND DELICIOUS LENTIL
SAUCE.*

SERVES 6

INGREDIENTS
Lentil Bolognese Sauce (see Index)
1 small cauliflower, in florets
8 ounces broccoli florets
2 leeks, thickly sliced
8 ounces Brussels sprouts, halved if
  large

1 Make up the sauce and keep warm.

2 Place all the vegetables in a steamer over a pan of boiling water and cook for 8–10 minutes, until just tender.

3 Drain and place in a shallow serving dish. Spoon the sauce over the top, stirring slightly to mix. Serve hot.

FALAFELS

MADE WITH GROUND CHICKPEAS, HERBS AND SPICES, FALAFELS ARE A MIDDLE EASTERN STREET FOOD, NORMALLY SERVED TUCKED INTO WARM PITA BREADS WITH SPOONFULS OF SALAD. THEY ARE DELICIOUS SERVED WITH TAHINI CREAM OR DOLLOPS OF PLAIN YOGURT.

MAKES EIGHT

INGREDIENTS
    1 can (15 ounces) chickpeas, drained
    1 garlic clove, crushed
    2 tablespoons chopped fresh parsley
    2 tablespoons chopped fresh cilantro
    1 tablespoon chopped fresh mint
    1 teaspoon cumin seeds
    2 tablespoons fresh bread crumbs
    1 teaspoon salt
    freshly ground black pepper
    oil, for deep-frying

1 Grind the chickpeas in a food processor until they are just smooth, then mix them with all the other ingredients until you have a thick, creamy paste. Add pepper to taste.

2 Using wet hands, shape the chickpea mixture into 8 rounds and chill for 30 minutes so that they become firm.

3 Meanwhile, heat about ¼ inch of oil in a shallow frying pan and fry the falafels a few at a time. Cook each one for about 8 minutes, turning the falafels carefully just once.

4 Drain the falafels on paper towels and fry the rest in batches, reheating the oil in between. Serve tucked inside warm pita breads with salad, tomatoes and tahini or yogurt.

COOK'S TIP
Falafels can be made in batches and frozen. Let them cool, spread out on wire cooling racks. Open-freeze until solid, then place in a freezer-proof plastic container. To reheat, bake in a moderate oven for 10–15 minutes.

CARIBBEAN RICE AND PEAS

A GREAT FAMILY FAVORITE IN WEST INDIAN CULTURE, THIS DISH IS NOT ONLY TASTY, BUT NUTRITIONALLY WELL BALANCED.

SERVES FOUR

INGREDIENTS
    1¼ cups long grain rice
    ¾ cup dried pigeon peas or red kidney
        beans, soaked and cooked
    3⅔ cups water
    2 ounces creamed coconut, chopped
    1 teaspoon dried thyme or 1 tablespoon
        fresh thyme leaves
    1 small onion stuck with 6 whole
        cloves
    salt and ground black pepper

1 Put the rice and peas or kidney beans in a large saucepan with the water, coconut, thyme, onion and seasoning.

2 Bring to a boil, stirring until the coconut melts, then cover and simmer gently for 20 minutes.

3 Remove the lid and allow to cook uncovered for 5 minutes to reduce any excess liquid. Remove from the heat and stir occasionally to separate the grains. The rice should be quite dry.

GREEK STUFFED VEGETABLES

VEGETABLES SUCH AS BELL PEPPERS MAKE WONDERFUL CONTAINERS FOR SAVORY FILLINGS. THICK, CREAMY GREEK YOGURT IS THE IDEAL ACCOMPANIMENT.

SERVES THREE TO SIX

INGREDIENTS
1 medium eggplant
1 large green bell pepper
2 large tomatoes
1 large onion, chopped
2 garlic cloves, crushed
3 tablespoons olive oil
1 cup brown rice
2½ cups vegetable stock
¾ cup pine nuts
⅓ cup currants
salt and freshly ground black pepper
3 tablespoons chopped fresh dill
3 tablespoons chopped fresh parsley
1 tablespoon chopped fresh mint
extra olive oil, to sprinkle
plain yogurt, to serve
fresh sprigs of dill

1 Halve the eggplant, scoop out the flesh with a sharp knife and chop finely. Salt the insides and leave to drain upside down for 20 minutes while you prepare the other ingredients.

2 Halve the pepper, seed and core. Cut the tops from the tomatoes, scoop out the insides and chop coarsely along with the tomato tops.

3 Fry the onion, garlic and chopped eggplant in the oil for 10 minutes, then stir in the rice and cook for 2 minutes.

4 Add the tomatoes, stock, pine nuts, currants and seasoning. Bring to a boil, cover and simmer for 15 minutes, then stir in the fresh herbs.

5 Blanch the eggplant and green pepper halves in boiling water for about 3 minutes, then drain them upside down.

6 Spoon the rice filling into all six vegetable containers and place in a lightly greased shallow ovenproof dish.

7 Heat the oven to 375°F. Drizzle some olive oil over the vegetables and bake for 25–30 minutes. Serve hot, topped with spoonfuls of plain yogurt and dill sprigs.

RED ONION AND ZUCCHINI PIZZA

*IT'S EASY TO MAKE A HOMEMADE
PIZZA USING ONE OF THE NEW
FAST-ACTING YEASTS. YOU CAN
EITHER ADD THE TRADITIONAL
CHEESE AND TOMATO TOPPING OR
TRY SOMETHING DIFFERENT, SUCH
AS THE ONE DESCRIBED HERE.*

SERVES FOUR

INGREDIENTS

    3 cups all-purpose flour
    1 package fast-acting/easy-blend yeast
    2 teaspoons salt
    lukewarm water to mix
For the topping
    2 red onions, thinly sliced
    ¼ cup olive oil
    2 zucchini, thinly sliced
    salt and freshly ground black pepper
    fresh nutmeg, grated
    4 ounces semisoft goat cheese
    6 sun-dried tomatoes in oil, snipped
    dried oregano
    extra olive oil, to sprinkle

1 Preheat the oven to 400°F. Mix
the flour, yeast and salt together,
then mix to a firm dough with
warm water.

2 Knead the dough for about 5 minutes,
until it is smooth and elastic, then roll it
out to a large circle and place on a
lightly greased baking sheet. Set aside
somewhere warm to rise slightly while you
make the topping.

3 Gently fry the onions in half the oil for
5 minutes, then add the zucchini and fry
for another 2 minutes. Season and add
nutmeg to taste.

4 Spread the pizza base with fried
vegetable mixture and dot with the
cheese, tomatoes and oregano. Sprinkle
with the rest of the olive oil and bake for
12–15 minutes, until golden and crisp.

BEAN SPROUTS AND BOK CHOY

SUPERMARKETS ARE FAST BECOMING COSMOPOLITAN, AND MANY STOCK EXOTIC VEGETABLES.

SERVES FOUR

INGREDIENTS

3 tablespoons peanut oil
3 scallions, sliced
2 garlic cloves, cut into slivers
1-inch cube fresh ginger,
 cut into slivers
1 carrot, cut into thin sticks
⅔ cup bean sprouts
7 ounces bok choy, shredded
½ cup unsalted cashew nuts or
 halved almonds
For the sauce
3 tablespoons light soy sauce
2 tablespoons dry sherry
1 tablespoon sesame oil
⅔ cup cold water
1 teaspoon cornstarch
1 teaspoon honey
freshly ground black pepper

1 Heat the oil in a large wok and stir-fry the onions, garlic, ginger and carrot for 2 minutes. Add the bean sprouts and fry for another 2 minutes, stirring and tossing ingredients together.

2 Add the bok choy and nuts and stir-fry until the cabbage leaves are just wilting. Quickly mix all the sauce ingredients together in a bowl and pour them into the wok, stirring immediately.

3 The vegetables will be coated in a thin, glossy sauce. Season and serve as soon as possible.

THAI TOFU CURRY

THAI FOOD IS A MARVELOUS MIXTURE OF CHINESE AND INDIAN STYLES.

SERVES FOUR

INGREDIENTS

2 packages (7 ounces each) tofu, cubed
2 tablespoons light soy sauce
2 tablespoons peanut oil
For the paste
1 small onion, chopped
2 green chilies, seeded and chopped
2 garlic cloves, chopped
1 tablespoon grated fresh galangal or
 1 teaspoon grated fresh ginger
1 teaspoon grated lime rind
2 teaspoons coriander berries, crushed
2 teaspoons cumin seeds, crushed
3 tablespoons chopped fresh cilantro
juice of 1 lime or small lemon
1 teaspoon sugar
1 ounce creamed coconut dissolved in
 ⅔ cup boiling water
For the garnish
thin slices fresh red chili or red pepper
fresh cilantro leaves

1 Toss the tofu cubes in soy sauce and leave to marinate for 15 minutes or so while you prepare the paste.

2 Put all the paste ingredients in a food processor and grind until smooth.

3 To cook, heat the oil in a wok until quite hot. Drain the tofu cubes and stir-fry at a high temperature until well browned on all sides and just firm. Drain on paper towels.

4 Wipe the wok clean. Pour in the paste and stir well. Return the tofu to the wok and mix it into the paste, reheating the ingredients as you stir.

5 Serve this dish on a flat platter garnished with red chili or pepper and chopped cilantro. Bowls of Thai fragrant or jasmine rice are the perfect accompaniment to the curry.

FESTIVE JALOUSIE

AN EXCELLENT PIE TO SERVE DURING THE HOLIDAY PERIOD. USE CHINESE DRIED CHESTNUTS, SOAKED AND COOKED, INSTEAD OF FRESH ONES.

SERVES SIX

INGREDIENTS

    1 pound puff pastry, thawed if frozen
    1 pound Brussels sprouts, trimmed
    16 whole chestnuts, peeled if fresh
    1 large red bell pepper, sliced
    1 large onion, sliced
    3 tablespoons sunflower oil
    1 egg yolk, beaten with 1 tablespoon
      water
For the sauce
    scant ½ cup all-purpose flour
    3 tablespoons butter
    ½ pint milk
    3 ounces Cheddar cheese, grated
    2 tablespoons dry sherry
    generous pinch of dried sage
    salt and freshly ground black pepper
    3 tablespoons chopped fresh parsley

2 Blanch the Brussels sprouts for 4 minutes in 1 cup boiling water, then drain, reserving the water. Refresh the sprouts under cold running water.

3 Cut each chestnut in half. Lightly fry the red pepper and onion in the oil for 5 minutes. Set aside.

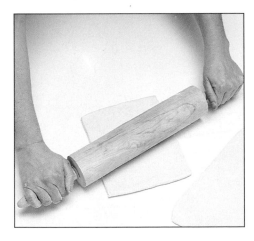

1 Roll out the pastry to make two large rectangles, roughly the size of your dish. The pastry should be about ¼ inch thick and one rectangle should be slightly larger than the other. Set the pastry aside in the refrigerator.

4 Make the sauce by beating the flour, butter and milk together over medium heat. Beat the sauce continuously, bringing it to a boil and stirring until it is thickened and smooth.

5 Stir in the reserved sprout water and the cheese, sherry, sage and seasoning. Simmer for 3 minutes to reduce and stir in the parsley.

6 Fit the larger piece of pastry into a pie dish and layer the Brussels sprouts, chestnuts, peppers and onions on top. Drizzle with the sauce, making sure it seeps through to wet the vegetables.

7 Brush the pastry edges with beaten egg yolk and fit the second pastry sheet on top, pressing the edges well to seal them.

8 Crimp the edges, then mark the center. Glaze well with egg yolk. Set aside to rest somewhere cool while you preheat the oven to 400°F. Bake for 30–40 minutes, until golden brown and crisp.

SHEPHERDESS PIE

A NO-MEAT VERSION OF THE TIMELESS CLASSIC, THIS DISH CONTAINS NO DAIRY PRODUCTS, SO IS SUITABLE FOR VEGANS.

SERVES SIX TO EIGHT

INGREDIENTS

2 pounds potatoes
3 tablespoons extra-virgin olive oil
salt and freshly ground black pepper
1 large onion, chopped
1 green bell pepper, chopped
2 carrots, coarsely grated
2 garlic cloves
3 tablespoons sunflower oil or
  margarine
4 ounces mushrooms, chopped
2 cans (14 ounces each) aduki beans
2½ cups vegetable stock
1 teaspoon vegetable yeast extract
2 bay leaves
1 teaspoon dried Italian herbs
dried bread crumbs or chopped nuts,
  to sprinkle

1 Boil the potatoes in their skins until tender, then drain, reserving a little of the water to moisten them.

2 Mash well, mixing in the olive oil and seasoning until you have a smooth purée.

3 Gently fry the onion, pepper, carrots and garlic in the sunflower oil or margarine for about 5 minutes, until they are soft. Preheat the broiler.

4 Stir in the mushrooms and drained beans and cook for another 2 minutes, then add the stock, yeast extract, bay leaves and mixed herbs. Simmer for 15 minutes.

5 Remove the bay leaves and empty the vegetables into a shallow ovenproof dish. Spoon on the potatoes in dollops and sprinkle with the bread crumbs or nuts. Broil until golden brown.

GREAT SQUASH

*At summer time, zucchini —
and summer squash — look so
attractive and tempting.
They make delicious and
inexpensive main courses, just
right for a satisfying family
Sunday lunch.*

SERVES FOUR TO SIX

INGREDIENTS

3 cups pasta shells
3–4 pounds zucchini or summer squash
1 onion, chopped
1 bell pepper, seeded and chopped
1 tablespoon grated fresh ginger
2 garlic cloves, crushed
3 tablespoons sunflower oil
4 large tomatoes, peeled and chopped
salt and freshly ground black pepper
½ cup pine nuts
1 tablespoon chopped fresh basil
grated, cheese, to serve (optional)

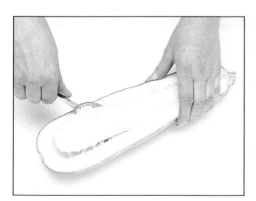

1 Preheat the oven to 375°F. Boil
the pasta according to the instructions
on the package, slightly overcooking
it so it is just a little soft. Drain and
reserve.

2 Cut the zucchini in half lengthwise and
scoop out the seeds. These can be
discarded. Use a small sharp knife and
tablespoon to scoop out the zucchini
flesh. Chop the flesh roughly.

3 Gently fry the onion, pepper, ginger
and garlic in the oil for 5 minutes.

4 Add the zucchini flesh, tomatoes and
seasoning. Cover and cook for 10–12
minutes, until the vegetables are soft. Add
to the pan the pasta, pine nuts and basil,
stir well and set aside.

5 Meanwhile, place the zucchini halves
in a roasting pan, season lightly and pour
a little water around the zucchini, taking
care it does not spill inside. Cover with foil
and bake for 15 minutes.

6 Remove the foil, discard the water and
fill the shells with the vegetable mixture.
Recover with foil and return to the oven
for another 20–25 minutes.

7 If you wish, serve this dish topped with
grated cheese. The zucchini can either be
served cut into sections or scooped out of
the "shell."

GREEK SPINACH PIES

*THESE LITTLE HORNS OF FILO
PASTRY ARE STUFFED WITH A
SIMPLE SPINACH AND FETA
CHEESE FILLING TO MAKE A
QUICK AND EASY MAIN COURSE.*

SERVES EIGHT

INGREDIENTS
    8 ounces fresh leaf spinach
    2 scallions, chopped
    6 ounces feta cheese, crumbled
    1 egg, beaten
    1 tablespoon fresh dill, chopped
    freshly ground black pepper
    4 large sheets or 8 small sheets of filo
        pastry
    olive oil, for brushing

1 Preheat the oven to 375°F. Blanch the spinach in the tiniest amount of water until just wilted, then drain very well, pressing it against a colander with the back of a wooden spoon.

2 Chop the spinach finely and mix with the onions, feta, egg, dill and ground black pepper.

3 Lay out a sheet of filo pastry and brush with olive oil. If large, cut the pieces in two and sandwich them together. If small, fit another sheet on top and brush with olive oil.

4 Spread a quarter of the filling on the bottom edge of the filo. Roll up. Shape into a crescent and place on a baking sheet. Repeat with remaining filo and filling.

5 Brush the pastry well with oil and bake for 20–25 minutes in the preheated oven, until golden and crisp. Cool slightly, then remove to a wire rack to cool further.

CHUNKY VEGETABLE PAELLA

*THIS SPANISH RICE DISH HAS
BECOME A FAMILY FAVORITE.*

SERVES SIX

INGREDIENTS
    generous pinch saffron strands
    1 eggplant, cut into thick chunks
    salt
    6 tablespoons olive oil
    1 large onion, sliced
    3 garlic cloves, crushed
    1 yellow bell pepper, sliced
    1 red bell pepper, sliced
    2 teaspoons paprika
    1¼ cups Arborio rice
    2½ cups vegetable stock
    1 pound fresh tomatoes, peeled
        and chopped
    ground black pepper
    ½ cup sliced mushrooms
    ½ cup cut green beans
    1 can (14 ounces) chickpeas

1 Steep the saffron in 3 tablespoons hot water. Sprinkle the eggplant with salt, leave to drain in a colander for 30 minutes, then rinse and dry.

2 In a large paella or frying pan, heat the oil and fry the onion, garlic, peppers and eggplant for about 5 minutes, stirring occasionally. Sprinkle in the paprika and stir again.

3 Mix in the rice, then pour in the stock, tomatoes, saffron and seasoning. Bring to a boil, then simmer for 15 minutes, uncovered, shaking the pan frequently and stirring occasionally.

4 Stir in the mushrooms, green beans and chickpeas (with their liquid). Continue cooking for another 10 minutes, then serve hot from the pan.

GREEN LENTIL KULBYAKA

This traditional Russian fish dish can be adapted to make a light, crisp vegetarian centerpiece.

SERVES SIX

INGREDIENTS
  1 cup green lentils
  2 bay leaves
  2 onions, sliced
  5 cups vegetable stock
  ¾ cup butter, melted
  1¼ cups Basmati or other long-grain rice
  salt and freshly ground black pepper
  4 tablespoons chopped fresh parsley
  2 tablespoons chopped fresh dill
  1 egg, beaten
  1 cup sliced mushrooms
  about 8 sheets filo pastry
  3 eggs, hard-cooked and sliced

1 Soak the lentils for 30 minutes, drain them, then simmer with the bay leaves, one onion and half the stock for 25 minutes, until cooked and thick. Season well, cool and set aside.

2 Gently fry the remaining onion in another saucepan with 2 tablespoons of the butter for 5 minutes. Stir in the rice, then the rest of the stock.

3 Season, bring to a boil, then cover and cook gently for 12 minutes (for basmati) or 15 minutes (for long-grain). Let stand, uncovered, for 5 minutes, then stir in the fresh herbs. Cool, then beat in the egg.

4 Fry the mushrooms in 3 tablespoons of the butter for 5 minutes, until they are just soft. Cool and set aside.

5 Brush the inside of a large, shallow ovenproof dish with more butter. Lay the sheets of filo inside, covering the base and making sure most of the pastry overhangs the sides. Brush well with butter in between and overlap the pastry as required. Make sure there is a lot of pastry to fold over the mounded filling.

6 In the pastry lining, layer rice, lentils and mushrooms, repeating the layers at least once and tucking the sliced egg in between. Season as you layer and form an even mound of filling.

7 Bring up the sheets of pastry over the filling, scrunching the top into attractive folds. Brush all over with the rest of the butter and set aside to chill and firm up.

8 Preheat the oven to 375°F. When ready, bake the kulbyaka for about 45 minutes, until golden and crisp. Allow to stand for 10 minutes before you cut it and serve.

TURNIP AND CHICKPEA COBBLER

A GOOD MIDWEEK MEAL.

SERVES FOUR TO SIX

INGREDIENTS

    1 onion, sliced
    2 carrots, chopped
    3 medium size turnips, chopped
    1 small sweet potato or rutabaga, chopped
    2 celery stalks, sliced thinly
    3 tablespoons sunflower oil
    ½ teaspoon ground coriander
    ½ teaspoon dried Italian herbs
    1 can (14 ounces) tomatoes, chopped
    1 can (14 ounces) chickpeas
    1 vegetable bouillon cube
    salt and freshly ground black pepper
For the topping
    2 cups self-rising flour
    1 teaspoon baking powder
    4 tablespoons margarine
    3 tablespoons sunflower seeds
    2 tablespoons grated Parmesan cheese
    ⅔ cup milk

1 Fry all the vegetables in the oil for about 10 minutes, until they are soft. Add the coriander, herbs, tomatoes, chickpeas with their liquid and bouillon cube. Season well and simmer for 20 minutes.

2 Pour the vegetables into a shallow casserole dish while you make the topping. Preheat the oven to 375°F.

3 Mix together the flour and baking powder, then rub in the margarine until the mixture resembles fine crumbs. Stir in the seeds and Parmesan cheese. Add the milk and mix to a firm dough.

4 Lightly roll out the dough to a thickness of ½ inch and stamp out star shapes or circles, or simply cut it into small squares.

5 Place the shapes on top of the vegetable mixture and brush with a little extra milk. Bake for 12–15 minutes, until risen and golden brown. Serve hot with green, leafy vegetables.

TANGY FRICASSEE

VEGETABLES IN A LIGHT, TANGY
SAUCE COVERED WITH A CRISPY
CRUMB TOPPING MAKE A SIMPLE
AND EASY MAIN COURSE TO
SERVE WITH CRUSTY BREAD
AND SALAD.

SERVES FOUR

INGREDIENTS
4 zucchini, sliced
4 ounces green beans, sliced
4 large tomatoes, peeled and sliced
1 onion, sliced
4 tablespoons butter or sunflower
  margarine
⅓ cup all-purpose flour
2 teaspoons coarse-grained mustard
2 cups milk
⅔ cup plain yogurt
1 teaspoon dried thyme
4 ounces aged cheese, grated
salt and freshly ground black pepper
¼ cup fresh whole-wheat bread crumbs
  tossed with
1 tablespoon sunflower oil

1 Blanch the zucchini and beans in a small amount of boiling water for just 5 minutes, then drain and arrange in a shallow ovenproof dish. Arrange all but three slices of tomato on top. Put the onion in a saucepan with the butter or margarine and fry gently for 5 minutes.

2 Stir in the flour and mustard, cook for a minute, then add the milk gradually until the sauce has thickened. Simmer for another 2 minutes.

3 Remove the pan from the heat and add the yogurt, thyme and cheese, stirring until melted. Season to taste. Reheat gently if you wish, but do not allow the sauce to boil or it will curdle.

4 Pour the sauce over the vegetables and scatter the bread crumbs on top. Brown under a preheated broiler until golden and crisp, taking care not to let the bread crumbs burn. Garnish with the reserved tomato slices if desired.

CHILI CON QUESO

THIS CLASSIC MEXICAN DISH IS JUST AS TASTY WHEN MADE WITH ALL-RED BEANS. FOR AN EXTRA GOOD FLAVOR, USE SMALL CUBES OF SMOKED CHEESE, AND SERVE WITH RICE.

SERVES FOUR

INGREDIENTS
    2 cups red kidney beans, soaked
      and drained
    3 tablespoons sunflower oil
    1 onion, chopped
    1 red bell pepper, chopped
    2 garlic cloves, crushed
    1 fresh red chili, chopped (optional)
    1 tablespoon chili powder (mild or hot)
    1 teaspoon ground cumin
    4 cups vegetable stock or water
    1 teaspoon crushed dried epazote
      leaves (optional)
    freshly ground black pepper and salt
    1 tablespoon granulated sugar
    4 ounces cheese, cubed, to serve

1 Rinse the beans. In a large saucepan, heat the oil and fry the onion, pepper, garlic and fresh chili for about 5 minutes.

2 Stir in the spices and cook for another minute, then add the beans, stock or water, epazote (if using) and a grinding of pepper. Don't add salt at this stage. Boil for 10 minutes, cover and turn down to a gentle simmer. Cook for about 50 minutes, checking the water level and adding more if necessary.

3 When the beans are tender, season them well with salt. Remove about a quarter of the mixture and mash to a pulp.

4 Return the purée to the pan and stir well. Add sugar and serve hot with the cheese sprinkled on top. Great with plain boiled long-grain rice.

COOK'S TIP
Epazote is a traditional Mexican herb, found in specialty stores.

BIG BARLEY BOWL

BARLEY SEEMS TO HAVE FALLEN OUT OF FASHION IN RECENT YEARS — A PITY, AS IT HAS A DELICIOUS, NUTTY TEXTURE.

SERVES SIX

INGREDIENTS
    1 red onion, sliced
    ½ fennel bulb, sliced
    2 carrots, cut into sticks
    1 parsnip, sliced
    3 tablespoons sunflower oil
    1 cup pearl barley
    4 cups vegetable stock
    1 teaspoon dried thyme
    chopped fresh parsley, to garnish
    salt and freshly ground black pepper
    ⅔ cup sliced green beans
    1 can (14 ounces) pinto beans
For the croutons
    1 medium-size baguette, sliced
    olive oil, for brushing
    1 garlic clove, cut in half
    4 tablespoons grated Parmesan cheese

1 In a large heatproof casserole, sauté the onion, fennel, carrots and parsnip gently in the oil for 10 minutes.

2 Stir in the barley and stock. Bring to a boil, add the herbs and seasoning, then cover and simmer gently for 40 minutes.

3 Stir in the green beans and drained pinto beans and continue cooking, covered, for another 20 minutes.

4 Meanwhile, preheat the oven to 375°F. Brush the baguette slices with olive oil and place them on a baking sheet.

5 Bake for about 15 minutes, until light golden and crisp. Remove from the oven and quickly rub each crouton with the garlic halves. Sprinkle with the cheese and return to the oven to melt.

6 Ladle the barley into warm bowls and serve sprinkled with parsley, accompanied by the cheese croutons. This dish is best eaten with a spoon.

VEGETABLES JULIENNE WITH A RED PEPPER COULIS

JUST THE RIGHT COURSE FOR THOSE WATCHING THEIR WEIGHT. CHOOSE A SELECTION OF AS MANY VEGETABLES AS YOU FEEL YOU CAN EAT.

SERVES TWO

INGREDIENTS

A selection of vegetables (choose from: carrots, turnips, asparagus, parsnips, zucchini, green beans, broccoli, salsify, cauliflower, snow peas)

For the red pepper coulis
1 small onion, chopped
1 garlic clove, crushed
1 tablespoon sunflower oil
1 tablespoon water
3 red bell peppers, roasted and skinned
8 tablespoons fromage blanc
squeeze of fresh lemon juice
salt and freshly ground black pepper
sprigs of fresh rosemary and thyme
2 bay leaves
fresh green herbs, to garnish

1 Prepare the vegetables by cutting them into thin fingers or small, bite-size pieces.

2 Make the coulis. Lightly sauté the onion and garlic in the oil and water for 3 minutes, then add the peppers and cook for another 2 minutes.

3 Purée the coulis in a food processor, then work in the fromage blanc, lemon juice and seasoning.

4 Boil some salted water with the fresh rosemary, thyme and bay leaves, and fit a steamer over the top.

5 Arrange the prepared vegetables on the steamer, placing the harder root vegetables at the bottom and steaming these for about 3 minutes.

6 Add the other vegetables according to their natural tenderness and cook for another 2–4 minutes.

7 Serve the vegetables on plates with the sauce to one side. Garnish with fresh green herbs, if you wish.

VARIATION
The red pepper coulis makes a wonderful sauce for many other dishes. Try it spooned over fresh pasta with lightly steamed or fried zucchini, or use it as a pouring sauce for savory filled crêpes.

PISTACHIO PILAF IN A SPINACH CROWN

SAFFRON AND GINGER ARE DELICIOUS WHEN MIXED WITH FRESH PISTACHIOS. THIS IS A GOOD LIGHT MAIN COURSE.

SERVES FOUR

INGREDIENTS
   3 onions
   ¼ cup olive oil
   2 garlic cloves, crushed
   1 tablespoon grated fresh ginger
   1 fresh green chili, chopped
   2 carrots, coarsely grated
   1¼ cups basmati rice
   ¼ teaspoon saffron strands, crushed
   2 cups vegetable stock
   1 cinnamon stick
   1 teaspoon ground coriander
   salt and ground black pepper
   ¼ cup fresh pistachio nuts
   1 pound fresh leaf spinach
   1 teaspoon garam masala

1 Coarsely chop two of the onions. Heat half the oil in a large saucepan and fry the onion with half the garlic, the grated ginger and the chili for 5 minutes.

2 Mix in the carrots and rinsed rice, cook for 1 more minute and then add the saffron, stock, cinnamon and coriander. Season well. Bring to a boil, then cover and simmer gently for 10 minutes, without lifting the lid.

3 Remove from the heat and let stand, uncovered, for 5 minutes. Add the pistachio nuts, mixing them in with a fork. Remove the cinnamon stick and keep the rice warm.

4 Thinly slice the third onion and fry in the remaining oil for about 3 minutes. Stir in the spinach. Cover and cook for another 2 minutes.

5 Add the garam masala. Cook until just tender, then drain and roughly chop the spinach.

6 Spoon the spinach around the edge of a round serving dish and pile the pilaf in the center. Serve hot, accompanied by a simple tomato salad.

SPINACH BREAD <u>AND</u> BUTTER CASSEROLE

IDEALLY USE CIABATTA BREAD FOR THIS, OR IF UNAVAILABLE, A FRENCH-STYLE BAGUETTE.

<u>SERVES FOUR TO SIX</u>

INGREDIENTS
1 pound fresh leaf spinach
1 ciabatta loaf, thinly sliced
4 tablespoons softened butter, olive oil or margarine
1 red onion, thinly sliced
4 ounces mushrooms, thinly sliced
2 tablespoons olive oil
1 teaspoon cumin seeds
salt and ground black pepper
4 ounces Gruyère cheese, grated
3 eggs
2¼ cups milk
grated fresh nutmeg

1 Rinse the spinach well and blanch it in the tiniest amount of water for 2 minutes. Drain well, pressing out any excess water, and chop roughly.

2 Spread the bread slices thinly with the butter or margarine. Grease a large shallow ovenproof dish and line the bottom and sides with bread.

3 Fry the onion and mushrooms lightly in the oil for 5 minutes, then add the cumin seeds and spinach. Season well.

4 Layer the spinach mixture with the remaining bread and half the cheese. For the top, mix everything together and sprinkle the remaining cheese on top.

5 Beat the eggs with the milk, adding seasoning and nutmeg to taste. Pour slowly over the whole dish and set aside for at least an hour to let the custard be absorbed into the bread.

6 Preheat the oven to 375°F. Stand the dish in a roasting pan and pour boiling water around it for a bain marie. Bake for 40–45 minutes, until risen, golden brown and crispy on top.

CURRIED PARSNIP PIE

SWEET, CREAMY PARSNIPS ARE BEAUTIFULLY COMPLEMENTED BY THE CURRY SPICES AND CHEESE.

SERVES FOUR

INGREDIENTS
For the pastry
    8 tablespoons butter or margarine
    1 cup all-purpose flour
    salt and freshly ground black pepper
    1 teaspoon dried thyme or oregano
    cold water, to mix
For the filling
    8 baby onions or shallots, peeled
    2 large parsnips, thinly sliced
    2 carrots, thinly sliced
    2 tablespoons butter or margarine
    2 tablespoons whole-wheat flour
    1 tablespoon mild curry or tikka paste
    1¼ cups milk
    4 ounces aged cheese, grated
    salt and freshly ground black pepper
    3 tablespoons fresh cilantro or parsley
    1 egg yolk, beaten with
    2 teaspoons water

2 Blanch the baby onions or shallots with the parsnips and carrots in just enough water to cover for about 5 minutes. Drain, reserving about 1¼ cups of the liquid.

3 In a clean pan, melt the butter or margarine and stir in the flour and spice paste to make a roux. Gradually whisk in the reserved stock and milk until smooth. Simmer for a minute or two.

1 Make the pastry by rubbing the butter or margarine into the flour until it resembles fine bread crumbs. Season and stir in the thyme or oregano, then mix to a firm dough with cold water.

4 Take the pan off the heat, stir in the cheese and seasoning, then mix in the chopped cilantro or parsley.

COOK'S TIP
This pie freezes well and makes a good standby for a midweek meal. For best results, make up to the final stage and freeze unbaked. Open freeze until solid, then wrap well in plastic wrap, seal and label. Use within one month.
    Cauliflower, broccoli or any other favorite vegetable can be added to the filling to give a variety of flavours and textures.

5 Pour into a pie dish, put a pie funnel in the center and allow to cool.

6 Roll out the pastry large enough to fit the top of the pie dish. Re-roll the trimmings into long strips.

7 Brush the pastry edges with egg yolk wash and fit on the pastry strips. Brush again with egg yolk wash.

8 Using a rolling pin, lift the rolled-out pastry over the pie top and fit over the funnel, pressing it down well onto the strips underneath.

9 Cut off the overhanging pastry and crimp the edges. Cut a hole for the funnel, brush well all over with the remaining egg yolk wash and make decorations with the trimmings, glazing them too.

10 Place the pie dish on a baking sheet and chill for 30 minutes while you preheat the oven to 400°F. Bake the pie for 25–30 minutes, until golden brown and crisp on top.

VEGETABLES UNDER A LIGHT CREAMY CRUST

THE SUBTLE FLAVORS OF LEEKS,
ZUCCHINI AND MUSHROOMS ARE
TOPPED BY RICOTTA, CHEESE AND
BREAD CRUMBS.

SERVES FOUR

INGREDIENTS
  2 leeks, thinly sliced
  3 zucchini, thickly sliced
  1½ cups sliced mushrooms
  2 garlic cloves, crushed
  2 tablespoons olive oil
  2 tablespoons butter
  1 tablespoon all-purpose flour
  1¼ cups vegetable stock
  1 teaspoon dried thyme
  salt and freshly ground black pepper
  2 tablespoons fromage blanc
For the topping
  1 pound fromage blanc
  2 tablespoons butter, melted
  3 eggs, beaten
  salt and freshly ground black pepper
  fresh nutmeg, grated
  freshly grated cheese and dried bread
    crumbs, to sprinkle

1 Preheat the oven to 375°F. In a saucepan, gently fry the leeks, zucchini, mushrooms and garlic in the oil and butter for about 7 minutes, stirring occasionally, until the vegetables are just soft.

2 Stir in the flour, then gradually mix in the stock. Bring to a boil, stirring until thickened. Add the thyme and seasoning. Take the pan off the heat and stir in the fromage blanc. Pour the vegetable mixture into a shallow ovenproof dish.

3 Beat the topping ingredients together, seasoning them well and adding the nutmeg to taste. Spoon on top of the vegetables and sprinkle with cheese and bread crumbs.

4 Bake for about 30 minutes, until a light golden, firm crust forms. Serve hot with pasta or crusty bread.

POTATO AND PARSNIP AMANDINE

SHELLS OF BAKED POTATOES,
FILLED WITH A PARSNIP
AND ALMOND MIX, MAKE
AN UNUSUAL ALTERNATIVE TO
PLAIN POTATOES.

SERVES FOUR

INGREDIENTS
  4 large baking potatoes
  olive oil, for greasing
  8 ounces parsnips, diced
  2 tablespoons butter
  1 teaspoon cumin seeds
  1 teaspoon ground coriander
  2 tablespoons light cream,
    half-and-half or plain yogurt
  salt and freshly ground black pepper
  4 ounces Gruyère or Cheddar cheese,
    grated
  1 egg, beaten
  ¼ cup flaked almonds

1 Rub the potatoes all over with oil, score in half, then bake at 400°F for about 1 hour, until cooked.

2 Meanwhile, boil the parsnips until tender, then drain well, mash and mix with the butter, spices and cream or plain yogurt.

3 When the potatoes are cooked, halve, scoop out and mash the flesh, then mix with the parsnip, seasoning well.

4 Stir in the cheese, egg and three-quarters of the almonds. Fill the potato shells with the mixture and sprinkle with the remaining almonds.

5 Return to the oven and bake for about 15–20 minutes, until golden brown and the filling has set lightly. Serve hot with a salad on the side.

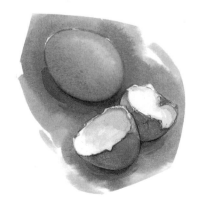

AUTUMN GLORY

*PUMPKIN AND PASTA MAKE
MARVELOUS PARTNERS, ESPECIALLY
AS A MAIN COURSE SERVED FROM
THE BAKED SHELL.*

SERVES FOUR

INGREDIENTS
1 pumpkin, about 4 pounds
1 onion, sliced
1-inch cube fresh ginger
3 tablespoons extra-virgin olive oil
1 zucchini, sliced
4 ounces sliced mushrooms
1 can (14 ounces) tomatoes, chopped
1 cup pasta shells
2 cups vegetable stock
salt and freshly ground black pepper
¼ cup fromage blanc
2 tablespoons chopped fresh basil

1 Preheat the oven to 350°F. Cut the top off the pumpkin with a large, sharp knife and scoop out and discard the seeds.

2 Using a small sharp knife and a sturdy tablespoon, extract as much of the pumpkin flesh as possible, then chop it into chunks.

3 Bake the pumpkin shell with its lid on for 45 minutes to one hour, until the inside begins to soften.

4 Meanwhile, make the filling. Gently fry the onion, ginger and pumpkin flesh in the olive oil for about 10 minutes, stirring occasionally.

5 Add the zucchini and mushrooms and cook for another 3 minutes, then stir in the tomatoes, pasta shells and stock. Season well, bring to a boil, then cover and simmer gently for 10 minutes.

6 Stir the fromage blanc and basil into the pasta and spoon the mixture into the pumpkin. (It may not be possible to fit all the filling into the pumpkin shell; serve the rest separately if this is the case.)

FESTIVE LENTIL AND NUT ROAST

SERVE WITH VEGETARIAN GRAVY,
CRANBERRIES AND FRENCH
PARSLEY.

SERVES SIX TO EIGHT

INGREDIENTS
⅔ cup red lentils
1 cup hazelnuts
1 cup walnuts
1 large carrot
2 celery stalks
1 large onion, sliced
4 ounces mushrooms
¼ cup butter
2 teaspoons mild curry powder
2 tablespoons ketchup
2 tablespoons Worcestershire sauce
1 egg, beaten
2 teaspoons salt
4 tablespoons chopped fresh parsley
⅔ cup water

1 Soak the lentils for 1 hour in cold water, then drain well. Grind the nuts in a food processor until very fine but not too smooth. Set the nuts aside.

2 Chop the carrot, celery, onion and mushrooms into small chunks, then process them in a food processor or blender until they are finely chopped.

3 Fry the vegetables gently in the butter for 5 minutes, then stir in the curry powder and cook for a minute. Cool.

4 Mix the lentils with the nuts, vegetables and remaining ingredients.

5 Grease and line the bottom and sides of a long 2-pound loaf pan with waxed paper or a sheet of foil. Press the mixture into the pan. Preheat the oven to 375°F.

6 Bake for 1–1¼ hours, until just firm, covering the top with a buttered piece of waxed paper or foil if it starts to burn. Let the mixture stand for about 15 minutes before you turn it out and peel off the paper. It will be fairly soft when cut, as it is a moist loaf.

VEGETARIAN GRAVY

MAKE UP A LARGE BATCH AND
FREEZE IT IN SMALL CONTAINERS
READY TO REHEAT AND SERVE.

MAKES ABOUT 1 QUART

INGREDIENTS
1 large red onion, sliced
3 turnips, sliced
3 celery stalks, sliced
4 ounces white mushrooms, halved
2 whole garlic cloves
6 tablespoons sunflower oil
6 cups vegetable stock or water
3 tablespoons soy sauce
generous pinch of granulated sugar
salt and freshly ground black pepper

1 Cook the vegetables and garlic with the oil in a large saucepan over medium high heat, stirring occasionally, until nicely browned but not singed. This should take 15-20 minutes.

2 Add the stock or water and soy sauce, bring to a boil, then cover and simmer for another 20 minutes.

3 Purée the vegetables, adding a little of the stock, and return them to the pan by rubbing the pulp through a sieve with the back of a ladle or wooden spoon.

4 Taste for seasoning and add the sugar. Freeze at least half of the gravy to use later and reheat the rest to serve with rice and peas or the lentil and nut roast.

HOMEMADE RAVIOLI

IT IS A PLEASURE TO MAKE YOUR OWN FRESH PASTA, AND YOU WILL BE SURPRISED AT HOW EASY IT IS TO FILL AND SHAPE RAVIOLI. ALLOW A LITTLE MORE TIME THAN YOU WOULD FOR READY-MADE OR DRIED PASTA.

SERVES SIX

INGREDIENTS
   1½ cups all-purpose flour
   ½ teaspoon salt
   1 tablespoon olive oil
   2 eggs, beaten
For the filling
   1 small red onion, finely chopped
   1 small green bell pepper, seeded and
      finely chopped
   1 carrot, coarsely grated
   1 tablespoon olive oil
   ½ cup walnuts, chopped
   ½ cup ricotta cheese
   2 tablespoons grated fresh Parmesan or
      Pecorino cheese
   1 tablespoon fresh marjoram or basil
   salt and freshly ground black pepper
   extra oil or melted butter, to serve

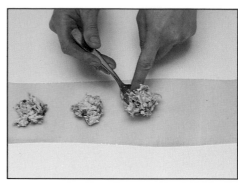

3 If you are using a pasta machine, break off small balls of dough and feed them through the rollers several times, according to the manufacturer's instructions.

4 If rolling the pasta by hand, divide the dough in two and roll out on a lightly floured surface to a thickness of about ¼ inch.

5 Fold the pasta in thirds and re-roll. Repeat up to six times, until the dough is smooth and no longer sticky. Roll the pasta slightly more thinly each time.

6 Keep the rolled dough under clean, dry dish towels while you complete the rest and make the filling. You should aim to have an even number of pasta sheets, all the same size if rolling by machine.

7 Fry the onion, pepper and carrot in the oil for 5 minutes, then allow to cool. Mix with the walnuts, cheeses, chopped herbs and seasoning.

8 Lay out a pasta sheet and place small scoops of the filling in neat rows about 2 inches apart. Brush in between with a little water and then place another pasta sheet on the top.

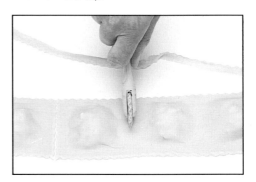

9 Press down well in between the rows, then, using a ravioli or pastry cutter, cut into squares. If the edges pop open occasionally, press them back gently with your fingers.

1 Sift the flour and salt into a food processor. With the machine running, trickle in the oil and eggs and blend to a stiff but smooth dough.

2 Allow the machine to run for at least a minute if possible, otherwise remove the dough and knead it by hand for 5 minutes.

COOK'S TIP
A food processor will save you time and effort in making and kneading the dough. A pasta-rolling machine helps with the rolling out, but both these jobs can be done by hand if necessary.

10 Leave the ravioli to dry in the refrigerator, then boil in plenty of lightly salted water for just 5 minutes.

11 Toss the cooked ravioli in a little oil or melted butter before serving with either homemade tomato sauce or extra cheese.

MUSHROOM PUFF PASTIES

*IF POSSIBLE, USE FULL-
FLAVORED CRIMINI
MUSHROOMS.*

<u>MAKES EIGHT</u>

INGREDIENTS
    2 blocks (8 ounces each) frozen puff
      pastry
    1 egg, beaten
For the filling
    1 onion, chopped
    1 carrot, coarsely grated
    1 medium potato, coarsely grated
    3 tablespoons sunflower oil
    1 cup sliced mushrooms
    2 tablespoons soy sauce
    1 tablespoon ketchup
    1 tablespoon dry sherry (optional)
    generous pinch of dried thyme
    salt and freshly ground black pepper

1 Roll out the thawed pastry blocks until they are ¼ inch thick and cut each block into four 6-inch squares. Reserve a little pastry for decoration. Cover the rolled pastry squares and trimmings and set aside in a cool place.

2 To make the filling, gently fry the onion, carrot and potato in the oil for 5 minutes, then add the mushrooms, soy sauce, ketchup, sherry (if using), thyme and seasoning.

3 Cook, stirring occasionally, until the mushrooms and vegetables have softened and feel quite tender. Cool.

4 Divide the filling between the eight squares, placing it to one side across the diagonal. Brush the pastry edges with egg, then fold over into triangles and press well to seal. From the pastry scraps, cut out little shapes, such as mushrooms, to decorate the pasties.

5 Crimp each pastie edge and top with the cut out shapes. Set on two baking sheets. Preheat the oven to 400°F and in the meantime, let the pasties rest somewhere cool.

6 Glaze the pasties with beaten egg, then bake for 15–20 minutes, until golden brown and crisp.

WINTER CASSEROLE <u>WITH</u> HERB DUMPLINGS

*WHEN THE COLD WEATHER
ARRIVES, GATHER A GOOD
SELECTION OF VEGETABLES AND
MAKE THIS COMFORTING
CASSEROLE WITH SOME HEARTY
OLD-FASHIONED DUMPLINGS.*

<u>SERVES SIX</u>

INGREDIENTS
    2 potatoes
    2 carrots
    1 small fennel bulb
    1 small rutabaga
    2 leeks
    2 zucchini
    ¼ cup butter or margarine
    2 tablespoons all-purpose flour
    1 can (15 ounces) lima beans, with
      liquid
    2½ cups vegetable stock
    2 tablespoons tomato paste
    1 cinnamon stick
    2 teaspoons ground coriander
    ½ teaspoon ground ginger
    2 bay leaves
    salt and freshly ground black pepper
For the dumplings
    1½ cups all-purpose flour
    4 ounces vegetarian suet, shredded, or
      chilled butter, grated
    1 teaspoon dried thyme
    1 teaspoon salt
    ½ cup milk

1 Cut all the vegetables into even,
bite-size chunks, then fry gently in the
butter or margarine for about 10 minutes.

2 Stir in the flour, then the liquid from
the beans, the stock, tomato paste,
spices, bay leaves and seasoning. Bring to
a boil, stirring.

3 Cover and simmer for 10 minutes, then
add the beans and cook for another
5 minutes.

4 Meanwhile, to make the dumplings,
simply mix the flour, suet or butter, thyme
and salt into a firm but moist dough with
the milk and knead with your hands until
it is smooth.

5 Divide the dough into 12 pieces, rolling
each one into a ball with your fingers.
Uncover the simmering stew and then
add the dumplings, allowing space
between each one for expansion.

6 Replace the lid and cook at a gentle
simmer for another 15 minutes. Do not
peek – or you will let out all the steam.
Nor should you cook dumplings too fast,
or they will break up. Remove the
cinnamon stick and bay leaves before you
serve this dish, steaming hot.

LASAGNE ROLLS

*PERHAPS A MORE ELEGANT
PRESENTATION THAN ORDINARY
LASAGNE, BUT JUST AS TASTY AND
POPULAR. YOU WILL NEED TO
BOIL FRESH LASAGNE, AS IT NEEDS
TO BE SOFT ENOUGH TO ROLL.*

SERVES FOUR

INGREDIENTS
    8–10 lasagne sheets
    Lentil Bolognese Sauce (see below)
    8 ounces fresh leaf spinach
    ½ cup sliced mushrooms
    4 ounces mozzarella cheese, thinly
      sliced
For the béchamel sauce
    scant ½ cup all-purpose flour
    3 tablespoons butter or margarine
    2½ cups milk
    bay leaf
    salt and freshly ground black pepper
    fresh nutmeg, grated
    freshly grated Parmesan or Pecorino
      cheese, to serve

1 Cook the lasagne sheets according to the instructions on the package, or for about 10 minutes. Drain and allow to cool.

2 Cook the spinach in the tiniest amount of water for 2 minutes, then add the sliced mushrooms and cook for another 2 minutes. Drain very well, pressing out all the excess liquid, and chop roughly.

3 Put all the béchamel ingredients in a saucepan and bring slowly to a boil, stirring continuously until the sauce is thick and smooth. Simmer for 2 minutes with the bay leaf, then season well and stir in grated nutmeg to taste.

4 Lay out the pasta sheets and spread with the bolognese, spinach and mushrooms and mozzarella. Roll up each one and place in a large shallow casserole dish with the join face down.

5 Remove and discard the bay leaf and then pour the sauce over the pasta. Sprinkle with the cheese and place under a hot broiler to brown.

LENTIL BOLOGNESE SAUCE

*THIS IS A VERY USEFUL SAUCE TO
SERVE WITH PASTA, AS A CRÊPE
STUFFING OR EVEN AS A PROTEIN-
PACKED SAUCE FOR VEGETABLES.*

SERVES SIX

INGREDIENTS
    1 onion, chopped
    2 garlic cloves, crushed
    2 carrots, coarsely grated
    2 celery stalks, chopped
    3 tablespoons olive oil
    ⅔ cup red lentils
    1 can (14 ounces) tomatoes, chopped
    2 tablespoons tomato paste
    2 cups vegetable stock
    1 tablespoon chopped fresh marjoram
      or 1 teaspoon dried marjoram
    salt and freshly ground black pepper

1 In a large saucepan, gently fry the onion, garlic, carrots and celery in the oil for about 5 minutes, until they are soft.

2 Add the lentils, tomatoes, tomato paste, stock, marjoram and seasoning.

3 Bring the mixture to a boil, then partially cover with a lid and simmer for 20 minutes, until thick and soft. Use the bolognese as required.

ARTICHOKE AND LEEK CRÊPES

*THIN CRÊPES WITH A MOUTH-
WATERING SOUFFLÉ MIXTURE OF
ARTICHOKES AND LEEKS.*

SERVES FOUR

INGREDIENTS
   1 cup all-purpose flour
   pinch of salt
   1 egg
   1¼ cup milk
   oil, for brushing
For the soufflé filling
   1 pound Jerusalem artichokes
   1 large leek, thinly sliced
   ¼ cup butter
   2 tablespoons self-rising flour
   2 tablespoons light cream or half-and-half
   3 ounces aged Cheddar cheese, grated
   2 tablespoons chopped fresh parsley
   fresh nutmeg, grated
   2 eggs, separated
   salt and freshly ground black pepper

1 Make the crêpe batter by blending the flour, salt, egg and milk to a smooth batter in a food processor or blender.

2 In a crêpe or omelet pan with a diameter of about 8 inches, make a batch of thin crêpes. You will need about 2 tablespoons of batter for each one.

3 Stack the crêpes under a clean dish-towel as you make them. Reserve eight for this dish and freeze the rest.

4 Cook the artichokes and leek with the butter in a covered saucepan over low heat for about 12 minutes, until very soft. Mash with the back of a wooden spoon. Season well.

5 Stir the flour into the vegetables and cook for 1 minute. Take the pan off the heat and beat in the cream, grated cheese, parsley and nutmeg to taste. Cool, then add the egg yolks.

6 Whisk the egg whites until they form soft peaks and carefully fold them into the artichoke mixture.

7 Lightly grease a small ovenproof dish and preheat the oven to 375°F. Fold each pancake in four, hold the top open and spoon the mixture into the center.

8 Arrange the crêpes in the prepared dish with the filling uppermost if possible. Bake for about 15 minutes, until risen and golden. Eat immediately!

COOK'S TIP
Make sure the pan is at a good steady heat and is well oiled before you pour in the batter. It should sizzle as it hits the pan. Swirl the batter around to coat the pan, and then cook quickly.

BROCCOLI RISOTTO TORTE

LIKE A SPANISH OMELET, THIS IS A SAVORY CAKE SERVED IN WEDGES. IT IS GOOD COLD OR HOT, AND NEEDS ONLY A SALAD AS AN ACCOMPANIMENT.

SERVES SIX

INGREDIENTS

8 ounces broccoli, cut into very small florets
1 onion, chopped
2 garlic cloves, crushed
1 large yellow bell pepper, sliced
2 tablespoons olive oil
¼ cup butter
1¼ cups Arborio rice
½ cup dry white wine
4½ cups vegetable stock
salt and freshly ground black pepper
½ cup coarsely grated Parmesan cheese
4 eggs, separated
oil, for greasing
sliced tomato and chopped parsley, to garnish

1 Blanch the broccoli for 3 minutes, then drain and reserve.

2 In a large saucepan, gently fry the onion, garlic and pepper in the oil and butter for 5 minutes, until they are soft.

3 Stir in the rice, cook for a minute, then pour in the wine. Cook, stirring the mixture, until the liquid is absorbed.

4 Pour in the stock, season well, bring to a boil, then lower to a simmer. Cook for 20 minutes, stirring occasionally.

5 Meanwhile, grease a deep 10-inch round cake pan and line the bottom with a circle of waxed paper. Preheat the oven to 350°F.

6 Stir the cheese into the rice, allow the mixture to cool for 5 minutes, then beat in the egg yolks.

7 Whisk the egg whites until they form soft peaks and carefully fold into the rice. Turn into the prepared pan and bake for about 1 hour, until risen, golden brown and slightly wobbly in the center.

8 Allow the torte to cool in the pan, then chill if serving cold. Run a knife around the edge of the pan and shake out onto a serving plate. If desired, garnish with sliced tomato and chopped parsley.

LEEK AND GOAT CHEESE LASAGNE

*AN UNUSUAL AND LIGHTER THAN
AVERAGE LASAGNE MADE USING A
SOFT FRENCH GOAT CHEESE. THE
PASTA SHEETS ARE NOT SO CHEWY
IF BOILED BRIEFLY FIRST.*

SERVES SIX

INGREDIENTS

    6–8 lasagne sheets
    salt
    1 large eggplant
    3 leeks, thinly sliced
    2 tablespoons olive oil
    2 red bell peppers, roasted and peeled
    7 ounces goat cheese, broken into pieces
    ¼ cup freshly grated Pecorino or
      Parmesan cheese
For the sauce
    ½ cup all-purpose flour
    5 tablespoons butter
    3¾ cups milk
    ½ teaspoon ground bay leaves
    fresh nutmeg, grated
    freshly ground black pepper

1 Blanch the pasta sheets in plenty of boiling water for just 2 minutes. Drain and place on a clean dish towel.

2 Lightly salt the eggplant and lay in a colander to drain for 30 minutes, then rinse and pat dry with paper towels.

3 Lightly fry the leeks in the oil for about 5 minutes, until softened. Peel the roasted peppers and cut into strips.

4 Make the sauce. Put the flour, butter and milk in a saucepan and bring to a boil, stirring constantly, until the sauce has thickened. Add the ground bay leaves, nutmeg and seasoning. Simmer for another 2 minutes.

5 In a greased shallow casserole, layer the leeks, pasta, eggplant, goat cheese and Pecorino or Parmesan. Drizzle the sauce over the layers, ensuring that plenty goes in between.

6 Finish with a layer of sauce and grated cheese. Bake in the oven at 375°F for 30 minutes or until browned on top. Serve immediately.

GLAMORGAN SAUSAGES

THIS OLD WELSH RECIPE TASTES PARTICULARLY GOOD SERVED WITH CREAMY MASHED POTATOES AND LIGHTLY COOKED GREEN CABBAGE.

SERVES FOUR

INGREDIENTS

2 cups fresh whole-wheat bread crumbs
6 ounces aged Cheddar cheese, grated
2 tablespoons finely chopped leek or scallion
2 tablespoons chopped fresh parsley
1 tablespoon chopped fresh marjoram
1 tablespoon coarse-grained mustard
2 eggs, 1 separated
freshly ground black pepper
½ cup dried bread crumbs
oil, for deep-frying

1 Mix the fresh bread crumbs with the cheese, leek or onion, parsley, marjoram, mustard, whole egg, one egg yolk and ground black pepper to taste. The mixture may appear dry at first, but knead it lightly with your fingers and it will come together. Make 8 small sausage shapes.

2 Whisk the egg white until lightly frothy and put the dried bread crumbs in a bowl. Dip the sausages first into the egg white, then coat them evenly in bread crumbs, shaking off any excess.

3 Heat a deep-frying pan one-third full of oil and carefully fry four sausages at a time for 2 minutes each. Drain on paper towels and reheat the oil to repeat.

4 Keep the sausages warm in the oven, uncovered. Alternatively, open-freeze, bag and seal; then, to reheat, thaw for 1 hour and cook in a medium-hot oven for 10–15 minutes.

BRAZILIAN STUFFED PEPPERS

COLORFUL AND FULL OF FLAVOR, THESE STUFFED PEPPERS ARE EASY TO MAKE IN ADVANCE. THEY CAN BE REHEATED QUICKLY IN A MICROWAVE OVEN AND BROWNED UNDER A BROILER.

SERVES FOUR

INGREDIENTS

4 bell peppers, halved and seeded
1 eggplant, cut into chunks
1 onion, sliced
1 garlic clove, crushed
2 tablespoons olive oil
1 can (14 ounces) tomatoes, chopped
1 teaspoon ground coriander
salt and freshly ground black pepper
1 tablespoon chopped fresh basil
4 ounces goat cheese, coarsely grated
2 tablespoons dried bread crumbs

1 Blanch the pepper halves in boiling water for 3 minutes, then drain well.

2 Sprinkle the eggplant chunks with salt, place in a colander and leave to drain for 20 minutes. Rinse and pat dry.

3 Fry the onion and garlic in the oil for 5 minutes until they are soft, then add the eggplant and cook for another 5 minutes, stirring occasionally.

VARIATION
There are all sorts of delicious stuffings for peppers. Rice or pasta make a good base, mixed with some lightly fried onion, garlic and spices. Mixed nuts, finely chopped, can be added and a beaten egg or grated cheese helps to bind it all together. Vegans can leave out the last two ingredients.

4 Pour in the tomatoes, coriander and seasoning. Bring to a boil, then simmer for 10 minutes, until the mixture is thick. Cool slightly and stir in the basil and half of the cheese.

5 Spoon filling into the pepper halves and place on a shallow heatproof serving dish. Sprinkle with cheese and bread crumbs, then brown lightly under the grill. Serve with rice and salad.

MUSHROOM GOUGÈRE

A SAVORY CHOUX PASTRY RING MAKES A MARVELOUS MAIN COURSE DISH THAT CAN BE MADE AHEAD, THEN BAKED WHEN REQUIRED. WHY NOT TRY IT FOR A DINNER PARTY? IT LOOKS SO VERY SPECIAL.

SERVES FOUR

INGREDIENTS
- ½ cup all-purpose flour
- ½ teaspoon salt
- 6 tablespoons butter
- ¾ cup cold water
- 3 eggs, beaten
- ¾ cup diced Gruyère or aged Gouda cheese

For the filling
- 1 small onion, sliced
- 1 carrot, coarsely grated
- 1 cup sliced white mushrooms
- 3 tablespoons butter or margarine
- 1 teaspoon tikka or mild curry paste
- 2 tablespoons all-purpose flour
- 1¼ cups milk
- 2 tablespoons chopped fresh parsley
- salt and freshly ground black pepper
- 2 tablespoons flaked almonds

1 Preheat the oven to 400°F. Grease a shallow ovenproof dish about 9 inches long.

2 To make the choux pastry, first sift the flour and salt onto a sheet of waxed paper. In a large saucepan, heat the butter and water until the butter melts. Do not let the water boil. Fold the paper and shoot the flour into the pan all at once.

3 With a wooden spoon, beat the mixture rapidly until the lumps become smooth and the mixture comes away from the sides of the pan. Cool for 10 minutes.

4 Beat the eggs gradually into the mixture until the dough has a soft, but still quite stiff consistency. You may not need all the egg.

5 Stir in the cheese, then spoon the mixture around the sides of the greased ovenproof dish.

6 To make the filling, sauté the onion, carrot and mushrooms in the butter or margarine for 5 minutes. Stir in the curry paste, then the flour.

7 Gradually stir in the milk and heat until thickened. Mix in the parsley, season well, then pour into the center of the choux pastry.

8 Bake for 35–40 minutes, until risen and golden brown, sprinkling on the almonds for the last 5 minutes or so. Serve at once.

COOK'S TIP
Choux pastry is remarkably easy to make, as no rolling out is required. The secret of success is to let the flour and butter mixture cool before beating in the eggs, to prevent them from setting.

COUSCOUS-STUFFED CABBAGE

CUT INTO WEDGES AND SERVE ACCOMPANIED BY A FRESH TOMATO OR CHEESE SAUCE OR EVEN A VEGETARIAN GRAVY.

SERVES FOUR

INGREDIENTS
1 medium-size cabbage
1 cup couscous
1 onion, chopped
1 small red bell pepper, chopped
2 garlic cloves, crushed
2 tablespoons olive oil
1 teaspoon ground coriander
½ teaspoon ground cumin
generous pinch ground cinnamon
½ cup green lentils, soaked
2½ cups vegetable stock
2 tablespoons tomato paste
salt and freshly ground black pepper
2 tablespoons chopped fresh parsley
2 tablespoons pine nuts
3 ounces aged Cheddar cheese, grated
1 egg, beaten

1 Cut the top quarter off the cabbage and remove any loose outer leaves. Using a small sharp knife, cut out as much of the middle as you can. Reserve a few larger leaves for later.

2 Blanch the cabbage in a pan of boiling water for 5 minutes, then drain it well, upside down.

COOK'S TIP
A whole stuffed cabbage makes a wonderful main dish, especially for a Sunday lunch. It can be made ahead and steamed when required.

3 Steam the couscous according to the instructions on the package, making sure the grains are light and fluffy.

4 Lightly fry the onion, pepper and garlic in the oil for 5 minutes, until soft, then stir in the spices and cook for another 2 minutes.

5 Add the lentils and pour in the stock and tomato paste. Bring to a boil, season and simmer for 25 minutes, until the lentils are cooked.

6 Mix in the couscous, parsley, pine nuts, grated cheese and egg. Check the seasoning again. Open up the cabbage and spoon in the stuffing.

7 Blanch the leftover outer cabbage leaves and place these over the top of the stuffing, then wrap the whole thing in a sheet of buttered foil.

8 Place in a steamer over simmering water and cook for about 45 minutes. Remove from the foil and serve cut into wedges.

COUSCOUS AROMATIQUE

*MOROCCO AND TUNISIA HAVE
MANY WONDERFUL DISHES MADE
USING COUSCOUS, WHICH IS
STEAMED OVER SIMMERING
SPICY STEWS.*

SERVES FOUR TO SIX

INGREDIENTS
1 pound couscous
¼ cup olive oil
1 onion, cut into chunks
2 carrots, cut into thick slices
4 baby turnips, halved
8 small new potatoes, halved
1 green bell pepper, cut into chunks
4 ounces green beans, halved
1 small fennel bulb, thickly sliced
1-inch cube fresh ginger, grated
2 garlic cloves, crushed
1 teaspoon ground turmeric
1 tablespoon ground coriander
1 teaspoon cumin seeds
1 teaspoon ground cinnamon
3 tablespoons red lentils
1 can (14 ounces) tomatoes, chopped
4½ cups vegetable stock
4 tablespoons raisins
salt and freshly ground black pepper
rind and juice of 1 lemon
harissa paste, to serve (optional)

1 Cover the couscous with cold water
and soak for 10 minutes. Drain and
spread out on a tray for 20 minutes,
stirring it occasionally with your fingers.

2 Meanwhile, in a large saucepan, heat
the oil and fry the vegetables for about
10 minutes, stirring from time to time.

3 Add the grated ginger, garlic and
spices, stir well and cook for 2 minutes.
Pour in the lentils, tomatoes, stock and
raisins and add seasoning.

4 Bring to a boil, then turn down to a
simmer. By this time the couscous should
be ready for steaming. Place in a steamer
and fit this on top of the stew.

5 Cover and steam gently for about 20
minutes. The grains should be swollen
and soft. Fork through and season well.
Spoon into a serving dish.

6 Add the lemon rind and juice to the
stew and check the seasoning. If desired,
add harissa paste to taste; it is quite hot,
so beware! Serve the stew separately in a
casserole dish. Spoon the couscous onto
a plate and ladle the stew on top.

CABBAGE ROULADES WITH LEMON SAUCE

CABBAGE OR CHARD LEAVES FILLED WITH RICE AND LENTILS MAKE A TASTY MAIN COURSE.

SERVES FOUR TO SIX

INGREDIENTS
    12 large cabbage or chard leaves
    salt
    2 tablespoons sunflower oil
    1 onion, chopped
    1 large carrot, grated
    ½ cup sliced mushrooms
    2½ cups vegetable stock
    ½ cup long-grain rice
    4 tablespoons red lentils
    1 teaspoon dried oregano or marjoram
    freshly ground black pepper
    ½ cup cream cheese with garlic
For the sauce
    3 tablespoons all-purpose flour
    juice of 1 lemon
    3 eggs, beaten

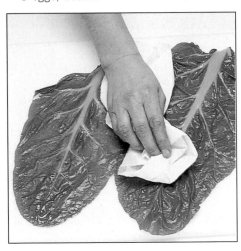

1 Remove the stalks and blanch the leaves in boiling salted water until they begin to wilt. Drain, reserve the water and pat the leaves dry with paper towels.

2 Heat the oil and lightly fry the onion, carrot and mushrooms for 5 minutes, then pour in the stock.

3 Add the rice, lentils, herbs and seasoning. Bring to a boil, cover and simmer gently for 15 minutes. Remove, then stir in the cheese. Preheat the oven to 375°F.

4 Lay out the chard or cabbage leaves, rib side down, and spoon on the filling at the stalk end. Fold the sides in and roll up.

5 Place the leaves seam side down in a small roasting pan and pour in the reserved cabbage water. Cover with lightly greased foil and bake for 30–45 minutes, until the leaves are tender.

6 Remove the cabbage rolls from the oven, drain and place on a serving dish. Strain 2½ cups of the cooking water into a saucepan and bring to a boil.

7 Blend the flour to a runny paste with a little cold water and whisk into the boiling stock, together with the lemon juice.

8 Beat the eggs in a heatproof bowl and slowly pour on the hot stock, whisking well as you go.

9 Return to the stove and over the lowest heat, stir until smooth and thick. Do not allow the sauce to boil or it will curdle. Serve the rolls with some of the sauce poured on top and the rest handed separately.

IRISH COLCANNON

This lovely, warming winter's dish is a lot like Eggs Florentine. Here, baked eggs nestle among creamy potatoes with curly kale or cabbage and a topping of grated cheese.

SERVES FOUR

INGREDIENTS
- 2 pounds potatoes, cut into even pieces
- 8 ounces curly kale or crisp green cabbage, shredded
- 2 scallions, chopped
- butter or margarine, to taste
- fresh nutmeg, grated
- salt and freshly ground black pepper
- 4 large eggs
- 3 ounces aged cheese, grated

1 Boil the potatoes until just tender, then drain and mash well.

2 Lightly cook the kale or cabbage until just tender but still crisp. Preheat the oven to 375°F.

3 Drain the greens and mix them into the potato with the onions, butter or margarine and nutmeg. Season to taste.

4 Spoon the mixture into a shallow ovenproof dish and make four hollows in the mixture. Crack an egg into each and season well.

5 Bake for about 12 minutes or until the eggs are just set, then serve sprinkled with the cheese.

PASTA WITH CAPONATA

This excellent sweet and sour vegetable dish goes wonderfully well with pasta.

SERVES FOUR

INGREDIENTS
- 1 medium eggplant, cut into sticks
- 2 medium zucchini, cut into sticks
- 8 baby onions, peeled, or 1 large onion, sliced
- 2 garlic cloves, crushed
- 1 large red bell pepper, sliced
- ¼ cup olive oil
- scant 2 cups tomato juice or 1 can (17 ounces) crushed tomatoes
- ⅔ cup water
- 2 tablespoons balsamic vinegar
- juice of 1 lemon
- 1 tablespoon sugar
- 2 tablespoons sliced black olives
- 2 tablespoons capers
- salt and freshly ground black pepper
- 14 ounces tagliatelle or pasta ribbons

1 Lightly salt the eggplant and zucchini and leave them to drain in a colander for 30 minutes. Rinse and pat dry with paper towels.

2 In a large saucepan, lightly fry the onions, garlic and pepper in the oil for 5 minutes, then stir in the eggplant and zucchini and fry for another 5 minutes.

3 Stir in the tomato juice or crushed tomatoes plus the water. Stir well, bringing the mixture to the boil, then add all the rest of the ingredients except the pasta. Season to taste and simmer for 10 minutes.

4 Meanwhile, boil the pasta according to the instructions on the package, then drain. Serve the caponata with the pasta.

SPINACH GNOCCHI

THIS WHOLESOME ITALIAN DISH IS IDEAL FOR MAKING IN ADVANCE. SERVE IT WITH A FRESH TOMATO SAUCE.

SERVES FOUR TO SIX

INGREDIENTS

14 ounces fresh leaf spinach
  or 6 ounces frozen spinach, thawed
3 cups milk
1¼ cups semolina
¼ cup butter, melted
¼ cup freshly grated Parmesan cheese,
  plus extra to serve
fresh nutmeg, grated
salt and freshly ground black pepper
2 eggs, beaten

2 In a large saucepan, heat the milk and when just on the point of boiling, sprinkle in the semolina in a steady stream, stirring it briskly with a wooden spoon.

5 Stamp out shapes using a plain round cutter with a diameter of about 1½ inches. Reserve the trimmings.

1 Blanch the spinach in the tiniest amount of water, then drain and squeeze dry through a sieve with the back of a ladle. Chop the spinach coarsely.

3 Simmer the semolina for 2 minutes, then remove from the heat and stir in half the butter, most of the cheese, nutmeg and seasoning to taste and the spinach. Allow to cool for 5 minutes.

6 Grease a shallow ovenproof dish. Place the trimmings on the bottom and arrange the gnocchi rounds on top with each one overlapping.

7 Brush the tops with the remaining butter and sprinkle with the last of the cheese.

8 Preheat the oven to 375°F when ready to bake and cook for about 35 minutes, until golden and crisp on top. Serve hot with fresh tomato sauce and extra cheese.

VARIATION

For a special occasion, make half plain and half spinach gnocchi and arrange in an attractive pattern to serve. Use the same recipe as above but halve the amount of spinach and add to half the mixture in a separate bowl to make two batches. Stamp out and cook the gnocchi as usual. For a more substantial, healthy meal, make a tasty vegetable base of lightly sautéed peppers, zucchini and mushrooms and place the gnocchi on top.

4 Stir in the eggs, then pour the mixture out onto a shallow baking sheet, spreading it to a ½-inch thickness. Let cool completely, then chill until solid.

RED RICE RISSOLES

Risotto rice chills to a firm texture yet remains light and creamy when reheated as crisp rissoles.

SERVES ABOUT EIGHT

INGREDIENTS

1 large red onion, chopped
1 red bell pepper, chopped
2 garlic cloves, crushed
1 red chili, finely chopped
2 tablespoons olive oil
2 tablespoons butter
1¼ cups Arborio rice
4½ cups vegetable stock
4 sun-dried tomatoes, chopped
2 tablespoons tomato paste
2 teaspoons dried oregano
salt and freshly ground black pepper
3 tablespoons chopped fresh parsley
6 ounces cheese (e.g. Cheddar)
1 egg, beaten
1 cup dried bread crumbs
oil, for deep-frying

1 Fry the onion, pepper, garlic and chili in the oil and butter for 5 minutes. Stir in the rice and fry for another 2 minutes.

2 Pour in the stock and add the tomatoes, tomato paste, oregano and seasoning. Bring to a boil, stirring occasionally. Cover and simmer for 20 minutes.

3 Stir in the parsley, then pour into a shallow dish, cool and chill until firm. When cold, divide into 12 and shape into balls.

4 Cut the cheese into 12 pieces and press a nugget into the center of each of the rissoles.

5 Put the beaten egg in one bowl and the bread crumbs into another. Dip the rissoles first into the egg, then into the bread crumbs, coating each one evenly.

6 Lay the coated rissoles on a plate and chill again for 30 minutes. Fill a deep-frying pan one-third full of oil and heat until a cube of day-old bread browns in under a minute.

7 Fry the rissoles in batches, reheating the oil in between, for about 3–4 minutes. Drain on paper towels and keep warm, uncovered, before serving.

Fava Bean <u>and</u> Cauliflower Curry

A tasty midweek curry to serve with rice, small poppadums and maybe a cucumber raita.

SERVES FOUR

INGREDIENTS

2 garlic cloves, chopped
1-inch cube fresh ginger
1 fresh green chili, seeded and chopped
1 tablespoon oil
1 onion, sliced
1 large potato, chopped
2 tablespoons ghee or softened butter
1 tablespoon curry powder, mild or hot
1 medium-size cauliflower, cut into small florets
2½ cups vegetable stock
2 tablespoons creamed coconut
salt and ground black pepper
1 can (10 ounces) fava beans
juice of half a lemon (optional)
fresh cilantro or parsley, to serve

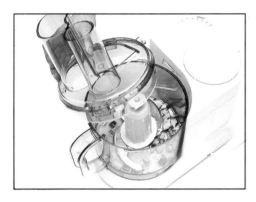

1 Blend the garlic, ginger, chili and oil in a food processor until they form a smooth paste.

2 In a large saucepan, fry the onion and potato in the ghee or butter for 5 minutes, then stir in the garlic paste and curry powder. Cook for 1 minute.

3 Add the cauliflower florets and stir well into the spicy mixture, then pour in the stock. Bring to a boil and mix in the coconut, stirring until it melts.

4 Season well, then cover and simmer for 10 minutes. Add the beans and their liquid and cook uncovered for another 10 minutes.

5 Check the seasoning and add a good squeeze of lemon juice, if desired. Serve hot, garnished with chopped cilantro or parsley.

BAKED ONIONS STUFFED WITH FETA

RED ONIONS HAVE A MILD FLAVOR AND ATTRACTIVE APPEARANCE. THE RED FLESH LOOKS ESPECIALLY APPEALING WITH THIS FETA AND BREAD CRUMB STUFFING.

SERVES FOUR

INGREDIENTS
  4 large red onions
  1 tablespoon olive oil
  2 tablespoons pine nuts
  4 ounces feta cheese, crumbled
  2 tablespoons white bread crumbs
  1 tablespoon chopped fresh cilantro
  salt and freshly ground black pepper

1 Preheat the oven to 350°F and lightly grease a shallow ovenproof dish. Peel the onions and cut a thin slice from the top and base of each. Place in a large saucepan of boiling water and cook for 10–12 minutes, until just tender. Remove with a slotted spoon. Drain on paper towels and leave to cool slightly.

2 Using a small knife or your fingers, remove the inner sections of the onions, leaving about two or three outer rings. Finely chop the inner sections and place the shells in an ovenproof dish.

3 Heat the oil in a medium frying pan and fry the chopped onions for 4–5 minutes, until golden, then add the pine nuts and stir-fry for a few minutes.

4 Place the feta cheese in a small bowl and stir in the onions and pine nuts, bread crumbs and cilantro. Season well with salt and pepper and then spoon the mixture into the onion shells. Cover loosely with foil and bake in the oven for 30 minutes, removing the foil for the last 10 minutes.

5 Serve as an appetizer or as a light lunch with warm olive bread.

ONION TARTS WITH GOAT CHEESE

A VARIATION OF A CLASSIC FRENCH DISH, TARTE A L'OIGNON, THIS DISH USES FRESH GOAT CHEESE INSTEAD OF CREAM, SINCE IT IS MILD AND CREAMY AND COMPLEMENTS THE FLAVOR OF THE ONIONS. THIS RECIPE MAKES EITHER EIGHT INDIVIDUAL TARTS OR ONE LARGE 9-INCH TART.

SERVES EIGHT

INGREDIENTS
For the pastry
  3/4 cup all-purpose flour
  5 tablespoons butter
  1 ounce goat Cheddar or Cheddar
    cheese, grated
For the filling
  1–1½ tablespoons olive or
    sunflower oil
  3 onions, finely sliced
  6 ounces fresh goat cheese
  2 eggs, beaten
  1 tablespoon light cream
  2 ounces goat Cheddar, grated
  1 tablespoon chopped fresh tarragon
  salt and ground black pepper

1 To make the pastry, sift the flour into a bowl and rub in the butter until the mixture resembles fine bread crumbs. Stir in the grated cheese and add enough cold water to make a dough. Knead lightly, put in a plastic bag and chill. Preheat the oven to 375°F.

2 Roll out the dough on a lightly floured surface, and then cut into eight rounds using a 4½-inch pastry cutter and line eight 4-inch tart tins. Prick the bottoms with a fork and bake in the oven for 10–15 minutes, until firm but not browned. Reduce the oven temperature to 350°F.

3 Heat the olive or sunflower oil in a large frying pan and fry the onions over a low heat for 20–25 minutes, until they are a deep golden brown. Stir occasionally to prevent them from burning.

4 Beat the goat cheese with the eggs, cream, goat Cheddar and tarragon. Season with salt and pepper and then stir in the fried onions.

5 Pour the mixture into the partly-baked pastry shells and bake for 20–25 minutes, until golden. Serve warm or cold with a green salad.

PARSNIP AND CHESTNUT CROQUETTES

THE SWEET NUTTY TASTE OF CHESTNUTS BLENDS PERFECTLY WITH THE SIMILARLY SWEET BUT EARTHY FLAVOR OF PARSNIPS. FRESH CHESTNUTS NEED TO BE PEELED BUT FROZEN CHESTNUTS ARE EASY TO USE AND ARE NEARLY AS GOOD AS FRESH FOR THIS RECIPE.

MAKES TEN TO TWELVE

INGREDIENTS
1 pound parsnips, cut roughly into
    small pieces
4 ounces frozen chestnuts
1 ounce butter
1 garlic clove, crushed
1 tablespoon chopped fresh cilantro
1 egg, beaten
1½–2 ounces fresh white bread
    crumbs
vegetable oil, for frying
salt and freshly ground black pepper
sprig of cilantro, to garnish

1 Place the parsnips in a saucepan with enough water to cover. Bring to a boil, cover and simmer for 15–20 minutes until completely tender.

2 Place the frozen chestnuts in a pan of water, bring to a boil and simmer for 8–10 minutes until very tender. Drain, place in a bowl and mash roughly.

3 Melt the butter in a small saucepan and cook the garlic for 30 seconds. Drain the parsnips and mash with the garlic butter. Stir in the chestnuts, chopped cilantro and season well.

4 Take about 1 tablespoon of mixture at a time and form into small croquettes, about 3 inches long. Dip each croquette into the beaten egg and then roll in the bread crumbs.

5 Heat a little oil in a frying pan and fry the croquettes for 3–4 minutes until golden, turning frequently so they brown evenly. Drain on paper towels and then serve at once, garnished with cilantro.

PARSNIP, EGGPLANT AND CASHEW BIRYANI

SERVES FOUR TO SIX

INGREDIENTS

1 small eggplant, sliced
10 ounces basmati rice
3 parsnips
3 onions
2 garlic cloves
1-inch piece fresh ginger, peeled
about 4 tablespoons vegetable oil
6 ounces unsalted cashew nuts
1½ ounces golden raisins
1 red bell pepper, seeded and sliced
1 teaspoon ground cumin
1 teaspoon ground coriander
½ teaspoon chili powder
½ cup plain yogurt
1¼ cups vegetable or chicken stock
1 ounce butter
salt and freshly ground black pepper
sprigs of cilantro, to garnish
2 hard-boiled eggs, quartered

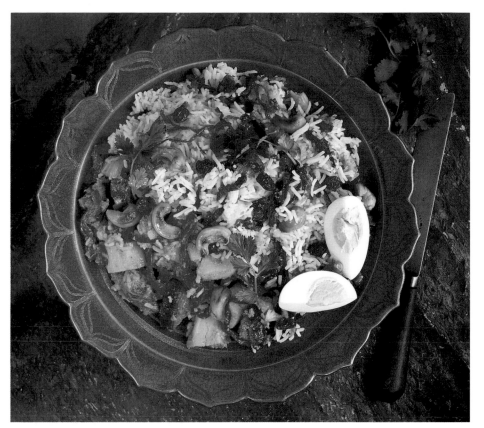

1 Sprinkle the eggplant with salt and leave for 30 minutes. Rinse, pat dry and cut into bite-size pieces. Soak the rice in a bowl of cold water for 40 minutes. Peel and core the parsnips. Cut into ½-inch pieces. Roughly chop 1 onion and put in a food processor or blender with the garlic and ginger. Add 2–3 tablespoons water and process to a paste.

2 Finely slice the remaining onions. Heat 3 tablespoons of the oil in a large flameproof casserole and fry gently for 10–15 minutes until deep golden brown. Remove and drain. Add 1½ ounces of the cashew nuts to the pan, stir-fry for 2 minutes. Add the golden raisins and fry until they swell. Remove and drain.

3 Add the eggplant and pepper to the pan and stir-fry for 4–5 minutes. Drain on paper towels. Fry the parsnips for 4–5 minutes. Stir in the remaining cashew nuts and fry for 1 minute. Transfer to the plate with the eggplants.

4 Add the remaining 1 tablespoon of oil to the pan. Add the onion paste. Cook, stirring over moderate heat for 4–5 minutes until the mixture turns golden. Stir in the cumin, cilantro and chili powder. Cook, stirring, for 1 minute, then reduce the heat and add the yogurt.

5 Bring the mixture slowly to a boil and stir in the stock, parsnips, eggplant and peppers. Season, cover and simmer for 30–40 minutes until the parsnips are tender and then transfer to an ovenproof casserole.

6 Preheat the oven to 300°F. Drain the rice and add to 1¼ cups of salted boiling water. Cook gently for 5–6 minutes until it is tender but slightly undercooked.

7 Drain the rice and pile it in a mound on top of the parsnips. Make a hole from the top to the base using the handle of a wooden spoon. Scatter the reserved fried onions, cashew nuts and golden raisins over the rice and dot with butter. Cover with a double layer of foil and then secure in place with a lid.

8 Cook in the oven for 35–40 minutes. To serve, spoon the mixture onto a warmed serving dish and garnish with cilantro sprigs and quartered eggs.

CELERY ROOT AND BLUE CHEESE ROULADE

CELERY ROOT ADDS A DELICATE AND SUBTLE FLAVOR TO THIS ATTRACTIVE DISH. THE SPINACH ROULADE MAKES AN ATTRACTIVE CONTRAST TO THE CREAMY FILLING, BUT YOU COULD USE A PLAIN OR CHEESE ROULADE BASE INSTEAD. BE SURE TO ROLL UP THE ROULADE WHILE IT IS STILL WARM AND PLIABLE.

SERVES SIX

INGREDIENTS
- ½ ounce butter
- 8 ounces cooked spinach, drained and chopped
- ⅔ cup light cream
- 4 large eggs, separated
- ½ ounce Parmesan cheese, grated
- pinch of nutmeg
- salt and freshly ground black pepper

For the filling
- 8 ounces celery root
- lemon juice
- 3 ounces blue cheese
- 4 ounces ricotta cheese
- freshly ground black pepper

1 Preheat the oven to 400°F and line a 13 x 9-inch jelly roll tin with non-stick baking parchment.

2 Melt the butter in a saucepan and add the spinach. Cook gently until all the liquid has evaporated, stirring frequently. Remove the pan from the heat and stir in the cream, egg yolks, Parmesan cheese, nutmeg and seasoning.

3 Whisk the egg whites until stiff, fold them gently into the spinach mixture and then spoon into the prepared pan. Spread the mixture evenly and use a metal spatula to smooth the surface.

4 Bake in the oven for 10–15 minutes until the roulade is firm to the touch and lightly golden on top. Carefully turn out onto a sheet of wax paper and peel away the lining paper. Roll it up with the paper inside and leave to cool slightly.

5 To make the filling, peel and grate the celery root into a bowl and sprinkle well with lemon juice. Blend the blue cheese and ricotta cheese together and mix with the celery root and a little black pepper.

6 Unroll the roulade, spread with the filling and roll up again. Serve at once or wrap loosely and chill.

BAKED LEEKS WITH CHEESE AND YOGURT TOPPING

LIKE ALL VEGETABLES, THE FRESHER LEEKS ARE, THE BETTER THEIR FLAVOR, AND THE FRESHEST LEEKS
AVAILABLE SHOULD BE USED FOR THIS DISH. SMALL, YOUNG LEEKS ARE AROUND AT THE BEGINNING OF
THE SEASON AND ARE PERFECT TO USE HERE.

SERVES FOUR

INGREDIENTS
8 small leeks, about 1½ pounds
2 small eggs or 1 large one, beaten
5 ounces fresh goat cheese
⅓ cup plain yogurt
2 ounces Parmesan cheese, grated
1 ounce fresh white or brown bread
  crumbs
salt and freshly ground black pepper

1 Preheat the oven to 350°F and butter
a shallow ovenproof dish. Trim the leeks,
cut a slit from top to bottom and rinse
well under cold water.

2 Place the leeks in a saucepan of
water, bring to the boil and simmer
gently for 6–8 minutes until just tender.
Remove and drain well using a slotted
spoon, and arrange in the prepared dish.

3 Beat the eggs with the goat cheese,
yogurt and half the Parmesan cheese,
and season well with salt and pepper.

4 Pour the cheese and yogurt mixture
over the leeks. Mix the bread crumbs
and remaining Parmesan cheese together and sprinkle over the sauce. Bake in
the oven for 35–40 minutes until the top
is crisp and golden brown.

CASSAVA AND VEGETABLE KEBABS

THIS IS AN ATTRACTIVE AND DELICIOUS ASSORTMENT OF AFRICAN VEGETABLES, MARINATED IN A SPICY GARLIC SAUCE. IF CASSAVA IS UNAVAILABLE, USE SWEET POTATO OR YAM INSTEAD.

SERVES FOUR

INGREDIENTS
- 6 ounces cassava
- 1 onion, cut into wedges
- 1 eggplant, cut into bite-size pieces
- 1 zucchini, sliced
- 1 ripe plantain, sliced
- 1 red pepper or ½ red bell pepper,
  ½ green bell pepper, sliced
- 16 cherry tomatoes

For the marinade
- 4 tablespoons lemon juice
- 4 tablespoons olive oil
- 3–4 tablespoons soy sauce
- 1 tablespoon tomato paste
- 1 green chili, seeded and finely chopped
- ½ onion, grated
- 2 garlic cloves, crushed
- 1 teaspoon mixed spice
- pinch dried thyme
- rice or couscous, to serve

1 Peel the cassava and cut into bite-size pieces. Place in a bowl, cover with boiling water and leave to blanch for 5 minutes. Drain well.

2 Place all the vegetables, including the cassava, in a large bowl.

3 Blend together all the marinade ingredients and pour over the prepared vegetables. Set aside for 1–2 hours.

4 Preheat the broiler and thread all the vegetables and cherry tomatoes onto eight skewers.

5 Broil the vegetables under low heat for about 15 minutes until tender and browned, turning frequently and basting occasionally with the marinade.

6 Meanwhile, pour the remaining marinade into a small saucepan and simmer for 10 minutes until slightly reduced.

7 Arrange the vegetable kebabs on a serving plate and strain the sauce into a small jug. Serve with rice or couscous.

SALSIFY GRATIN

THE SPINACH IN THIS RECIPE ADDS COLOR AND MAKES THE SALSIFY GO FURTHER. HOWEVER, IF YOU CAN OBTAIN SALSIFY EASILY AND HAVE THE PATIENCE TO PEEL A LOT OF IT, INCREASE THE QUANTITY AND LEAVE OUT THE SPINACH.

<u>SERVES FOUR</u>

INGREDIENTS

1 pound salsify, cut into
  2-inch lengths
juice of 1½ lemons
1 pound spinach, trimmed and washed
⅔ cup vegetable stock
1¼ cups light cream or half-and-half
salt and freshly ground black pepper

3 Cook the spinach in a large saucepan over medium heat for 2–3 minutes, until the leaves have wilted, shaking the pan occasionally. Place the stock, cream and seasoning in a small saucepan over low heat and heat through, stirring.

4 Arrange the salsify and spinach in layers in the prepared dish. Add the stock and cream mixture and bake for about 1 hour, until the top is golden brown and bubbling.

1 Trim away the tops and bottoms of the salsify and peel or scrape away the outer skin. Immediately place each peeled root in water with a little lemon juice, to prevent discoloration.

2 Preheat the oven to 325°F and butter an ovenproof dish. Place the salsify in a saucepan of boiling water with the lemon juice. Simmer for about 10 minutes, until the salsify is just tender, then drain.

CELERY ROOT GRATIN

Although celery root has a rather unattractive appearance with its hard, knobbly skin, it is a vegetable that has a very delicious sweet and nutty flavor. This is accentuated in this dish by the addition of the sweet yet nutty Emmental cheese.

SERVES FOUR

INGREDIENTS
    1 pound celery root
    juice of ½ lemon
    1 ounce butter
    1 small onion, finely chopped
    2 tablespoons all-purpose flour
    1¼ cups milk
    1 ounce Emmental cheese, grated
    1 tablespoon capers
    salt and cayenne pepper

1 Preheat the oven to 375°F. Peel the celery root and cut into ¼-inch slices, immediately plunging them into a saucepan of cold water acidulated with the lemon juice.

2 Bring the water to a boil and simmer the celery root for 10–12 minutes until just tender. Drain and arrange the celery root in a shallow ovenproof dish.

3 Melt the butter in a small saucepan and fry the onion over low heat until soft but not browned. Stir in the flour, cook for 1 minute and then slowly stir in the milk to make a smooth sauce. Stir in the cheese, capers and seasoning to taste and then pour over the celery root. Cook in the oven for 15–20 minutes until the top is golden brown.

VARIATION
For a less strongly flavored dish, alternate the layers of celery root with potato. Slice the potato, cook until almost tender, then drain well before assembling the dish.

BAKED MARROW ᴵᴺ PARSLEY SAUCE

THIS IS A REALLY GLORIOUS WAY WITH A SIMPLE AND MODEST VEGETABLE. TRY TO FIND A SMALL, FIRM AND UNBLEMISHED MARROW FOR THIS RECIPE, AS THE FLAVOR WILL BE SWEET, FRESH AND DELICATE.

SERVES FOUR

INGREDIENTS
  1 small young marrow, about 2 pounds
  2 tablespoons olive oil
  ½ ounce butter
  1 onion, chopped
  1 tablespoon all-purpose flour
  1¼ cups milk and light cream mixed
  2 tablespoons chopped fresh parsley
  salt and freshly ground black pepper

1 Preheat the oven to 350°F and cut the marrow into pieces measuring about 2 x 1 inches.

2 Heat the oil and butter in a flameproof casserole and fry the onion over a gentle heat until very soft.

3 Add the marrow and sauté for 1–2 minutes and then stir in the flour. Cook for a few minutes and then stir in the milk and cream mixture.

4 Add the parsley and seasoning, stir well and then cover and cook in the oven for 30–35 minutes. If liked, remove the lid for the final 5 minutes of cooking to brown the top. Alternately, serve the marrow in its rich pale sauce.

COOK'S TIP
Chopped fresh basil or a mixture of basil and chervil also tastes good in this dish.

MARROWS <u>WITH</u> GNOCCHI

A SIMPLE WAY WITH MARROW, THIS DISH MAKES AN EXCELLENT ACCOMPANIMENT TO BROILED MEAT BUT IT IS ALSO GOOD WITH A VEGETARIAN DISH, OR SIMPLY SERVED WITH GRILLED TOMATOES.

SERVES FOUR

INGREDIENTS
    1 small marrow, cut into
      bite-size chunks
    2 ounces butter
    14-ounce packet gnocchi
    ½ garlic clove, crushed
    salt and freshly ground black pepper
    chopped fresh basil, to garnish

1 Preheat the oven to 350°F and butter a large ovenproof dish. Place the marrow, more or less in a single layer, in the dish. Dot all over with the remaining butter.

2 Place a double piece of buttered wax paper over the top. Cover with an oven-proof plate or lid so that it presses the marrow down, and then place a heavy, ovenproof weight on top of that. (Use a couple of old-fashioned scale weights.)

3 Put in the oven to bake for about 15 minutes, by which time the marrow should just be tender.

4 Cook the gnocchi in a large saucepan of boiling salted water for 2–3 minutes, or according to the instructions on the packet. Drain well.

5 Stir the garlic and gnocchi into the marrow. Season and then place the wax paper over the marrow and return to the oven for 5 minutes (the weights are not necessary).

6 Just before serving, sprinkle the top with a little chopped fresh basil.

PASTA WITH SAVOY CABBAGE AND GRUYÈRE

THIS IS AN INEXPENSIVE AND SIMPLE DISH WITH A SURPRISING TEXTURE AND FLAVOR. THE CABBAGE IS COOKED SO THAT IT HAS PLENTY OF "BITE" TO IT, CONTRASTING WITH THE SOFTNESS OF THE PASTA.

SERVES FOUR

INGREDIENTS

   1 ounce butter
   1 small Savoy or green cabbage,
      thinly sliced
   1 small onion, chopped
   12 ounces pasta, e.g. tagliatelle,
      fettucine, penne, etc.
   1 tablespoon chopped fresh parsley
   ⅔ cup light cream
   2 ounces Gruyère or Cheddar cheese,
      grated
   about 1¼ cups hot vegetable or
      chicken stock
   salt and freshly ground black pepper

1 Preheat the oven to 350°F and butter a large casserole. Place the cabbage in a mixing bowl.

2 Melt the butter in a small frying pan and fry the onion until softened. Stir into the cabbage in the bowl.

3 Cook the pasta according to the instructions, until *al dente*.

4 Drain well and stir into the bowl with the cabbage and onion. Add the parsley and mix well and then pour into the prepared casserole.

5 Beat together the cream and Gruyère or Cheddar cheese and then stir in the hot stock. Season well and pour over the cabbage and pasta, so that it comes about halfway up the casserole. If necessary, add a little more stock.

6 Cover tightly and cook in the oven for 30–35 minutes, until the cabbage is tender and the stock is bubbling. Remove the lid for the last 5 minutes of the cooking time to brown the top.

CORN IN A GARLIC BUTTER CRUST

WHETHER YOU ARE SERVING THIS AS A MAIN COURSE OR AS AN ACCOMPANIMENT, IT WILL DISAPPEAR IN A FLASH. EVEN PEOPLE WHO ARE NOT USUALLY FOND OF CORN ON THE COB HAVE BEEN WON OVER BY THIS RECIPE.

SERVES SIX

INGREDIENTS

6 ears corn
salt
1 cup butter
2 tablespoons olive oil
2 cloves garlic, peeled and crushed
2 teaspoons freshly ground black pepper
1 cup whole-wheat bread crumbs
1 tablespoon chopped parsley

1 Boil the corn in salted water until tender, then leave to cool.

2 Melt the butter and add the oil, garlic and black pepper. Pour the mixture into a shallow dish.

3 Mix the bread crumbs and parsley in another shallow dish. Roll the corn in the melted butter mixture and then in the bread crumbs.

4 Broil the corn under a high broiler until the bread crumbs are golden.

VARIATIONS
• Partially cut through a French loaf at regular intervals. Spread the garlic butter mixture between the slices and bake in a moderate oven for 30 minutes.
• To make garlic croutons, melt the garlic butter in a pan and add cubes of bread. Toss frequently over medium heat. When golden brown, add to soups or salads.

VEGETABLE AND HERB KEBABS WITH GREEN PEPPERCORN SAUCE

OTHER VEGETABLES CAN BE INCLUDED IN THESE KEBABS, DEPENDING ON WHAT IS AVAILABLE AT THE TIME.
THE GREEN PEPPERCORN SAUCE IS ALSO AN EXCELLENT ACCOMPANIMENT TO MANY OTHER DISHES.

SERVES FOUR

INGREDIENTS
    8 bamboo skewers soaked in water for
      1 hour
    24 mushrooms
    16 cherry tomatoes
    16 large basil leaves
    16 thick slices of zucchini
    16 large mint leaves
    16 squares of red bell pepper
To baste
    ½ cup melted butter
    1 clove garlic, peeled and crushed
    1 tablespoon crushed green peppercorns
    salt
For the green peppercorn sauce
    ¼ cup butter
    3 tablespoons brandy
    1 cup heavy cream
    1 teaspoon crushed green peppercorns

1 Thread the vegetables and herbs onto bamboo skewers: place the basil leaves next to the tomatoes, and wrap mint leaves around the zucchini slices.

2 Mix the basting ingredients and baste the kebabs thoroughly. Place the skewers on a grill or under the broiler, turning and basting regularly until the vegetables are just cooked, about 5–7 minutes.

3 Heat the butter for the sauce in a frying pan, then add the brandy and light it. When the flames have died down, stir in the cream and the peppercorns. Cook for approximately 2 minutes, stirring constantly. Serve the kebabs with the green peppercorn sauce.

SPINACH, WALNUT AND GRUYÈRE LASAGNE WITH BASIL

THIS NUTTY LASAGNE IS A DELICIOUS COMBINATION OF FLAVORS, WHICH EASILY EQUALS THE TRADITIONAL MEAT AND TOMATO VERSION.

SERVES EIGHT

INGREDIENTS
3 cups spinach lasagne
  (quick cooking)
For the walnut and tomato sauce
3 tablespoons walnut oil
1 large onion, chopped
8 ounces celeriac, finely chopped
1 can (14 ounces) tomatoes, chopped
1 large clove garlic, finely chopped
½ teaspoon sugar
⅔ cup chopped walnuts
⅔ cup Dubonnet
For the spinach and Gruyère sauce
generous ⅓ cup butter
2 tablespoons walnut oil
1 medium onion, chopped
generous ⅓ cup flour
1 teaspoon mustard powder
5 cups milk
2 cups grated Gruyère cheese
salt and ground black pepper
ground nutmeg
1 pound frozen spinach, thawed and
  puréed
2 tablespoons chopped basil

2 To make the spinach and Gruyère sauce, melt the butter with the walnut oil and add the onion. Cook for 5 minutes, then stir in the flour. Cook for another minute and add the mustard powder and milk, stirring vigorously. When the sauce has come to a boil, take off the heat and add three-quarters of the grated Gruyère. Season to taste with salt, pepper and nutmeg. Finally, add the puréed spinach.

3 Preheat the oven to 350°F. Layer the lasagne in an ovenproof dish. Start with a layer of the spinach and Gruyère sauce, then add a little walnut and tomato sauce, then a layer of lasagne, and continue until the dish is full, ending with a layer of one of the sauces.

4 Sprinkle the remaining Gruyère over the top of the dish, followed by the basil. Bake for 45 minutes.

1 First make the walnut and tomato sauce. Heat the walnut oil and sauté the onion and celeriac. Cook for about 8–10 minutes. Meanwhile, purée the tomatoes in a food processor. Add the garlic to the pan and cook for about 1 minute, then add the sugar, walnuts, tomatoes and Dubonnet. Season to taste. Simmer, uncovered, for 25 minutes.

KOHLRABI STUFFED WITH PEPPERS

IF YOU HAVEN'T SAMPLED KOHLRABI, OR HAVE ONLY EATEN IT IN STEWS WHERE ITS FLAVOR IS LOST, THIS DISH IS RECOMMENDED. THE SLIGHTLY SHARP FLAVOR OF THE PEPPERS IS AN EXCELLENT FOIL TO THE MORE EARTHY FLAVOR OF THE KOHLRABI.

SERVES FOUR

INGREDIENTS

4 small kohlrabi, about 6–8 ounces each
about 1⅔ cups hot vegetable stock
1 tablespoon olive or sunflower oil
1 onion, chopped
1 small red bell pepper, seeded and sliced
1 small green bell pepper, seeded and sliced
salt and freshly ground black pepper
flat leaf parsley, to garnish (optional)

1 Preheat the oven to 350°F. Trim and remove the ends of the kohlrabi, and arrange in the bottom of a medium-size ovenproof dish.

2 Pour over the stock to come about halfway up the vegetables. Cover and braise in the oven for about 30 minutes until tender. Transfer to a plate and allow to cool, reserving the stock.

3 Heat the oil in a frying pan and fry the onion for 3–4 minutes over low heat, stirring occasionally. Add the peppers and cook for a further 2–3 minutes, until the onion is lightly browned.

4 Add the reserved vegetable stock, and a little seasoning and simmer, uncovered, over moderate heat until the stock has almost evaporated.

5 Scoop out the flesh from the kohlrabis and roughly chop. Stir the flesh into the onion and pepper mixture, taste and adjust the seasoning. Arrange the shells in a shallow ovenproof dish.

6 Spoon the filling into the kohlrabi shells. Place in the oven for 5–10 minutes to heat through and then serve, garnished with flat leaf parsley, if liked.

SPINACH ROULADE

A simple purée of spinach baked with eggs rolled around a creamy red bell pepper filling makes an exotic and colorful supper dish. This can be prepared in advance and then reheated when required.

INGREDIENTS
1 pound leaf spinach, well washed and
  drained
fresh nutmeg, grated
pat of butter
3 tablespoons grated Parmesan cheese
3 tablespoons heavy cream
salt and ground black pepper
2 eggs, separated
1 small red bell pepper, chopped
1 cup cream cheese with garlic and herbs

1 Line and then grease a medium-sized jelly roll pan. Preheat the oven to 375°F. Cook the spinach with a tiny amount of water, then drain well, pressing it through a sieve with the back of a ladle. Chop the spinach finely.

2 Mix the spinach with the nutmeg, butter, Parmesan cheese, cream and seasoning. Cool for 5 minutes, then beat in the egg yolks.

3 Whisk the egg whites until they form soft peaks and carefully fold into the spinach mixture. Spread in the prepared pan, level and bake for 12–15 minutes, until firm.

4 Turn the spinach out upside down onto a clean dish towel and let it cool in the pan for half an hour.

5 Meanwhile, simmer the pepper in about 2 tablespoons of water in a covered pan until just soft, then either purée it in a blender or chop it finely. Mix with the soft cheese and season well.

6 When the spinach has cooled, peel off the paper. Trim any hard edges and spread it with the red pepper cream.

7 Carefully roll up the spinach and pepper in the dish towel, leave for 10 minutes to firm up, then serve on a long platter, cut in thick slices.

VARIATION
A thick purée of any root vegetable also works well as a roulade. Try cooked beets or parsnips, flavoring lightly with a mild curry-style spice such as cumin or coriander. The fillings can be varied too, for example, finely chopped and sautéed mushroom and onion or grated carrot mixed with fromage blanc and chives. Roulades are delicious served warm as well. Sprinkle with cheese and bake in a moderately hot oven for 15 minutes or so.

SALADS
AND
VEGETABLE DISHES

*Brighten your menus with this delightful range of colorful
salads and scrumptious vegetable dishes. Varied
but easy-to-obtain ingredients will guarantee that you
have the perfect recipe and accompaniment for every
style of meal — whatever the season.*

USEFUL DRESSINGS

A GOOD DRESSING CAN MAKE EVEN THE SIMPLEST COMBINATION OF FRESH VEGETABLES A MEMORABLE TREAT. REMEMBER THAT LIGHTLY COOKED VEGETABLES ABSORB MORE FLAVOR AND ARE LESS GREASY IF DRESSED WHILE HOT.

HOMEMADE MAYONNAISE
Make this by hand, if possible. If you make it in a food processor, it will be noticeably lighter.

INGREDIENTS
  2 egg yolks
  ½ teaspoon salt
  ½ teaspoon dry mustard
  ground black pepper
  1¼ cups sunflower oil or half olive and
    half sunflower oil
  1 tablespoon wine vinegar
  1 tablespoon hot water

1 Put the yolks in a bowl with the salt and mustard and a grinding of pepper.

2 Set the bowl on a damp dish towel. Using a whisk, beat the yolks and the seasoning thoroughly, then beat in a small trickle of oil.

3 Continue drizzling in the oil, adding it in very small amounts. The secret of a good, thick mayonnaise is to add the oil very slowly, beating each addition well before you add more. When all the oil is added, mix in the vinegar and hot water. To make mayonnaise in a blender, use one whole egg and one yolk instead of two yolks. Blend the eggs with the seasonings. Then, with the blades running, drizzle in the oil very slowly. Add the vinegar.

ORIGINAL THOUSAND ISLANDS DRESSING

INGREDIENTS
  ¼ cup sunflower oil
  1 tablespoon fresh orange juice
  1 tablespoon fresh lemon juice
  2 teaspoons grated lemon rind
  1 tablespoon finely chopped onion
  1 teaspoon paprika
  1 teaspoon Worcestershire sauce
  1 tablespoon finely chopped parsley
  salt and ground black pepper

Put all the ingredients into a screw-topped jar, season to taste and shake vigorously. Great with green salads, grated carrot, baked potato, pasta and rice salads.

YOGURT DRESSING

INGREDIENTS
  ⅔ cup plain yogurt
  2 tablespoons mayonnaise
  2 tablespoons milk
  1 tablespoon fresh parsley, chopped
  1 tablespoon fresh chives or scallions,
  salt and ground black pepper

Simply combine all the ingredients thoroughly in a bowl.

PEPERONATA WITH RAISINS

SLICED ROASTED PEPPERS IN DRESSING WITH VINEGAR-SOAKED RAISINS MAKE A TASTY SIDE SALAD THAT COMPLEMENTS MANY OTHER DISHES.

SERVES TWO TO FOUR

INGREDIENTS

    6 tablespoons sliced peppers in olive
      oil, drained
    1 tablespoon chopped onion
    2 tablespoons balsamic vinegar
    3 tablespoons raisins
    2 tablespoons chopped fresh parsley
    ground black pepper

1 Toss the peppers with the onion and let steep for an hour.

2 Put the vinegar and raisins in a small saucepan and heat for a minute, then let cool.

3 Mix all the ingredients together thoroughly and spoon into a serving bowl. Serve lightly chilled.

COOK'S TIP
Peperonata is one of the classic Italian antipasto dishes, served at the start of each meal with crusty bread to mop up the delicious juices. Try serving shavings of fresh Parmesan cheese alongside, or buy a good selection of green and black olives to accompany the peperonata. Small baby tomatoes will complete the antipasto.

BEAN SPROUT STIR-FRY

HOMEGROWN BEAN SPROUTS TASTE SO GOOD, TOSSED INTO A TASTY STIR-FRY. THEY HAVE MORE FLAVOR AND TEXTURE THAN STORE-BOUGHT VARIETIES AND ARE VERY NUTRITIOUS, BEING RICH IN VITAMINS AND HIGH IN FIBER. OLD DRIED BEANS WILL NOT SPROUT, SO USE BEANS THAT ARE WELL WITHIN THEIR "USE BY" DATE.

SERVES THREE TO FOUR

INGREDIENTS
    2 tablespoons sunflower or peanut oil
    1 cup mixed bean sprouts
    2 scallions, chopped
    1 garlic clove, crushed
    2 tablespoons soy sauce
    2 teaspoons sesame oil
    1 tablespoon sesame seeds
    2 tablespoons chopped fresh cilantro or
      parsley
    salt and ground black pepper

1 Heat the sunflower oil in a large wok and stir-fry the bean sprouts, onion and garlic for 3–5 minutes.

2 Add the remaining ingredients, cook for 1–2 more minutes and serve hot.

GROWING BEAN SPROUTS AT HOME
Use any of the following pulses to grow your own sprouts: green or brown lentils, aduki beans, mung beans, chickpeas, flageolet and haricot beans, soy beans or Indian massor dal.

Cover 3 tablespoons of your chosen pulses with lukewarm water. Let soak overnight, then drain and rinse.

Place in a large clean jam jar or special sprouting tray. Cover with muslin and secure with a rubber band. If using a jam jar, lay the jar on its side and shake it so the beans spread along the length. Leave somewhere warm.

Rinse the beans night and morning with plenty of cold water, running this through the muslin, and drain. Carefully place the jar back on its side.

Repeat this twice a day until roots and shoots appear. (If nothing happens after 48 hours, the beans are probably too old.) When the shoots are at least twice the length of the bean, rinse once more and store in the fridge for up to two days.

PANZANELLA SALAD

SLICED JUICY TOMATOES LAYERED WITH DAY-OLD BREAD SOUNDS STRANGE FOR A SALAD, BUT IT'S QUITE DELICIOUS.

SERVES FOUR TO SIX

INGREDIENTS
    4 thick slices day-old bread, either
      white, brown or rye
    1 small red onion, thinly sliced
    1 pound ripe tomatoes, thinly sliced
    4 ounces mozzarella cheese
    1 tablespoon fresh basil, shredded, or
      marjoram
    salt and ground black pepper
    ½ cup extra-virgin olive oil
    3 tablespoons balsamic vinegar
    juice of 1 small lemon
    pitted and sliced black olives or salted
      capers, to garnish

1 Dip the bread briefly in cold water, then carefully squeeze out the excess water. Arrange on the bottom of a shallow salad bowl.

2 Soak the onion slices in cold water for about 10 minutes while you prepare the other ingredients. Drain and reserve.

3 Layer the tomatoes, thinly sliced cheese, onion, and basil, seasoning well in between each layer. Sprinkle with oil, vinegar and lemon juice.

4 Top with the olives or capers, cover with plastic wrap and chill in the refrigerator overnight, if possible.

CAESAR SALAD

SERVES FOUR

INGREDIENTS

   2 thick slices crustless bread
   2 garlic cloves
   sunflower oil, for frying
   1 head romaine lettuce, torn in pieces
   ½ cup coarsely grated fresh Parmesan
     cheese
   2 eggs
For the dressing
   2 tablespoons extra-virgin olive oil
   2 teaspoons French mustard
   2 teaspoons Worcestershire sauce
   2 tablespoons fresh lemon juice

1 Cut the bread into cubes. Heat one of the garlic cloves slowly in about 3 tablespoons of the sunflower oil, then toss in the bread cubes. Remove the garlic clove.

2 Heat the oven to 375°F. Spread the garlicky cubes on a baking sheet and bake for 10–12 minutes, until golden and crisp. Remove and let cool.

3 Rub the inside of a large salad bowl with the remaining garlic clove and then discard it.

4 Toss in the torn lettuce, sprinkling the cheese between the leaves. Cover and set the salad aside.

5 Boil a small saucepan of water and cook the eggs for 1 minute only. Remove the eggs, and crack them open into a bowl. The whites should be milky and the yolks raw.

6 Whisk the dressing ingredients into the eggs. When ready to serve, pour the dressing over the leaves, toss well and serve topped with the croutons.

VARIATION

Why not try a refreshing Italian version of this salad? Use cubed ciabatta bread for the croutons. Rub the inside of a salad bowl with garlic and spoon in 2–3 tablespoons of good olive oil. Add a selection of torn salad leaves, including romaine, together with some shaved Parmesan cheese. Do not mix yet. Just before serving, add the croutons, season well, then toss the leaves with the oil, coating well. Finally, top with the juice of a fresh lemon.

CHEF'S SALAD

*THIS IS A GOOD OPPORTUNITY
TO USE UP LEFTOVER VEGETABLES
AND PIECES OF CHEESE.*

SERVES SIX

INGREDIENTS

- 1 pound new potatoes, halved if large
- 2 carrots, grated coarsely
- ½ small fennel bulb or 2 stalks celery, sliced thinly
- ¼ cup sliced white mushrooms
- ¼ cucumber, sliced or chopped
- small green or red bell pepper, sliced
- ¼ cup peas
- 1 cup cooked pulses (e.g. red kidney beans or green lentils)
- 1 baby lettuce or 1 head chicory
- 2–3 hard-cooked eggs, quartered, and/or grated cheese, to serve
- ½ bunch watercress, snipped

For the dressing
- ¼ cup mayonnaise
- 3 tablespoons plain yogurt
- 2 tablespoons milk
- 2 tablespoons chopped fresh chives or scallion tops
- salt and ground black pepper

1 Put all the vegetables and pulses (except the lettuce or chicory) into a large mixing bowl.

2 Line a large platter with the lettuce or chicory leaves – creating a nest for the other salad ingredients. Mix the dressing ingredients together and pour over the salad in the mixing bowl.

3 Toss the salad thoroughly in the dressing, season well, then pile into the center of the lettuce nest.

4 Top the salad with the eggs, cheese or both, and sprinkle with the snipped watercress. Serve lightly chilled.

POTATO AND RADISH SALAD

MANY POTATO SALADS ARE DRESSED IN A THICK SAUCE. THIS ONE IS QUITE LIGHT, WITH A FLAVORFUL YET DELICATE DRESSING.

SERVES FOUR TO SIX

INGREDIENTS

1 pound new potatoes, scrubbed
3 tablespoons olive oil
1 tablespoon walnut or hazelnut oil (optional)
2 tablespoons wine vinegar
2 teaspoons coarse-grain mustard
1 teaspoon honey
salt and freshly ground black pepper
6–8 radishes, thinly sliced
2 tablespoons chopped fresh chives

1 Boil the potatoes until just tender. Drain, return to the pan and cut any large potatoes in half.

2 Make a dressing with the oils, vinegar, mustard, honey and seasoning. Combine them thoroughly in a bowl.

3 Toss the potatoes in the dressing while they are still cooling and let them stand for an hour or so.

4 Mix in the radishes and chives, chill lightly, toss again and serve.

COOK'S TIP
The secret of a good potato salad is to dress the potatoes in a vinaigrette-style dressing while they are still warm in order to let them soak up the flavor as they cool. You can then mix in an additional creamy dressing of mayonnaise and plain yogurt, if desired. Sliced celery, red onion and chopped walnuts would make a good alternative to the radishes. For the best effect, serve on a platter lined with frilly lettuce leaves.

THAI RICE <u>AND</u> BEAN SPROUTS

THAI RICE HAS A DELICATE FRAGRANCE AND TEXTURE. THIS SALAD IS A COLORFUL COLLECTION OF THAI FLAVORS AND TEXTURES.

<u>SERVES SIX</u>

INGREDIENTS

2 tablespoons sesame oil
2 tablespoons fresh lime juice
1 small fresh red chili
1 garlic clove, crushed
2 teaspoons grated fresh ginger
2 tablespoons light soy sauce
1 teaspoon honey
3 tablespoons pineapple juice
1 tablespoon wine vinegar
1¼ cups Thai fragrant rice
2 scallions, sliced
2 rings canned pineapple in natural juice, chopped
1¼ cups sprouted lentils
1 small red bell pepper, sliced
1 stalk celery, sliced
½ cup unsalted cashews, roughly chopped
2 tablespoons toasted sesame seeds
salt and freshly ground black pepper

1 Whisk together the sesame oil, lime juice, the seeded and chopped chili, · garlic, ginger, soy sauce, honey, pineapple juice and vinegar in a large bowl. Stir in the lightly boiled rice.

2 Toss in all the remaining ingredients and mix well. This dish can be served warm or lightly chilled. If the rice grains stick together as they cool, simply stir them with a metal spoon.

CHICORY, CARROT <u>AND</u> ARUGULA SALAD

A BRIGHT AND COLORFUL SALAD, IDEAL FOR A BUFFET OR BARBECUE.

<u>SERVES FOUR TO SIX</u>

INGREDIENTS

3 carrots, coarsely grated
about ¼ cup chopped fresh arugula or watercress
1 large head chicory
For the dressing
3 tablespoons sunflower oil
1 tablespoon hazelnut or walnut oil (optional)
2 tablespoons cider or wine vinegar
2 teaspoons honey
1 teaspoon grated lemon rind
1 tablespoon poppy seeds
salt and freshly ground black pepper

1 Combine the carrot and arugula in a large bowl and season well.

2 Shake the dressing ingredients together in a screw-topped jar, then pour onto the carrot and greens. Toss the salad thoroughly.

3 Line a shallow salad bowl with the chicory leaves and spoon the salad into the center. Serve lightly chilled.

BOUNTIFUL BEAN AND NUT SALAD

*THIS IS A GOOD MULTIPURPOSE
DISH. IT CAN BE A COLD MAIN
COURSE, A BUFFET DISH
OR A SALAD ON THE SIDE. IT
ALSO KEEPS WELL FOR UP TO
THREE DAYS IF STORED IN THE
REFRIGERATOR.*

SERVES SIX

INGREDIENTS
   ½ cup red kidney or pinto beans
   ½ cup white cannellini or lima beans
   2 tablespoons olive oil
   6 ounces cut fresh green beans
   3 scallions, sliced
   1 small yellow or red bell pepper,
     sliced
   1 carrot, coarsely grated
   2 tablespoons chopped sun-dried
     tomatoes
   ½ cup unsalted cashews or
     almonds, split

1 Soak the beans, overnight if possible, then drain and rinse well, cover with a lot of cold water and cook according to the instructions on the package.

For the dressing
   3 tablespoons sunflower oil
   2 tablespoons red wine vinegar
   1 tablespoon coarse-grain mustard
   1 teaspoon superfine sugar
   1 teaspoon dried mixed herbs
   salt and ground black pepper

2 When cooked, drain and season the beans and toss them in the olive oil. Let cool for 30 minutes.

3 In a large bowl, mix in the other vegetables, including the sun-dried tomatoes but not the nuts.

4 Make the dressing by shaking all the ingredients together in a screw-topped jar. Toss the dressing with the salad and check the seasoning again. Serve sprinkled with the split nuts.

GARDEN SALAD AND GARLIC CROSTINI

DRESS A COLORFUL MIXTURE OF SALAD LEAVES WITH GOOD OLIVE OIL AND FRESH LEMON JUICE.

SERVES FOUR TO SIX

INGREDIENTS

   3 thick slices day-old bread
   ½ cup extra-virgin olive oil
   garlic clove, cut
   ½ small head romaine lettuce
   ½ small oak leaf lettuce
   2 tablespoons arugula leaves or watercress
   2 tablespoons fresh flat-leaf parsley
   a few leaves and flowers of nasturtium
   flowers of pansy and pot marigold
   a handful of young dandelion leaves
   sea salt flakes and freshly ground
    black pepper
   juice of 1 fresh lemon

1 Cut the bread into medium-size dice about ½-inch square.

2 Heat half the oil gently in a frying pan and fry the bread cubes in it, tossing them until they are well coated and lightly browned. Remove and cool.

3 Rub the inside of a large salad bowl with the garlic and discard. Pour the rest of the oil into the bottom of the bowl.

4 Wash, dry and tear the leaves into bite-size pieces and pile them into the bowl. Season with salt and pepper. Cover and keep chilled until ready to serve.

5 To serve, toss the leaves in the oil at the bottom of the bowl, then sprinkle with the lemon juice and toss again. Scatter over the crostini and serve immediately.

CALIFORNIAN VIM <u>AND</u> VIT SALAD

FULL OF VITALITY AND VITAMINS, THIS IS A LOVELY LIGHT, HEALTHY SALAD FOR SUNNY DAYS WHEN YOU FEEL FULL OF ENERGY OR WHEN YOU NEED AN EXTRA BOOST.

<u>SERVES FOUR</u>

INGREDIENTS
    1 small crisp lettuce, torn in pieces
    8 ounces young spinach leaves
    2 carrots, coarsely grated
    4 ounces cherry tomatoes, halved
    2 celery stalks, thinly sliced
    ½ cup raisins
    ½ cup blanched almonds or unsalted
      cashews, halved
    2 tablespoons sunflower seeds
    2 tablespoons sesame seeds, lightly
      toasted

For the dressing
    3 tablespoons extra-virgin olive oil
    2 tablespoons cider vinegar
    2 teaspoons honey
    juice of 1 small orange
    salt and freshly ground black pepper

1 Put the salad vegetables, raisins, almonds and seeds into a large bowl.

2 Put all the dressing ingredients into a screw top jar, shake them up well and pour over the salad.

3 Toss the salad thoroughly and divide it between four small salad bowls. Season and serve lightly chilled.

SCANDINAVIAN CUCUMBER <u>AND</u> DILL

IT'S AMAZING WHAT A LIGHT TOUCH OF SALT CAN DO TO SIMPLE CUCUMBER SLICES. THEY TAKE ON A CONTRADICTORY SOFT YET CRISP TEXTURE AND DEVELOP A GOOD, FULL FLAVOR. HOWEVER, JUICES CONTINUE TO FORM AFTER SALTING, SO THIS SALAD IS BEST DRESSED JUST BEFORE SERVING.

<u>SERVES FOUR</u>

INGREDIENTS
    2 cucumbers
    salt
    2 tablespoons chopped fresh chives
    2 tablespoons chopped fresh dill
    ⅔ cup sour cream
    freshly ground black pepper

1 Slice the cucumbers as thinly as possible, preferably in a food processor or a slicer.

2 Place the slices in layers in a colander set over a plate to catch the juices. Sprinkle each layer well, but not too heavily, with salt.

3 Let the cucumber drain for up to 2 hours, then lay out the slices on a clean dish towel and pat them dry.

4 Mix the cucumber with the herbs, sour cream and plenty of pepper. Serve as soon as possible.

COOK'S TIP
Lightly salted (or degorged) cucumbers are also delicious as sandwich fillings in wafer thin buttered brown bread. These sandwiches were always served at the traditional British tea-time.

POTATO SALAD WITH CURRY PLANT MAYONNAISE

POTATO SALAD CAN BE MADE WELL IN ADVANCE AND IS THEREFORE A USEFUL BUFFET DISH. ITS POPULARITY MEANS THAT THERE ARE VERY RARELY ANY LEFTOVERS.

SERVES SIX

INGREDIENTS
   salt
   2 pounds new potatoes,
    in skins
   1¼ cups mayonnaise
   6 curry-plant leaves, roughly chopped
   black pepper
   mixed lettuce or other salad greens, to
    serve

1 Place the potatoes in a pan of salted water and boil for 15 minutes, or until tender. Drain and place in a large bowl to cool slightly.

2 Mix the mayonnaise with the curry-plant leaves and black pepper. Stir these into the potatoes while they are still warm. Let cool, then serve on a bed of mixed lettuce or other assorted salad leaves.

TOMATO, SAVORY AND GREEN BEAN SALAD

SAVORY AND BEANS MUST HAVE BEEN INVENTED FOR EACH OTHER. THIS SALAD MIXES THEM WITH RIPE TOMATOES, MAKING A SUPERB ACCOMPANIMENT FOR ALL VEGETABLE DISHES.

<u>SERVES FOUR</u>

INGREDIENTS
    1 pound green beans
    2 pounds ripe tomatoes
    3 scallions, sliced
    1 tablespoon pine nuts
    4 sprigs fresh savory
For the dressing
    2 tablespoons extra-virgin olive oil
    juice of 1 lime
    3 ounces soft blue cheese
    1 clove garlic, peeled and crushed
    salt and pepper

1 Prepare the dressing first so that it can stand for a while before using. Place all the dressing ingredients in the bowl of a food processor, season to taste and blend until all the cheese has been finely chopped and you have a smooth dressing. Pour it into a bowl.

2 Trim and clean the beans and boil in salted water until they are just cooked. Drain them and run cold water over them until they have completely cooled. Slice the tomatoes, or, if they are fairly small, quarter them.

3 Toss the salad ingredients together, except for the pine nuts and savory. Pour on the salad dressing. Sprinkle the pine nuts over the top, followed by the savory.

GREEN BEAN SALAD

ALTHOUGH BEAN SALADS ARE DELICIOUS SERVED WITH A SIMPLE VINAIGRETTE DRESSING, THIS DISH IS A LITTLE MORE ELABORATE. IT DOES, HOWEVER, ENHANCE THE FRESH FLAVOR OF THE BEANS.

SERVES FOUR

INGREDIENTS
    1 pound green beans
    1 tablespoon olive oil
    1 ounce butter
    ½ garlic clove, crushed
    2 ounces fresh white bread crumbs
    1 tablespoon chopped fresh parsley
    1 egg, hard-boiled and finely chopped
    For the dressing
    2 tablespoons olive oil
    2 tablespoons sunflower oil
    2 teaspoons white wine vinegar
    ½ garlic clove, crushed
    ¼ teaspoon Dijon mustard
    pinch of sugar
    pinch of salt

1 Trim the green beans and cook in boiling salted water for 5–6 minutes until tender. Drain the beans and refresh them under cold running water and place in a serving bowl.

2 Make the salad dressing by blending the oils, vinegar, garlic, mustard, sugar and salt thoroughly together. Pour over the beans and toss to mix.

COOK'S TIP
For a more substantial salad, boil about 1 pound scrubbed new potatoes until tender, cool and then cut them into bite-size chunks. Stir into the green beans and then add the dressing.

3 Heat the oil and butter in a frying pan and fry the garlic for 1 minute. Stir in the bread crumbs and fry over moderate heat for about 3–4 minutes until golden brown, stirring frequently.

4 Remove the pan from the heat and stir in the parsley and then the egg. Sprinkle the breadcrumb mixture over the green beans. Serve warm or at room temperature.

RADISH, MANGO AND APPLE SALAD

RADISH IS AVAILABLE ALL YEAR THROUGH AND THIS SALAD CAN BE SERVED ANY TIME OF YEAR, WITH ITS CLEAN, CRISP TASTES AND MELLOW FLAVORS. SERVE WITH SMOKED FISH, SUCH AS ROLLS OF SMOKED SALMON OR WITH CONTINENTAL HAM OR SALAMI.

SERVES FOUR

INGREDIENTS
    10–15 radishes
    1 eating apple, peeled cored and
      thinly sliced
    2 celery stalks, thinly sliced
    1 small ripe mango, peeled and cut
      into small chunks
For the dressing
    ½ cup sour cream
    2 teaspoons creamed horseradish
    1 tablespoon chopped fresh dill
    salt and fresh ground black pepper
    sprig of dill, to garnish

3 Cut through the mango lengthwise either side of the pit. Make even criss-cross cuts through each side section. Take each one and bend it back to separate the cubes. Remove the mango cubes with a small knife and add to the bowl. Pour the dressing over the vegetables and fruit and stir gently so that all the ingredients are coated in the dressing. When ready to serve, spoon the salad into an attractive salad bowl and garnish with a sprig of dill.

1 To prepare the dressing, blend together the sour cream, horseradish and dill in a small jug or bowl and season with a little salt and pepper.

2 Remove the ends of the radishes and then slice them thinly. Add to a bowl together with the thinly sliced apple and celery.

CRUNCHY CABBAGE SALAD WITH PESTO MAYONNAISE

BOTH THE PESTO AND THE MAYONNAISE CAN BE MADE FOR THIS DISH. HOWEVER, IF TIME IS SHORT, YOU CAN BUY THEM BOTH READY-PREPARED AND IT WILL TASTE JUST AS GOOD.

SERVES FOUR TO SIX

INGREDIENTS

    1 small or ½ medium white cabbage
    3–4 carrots, grated
    4 scallions, finely sliced
    1–1½ ounces pine nuts
    1 tablespoon chopped fresh mixed
      herbs; parsley, basil and chervil
For the pesto dressing
    1 egg yolk
    about 2 teaspoons lemon juice
    ⅞ cup sunflower oil
    2 teaspoons pesto
    4 tablespoons plain yogurt
    salt and freshly ground black pepper

1 To make the mayonnaise, place the egg yolk in a blender or food processor and process with the lemon juice. With the machine running, very slowly add the oil, pouring it more quickly as the mayonnaise emulsifies. Season to taste with salt and pepper and a little more lemon juice if necessary. Alternately, make by hand using a balloon whisk.

2 Spoon 5 tablespoons of mayonnaise into a bowl and stir in the pesto and yogurt, beating well to make a fairly thin dressing. (The remaining mayonnaise will keep for about 3–4 weeks in a screw-top jar in the fridge.)

3 Using a food processor or a sharp knife, thinly slice the cabbage and place in a large salad bowl.

4 Add the carrots and scallions, together with the herbs and pine nuts, mixing thoroughly with your hands. Stir the pesto dressing into the salad or serve separately in a small dish if preferred.

ARUGULA AND GRILLED GOAT CHEESE SALAD

GOAT CHEESE CAN BE BOUGHT IN MANY DIFFERENT FORMS. FOR THIS RECIPE, LOOK OUT FOR CYLINDER-SHAPED GOAT CHEESE FROM A DELICATESSEN OR FOR SMALL ROLLS THAT CAN BE CUT INTO PIECES WEIGHING ABOUT 2 OUNCES.

SERVES FOUR

INGREDIENTS
    about 1 tablespoon olive oil
    about 1 tablespoon vegetable oil
    4 slices Italian bread
    3 tablespoons walnut oil
    1 tablespoon lemon juice
    8-ounce cylinder-shape goat cheese
    generous handful of arugula leaves
    about 4 ounces frisée
For the sauce
    3 tablespoons apricot jam
    4 tablespoons white wine
    2 teaspoons Dijon mustard

1 Heat the olive and vegetable oils in a frying pan and fry the slices of Italian bread on one side only, until lightly golden brown. Transfer to a plate lined with paper towels.

4 Preheat the broiler a few minutes before serving the salad. Cut the goat cheese into 2-ounce rounds and place each piece on a croûton, untoasted side up. Place under the broiler and cook for 3–4 minutes until the cheese melts.

5 Toss the arugula and frisée in the walnut oil dressing and arrange attractively on four individual serving plates. When the croûtons are ready, arrange on each plate and pour over a little of the apricot sauce.

2 To make the sauce, heat the jam in a small saucepan until warm but not boiling. Push through a strainer, into a clean pan, to remove the pieces of fruit, and then stir in the white wine and mustard. Heat gently and then keep warm until ready to serve.

3 Blend the walnut oil and lemon juice and season with a little salt and pepper.

BRAISED CELERY WITH GOAT CHEESE

THE SHARP FLAVOR OF THE CELERY IN THIS DISH IS PERFECTLY COMPLEMENTED BY THE MILD YET TANGY GOAT CHEESE. THIS RECIPE IS AN EXAMPLE OF A QUICK AND EASY PREPARATION TO MAKE A DELICIOUS ACCOMPANIMENT TO GRILLED MEAT OR STUFFED CRÊPES.

SERVES FOUR

INGREDIENTS
2 tablespoons butter
1 head of celery, thinly sliced
6 ounces mild medium-fat goat cheese
3–4 tablespoons light cream or half-and-half
salt and freshly ground black pepper

1 Preheat the oven to 350°F and lightly butter a medium-size shallow ovenproof dish.

2 Melt the butter in a heavy saucepan and fry the celery for 2–3 minutes, stirring frequently. Add 3–4 tablespoons water to the pan, heat gently and then cover and simmer over low heat for 5–6 minutes, until the celery is nearly tender and the water has almost evaporated.

3 Remove the pan from the heat and stir in the goat cheese and cream. Taste and season with salt and pepper, and then turn into the prepared dish.

4 Cover the dish with buttered waxed paper and bake for 10–12 minutes. Serve at once.

CELERY, AVOCADO AND WALNUT SALAD

THE CRUNCHINESS OF THE CELERY AND WALNUTS CONTRASTS PERFECTLY WITH THE SMOOTH AVOCADO. SERVE THIS SALAD WITH A SOUR CREAM DRESSING AS SUGGESTED, OR SIMPLY DRESSED WITH A LITTLE OLIVE OIL AND FRESHLY SQUEEZED LEMON JUICE.

SERVES FOUR

INGREDIENTS
8 tender white celery stalks, very thinly sliced
3 scallions, finely chopped
2 ounces walnut halves
1 ripe avocado
lemon juice
For the dressing
½ cup sour cream
1 tablespoon olive oil
pinch of cayenne pepper

1 Place the celery, scallions and walnuts in a large salad bowl.

2 Halve the avocado and, using a very sharp knife, cut into thin slices. Peel away the skin from each slice and then sprinkle generously with lemon juice and add to the celery mixture.

3 Lightly beat the sour cream, olive oil and cayenne pepper together in a pitcher or small bowl. Either fold carefully into the salad or serve separately.

SPINACH AND CANNELLINI BEANS

THIS HEARTY DISH CAN BE MADE WITH ALMOST ANY DRIED BEAN OR PEA, SUCH AS BLACK-EYED PEAS, HARICOTS OR CHICK-PEAS. IT IS A GOOD DISH TO SERVE ON A COLD EVENING.

SERVES FOUR

INGREDIENTS

8 ounces cannellini beans,
  soaked overnight
3 tablespoons olive oil
1 slice white bread
1 onion, chopped
3–4 tomatoes, peeled and chopped
a good pinch of paprika
1 pound spinach
1 garlic clove, halved
salt and freshly ground black pepper

1 Drain the beans, place in a saucepan and cover with water. Bring to a boil and boil rapidly for 10 minutes. Cover and simmer for about 1 hour until the beans are tender. Drain.

2 Heat 2 tablespoons of the oil in a frying pan and fry the bread until golden brown. Transfer to a plate.

3 Fry the onion in the remaining oil over low heat until soft but not brown, then add the tomatoes and continue cooking over low heat.

4 Heat the remaining oil in a large pan, stir in the paprika and then add the spinach. Cover and cook for a few minutes until the spinach has wilted.

5 Add the onion and tomato mixture to the spinach, mix well and stir in the cannellini beans. Place the garlic and fried bread in a food processor and process until smooth. Stir into the spinach and bean mixture. Add ⅔ cup cold water and then cover and simmer gently for 20–30 minutes, adding more water if necessary.

SPINACH IN FILO WITH THREE CHEESES

A GOOD CHOICE TO SERVE WHEN VEGETARIANS AND MEAT EATERS ARE GATHERED FOR A MEAL, AS WHATEVER THEIR PREFERENCE, EVERYONE SEEMS PARTIAL TO THIS TASTY DISH.

SERVES FOUR

INGREDIENTS

1 pound spinach
1 tablespoon sunflower oil
½ ounce butter
1 small onion, finely chopped
6 ounces ricotta cheese
4 ounces feta cheese, cut into
    small cubes
3 ounces Gruyère or Emmenthal
    cheese, grated
1 tablespoon fresh chopped chervil
1 teaspoon fresh chopped marjoram
salt and freshly ground black pepper
5 large or 10 small sheets filo pastry
1½–2 ounces butter, melted

1 Preheat the oven to 375°F. Cook the spinach in a large saucepan over moderate heat for 3–4 minutes until the leaves have wilted, shaking the saucepan occasionally. Strain and press out the excess liquid.

2 Heat the oil and butter in a saucepan and fry the onion for 3–4 minutes until softened. Remove from the heat and add half of the spinach. Combine using a metal spoon, breaking up the spinach.

3 Add the ricotta cheese and stir until evenly combined. Stir in the remaining spinach, again chopping it into the mixture with a metal spoon. Fold in the feta and Gruyère or Emmenthal cheeses, chervil, marjoram and seasoning.

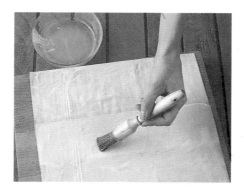

4 Lay a sheet of filo pastry measuring about 12 inches square on a work surface. (If you have small filo sheets, lay them side by side, overlapping by about 1 inch in the middle.) Brush with melted butter and cover with a second sheet; brush this with butter and build up five layers of pastry in this way.

5 Spread the filling over the pastry, leaving a 1-inch border. Fold the two shorter sides inward and then roll up.

6 Place the roll, seam side down, on a greased baking sheet and brush with the remaining butter. Bake in the oven for about 30 minutes until golden brown.

MIGHTY MUSHROOMS

THERE IS NOW A WIDE VARIETY OF CULTIVATED MUSHROOMS AVAILABLE AT LARGER SUPERMARKETS, SO A SIMPLE SIDE DISH OF MUSHROOMS BECOMES QUITE EXCITING.

SERVES FOUR

INGREDIENTS
½ ounce dried porcini mushrooms
¼ cup olive oil
1 cup halved or sliced button mushrooms
4 ounces oyster mushrooms
4 ounces fresh shiitake mushrooms, or 1 ounce dried shiitake mushrooms
2 garlic cloves, crushed
2 teaspoons ground coriander
salt and freshly ground black pepper
3 tablespoons chopped fresh parsley

1 If you are using porcini mushrooms (and they do give a good, rich flavor), soak them in a little hot water just to cover for 20 minutes.

2 In a large saucepan, heat the oil and add all the mushrooms, including the soaked porcinis. Stir well, cover and cook gently for 5 minutes.

3 Stir in the garlic, coriander and seasoning. Cook for another 5 minutes, until the mushrooms are tender and much of the liquor has been reduced.

4 Mix in the parsley, let cool slightly and serve.

TOMATO SAUCE

THIS BASIC SAUCE CAN BE EITHER PART OF A LARGER RECIPE OR SERVED AS A SIDE SAUCE. FOR EXTRA FLAVOR, ADD RED BELL PEPPER, OR ENLIVEN WITH ORANGE RIND AND JUICE AND CHOPPED FRESH HERBS SUCH AS BASIL.

SERVES FOUR TO SIX

INGREDIENTS
1 onion, chopped
2 garlic cloves, crushed
1 small red bell pepper (optional), chopped
3 tablespoons olive oil
1½ pounds fresh tomatoes, skinned and chopped or 1 can (14 ounces) tomatoes, chopped
1 tablespoon sugar
salt and freshly ground black pepper
2 tablespoons chopped fresh herbs (e.g. basil, parsley, marjoram)

1 Gently fry the onion, garlic and red pepper, if using, in the oil for 5 minutes until they are soft.

2 Stir in the tomatoes, add the sugar and seasoning to taste, bring to a boil, then cover and simmer for 15–20 minutes.

3 The sauce should now be thick and pulpy. If it is a little thin, then boil it – uncovered – so it reduces down. Stir in the fresh herbs, if using, and then check the seasoning.

COOK'S TIP
Why not make up a large batch of this sauce and freeze it in two-portion sizes?

SPICED OKRA WITH ALMONDS

LONG AND ELEGANTLY SHAPED, IT'S NOT SURPRISING THESE VEGETABLES HAVE THE POPULAR NAME OF "LADY'S FINGERS."

SERVES TWO TO FOUR

INGREDIENTS

8 ounces okra
½ cup blanched almonds, chopped
2 tablespoons butter
1 tablespoon sunflower oil
2 garlic cloves, crushed
1-inch cube fresh ginger, grated
1 teaspoon cumin seeds
1 teaspoon ground coriander
1 teaspoon paprika

1 Trim just the tops of the okra stems and around the edges of the stalks. They have a sticky liquid that seeps out if prepared too far ahead, so trim them immediately before cooking.

2 Fry the almonds in the butter until they are lightly golden, then remove.

3 Add the oil to the pan and fry the okra, stirring constantly, for 2 minutes.

4 Add the garlic and ginger and fry gently for a minute, then add the spices and cook for another minute or so, stirring constantly.

VARIATION
Okra is also popular in Louisiana cooking and is an essential ingredient in gumbo, a thick, spicy stew served over hot, steaming rice. Indeed, "gumbo" was the old African word for okra used by the American slaves. You can make a ratatouille-style vegetable stew using okra instead of eggplant, and adding onions, bell peppers, garlic and tomatoes. Or try them sliced, fried with garlic and spices, then stirred into a pilaf of basmati rice with cauliflower florets and carrots. This makes a colorful and delicious dish – especially when topped with crushed grilled poppadums.

5 Pour in about 1¼ cups water. Season well, cover and simmer for about 5 minutes or so until the okra feel just tender.

6 Finally, mix in the fried almonds and serve piping hot.

Salads and Vegetable Dishes

STIR-FRY CABBAGE

*AN OFTEN UNDERRATED
VEGETABLE, CRISP CABBAGE IS
WONDERFUL WHEN LIGHTLY
COOKED THE CHINESE WAY IN A
WOK. ANY CABBAGE WILL DO,
BUT SAVOY CABBAGE IS MAYBE
THE BEST.*

<u>SERVES FOUR</u>

INGREDIENTS
  ½ small cabbage
  2 tablespoons sunflower oil
  1 tablespoon light soy sauce
  1 tablespoon fresh lemon juice
    (optional)
  2 teaspoons caraway seeds
  freshly ground black pepper

1 Cut the central core from the cabbage and shred the leaves finely.

2 Heat the oil until quite hot in a wok and then stir-fry the cabbage for about 2 minutes.

3 Toss in the soy sauce, lemon juice, if using, caraway seeds and pepper, to taste.

PERFECT CREAMED POTATOES

*IF A BOWL OF PLAIN, MASHED
POTATOES SOUNDS BORING, THEN
TRY SERVING IT THIS WAY — IN
THE FRENCH STYLE. IT IS
ABSOLUTELY SCRUMPTIOUS! USE
GOOD QUALITY, FLOURY
POTATOES.*

<u>SERVES FOUR</u>

INGREDIENTS
  2 pounds potatoes, peeled and diced
  3 tablespoons extra-virgin olive oil
  about ⅔ cup milk
  fresh nutmeg, grated
  salt and freshly ground black pepper
  a few leaves fresh basil or sprigs fresh
    parsley, chopped

1 Boil the potatoes until just tender and not too mushy. Drain very well. Ideally, press the potatoes through a special potato ricer (something like a large garlic press) or mash them well with a potato masher. Do not pass them through a food processor or you will have a gluey mess.

2 Beat the olive oil into the potatoes with just enough hot milk to make a smooth, thick purée.

3 Flavor to taste with the nutmeg and seasoning, then stir in the fresh chopped herbs. Spoon into a warm serving dish and serve as soon as possible.

ROASTED PEPPERS IN OIL

PEPPERS TAKE ON A DELICIOUS, SMOKY FLAVOR IF ROASTED IN A VERY HOT OVEN. THE SKINS CAN BE EASILY PEELED OFF AND THE FLESH STORED IN OLIVE OIL.

INGREDIENTS
6 large peppers of differing colors
scant 2 cups olive oil

1 Preheat the oven to the highest temperature, about 450°F. Lightly grease a large baking sheet.

3 Roast the peppers at the top of the oven until the skins blacken and blister. This will take 12-15 minutes.

6 Add the oil to the jar to cover the peppers completely, then seal the lid tightly.

4 Remove the peppers from the oven, cover with a clean dish towel until they are cool, then peel off the skins.

5 Slice the peppers and pack them in a clean preserving jar.

7 Store the peppers in the refrigerator and use them within 2 weeks. Use the oil in dressing or for cooking once the peppers have been eaten.

2 Quarter the peppers, remove the cores and seeds, then squash them flat with the backs of your hands. Lay the peppers skin side up on the baking tray.

COOK'S TIP
These pepper slices make very attractive presents, especially around Christmas time. You can either buy special preserving jars at kitchen equipment stores or wash out large jam jars, soaking off the labels at the same time. The jars should then be sterilized by placing them upside down in a warm oven for about half an hour. Fill the jars while they are still hot with the sliced peppers, and top with a good olive oil. Cover immediately with the lid and attach an attractive label.

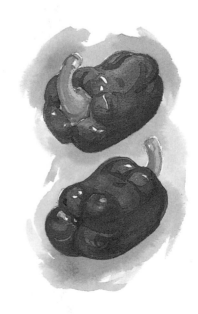

OVEN CHIP ROASTIES

*VERY POPULAR WITH CHILDREN
AND A MUCH BETTER
ALTERNATIVE FOR THE WHOLE
FAMILY TO HIGH-FAT ROASTED
POTATOES.*

SERVES FOUR TO SIX

INGREDIENTS
    4 medium to large baking potatoes
    ⅔ cup olive oil
    1 teaspoon mixed dried herbs (optional)
    sea salt flakes

1 Preheat the oven to the highest possible temperature, generally 450°F. Place a lightly-oiled roasting pan in the oven to get very hot.

2 Cut the potatoes in half lengthwise, then into long, thin wedges. Brush each side lightly with oil.

3 When the oven is very hot, remove the pan carefully and lay the potato slices over it in a single layer.

4 Sprinkle the potatoes with the herbs and salt and place in the oven for about 20 minutes or until they are golden brown, crisp and lightly puffy. Serve immediately.

VARIATION
Parsnips also make fine oven chips. Choose large parsnips, which tend to have more flavor. Slice thinly on a diagonal and roast in the same way as above, although you may find they do not take as long to cook. They make great mid-week suppers for kids and grown-ups served with fried eggs, mushrooms and tomatoes.

WARM SPICY DAL

IF YOU THOUGHT YELLOW SPLIT PEAS WERE ONLY FOR SOUPS, TRY THIS INDIAN-INSPIRED DISH. SERVE WITH RICE, CHAPATIS OR NAAN AND WHATEVER MAIN DISH YOU LIKE.

SERVES FOUR TO SIX

INGREDIENTS

8 ounces yellow split peas
2 onions, chopped
1 large bay leaf
2½ cups stock or water
salt and freshly ground black pepper
2 teaspoons black mustard seeds
2 tablespoons melted butter
1 garlic clove, crushed
1-inch cube fresh ginger
1 small green bell pepper, sliced
1 teaspoon ground turmeric
1 teaspoon garam masala
3 tomatoes, skinned and chopped
fresh cilantro or parsley, to serve

1 Put the split peas, 1 onion and the bay leaf in the stock, in a covered pan. Simmer for 25 minutes, seasoning lightly towards the end.

2 In a separate pan, fry the mustard seeds in the butter for about 30 seconds until they start to pop, then add all the remaining onion, along with the garlic, grated ginger and green pepper.

3 Sauté for about 5 minutes, until softened, then stir in the remaining spices and fry for a few seconds more.

4 Add the split peas, tomatoes, and a little extra water if needed. Cover and simmer for another 10 minutes, then check the seasoning and serve hot garnished with cilantro or parsley.

POTATO LATKES

THESE LITTLE POTATO PANCAKES MAKE A PLEASANT AND UNUSUAL ALTERNATIVE TO FRENCH FRIES OR ROAST POTATOES.

MAKES ABOUT 24

INGREDIENTS
2 pounds potatoes, peeled and coarsely grated
scant ½ cup self-rising flour
2 eggs
1 tablespoon onion, grated
fresh nutmeg, grated
salt and freshly ground black pepper
oil, for shallow frying

1 Soak the grated potato in plenty of cold water for about an hour, then drain well and pat dry with a clean dish towel.

2 Beat together the flour, eggs, onion and nutmeg, then mix in the potato. Season well.

3 Heat a thin layer of oil in a heavy frying pan and drop about a tablespoon of potato-batter into the pan, squashing it flat, if necessary.

4 Cook the potato until golden brown, then flip over and cook the other side. Drain on paper towels and keep warm, uncovered, in the oven. Repeat with the rest of the mixture.

STIR-FRY EGGPLANT

A SPEEDY SIDE DISH WITH AN ASIAN TOUCH. THE EGGPLANT IS STIR-FRIED WITH RED BELL PEPPER AND BLACK BEANS, WHICH GIVES IT AN EXOTIC AND COLORFUL APPEARANCE. SALTED BLACK BEANS ARE SOLD EITHER DRIED OR CANNED. DRIED ONES WILL NEED SOAKING.

SERVES FOUR

INGREDIENTS
2 tablespoons peanut oil
1 eggplant, sliced
2 scallions, sliced diagonally
1 garlic clove, crushed
1 small red bell pepper, sliced
2 tablespoons mushroom sauce
1 tablespoon Chinese salted black beans, soaked if dried
freshly ground black pepper
1 tablespoon chopped fresh cilantro or parsley, to garnish

1 Heat the oil in a wok and stir-fry the eggplant for 2 minutes. Add the onions, garlic and pepper and cook for another 2 minutes.

2 Add the mushroom sauce, black beans and pepper. Cook for another minute, season with pepper only and serve with fresh cilantro.

PEAS AND LETTUCE

*DO NOT DISCARD THE TOUGH,
OUTER LEAVES OF LETTUCE —
THEY ARE DELICIOUS IF THEY ARE
SHREDDED AND COOKED WITH
PEAS.*

SERVES FOUR

INGREDIENTS
    6 outer leaves of a Romaine lettuce
    1 small onion or shallot, sliced
    2 tablespoons butter or sunflower
      margarine (for vegans)
    8 ounces frozen garden peas
    fresh nutmeg, grated
    salt and freshly ground black pepper

1 Pull off the outer lettuce leaves and wash them well. Roughly shred the leaves with your hands.

2 In a saucepan, lightly fry the lettuce and onion in the butter for 3 minutes.

3 Add the peas, nutmeg to taste and seasoning. Stir, cover and simmer for about 5 minutes. This dish can be drained or served slightly wet.

HASH BROWNS

A TRADITIONAL BREAKFAST DISH, HASH BROWNS CAN BE SERVED ANY TIME OF DAY.

SERVES FOUR

INGREDIENTS
¼ cup sunflower or olive oil
1 pound potatoes, cooked and diced
1 small onion, chopped
salt and freshly ground black pepper

1 Heat the oil in a large, heavy frying pan and when it is quite hot add the potatoes in a single layer. Scatter the onion on top and season well.

2 Cook over medium heat until browned underneath, pressing down on the potatoes with a spoon or spatula to squash them together.

3 When the potatoes are nicely browned, turn them over in sections and fry on the other side, pressing them down once again. Serve when heated through and lightly crispy.

POTATO AND PARSNIP DAUPHINOIS

LAYERS OF POTATOES AND PARSNIPS ARE BAKED SLOWLY IN CREAMY MILK WITH GRATED CHEESE. THIS IS AN IDEAL SPECIAL SIDE DISH OR LIGHT SUPPER DISH.

SERVES FOUR TO SIX

INGREDIENTS
2 pounds potatoes, thinly sliced
1 onion, thinly sliced
1 pound parsnips, thinly sliced
2 garlic cloves, crushed
¼ cup butter
½ cup grated Gruyère or Cheddar
  cheese
fresh nutmeg, grated
salt and freshly ground black pepper
½ pint light cream or half-and-half
½ pint milk

1 Lightly grease a large shallow ovenproof dish. Preheat the oven to 350°F.

2 Layer the potatoes with the onion and parsnips. In between each layer, dot the vegetables with garlic and butter. Sprinkle on most of the cheese, add the nutmeg and season well.

3 Heat the cream and milk together in a saucepan until hot but not boiling. Slowly pour the creamy mixture over the vegetables, making sure it seeps underneath them.

4 Scatter the remaining cheese over the vegetables and grate a little more nutmeg on top. Bake for about an hour or so, until the potatoes are tender and the top is bubbling and golden.

ASPARAGUS MIMOSA

PRETTY SPEARS OF FRESH, TENDER ASPARAGUS ARE TOSSED IN A BUTTERY SAUCE AND SERVED WITH A CHOPPED EGG AND CHERVIL DRESSING. THIS ALSO MAKES AN EXCELLENT APPETIZER.

SERVES TWO

INGREDIENTS
8 ounces fresh asparagus
salt
ground black pepper
¼ cup butter, melted
squeeze of fresh lemon juice
2 eggs, hard-cooked and chopped
1 tablespoon chopped fresh chervil

1 Trim the asparagus stalks and peel off the tough outer layers at the base with a vegetable peeler.

2 Poach the asparagus spears in lightly salted water, until just tender. This will take between 3–6 minutes. (Use a clean, deep frying pan if you don't have an asparagus steamer.)

3 Drain the asparagus well and arrange it on two small plates or one large one. Season well.

4 Mix the melted butter with the lemon juice. Trickle over the spears, sprinkle with the eggs and garnish with the chervil. Serve warm.

STIR-FRIED BRUSSELS SPROUTS

SERVES FOUR

INGREDIENTS
    1 pound Brussels sprouts
    1 tablespoon sunflower oil
    6–8 scallions, cut into
      1-inch lengths
    2 slices fresh ginger
    ¼ cup slivered almonds
    ¾ cup vegetable stock
    salt

1 Remove any large outer leaves and trim the bases of the Brussels sprouts. Cut into slices about ⅓ inch thick.

2 Heat the oil in a wok or heavy frying pan and fry the scallions and the ginger for 2–3 minutes, stirring frequently. Add the almonds and stir-fry over medium heat until both the onions and almonds begin to brown.

3 Remove and discard the ginger, reduce the heat and stir in the Brussels sprouts. Stir-fry for a few minutes and then pour in the stock and cook over low heat for 5–6 minutes or until the sprouts are nearly tender.

4 Add a little salt, if necessary, and then increase the heat to boil off the excess liquid. Spoon into a warmed serving dish and serve immediately.

BRUSSELS SPROUTS GRATIN

SERVES FOUR

INGREDIENTS
    1 tablespoon butter
    ⅔ cup heavy cream
    ⅔ cup milk
    2 tablespoons grated Parmesan cheese
    salt and freshly ground black pepper
    1½ pounds Brussels sprouts, thinly
      sliced
    1 garlic clove, finely chopped

1 Preheat the oven to 300°F and butter a shallow ovenproof dish. Blend together the cream, milk, Parmesan cheese and seasoning.

2 Place a layer of Brussels sprouts in the base of the prepared dish, sprinkle with a little garlic and pour over about a quarter of the cream mixture. Add another layer of sprouts and continue building layers in this way, ending with the remaining cream and milk

3 Cover loosely with waxed paper and bake for 1–1¼ hours. Halfway through cooking, remove the paper and press the sprouts under the liquid in the dish. Return to the oven to brown.

PUFFY CREAMED POTATOES

THIS ACCOMPANIMENT CONSISTS OF CREAMED POTATOES INCORPORATED INTO MINI YORKSHIRE PUDDINGS. SERVE THEM WITH ROAST DUCK OR BEEF, OR WITH A VEGETARIAN CASSEROLE. FOR A MEAL ON ITS OWN, SERVE TWO OR THREE PER PERSON AND ACCOMPANY WITH SALADS.

MAKES SIX

INGREDIENTS
    10 ounces potatoes
    whole milk and butter for mashing
    1 teaspoon chopped fresh parsley
    1 teaspoon chopped fresh tarragon
    3 ounces all-purpose flour
    1 egg
    about ½ cup milk
    oil or sunflower fat, for baking
    salt and freshly ground black pepper

1 Boil the potatoes until tender and mash with a little milk and butter. Stir in the chopped parsley and tarragon and season well to taste. Preheat the oven to 400°F.

2 Process the flour, egg, milk and a little salt in a food processor or blender to make a smooth batter.

3 Place about ½ teaspoon oil or a small pat of sunflower fat in each of six ramekin dishes and place in the oven on a baking sheet for 2–3 minutes until the oil or fat is very hot.

4 Working quickly, pour a small amount of batter (about 4 teaspoons) into each ramekin dish. Add a heaped tablespoon of mashed potatoes and then pour an equal amount of the remaining batter in each dish. Place in the oven and bake for 15–20 minutes until the puddings are puffy and golden brown.

5 Using a metal spatula, carefully ease the puddings out of the ramekin dishes and arrange on a large warm serving dish. Serve at once.

HASSLEBACK POTATOES

*THESE SPLENDID ROAST POTATOES
ARE IDEAL TO SERVE AT DINNER
PARTIES OR ON SPECIAL
OCCASIONS SUCH AS CHRISTMAS.*

SERVES FOUR

INGREDIENTS
olive or sunflower oil, for roasting
4 medium potatoes, peeled and halved
lengthwise
salt and ground black pepper
1 tablespoon dried bread crumbs

1 Pour enough oil into a small roasting
pan to just cover the bottom, then put into
an oven set at 400°F to heat.

2 Meanwhile, parboil the potato halves for
5 minutes, then drain. Cool slightly and
slash about four times from the rounded
tops almost down to the flat bottoms.

3 Place the potatoes in the heated
roasting pan and spoon the hot oil over
them. Season well and return the potatoes
to the oven for about 20 minutes.

4 Remove the potatoes once more from
the oven, pry open the slashes slightly
and spoon the hot oil over them. Sprinkle
the potato tops lightly with bread crumbs
and return to the oven for another
15 minutes or so, until they are golden
brown, cooked and crispy.

COOK'S TIP
There are many different ways of roasting
potatoes in the oven. First, the choice of
potato is important. Choose a variety that
holds its shape well and yet is still slightly
floury inside. Details on the bag should
give you guidance. The oil is important
too – choose one that is either flavorless,
such as sunflower or peanut oil, or one
with a lot of good flavor, such as olive oil.
Just before serving, try drizzling a little
sesame seed, walnut or hazelnut oil over
the roasted potatoes for a delicious
nutty flavor.

BROCCOLI AND CAULIFLOWER WITH A CIDER AND APPLE MINT SAUCE

THE CIDER SAUCE MADE HERE IS IDEAL FOR OTHER VEGETABLES, SUCH AS CELERY OR BEANS. IT IS FLAVORED WITH TAMARI, A JAPANESE SOY SAUCE, AND APPLE MINT.

SERVES FOUR

INGREDIENTS

   1 large onion, chopped
   2 large carrots, chopped
   1 large garlic clove
   1 tablespoon dill seed
   4 large sprigs apple mint
   2 tablespoons olive oil
   2 tablespoons all-purpose flour
   1 cup dry cider
   1 pound broccoli florets
   1 pound cauliflower florets
   2 tablespoons tamari
   2 teaspoons mint jelly

1 Sauté the onions, carrots, garlic, dill seed and apple mint leaves in the olive oil until nearly cooked. Stir in the flour and cook for half a minute or so. Pour in the cider and simmer until the sauce looks glossy.

2 Boil the broccoli and cauliflower in separate pans until tender.

3 Pour the sauce into a food processor and add the tamari and the mint jelly. Blend until finely puréed. Pour over the broccoli and cauliflower.

ZUCCHINI <u>AND</u> CARROT RIBBONS <u>WITH</u> BRIE, BLACK PEPPER <u>AND</u> PARSLEY

THIS RECIPE PRODUCES A DELICIOUS VEGETARIAN MEAL OR SIMPLY A NEW WAY OF PRESENTING COLORFUL VEGETABLES AS AN ACCOMPANIMENT TO A MAIN COURSE.

SERVES FOUR

INGREDIENTS

1 large green bell pepper, diced
1 tablespoon sunflower oil
8 ounces Brie cheese
2 tablespoons crème fraîche
1 teaspoon lemon juice
4 tablespoons milk
2 teaspoons freshly ground black pepper
2 tablespoons parsley, very finely
  chopped, plus extra to garnish
salt and pepper
6 large zucchini
6 large carrots

1 Sauté the green pepper in the sunflower oil until just tender. Place the remaining ingredients, except for the zucchini and carrots, in a food processor and blend well. Place the mixture in a saucepan and add the green pepper.

2 Peel the zucchini. Use a potato peeler to slice them into long, thin strips. Do the same with the carrots. Put the zucchini and carrots in separate saucepans, add just enough water to cover, then simmer for 3 minutes, until barely cooked.

3 Heat the sauce and pour into a shallow vegetable dish. Toss the zucchini and carrot strips together and arrange them in the sauce. Garnish with a little finely chopped parsley.

BAKED ZUCCHINI

WHEN VERY SMALL AND VERY FRESH ZUCCHINI ARE USED FOR THIS RECIPE, IT IS WONDERFUL, BOTH SIMPLE AND DELICIOUS. THE CREAMY YET TANGY GOAT CHEESE CONTRASTS WELL WITH THE VERY DELICATE FLAVOR OF THE YOUNG ZUCCHINI.

SERVES FOUR

INGREDIENTS
    8 small zucchini, about 1 pound total
      weight
    1 tablespoon olive oil, plus extra
      for greasing
    4 ounces goat cheese, cut into
      thin strips
    small bunch fresh mint, finely
      chopped
    freshly ground black pepper

1 Preheat the oven to 350°F. Cut out eight rectangles of foil large enough to encase each zucchini and brush each with a little oil.

2 Trim the zucchini and cut a thin slit along the length of each.

3 Insert pieces of goat cheese in the slits. Add a little mint and sprinkle with the olive oil and black pepper.

4 Wrap each zucchini in the foil rectangles, place on a baking sheet and bake for about 25 minutes, until tender.

COOK'S TIP
Almost any cheese could be used in this recipe. Mild cheeses, however, such as a mild Cheddar or mozzarella, will best allow the flavor of the zucchini to be appreciated.

ZUCCHINI ITALIAN-STYLE

IF YOU GROW YOUR OWN ZUCCHINI AND HAVE HUGE QUANTITIES TO USE UP, THIS IS A QUICK AND EASY RECIPE. ITS SIMPLICITY BELIES ITS EXCELLENCE.

SERVES FOUR

INGREDIENTS

1 tablespoon virgin olive oil
1 tablespoon sunflower oil
1 large onion, chopped
1 garlic clove, crushed
4–5 medium zucchini, cut into ½-inch slices
⅔ cup chicken or vegetable stock
½ teaspoon chopped fresh oregano
salt and freshly ground black pepper
chopped fresh parsley, to garnish

3 Stir in the stock, oregano and seasoning and simmer gently for 8–10 minutes, until the liquid has almost evaporated. Spoon the zucchini into a serving dish, sprinkle with parsley and serve.

1 Heat the oils in a large frying pan and fry the onion and garlic over moderate heat for 5–6 minutes until the onion has softened and is beginning to brown.

2 Add the zucchini and fry for about 4 minutes until they just begin to be flecked with brown. Stir frequently.

PATATAS BRAVAS

THIS IS A CLASSIC SPANISH TAPAS DISH OF DEEP-FRIED CUBES OF POTATO WITH A SPICY TOMATO SAUCE. USE A VERSATILE MAIN-CROP VARIETY OF POTATO FOR THIS DISH — SUCH AS RUSSET — SO THAT THE FLESH RETAINS ITS TEXTURE.

SERVES FOUR

INGREDIENTS
  1½ pounds potatoes,
    such as russet
  oil, for deep frying
For the sauce
  1 tablespoon olive oil
  1 small onion, chopped
  1 garlic clove, crushed
  1 can (14 ounces) tomatoes
  2 teaspoons Worcestershire sauce
  1 teaspoon wine vinegar
  about 1 teaspoon Tabasco sauce

1 Peel and cut the potatoes into small cubes and place in a large bowl of cold water to remove the excess starch.

2 Heat the oil in a medium frying pan and fry the onion and garlic for 3–4 minutes, until the onion is soft and just beginning to brown.

3 Pour the tomatoes into a blender or processor, process until smooth and then pour into the pan with the onion. Simmer, uncovered, over medium heat for 8–10 minutes, stirring occasionally, until the mixture is thick and reduced.

4 Heat the oil in a deep fryer. Drain the potatoes and pat dry with paper towels. Fry the potatoes in the hot oil, in batches if necessary, until golden brown. Drain on paper towels.

5 Stir the Worcestershire sauce, wine vinegar and Tabasco sauce into the tomato mixture. Add the potatoes, stirring well so that all the potatoes are coated with the sauce. Spoon into individual serving dishes and serve at once.

POTATOES DAUPHINOIS

SERVES FOUR

INGREDIENTS
  1½ pounds potatoes, peeled and thinly
    sliced
  1 garlic clove
  2 tablespoons butter
  1¼ cups light cream or half-and-half
  ¼ cup milk
  salt and white pepper

1 Preheat the oven to 300°F. Place the potato slices in a bowl of cold water to remove the excess starch. Drain and pat dry with paper towels.

2 Cut the garlic in half and rub the cut side around the inside of a wide shallow ovenproof dish. Butter the dish generously. Blend the cream and milk in a bowl.

3 Cover the base of the dish with a layer of potatoes. Dot a little butter over the potato layer, season with salt and pepper and then top with a little of the cream and milk mixture.

4 Continue making layers until all the ingredients have been used up, ending with a layer of cream.

5 Bake in the oven for about 1¼ hours. If the dish browns too quickly and seems to be drying out, cover with a lid or with a piece of foil. The potatoes are ready when they are very soft and the top is pale golden brown.

COOK'S TIP
For a slightly speedier version of this recipe, parboil the potato slices for 3–4 minutes. Drain well and assemble as above. Cook at 325°F for 45–50 minutes, until the potatoes are completely tender.

GLAZED CARROTS WITH CIDER

THIS RECIPE IS EXTREMELY SIMPLE TO MAKE. THE CARROTS ARE COOKED IN THE MINIMUM OF LIQUID TO BRING OUT THE BEST OF THEIR FLAVOR, AND THE CIDER ADDS A PLEASANT SHARPNESS.

SERVES FOUR

INGREDIENTS
1 pound young carrots
1 ounce butter
1 tablespoon brown sugar
½ cup cider
4 tablespoons vegetable stock or water
1 teaspoon French mustard
1 tablespoon finely chopped fresh
  parsley

1 Trim the tops and bottoms off the carrots. Peel or scrape them. Using a sharp knife cut the carrots into julienne.

2 Melt the butter in a saucepan, add the carrots and sauté for 4–5 minutes, stirring frequently. Sprinkle over the sugar and cook, stirring for 1 minute or until the sugar has dissolved.

3 Add the cider and stock or water, bring to a boil and stir in the French mustard. Partially cover the pan and simmer for about 10–12 minutes until the carrots are just tender. Remove the lid and continue cooking until the liquid has reduced to a thick sauce.

4 Remove the saucepan from the heat, stir in the parsley and then spoon into a warmed serving dish. Serve as an accompaniment to broiled meat or fish or with a vegetarian dish.

COOK'S TIP
If the carrots are cooked before the liquid in the saucepan has reduced, transfer the carrots to a serving dish and rapidly boil the liquid until thick. Pour over the carrots and sprinkle with parsley.

CARROT, APPLE AND ORANGE COLESLAW

THIS DISH IS AS DELICIOUS AS IT IS EASY TO MAKE. THE GARLIC AND HERB DRESSING ADDS THE NECESSARY CONTRAST TO THE SWEETNESS OF THE SALAD.

SERVES FOUR

INGREDIENTS
12 ounces young carrots,
  finely grated
2 eating apples
1 tablespoon lemon juice
1 large orange
For the dressing
3 tablespoons olive oil
4 tablespoons sunflower oil
3 tablespoons lemon juice
1 garlic clove, crushed
4 tablespoons plain yogurt
1 tablespoon chopped mixed fresh
  herbs: tarragon, parsley, chives
salt and freshly ground black pepper

1 Place the carrots in a large serving bowl. Quarter the apples, remove the core and then slice thinly. Sprinkle with the lemon juice to prevent them discoloring and then add to the carrots.

2 Using a sharp knife, remove the peel and pith from the oranges and then separate into segments.

3 To make the dressing, place all the ingredients in a jar with a tight-fitting lid and shake vigorously to blend.

4 Just before serving, pour the dressing over the salad and toss well together.

Wax Beans <u>with</u> Garlic

Delicate and fresh tasting flageolet beans and garlic add a distinct French flavor to this simple side dish. Serve to accompany roast lamb or veal.

SERVES FOUR

INGREDIENTS

    8 ounces flageolet beans
    1 tablespoon olive oil
    1 ounce butter
    1 onion, finely chopped
    1–2 garlic cloves, crushed
    3–4 tomatoes, peeled and chopped
    12 ounces wax beans, prepared and
      sliced
    ⅔ cup white wine
    ⅔ cup vegetable stock
    2 tablespoons chopped fresh parsley
    salt and freshly ground black pepper

1 Place the flageolet beans in a large saucepan of water, bring to a boil and simmer for ¾–1 hour until tender. Drain.

2 Heat the oil and butter in a large frying pan and sauté the onion and garlic for 3–4 minutes until soft. Add the chopped tomatoes and continue cooking over low heat until they are soft.

3 Stir the flageolet beans into the onion and tomato mixture, then add the wax beans, wine, stock, and a little salt. Stir well. Cover and simmer for 5–10 minutes until the wax beans are tender.

4 Increase the heat to reduce the liquid, then stir in the parsley and season with a little more salt, if necessary, and pepper.

BALTI-STYLE CAULIFLOWER WITH TOMATOES

BALTI IS A TYPE OF MEAT AND VEGETABLE COOKING FROM PAKISTAN AND NORTHERN INDIA. IT CAN REFER BOTH TO THE PAN USED FOR COOKING, WHICH IS LIKE A LITTLE WOK, AND THE SPICES USED. IN THE ABSENCE OF A GENUINE BALTI PAN, USE EITHER A WOK OR A HEAVY FRYING PAN.

SERVES FOUR

INGREDIENTS

2 tablespoons vegetable oil
1 onion, chopped
2 garlic cloves, crushed
1 cauliflower, broken into florets
1 teaspoon ground coriander
1 teaspoon ground cumin
1 teaspoon ground fennel seeds
½ teaspoon garam masala
pinch of ground ginger
½ teaspoon chili powder
4 plum tomatoes, peeled, seeded and quartered
6 fluid ounces water
6 ounces fresh spinach, roughly chopped
1–2 tablespoons lemon juice
salt and freshly ground black pepper

1 Heat the oil in a balti pan, wok, or large frying pan. Add the onion and garlic and stir-fry for 2–3 minutes over high heat until the onion begins to brown. Add the cauliflower florets and stir-fry for a further 2–3 minutes until the cauliflower is flecked with brown.

2 Add the coriander, cumin, fennel seeds, garam masala, ginger and chili powder and cook over high heat for 1 minute, stirring all the time; then add the tomatoes, water and salt and pepper. Bring to a boil and then reduce the heat, cover and simmer for 5–6 minutes until the cauliflower is just tender.

3 Stir in the chopped spinach, cover and cook for 1 minute until the spinach is tender. Add enough lemon juice to sharpen the flavor and adjust the seasoning to taste.

4 Serve straight from the pan, with an Indian meal or with chicken or meat.

KALE WITH PARMESAN AND GARLIC

KALE IS A ROBUST, FULL-BODIED TYPE OF CABBAGE. IT HAS A VERY PRONOUNCED FLAVOR AND IS GOOD WHEN COOKED WITH OTHER STRONG-FLAVORED INGREDIENTS SUCH AS ONIONS, GARLIC AND PARMESAN CHEESE. IT DOES NOT NEED LONG COOKING AS THE LEAVES ARE QUITE TENDER.

SERVES FOUR

INGREDIENTS
    3 tablespoons olive oil
    2 garlic cloves, crushed
    4 scallions, sliced
    12 ounces curly kale, thinly sliced,
      tough stalk removed
    2 ounces Parmesan cheese, grated
    salt and freshly ground black pepper
    shavings of Parmesan cheese,
      to garnish

1 Heat the olive oil in a large saucepan or wok and fry the garlic gently for a few seconds. Add the scallions, stir-fry for 2 minutes and then add the kale.

2 Stir-fry for a few minutes so that the kale is coated in oil, and then add about ¼ cup water. Bring to a boil, cover and simmer until the kale is tender. Stir occasionally during cooking and do not allow the pan to boil dry.

3 Bring the liquid to the boil and allow the excess to evaporate and then stir in the Parmesan cheese. Serve at once with extra shavings of cheese, if liked.

INDIAN–STYLE OKRA

*WHEN OKRA (BHINDI) IS SERVED IN INDIAN RESTAURANTS IT IS OFTEN FLAT AND SOGGY BECAUSE IT HAS
BEEN OVERCOOKED OR LEFT STANDING. HOWEVER, WHEN YOU MAKE THIS DISH YOURSELF, YOU WILL
REALIZE HOW DELICIOUS OKRA CAN BE.*

SERVES FOUR

INGREDIENTS

    12 ounces okra
    2 small onions
    2 garlic cloves, crushed
    ½-inch piece fresh ginger
    1 green chili, seeded
    2 teaspoons ground cumin
    2 teaspoons ground coriander
    2 tablespoons vegetable oil
    juice 1 lemon

3 Reduce the heat and add the garlic
and ginger mixture. Cook for about
2–3 minutes, stirring frequently, and
then add the okra, lemon juice and
7 tablespoons water. Stir well, cover
tightly and simmer over low heat for
about 10 minutes until tender. Transfer
to a serving dish, sprinkle with the fried
onion rings and serve at once.

1 Trim the okra and cut into ½-inch
lengths. Roughly chop one of the onions
and place in a food processor or blender
with the garlic, ginger, chili and 6 tablespoons water. Process to a paste. Add
the cumin and coriander and blend again.

2 Thinly slice the remaining onion into
rings and fry in the oil for 6–8 minutes
until golden brown. Transfer to a plate
using a slotted spoon.

STUFFED TOMATOES <u>WITH</u> WILD RICE, CORN <u>AND</u> CILANTRO

THESE TOMATOES COULD BE SERVED AS A LIGHT MEAL WITH CRUSTY BREAD AND A SALAD, OR AS AN ACCOMPANIMENT TO A MAIN COURSE.

SERVES FOUR

INGREDIENTS
    8 medium tomatoes
    ⅓ cup corn
    2 tablespoons white wine
    ¼ cup cooked wild rice
    1 clove garlic
    ½ cup grated Cheddar cheese
    1 tablespoon chopped fresh cilantro
    salt and pepper
    1 tablespoon olive oil

1 Cut the tops off the tomatoes and remove the seeds with a small spoon. Scoop out all the flesh and chop finely – also chop the tops.

2 Preheat the oven to 350°F. Put the chopped tomato in a pan. Add the corn and the white wine. Cover with a close-fitting lid and simmer until tender. Drain.

3 Mix together all the remaining ingredients except the olive oil, adding salt and pepper to taste. Carefully spoon the mixture into the tomatoes, piling it higher in the center. Sprinkle the oil over the top, arrange the tomatoes in an ovenproof dish and bake at 350°F for 15–20 minutes, until cooked through. Let stand for a few minutes before serving.

PEAS <u>WITH</u> BABY ONIONS <u>AND</u> CREAM

IDEALLY, USE FRESH PEAS AND FRESH BABY ONIONS. FROZEN PEAS ARE AN ACCEPTABLE SUBSTITUTE IF FRESH ONES AREN'T AVAILABLE, BUT FROZEN ONIONS TEND TO BE INSIPID AND ARE NOT WORTH USING. ALTERNATELY, USE THE WHITE PART OF SCALLIONS.

SERVES FOUR

INGREDIENTS
6 ounces baby onions
½ ounce butter
2 pounds fresh peas (about 12 ounces shelled or frozen)
⅔ cup heavy cream
½ ounce all-purpose flour
2 teaspoons chopped fresh parsley
1–2 tablespoons lemon juice (optional)
salt and freshly ground black pepper

1 Peel the onions and halve them if necessary. Melt the butter in a flame-proof casserole and fry the onions for 5–6 minutes over moderate heat, until they begin to be flecked with brown.

3 Using a small whisk, blend the cream with the flour. Remove the pan from the heat and stir in the combined cream and flour, parsley and seasoning to taste.

4 Cook over low heat for about 3–4 minutes, until the sauce is thick. Taste and adjust the seasoning; add a little lemon juice to sharpen, if liked.

2 Add the peas and stir-fry for a few minutes. Add ¼ cup water and bring to a boil. Partially cover and simmer for about 10 minutes until both the peas and onions are tender. There should be a thin layer of water on the bottom of the pan – add a little more water if necessary or if there is too much liquid, remove the lid and increase the heat until the liquid is reduced.

BOK CHOY WITH LIME DRESSING

FOR THIS THAI RECIPE, THE COCONUT DRESSING IS TRADITIONALLY MADE USING FISH SAUCE, BUT VEGETARIANS COULD USE MUSHROOM SAUCE INSTEAD. BEWARE, THIS IS A FIERY DISH!

SERVES FOUR

INGREDIENTS
  6 scallions
  2 bok choy
  2 tablespoons oil
  3 fresh red chilies, cut into
    thin strips
  4 garlic cloves, thinly sliced
  1 tablespoon crushed peanuts
For the dressing
  1–2 tablespoons fish sauce
  2 tablespoons lime juice
  1 cup coconut milk

1 To make the dressing, blend together the fish sauce and lime juice, and then stir in the coconut milk.

2 Cut the scallions diagonally into slices, including all but the very tips of the green parts.

3 Using a large sharp knife, cut the bok choy into very fine shreds.

4 Heat the oil in a wok and stir-fry the chilies for 2–3 minutes, until crisp. Transfer to a plate using a slotted spoon.

5 Stir-fry the garlic for 30–60 seconds, until golden brown, and transfer to the plate with the chilies.

6 Stir-fry the white parts of the scallions for about 2–3 minutes, then add the green parts and stir-fry for another minute. Add to the plate with the chilies and garlic.

7 Bring a large pan of salted water to a boil and add the bok choy; stir twice and then drain immediately.

8 Place the warmed bok choy in a large bowl, add the coconut dressing and stir well. Spoon into a large serving bowl and sprinkle with the crushed peanuts and the stir-fried chili mixture. Serve either warm or cold.

COOK'S TIP
Coconut milk is available in cans at large supermarkets and Asian stores. Alternatively, creamed coconut is available in packages. To use creamed coconut, place about 4 ounces in a bowl and add 1 cup boiling water. Stir well until dissolved.

SHIITAKE FRIED RICE

SHIITAKE MUSHROOMS HAVE A STRONG MEATY MUSHROOMY AROMA AND FLAVOR. THIS IS A VERY EASY RECIPE TO MAKE, AND ALTHOUGH IT IS A SIDE DISH IT CAN ALMOST BE A MEAL IN ITSELF.

SERVES FOUR

INGREDIENTS
 2 eggs
 3 tablespoons vegetable oil
 12 ounces shiitake mushrooms
 8 scallions, sliced diagonally
 1 garlic clove, crushed
 ½ green bell pepper, chopped
 1 ounce butter
 12 ounces cooked long grain rice
 1 tablespoon medium dry sherry
 2 tablespoons dark soy sauce
 1 tablespoon chopped fresh cilantro
 salt

1 Beat the eggs with 1 tablespoon of cold water and season with a little salt.

2 Heat 1 tablespoon of the oil in a wok or large frying pan, pour in the eggs and cook to make a large omelet. Lift the sides of the omelet and tilt the wok so that the uncooked egg can run underneath and be cooked. Roll up the omelet and slice thinly.

3 Remove and discard the mushroom stalks if tough and slice the caps thinly, halving them if they are large.

4 Heat 1 tablespoon of the remaining oil in the wok and stir-fry the scallions and garlic for 3–4 minutes until softened but not brown. Transfer them to a plate using a slotted spoon.

5 Add the pepper, stir-fry for about 2–3 minutes, then add the butter and the remaining 1 tablespoon of oil. As the butter begins to sizzle, add the mushrooms and stir-fry over moderate heat for 3–4 minutes until soft.

6 Loosen the rice grains as much as possible. Pour the sherry over the mushrooms and then stir in the rice.

7 Heat the rice over moderate heat, stirring all the time to prevent the rice sticking. If the rice seems very dry, add a little more oil. Stir in the reserved onions and omelet slices, the soy sauce and cilantro. Cook for a few minutes until heated through and serve.

COOK'S TIP
Unlike risotto, for which rice is cooked along with the other ingredients, Chinese fried rice is always made using cooked rice. If you use 6–8 ounces uncooked long grain, you will get about 16–20 ounces of cooked rice, enough for four people.

PARTIES
AND
PICNICS

Whether you are planning an informal open-air meal or elegant, delicious dishes for a special party, you will find a variety of ideas and inspiration to add fun to any occasion.

HERBAL PUNCH

A GOOD PARTY DRINK THAT WILL HAVE PEOPLE COMING BACK FOR MORE, AND A DELIGHTFUL NON-ALCOHOLIC CHOICE FOR DRIVERS.

SERVES THIRTY PLUS

INGREDIENTS
    2 cups honey
    4 quarts water
    2 cups freshly squeezed lemon juice
    3 tablespoons fresh rosemary leaves,
      plus more to decorate
    8 cups sliced strawberries
    2 cups freshly squeezed lime juice
    2 quarts sparkling mineral water
    ice cubes
    3–4 scented geranium leaves

1 Combine the honey, 4 cups water, ¼ cup of the lemon juice and the rosemary leaves in a saucepan. Bring to a boil, stirring until all the honey is dissolved. Remove from the heat and allow to stand for about 5 minutes. Strain into a large punch bowl.

2 Press the strawberries through a fine sieve into the punch bowl, add the rest of the water and lemon juice, and the lime juice and sparkling water. Stir gently. Add the ice cubes 5 minutes before serving, and float the geranium and rosemary leaves on the surface.

ANGELICA LIQUEUR

THIS SHOULD BE DRUNK IN TINY GLASSES AFTER A LARGE MEAL. NOT ONLY WILL IT HELP THE DIGESTIVE SYSTEM, IT ALSO TASTES SUPERB.

ABOUT 1 QUART

INGREDIENTS

   1 teaspoon fennel seeds
   1 teaspoon aniseed
   20 coriander seeds
   2–3 cloves
   2 tablespoons crystallized angelica stems
   1 cup superfine sugar
   1 bottle vodka
   fine-mesh cheesecloth

1 Crush the fennel, aniseed and coriander seeds and cloves a little, and chop the crystallized angelica stems.

2 Put the seeds and angelica stems into a large preserving jar.

3 Add the sugar. Pour in the vodka and leave by a sunny window for 2 weeks, swirling the mixture daily.

4 Strain through the cheesecloth into a sterilized bottle and seal. Leave in a dark cupboard for at least 4 months. Drink in small quantities with a piece of angelica in each glass.

STRAWBERRY AND MINT CHAMPAGNE

THIS IS A SIMPLE CONCOCTION THAT MAKES A BOTTLE OF CHAMPAGNE GO A LOT FURTHER. IT TASTES VERY SPECIAL ON A HOT SUMMER'S EVENING.

SERVES FOUR TO SIX

INGREDIENTS
    1 pound strawberries
    6–8 fresh mint leaves
    1 bottle champagne or sparkling
      white wine

2 Strain through a fine sieve into a bowl. Half fill a glass with the mixture and top off with champagne. Decorate with a sprig of mint.

1 Purée the strawberries and mint leaves in a food processor.

MELON, GINGER AND BORAGE CUP

MELON AND GINGER COMPLEMENT EACH OTHER MAGNIFICENTLY. IF YOU PREFER, YOU CAN LEAVE OUT THE POWDERED GINGER — THE RESULT IS MILDER BUT EQUALLY DELICIOUS.

SERVES SIX TO EIGHT

INGREDIENTS
    ½ large honeydew melon
    1 quart ginger beer
    powdered ginger, to taste
    borage sprigs with flowers, to
      decorate

2 Pour the purée into a large pitcher and top off with ginger beer. Add powdered ginger to taste. Pour into glasses and decorate with borage.

1 Discard the seeds from the half melon and scoop the flesh into a food processor. Blend to a thin purée.

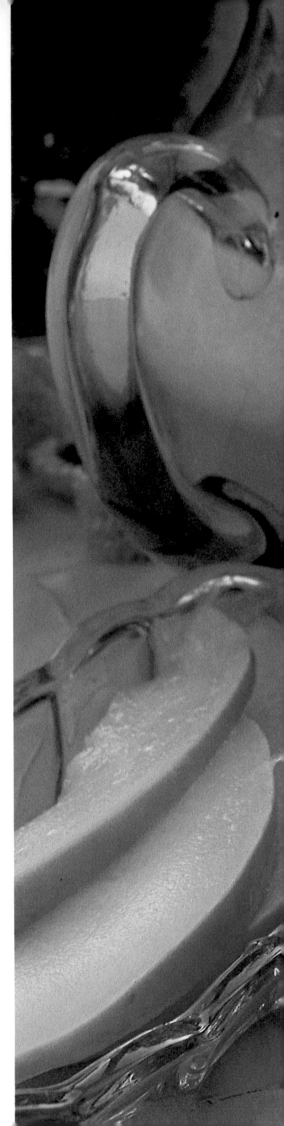

MINT CUP

MINT IS A PERENNIALLY POPULAR FLAVOR, AND THIS DELICATE DRINK IS A WONDERFUL MIXTURE WITH AN
INTRIGUING TASTE.

SERVES ONE

INGREDIENTS
4 sprigs fresh mint
½ teaspoon sugar
crushed ice
½ teaspoon lemon juice
2 tablespoons grapefruit juice
½ cup chilled tonic water
lemon slices, to decorate

1 Crush two of the sprigs of mint with the sugar and place in a glass. Fill the glass with crushed ice.

2 Add the lemon juice, grapefruit juice and tonic water. Stir gently and decorate with the remaining mint sprigs and lemon slices.

ELDERFLOWER SPARKLER

THE FLAVOR OF ELDERFLOWERS IS BECOMING POPULAR ONCE AGAIN. THIS RECIPE PRODUCES ONE OF THE MOST DELICIOUS DRINKS EVER CONCOCTED.

ABOUT 5 QUARTS

INGREDIENTS
3½ cups superfine sugar
2 cups hot water
4 large fresh elderflower heads
2 tablespoons white wine vinegar
juice and pared rind of 1 lemon
4 quarts water

1 Mix the sugar with the hot water. Pour the mixture into a large glass or plastic container. Add all the remaining ingredients. Stir well, cover and leave for about 5 days.

2 Strain the liquid into sterilized screw-top bottles (glass or plastic). Leave for another week or so. Serve very cold with slivers of lemon rind.

PASTA AND BEET SALAD

COLOR IS VITAL AT A PARTY TABLE, AND THIS SALAD IS CERTAINLY EYE-CATCHING. SERVE THE EGG AND AVOCADO AT THE LAST MOMENT TO AVOID DISCOLORATION.

SERVES EIGHT

INGREDIENTS
2 uncooked beets, scrubbed
8 ounces pasta shells or twists
3 tablespoons vinaigrette dressing
salt and freshly ground black pepper
2 celery stalks, thinly sliced
3 scallions, sliced
⅔ cup walnuts or hazelnuts, coarsely chopped
1 dessert apple, cored, halved and sliced

FOR THE DRESSING
¼ cup mayonnaise
3 tablespoons plain yogurt
2 tablespoons milk
2 teaspoons prepared horseradish

TO SERVE
curly lettuce leaves
3 eggs, hard-cooked and chopped
2 ripe avocados
1 bunch watercress

1 Boil the beets, without peeling them, in lightly salted water until they are just tender. Drain, cool, peel and chop. Set aside.

2 Cook the pasta according to the instructions on the pack, then drain,

toss with the vinaigrette and season well. Cool. Mix the pasta with the beets, celery, onions, nuts and apple.

3 Stir all the dressing ingredients together and mix into the pasta bowl. Chill well.

4 To serve, line a pretty salad bowl with the lettuce leaves and pile the salad in the center. When ready to serve, scatter the chopped egg on top. Peel and slice the avocados and arrange them on top, then sprinkle with the watercress.

GAZPACHO

THIS CLASSIC SPANISH NO-COOK SOUP IS IDEAL FOR TAKING ON PICNICS AS IT CAN BE PACKED STRAIGHT FROM THE REFRIGERATOR.

SERVES SIX

INGREDIENTS
1 slice white bread, crusts removed
cold water, to soak
1 garlic clove, crushed
2 tablespoons extra-virgin olive oil
2 tablespoons white wine vinegar
6 large ripe tomatoes, peeled and finely chopped
1 small onion, finely chopped
½ teaspoon paprika
generous pinch ground cumin
⅔ cup tomato juice
salt and freshly ground black pepper

CROUTONS
2 slices bread, cubed and deep-fried

TO GARNISH
1 green bell pepper, chopped
⅓ cucumber, peeled, seeded and chopped

1 Soak the bread slice in just enough cold water to cover and leave for about 5 minutes, then mash with a fork.

2 Purèe the garlic, oil and vinegar in a blender or food processor. Stir into the bread.

3 Spoon the mixture into a bowl and stir in the tomatoes, onion, spices and tomato juice. Season well and store in the refrigerator. Prepare the garnishes and store in separate containers.

4 For a picnic, pour the chilled soup into a thermos. Otherwise, pour into a chilled glass salad bowl and serve the garnishes in smaller bowls.

SPICY POTATO STRUDEL

THIS IS A PERFECT DISH FOR A SPECIAL FAMILY SUPPER.

SERVES FOUR

INGREDIENTS

1 onion, chopped
2 carrots, coarsely grated
1 zucchini, chopped
12 ounces potatoes, chopped
5 tablespoons butter
2 teaspoons mild curry paste
½ teaspoon dried thyme
⅔ cup water
salt and freshly ground black pepper
1 egg, beaten
2 tablespoons light cream
¼ cup grated Cheddar cheese
8 sheets filo pastry
sesame seeds, to sprinkle

1 Fry the onion, carrots, zucchini and potatoes in half the butter for 5 minutes, until they are soft, then add the curry paste and cook for another minute.

2 Add the thyme, water and seasoning. Continue to cook gently, uncovered, for another 10 minutes.

3 Let the mixture cool and mix in the egg, cream and cheese. Chill until ready to fill and roll.

4 Melt the remaining butter and lay out four sheets of filo pastry, slightly overlapping them to form a large rectangle. Brush with butter and fit the other sheets on top. Brush again.

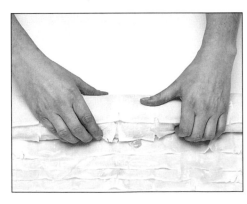

5 Spoon the filling along one long edge, then roll up the pastry. Form it into a circle and brush again with the last of the butter. Sprinkle with the sesame seeds and set on a baking sheet.

6 Heat the oven to 375°F, then bake the strudel for about 25 minutes, until golden and crisp. Allow to stand for 5 minutes or so before cutting.

CORONATION SALAD

THIS FAMOUS SALAD DRESSING WAS CREATED ESPECIALLY FOR THE CORONATION DINNER OF QUEEN ELIZABETH II. IT IS A WONDERFUL ACCOMPANIMENT TO EGGS AND VEGETABLES.

SERVES SIX

INGREDIENTS

    1 pound new potatoes
    salt
    3 tablespoons vinaigrette dressing
    3 scallions, chopped
    ground black pepper
    6 eggs, hard-boiled and halved
    frilly lettuce leaves, to serve
    ¼ cucumber, sliced, then cut into shreds
    6 large radishes, sliced
    1 bunch watercress
For the dressing
    2 tablespoons olive oil
    1 small onion, chopped
    1 tablespoon mild curry
Powder or korma spice mix
    2 teaspoons tomato paste
    2 tablespoons lemon juice
    2 tablespoons sherry
    1¼ cups mayonnaise
    ½ cup plain yogurt

1 Boil the potatoes in salted water until tender. Drain them and toss in the vinaigrette dressing.

2 Allow the potatoes to cool, stirring in the scallions and seasoning. Cool the mixture thoroughly.

3 Meanwhile, make the coronation dressing. Heat the oil and fry the onion for 3 minutes, until it is soft. Stir in the spice powder and fry for another minute. Mix in all the other dressing ingredients.

4 Stir the dressing into the potatoes; add the eggs, then chill. Line a serving platter with lettuce leaves and pile the salad in the center. Top with the cucumber, radishes and watercress.

PASTA AND WILD MUSHROOM MOLD

BAKE PASTA SHAPES IN A GOLDEN CRUMB COATING LAYERED WITH A RICH BÉCHAMEL SAUCE AND MUSHROOMS. SCRUMPTIOUS!

SERVES FOUR TO SIX

INGREDIENTS
   7 ounces pasta shapes
   2½ cups milk
   1 bay leaf
   small onion stuck with 6 cloves
   4 tablespoons butter
   3 tablespoons bread crumbs
   2 teaspoons dried mixed herbs
   ⅓ cup all-purpose flour
   ¼ cup freshly grated Parmesan cheese
   fresh nutmeg, grated
   salt and freshly ground black pepper
   2 eggs, beaten
   ½ ounce dried porcini mushrooms
   12 ounces button mushrooms, sliced
   2 garlic cloves, crushed
   2 tablespoons olive oil
   2 tablespoons chopped fresh parsley

1 Boil the pasta according to the instructions on the package. Drain and set aside. Heat the milk with the bay leaf and clove-studded onion and let stand for 15 minutes. Remove bay leaf and onion.

2 Melt the butter in a saucepan and use a little to brush the inside of a large oval baking dish. Mix the crumbs and mixed herbs together and use them to coat the inside of the dish.

3 Stir the flour into the butter, cook for a minute, then slowly add the hot milk to make a smooth sauce. Add the cheese, nutmeg, seasoning and cooked pasta. Cool for 5 minutes, then beat in the eggs.

4 Soak the porcini in a little hot water until they are soft. Reserve the liquid and chop the porcini.

5 Fry the porcini with the sliced mushrooms and garlic in the olive oil for about 3 minutes. Season well, stir in the liquid and reduce down. Add the parsley.

6 Spoon a layer of pasta into the dish. Sprinkle on a layer of the mushrooms, then more pasta and so on, finishing with pasta. Cover with greased foil. Heat the oven to 375°F and bake for 25–30 minutes. Let stand for 5 minutes before turning out to serve.

EGGPLANT BOATS

THESE CAN BE PREPARED AHEAD AND BAKED PRIOR TO EATING. THE HAZELNUT TOPPING CONTRASTS NICELY WITH THE SMOOTH EGGPLANT FILLING.

SERVES FOUR

INGREDIENTS
   ⅔ cup brown basmati rice
   2 medium-size eggplants, halved
     lengthwise
   1 onion, chopped
   2 garlic cloves, crushed
   1 small green bell pepper, chopped
   ½ cup sliced mushrooms
   3 tablespoons olive oil
   ½ cup grated Cheddar cheese
   1 egg, beaten
   ½ teaspoon marjoram
   salt and freshly ground black pepper
   2 tablespoons hazelnuts, chopped

1 Boil the rice according to the instructions on the package, drain and then cool. Scoop out the flesh from the eggplants and chop. Blanch the shells in boiling water for 2 minutes, then drain upside down.

2 Fry the eggplant flesh, onion, garlic, pepper and mushrooms in the oil for about 5 minutes.

3 Mix in the rice, cheese, egg, marjoram and seasoning. Arrange the eggplant shells in an ovenproof dish. Spoon the filling inside. Sprinkle with the nuts. Chill until ready to bake.

4 Heat the oven to 375°F and bake the eggplants for about 25 minutes, until the filling is set and the nuts are golden brown.

CHARGRILLED VEGETABLES <u>WITH</u> SALSA

ENJOY A BARBECUE WITH THESE CHARGRILLED VEGETABLES. SERVE HOT WITH SALSA.

SERVES FOUR

INGREDIENTS

   1 large sweet potato, cut into thick
     slices
   2 zucchini, halved lengthwise
   salt
   2 red bell peppers, quartered
   olive oil, to brush
For the salsa
   2 large tomatoes, peeled and finely
     chopped
   2 scallions, finely chopped
   1 small green chili, chopped
   juice of 1 small lime
   2 tablespoons chopped fresh cilantro
   salt and freshly ground black pepper

1 Parboil the sweet potato for 5 minutes, until it is barely tender. Drain and leave to cool.

2 Sprinkle the zucchini with a little salt and leave to drain in a colander for 20 minutes, then pat dry.

3 Make the salsa by mixing all the ingredients together, and allow them to stand for about 30 minutes to mellow.

4 Prepare the barbecue until the coals glow, or preheat a broiler. Brush the potato slices, zucchini and peppers with oil and cook them until they are lightly charred and softened, brushing with oil again and turning at least once. Serve hot, accompanied by the salsa.

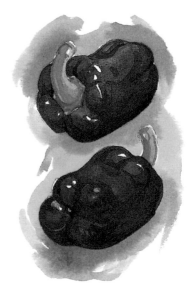

GARDEN VEGETABLE TERRINE

*PERFECT FOR A SPECIAL FAMILY
PICNIC OR BUFFET, THIS IS A
SOFTLY SET, CREAMY TERRINE OF
COLORFUL VEGETABLES WRAPPED
IN GLOSSY SPINACH LEAVES.
SELECT LARGE SPINACH LEAVES
FOR THE BEST RESULTS.*

SERVES SIX

INGREDIENTS
   8 ounces fresh leaf spinach
   3 carrots, cut into sticks
   3–4 long, thin leeks
   4 ounces long green beans, trimmed
   1 red bell pepper, cut into strips
   2 zucchini, cut into sticks
   4 ounces broccoli florets
For the sauce
   1 egg and 2 yolks
   1¼ cups light cream or half-and-half
   fresh nutmeg, grated
   1 teaspoon salt
   ¼ cup grated Cheddar cheese
   oil, for greasing
   freshly ground black pepper

1 Blanch the spinach quickly in boiling water, then drain, refresh in cold water and drain again, taking care not to break up the leaves, then carefully pat them dry.

2 Grease a 2-pound loaf pan and line the base with a sheet of waxed paper. Line the pan with the spinach leaves, trimming any thick stalks. Allow the leaves to overhang the pan.

3 Blanch the rest of the vegetables in boiling salted water until just tender. Drain and refresh in cold water then, when cool, pat dry with pieces of paper towel.

4 Place the vegetables into the loaf pan in a colorful mixture, making sure the sticks of vegetables lie lengthwise.

5 Beat the sauce ingredients together and slowly pour over the vegetables. Tap the loaf pan to make sure the sauce seeps into the gaps. Fold over the spinach leaves at the top of the terrine.

6 Cover the terrine with a sheet of greased foil, then bake in a roasting pan half full of boiling water at 350°F for 1–1¼ hours, until set.

7 Cool the terrine in the pan, then chill. To serve, loosen the sides and shake out gently. Serve cut into thick slices.

CRÊPES GALETTE

A STACK OF LIGHT CRÊPES LAYERED WITH A LENTIL FILLING MAKES AN IMPRESSIVE DINNER PARTY MAIN COURSE.

SERVES SIX

INGREDIENTS
   1 cup all-purpose flour
   generous pinch of salt
   1 egg
   1¼ cups buttermilk, or milk
      and water, mixed
   oil, for cooking
For the filling
   2 leeks, thinly sliced
   1 small fennel bulb, thinly sliced
   4 tablespoons olive oil
   ¾ cup red lentils
   ⅔ cup dry white wine
   1 can (14 ounces) tomatoes, chopped
   1¼ cups vegetable stock
   1 teaspoon dried oregano
   salt and freshly ground black pepper
   1 onion, sliced
   1 cup sliced mushrooms
   8 ounces frozen leaf spinach, thawed
   8 ounces low-fat cream cheese
   ¼ cup freshly grated Parmesan cheese

1 Make the crêpe batter by mixing the flour, salt, egg and buttermilk or milk and water in a blender until smooth. Set aside while you prepare the filling.

2 Gently fry the leeks and fennel in half the olive oil for 5 minutes, then add the lentils and wine. Cook for a minute, until reduced, then stir in the tomatoes and stock.

3 Bring the leek mixture to a boil, add the oregano and seasoning, then simmer for 20 minutes, stirring it occasionally until it thickens.

4 Fry the onion and mushrooms in the remaining olive oil for 5 minutes, stir in the squeezed-dry spinach and heat. Season well, then mix in the cream cheese.

5 Make 12–14 crêpes with the batter in a well-heated nonstick frying pan. Lightly grease a deep 8-inch round springform cake pan and line the bottom and sides with some of the crêpes, overlapping them as necessary.

6 Layer the remaining pancakes with the two fillings, sprinkling freshly grated Parmesan in between and pressing them down well. Finish with a pancake on top.

7 Cover with foil and set aside to rest. Preheat the oven to 375°F. Bake for about 40 minutes, then turn out and let firm up for 10 minutes before cutting into wedges. Serve with a homemade tomato sauce.

COOK'S TIP
This can be frozen already assembled, but it is probably better if frozen in parts – the crêpes separated by waxed paper and then wrapped in foil, and the sauce frozen separately.

POLENTA FINGERS WITH BEANS AND TOMATOES

POLENTA, OR CORNMEAL, IS A POPULAR FAMILY FAVORITE IN ITALY. IT IS EATEN HOT FROM A BOWL OR ALLOWED TO SET, CUT INTO FINGERS AND BROILED.

SERVES SIX

INGREDIENTS
    2 quarts milk and
        water, mixed
    2 teaspoons salt
    1½ cups polenta
    2 tablespoons butter, plus extra for
        spreading
    ¼ cup grated Parmesan cheese
    freshly ground black pepper
For the sauce
    1 onion, chopped
    2 garlic cloves, crushed
    2 tablespoons olive oil
    1 can (14 ounces) tomatoes, chopped
    salt and freshly ground black pepper
    generous pinch of dried sage
    8 ounces frozen fava beans

1 In a large saucepan, bring the milk and water to a boil. Stir in the salt. While stirring with a wooden spoon, trickle the polenta into the boiling liquid in a steady stream and continue stirring until the mixture has thickened.

2 Lower the heat and simmer for about 20 minutes, stirring frequently. Add the butter, freshly grated cheese and seasoning.

3 Lightly grease a shallow roasting pan and pour in the polenta mixture. Cool, then chill overnight.

4 For the sauce, fry the onion and garlic in the oil for 5 minutes. Add the tomatoes, seasoning and sage and cook for another 10 minutes. Stir in the fava beans and cook for 5 more minutes.

5 Turn out the polenta and cut into fingers. Broil both sides until brown and crisp. Spread with a little butter and serve accompanied by the tomatoes and beans.

PAPRIKA AND PARMESAN TARTLETS

PRETTY PINK PASTRY TARTS WITH A TANGY CREAM FILLING ARE IDEAL FOR SERVING AT COCKTAIL PARTIES. MAKE THE SHELLS AHEAD OF TIME AND FILL THEM JUST BEFORE SERVING.

MAKES 18

INGREDIENTS
    2 cups all-purpose flour
    2 teaspoons paprika
    10 tablespoons butter or sunflower
        margarine
    scant ½ cup freshly grated Parmesan
        cheese
    cold water, to bind
For the filling
    12 ounces goat cheese
    2 ounces arugula leaves,
        or watercress, chopped
    2 tablespoons chopped fresh chives
    salt and freshly ground black pepper
    1 pound tomatoes, sliced

1 Sift the flour with the paprika and rub in the butter or margarine. Stir in the Parmesan and mix to a firm dough with cold water.

2 Roll out the pastry and cut out 18 rounds, large enough to fit into muffin tins. Prick the bases well with a fork and chill while you preheat the oven to 375°F.

3 Bake the tartlet shells for 15 minutes, until crisp. Cool them on a wire rack.

4 Beat the cheese with the arugula or watercress, chives and seasoning. Slice the tomatoes, allowing roughly two slices per tart.

5 When ready to serve, spoon the filling into the tarts. Top each one with some tomato and garnish with extra arugula or watercress leaves.

TOFU SATAY

*GRILL CUBES OF TOFU UNTIL
CRISPY, THEN SERVE WITH A
THAI-STYLE PEANUT SAUCE.*

<u>SERVES FOUR TO SIX</u>

INGREDIENTS
    2 packages (7 ounces each) smoked tofu
    3 tablespoons light soy sauce
    2 teaspoons sesame oil
    1 garlic clove, crushed
    1 yellow and 1 red bell pepper, seeded
    8–12 fresh bay leaves
    sunflower oil, for grilling
For the sauce
    2 scallions, finely chopped
    2 garlic cloves, crushed
    generous pinch chili powder
    1 teaspoon granulated sugar
    1 tablespoon white vinegar
    2 tablespoons light soy sauce
    3 tablespoons crunchy peanut butter

1 To help them withstand the hot grilling, soak 8–12 wooden satay sticks in water for 20 minutes, then drain. Cut the tofu into bite-sized cubes and mix with the soy sauce, sesame oil and garlic. Cover and marinate for 20 minutes.

2 Beat the sauce ingredients together until well blended. Avoid using a food processor for this, as the texture should be slightly chunky.

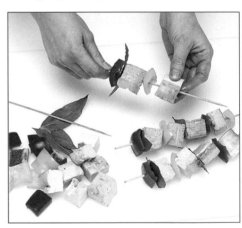

3 Seed and cut the peppers into squares. Drain the tofu and thread the cubes onto the sticks with the peppers and bay leaves. Larger leaves may need to be halved.

4 Heat a broiler or grill until quite hot. Brush the satays with oil. Grill, turning the sticks occasionally, until the ingredients are browned and crisp. Serve hot with the dipping sauce.

PARTY MOUSSAKA

*MOUSSAKA BENEFITS FROM BEING
MADE AHEAD OF TIME AND JUST
BEING REHEATED ON THE DAY.*

SERVES EIGHT

INGREDIENTS
2 large eggplants, thinly sliced
6 zucchini, cut into chunks
⅔ cup olive oil, plus extra if required
1½ pounds potatoes, thinly sliced
2 onions, sliced
3 garlic cloves, crushed
⅔ cup dry white wine
2 cans (14 ounces each) tomatoes,
  chopped
2 tablespoons tomato paste
1 can (15 ounces) green lentils
2 teaspoons dried oregano
4 tablespoons chopped fresh parsley
2 cups crumbled feta cheese
salt and freshly ground black pepper
For the béchamel sauce
3 tablespoons butter
4 tablespoons all-purpose flour
2½ cups milk
nutmeg, freshly grated
2 eggs, beaten
½ cup grated Parmesan cheese

2 Pour in the wine and cook until reduced, then add the tomatoes, tomato paste, lentils with their liquid, and the herbs and seasoning. Cover and simmer for 15 minutes.

1 Lightly salt the eggplants and zucchini in a colander and leave to drain for 30 minutes. Rinse and pat dry. Heat the oil until quite hot in a frying pan and quickly brown the eggplant and zucchini slices. Remove them with a slotted spoon and drain on paper towels. Brown the potato slices, remove and pat dry. Add the onion and garlic with a little extra oil, if required, and fry for about 5 minutes.

3 In a large ovenproof dish, layer the vegetables, trickling the tomato and lentil sauce in between and topping with the feta cheese. Finish with a layer of eggplant slices.

4 Cover the vegetables with a sheet of foil and bake at 375°F for 25 minutes or until the vegetables are quite soft but not overcooked.

5 Meanwhile, for the béchamel sauce, put the butter, flour and milk in a saucepan and bring slowly to a boil, stirring or whisking constantly. The mixture should thicken and become smooth. Season and add the nutmeg.

6 Remove the sauce and cool for 5 minutes, then beat in the eggs. Pour over the eggplants and sprinkle with the Parmesan. If cooking ahead, cool and chill at this stage.

7 To finish, return to the oven uncovered and bake for another 25–30 minutes, until golden and bubbling hot.

BASMATI AND BLUE LENTIL SALAD

*PUY LENTILS FROM FRANCE
(SOMETIMES KNOWN AS BLUE
LENTILS) ARE SMALL,
DELICIOUSLY NUTTY PULSES,
HIGHLY PRIZED BY GOURMETS.*

SERVES SIX

INGREDIENTS
⅔ cup puys de dôme lentils,
 soaked
1¼ cups basmati rice,
 rinsed well
2 carrots, coarsely grated
⅓ cucumber, halved, seeded and
 coarsely grated
3 scallions, sliced
3 tablespoons chopped fresh parsley
For the dressing
2 tablespoons sunflower oil
2 tablespoons extra-virgin olive oil
2 tablespoons wine vinegar
2 tablespoons fresh lemon juice
generous pinch of granulated sugar
salt and freshly ground black pepper

1 Soak the lentils for 30 minutes.
Meanwhile, make the dressing by shaking
all the ingredients together in a screw-top
jar. Set aside.

2 Boil the lentils in plenty of unsalted
water for 20–25 minutes or until soft.
Drain thoroughly.

3 Boil the basmati rice for 10 minutes,
then drain.

4 Mix together the rice and lentils in the
dressing and season well. Leave to cool.

5 Add the carrots, cucumber, onions and
parsley. Spoon into an attractive serving
bowl and chill before serving.

WILD RICE WITH JULIENNE VEGETABLES

*FOR THE BEST FLAVOR, BUY A
GOOD QUALITY WILD RICE
(WHICH IS ACTUALLY A CEREAL)
AND, TO SHORTEN THE COOKING
TIME, SOAK IT OVERNIGHT.*

SERVES FOUR

INGREDIENTS
½ cup wild rice
1 red onion, sliced
2 carrots, cut into julienne sticks
2 celery stalks, cut into julienne sticks
4 tablespoons butter
⅔ cup vegetable stock or water
salt and freshly ground black pepper
2 medium zucchini, cut into
 thicker sticks
a few toasted almond flakes, to serve

1 Drain the soaked rice, then boil in
plenty of unsalted water for 15–20
minutes, until it is soft and many of the
grains have burst open. Drain.

2 In another saucepan, gently fry the
onion, carrots and celery in the butter for
2 minutes, then pour in the stock or water
and season well.

3 Bring to a boil, simmer for 2 minutes,
then stir in the zucchini. Cook for 1 more
minute, then mix in the rice. Reheat and
serve hot, sprinkled with the almonds.

OVEN-CRISP ASPARAGUS ROLLS

BLANCHED SPEARS OF FRESH ASPARAGUS WRAPPED IN SLICES OF THIN BREAD AND BAKED IN A BUTTERY GLAZE UNTIL CRISP ARE DELICIOUS.

SERVES EIGHT

INGREDIENTS

    8 thick spears of fresh asparagus
    salt
    8 tablespoons butter, softened
    1 tablespoon coarse-grained mustard
    grated rind of 1 lemon
    freshly ground black pepper
    8 slices thin white bread, crusts
      removed

1 Trim the asparagus stalks, peeling the tough woody skin at the base. Blanch until just tender in a shallow pan of boiling salted water. Drain and refresh in cold water. Pat dry.

2 Blend two-thirds of the butter with the mustard, lemon rind and seasoning. Spread on the slices of bread.

3 Lay an asparagus spear on the edge of each bread slice and roll it up tightly. Place the rolls join side down on a lightly greased baking sheet.

4 Melt the remaining butter and brush over the rolls. Heat the oven to 375°F and bake for 12–15 minutes, until golden and crisp. Cool slightly before serving.

VARIATION

Asparagus has always been something of a luxury because its season is so short, but imports from across the world mean that it is available almost all year, albeit at a price!

    Thin baby asparagus can be eaten raw in salads or stir-fried quickly. Opinions differ about the merits of green or white asparagus spears. The latter are forced in the dark (hence their white color), but some people consider them to have a better flavor and texture.

RATATOUILLE TART

A DELICIOUS MEDITERRANEAN FILLING ON A PASTRY BASE.

SERVES SIX

INGREDIENTS
   1 cup all-purpose flour
   ¾ cup whole-wheat flour
   1 teaspoon dried Italian herbs
   salt and ground black pepper
   ½ cup sunflower margarine
   3–4 tablespoons cold water
For the filling
   1 small eggplant, thickly sliced
   salt
   3 tablespoons olive oil
   1 onion, sliced
   1 red or yellow bell pepper, sliced
   2 garlic cloves, crushed
   2 zucchini, thickly sliced
   2 tomatoes, peeled and sliced
   freshly ground black pepper
   2 tablespoons chopped fresh basil
   5 ounces mozzarella cheese, sliced
   2 tablespoons pine nuts

1 Mix the two flours with the herbs and seasoning, then rub in the margarine until it resembles fine crumbs. Mix to a firm dough with water.

2 Roll out the pastry and line a 9-inch round tart pan. Prick the base, line with foil and dried beans, then allow to rest in the fridge.

3 Meanwhile, sprinkle the eggplant lightly with salt and leave to drain for 30 minutes in a colander. Rinse and pat dry.

4 Heat the oil in a frying pan and fry the onion and pepper for 5 minutes, then add the garlic, zucchini and eggplant. Fry for another 10 minutes, stirring the mixture occasionally.

5 Stir in the tomatoes and seasoning, cook for another 3 minutes, add the basil, then remove the pan from the heat and allow to cool.

6 Heat the oven to 400°F. Place the tart on a baking sheet and bake for 25 minutes, removing the foil and dried beans for the last 5 minutes. Cool and then, if possible, remove the shell from the pan.

7 When ready to serve, spoon the vegetables into the shell using a slotted spoon, so any juices drain off and don't soak into the pastry. Top with the cheese slices and pine nuts. Toast under a preheated broiler until golden and bubbling. Serve warm.

FILO BASKETS WITH GINGER DILL VEGETABLES

MAKE UP SOME ELEGANT FILO BASKETS, THEN FILL WITH SOME CRISPLY STEAMED VEGETABLES TOSSED IN A TASTY SAUCE.

SERVES FOUR

INGREDIENTS
    4 sheets of filo pastry
    3 tablespoons butter, melted
For the filling
    2 tablespoons olive oil
    1 tablespoon grated fresh ginger
    2 garlic cloves, crushed
    3 shallots, sliced
    1 cup sliced mushrooms, chestnut or
      brown
    ½ cup sliced oyster mushrooms
    1 zucchini, sliced
    7 ounces crème fraîche
    2 tablespoons chopped fresh dill
    salt and freshly ground black pepper
    dill and parsley sprigs, to serve

1 Cut the filo sheets in fourths. Line four large muffin tins, angling the layers so that the corners form a pretty star shape. Brush between each layer with butter. Set aside.

2 Heat the oven to 375°F. Bake the pastry shells for about 10 minutes, until golden brown and crisp. Remove and cool.

3 For the filling, heat the oil and sauté the ginger, garlic and shallots for 2 minutes, then add the mushrooms and zucchini. Cook for another 3 minutes.

4 Mix in the crème fraîche, chopped dill and seasoning. Heat until just bubbling, then spoon into the filo baskets. Garnish with the dill and parsley and serve.

GADO GADO SALAD WITH PEANUT SAMBAL

INDONESIANS ENJOY A SALAD OF LIGHTLY STEAMED VEGETABLES TOPPED WITH A PEANUT SAUCE.

1 Fit a steamer or metal colander over a pan of gently boiling water. Cook the potatoes for 10 minutes.

SERVES SIX

INGREDIENTS
    8 ounces new potatoes, halved
    2 carrots, cut into sticks
    4 ounces green beans
    ½ small cauliflower, broken into florets
    ¼ firm white cabbage, shredded
    7 ounces bean or lentil sprouts
    4 eggs, hard-boiled and quartered
    1 bunch watercress, trimmed
For the sauce
    6 tablespoons crunchy peanut butter
    1¼ cups cold water
    1 garlic clove, crushed
    2 tablespoons dark soy sauce
    1 tablespoon dry sherry
    2 teaspoons superfine sugar
    1 tablespoon fresh lemon juice
    1 teaspoon anchovy paste

2 Add the rest of the vegetables and sprouts and steam for another 10 minutes, until tender. Cool and place on a serving platter with the egg quarters surrounded by the watercress.

3 Beat all the sauce ingredients together until smooth. Put the sauce in a small bowl and drizzle over each individual serving of salad.

PERSIAN RICE AND LENTILS WITH A TAHDEEG

PERSIAN OR IRANIAN CUISINE IS AN EXOTIC, DELICIOUS ONE. FLAVORS ARE INTENSE AND SOMEHOW MORE SOPHISTICATED THAN OTHER EASTERN STYLES. A TAHDEEG IS THE GOLDEN RICE CRUST THAT FORMS AT THE BOTTOM OF THE SAUCEPAN.

SERVES EIGHT

INGREDIENTS

    1 pound basmati rice, rinsed thoroughly and soaked
    2 onions, 1 chopped, 1 thinly sliced
    2 garlic cloves, crushed
    ⅔ cup sunflower oil
    1 cup green lentils, soaked
    2½ cups vegetable stock
    ⅓ cup raisins
    2 teaspoons ground coriander
    3 tablespoons tomato paste
    salt and freshly ground black pepper
    few strands of saffron
    1 egg yolk, beaten
    2 teaspoons plain yogurt
    6 tablespoons butter, melted and strained
    extra oil, for frying

1 Boil the rinsed and drained rice in plenty of well-salted water for 3 minutes only. Drain again.

2 Meanwhile, fry the chopped onion and garlic in 2 tablespoons of oil for 5 minutes, then add the lentils, stock, raisins, coriander, tomato paste and seasoning. Bring to a boil, then cover and simmer for 20 minutes. Set aside.

3 Soak the saffron strands in a little hot water. Remove about 8 tablespoons of the rice and mix with the egg yolk and yogurt. Season well.

4 In a large saucepan, heat about two-thirds of the remaining oil and scatter the egg and yogurt rice evenly over the bottom.

5 Scatter the remaining rice into the pan, alternating it with the lentils. Build up in a pyramid shape away from the sides of the pan, finishing with plain rice on top.

6 With a long wooden spoon handle, make three holes down to the bottom of the pan and drizzle with the butter. Bring to a high heat, then wrap the pan lid in a clean, wet dish towel and place firmly on top. When a good head of steam appears, turn the heat down to low. Cook for about 30 minutes.

7 Meanwhile, fry the sliced onion in the remaining oil until browned and crisp. Drain well and set aside.

8 Remove the rice pan from the heat, still covered, and stand it briefly in a sink of cold water for a minute or two to loosen the bottom. Remove the lid and mix a few spoons of the white rice with the saffron water prepared in Step 3.

9 Toss the rice and lentils together in the pan and spoon out onto a serving dish in a mound. Scatter the saffron rice on top. Break up the rice crust on the bottom (the prized tahdeeg) and place around the mound. Scatter the onions on top of the saffron rice and serve.

VEGETABLE FRITTERS WITH TZATZIKI

SPICY DEEP-FRIED EGGPLANT AND ZUCCHINI SLICES SERVED WITH A CREAMY PLAIN YOGURT AND DILL DIP MAKE A GOOD, SIMPLE PARTY APPETIZER.

SERVES FOUR TO SIX

INGREDIENTS

½ cucumber, coarsely grated
1 cup plain yogurt
1 tablespoon extra-virgin olive oil
2 teaspoons fresh lemon juice
2 tablespoons chopped fresh dill
1 tablespoon chopped fresh mint
1 garlic clove, crushed
salt and freshly ground black pepper
1 large eggplant, thickly sliced
2 zucchinis, thickly sliced
1 egg white, beaten
4 tablespoons all-purpose flour
2 teaspoons ground coriander
ground cumin

1 For the dip, mix the cucumber, yogurt, oil, lemon juice, dill, mint, garlic and seasoning. Spoon into a bowl, then set aside.

2 Layer the eggplant and zucchini in a colander and sprinkle them with salt. Leave for 30 minutes. Rinse in cold water, then pat dry.

3 Put the egg white in a bowl. Mix the flour, coriander and cumin with more seasoning and put into another bowl.

4 Dip the vegetables first into the egg white, then into the seasoned flour and set aside.

5 Heat about 1 inch of oil in a deep frying pan until quite hot, then fry the vegetables a few at a time until they are golden and crisp.

6 Drain and keep warm while you fry the remainder. Serve warm on a platter with a bowl of the tzatziki dip lightly sprinkled with paprika.

MUSHROOM SAUCERS

RECIPES THAT ARE ALREADY PORTIONED ARE A GREAT BOON FOR THE HOST, AS GUESTS CAN HELP THEMSELVES WITHOUT FEELING THEY ARE TAKING MORE THAN THEIR FAIR SHARE.

SERVES EIGHT

INGREDIENTS

8 large, flat mushrooms with stalks removed, wiped clean and chopped
3 tablespoons olive oil
salt and freshly ground black pepper
1 onion, sliced
1 teaspoon cumin seeds
1 pound leaf spinach, stalks trimmed, and shredded
1 can (15 ounces) red kidney beans, drained
1 cup cream cheese with garlic and herbs
2 medium tomatoes, halved, seeded and sliced into strips

1 Heat the oven to 375°F. Lightly grease a large, shallow ovenproof dish. Brush the mushrooms with some oil, place them in the dish and season well. Cover with foil and bake for 15–20 minutes. Uncover, drain and reserve the juices.

3 Stir in the spinach and fry until the leaves begin to wilt, then mix in the beans and heat well. Add the cheese, stirring until melted, and season again.

4 Divide the mixture among the mushroom cups and return to the oven to heat through. Serve garnished with tomato slices.

2 Fry the onion and chopped mushroom stalks in the remaining oil for 5 minutes, until soft. Then add the cumin seeds and mushroom juices and cook for a minute longer, until reduced.

BIRDS' NESTS

A RECIPE FROM AN OLD HANDWRITTEN COOKBOOK DATED 1887. THESE ARE ALSO KNOWN AS WELSH EGGS BECAUSE THEY RESEMBLE SCOTCH EGGS BUT THEY HAVE LEEKS IN THE FILLING.

SERVES SIX

INGREDIENTS

6 eggs, hard-cooked
flour, seasoned with salt and paprika
1 leek, chopped
2 teaspoons sunflower oil
2 cups fresh white bread crumbs
grated rind and juice of 1 lemon
½ cup shredded vegetarian suet
4 tablespoons chopped fresh parsley
1 teaspoon dried thyme
salt and freshly ground black pepper
1 egg, beaten
½ cup dried bread crumbs
oil, for deep-frying
lettuce and tomato slices, to garnish

1 Peel the hard-boiled eggs and toss in the seasoned flour.

2 Fry the leeks in the oil for about 3 minutes. Remove, cool, then mix with the fresh bread crumbs, lemon rind and juice, suet, herbs and seasoning. If the mixture is a little dry, add a little water.

3 Shape the mixture around the eggs, then roll first in the beaten egg, then the dried bread crumbs. Set aside on a plate to chill for 30 minutes.

4 Pour enough oil to fill one-third of a deep-fryer and heat to a temperature of 375°F, and fry the eggs, three at a time, for about 3 minutes. Remove and drain on paper towels.

5 Serve cool, cut in half on a platter lined with lettuce and garnished with tomato slices.

PORTABLE SALADS

A CLEVER VICTORIAN NOTION FOR TRANSPORTING DRESSED SALADS NEATLY TO A PICNIC SITE.

SERVES SIX

INGREDIENTS

    1 large, deep crusty loaf
    softened butter or margarine, for
      spreading
    few leaves of crisp lettuce
    4 eggs, hard-boiled and chopped
    12 ounces new potatoes, boiled and
      sliced
    1 green bell pepper, thinly sliced
    2 carrots, coarsely grated
    3 scallions, chopped
    ½ cup grated Gouda cheese
    salt and freshly ground black pepper
For the dressing
    2 tablespoons mayonnaise
    2 tablespoons plain yogurt
    2 tablespoons milk
    1 garlic clove, crushed (optional)
    1 tablespoon fresh dill, chopped

1 Cut the top from the loaf and scoop out the bread inside. Use this for making fresh bread crumbs and freeze for later.

2 Spread the inside of the loaf lightly with the softened butter or margarine, then line with the lettuce leaves.

3 Mix the eggs with the vegetables and cheese. Season well. Beat the dressing ingredients together and mix into the egg and vegetables.

4 Spoon the dressed salad into the hollow and lined loaf, replace the lid and wrap in plastic wrap. Chill until ready to transport. To serve, spoon the salad onto plates and cut the crust into chunks.

GUACAMOLE, BASIL AND TOMATO PITA BREADS

THIS IS A FAVORITE FAMILY RECIPE — THE FRESH BASIL AND TOMATOES ARE PERFECT PARTNERS FOR EACH OTHER AND FOR THE SPICY GUACAMOLE.

SERVES SIX

INGREDIENTS
    6 large pita breads
    1–2 large tomatoes, sliced
    12 basil leaves
    2 large ripe avocados
    1 tomato
    ½ red onion
    1 clove garlic, peeled and crushed
    1 tablespoon lime juice
    ¼ teaspoon chili powder
    2 tablespoons chopped fresh dill

1 Open the ends of the pita breads to make pockets and place a couple of slices of tomato and two basil leaves in each one.

2 Coarsely chop the avocados, the remaining tomato and the red onion. Mix all the remaining ingredients briefly in a food processor.

3 Add the mixture from the food processor to the coarsely chopped avocado, tomato and onions, and stir gently. Fill the pockets with the avocado mixture and serve immediately.

BRIE AND GRAPE SANDWICHES WITH MINT

A SLIGHTLY UNUSUAL SANDWICH COMBINATION WHICH WORKS WELL, JUDGING BY THE SPEED WITH WHICH THE SANDWICHES DISAPPEAR AT FAMILY PICNICS.

SERVES FOUR

INGREDIENTS
    8 slices whole-wheat bread
    butter for spreading
    12 ounces ripe Brie cheese
    30–40 large grapes
    16 fresh mint leaves

OTHER SANDWICH IDEAS
• Feta cheese, black olives, lettuce, tomato and freshly chopped mint in pita bread.
• Italian salami, cream cheese, tomato and fresh basil on ciabatta bread.
• Sliced chicken breast, mayonnaise and dill sprigs on whole-wheat bread.
• Grilled mozzarella and sun-dried tomato focaccia bread sandwich, with black olives, arugula and basil leaves.
• Hummus, lettuce and freshly chopped cilantro on French bread.
• Parma ham, green olives and arugula leaves on white bread with poppy seeds.

1 Butter the bread. Cut the Brie into thick slices, to be divided among the sandwiches.

2 Place the Brie slices on four slices of bread. Peel, halve and seed the grapes and place on top of the Brie. Chop the mint finely by hand or in a food processor, and sprinkle the mint over the Brie and grapes. Place the other four slices of bread over the top and cut each sandwich in half.

MARBLED QUAILS' EGGS

HARD-BOILED QUAILS' EGGS RE-BOILED IN SMOKY CHINA TEA ASSUME A PRETTY MARBLED SKIN. IT'S REALLY A TREAT TO DIP THEM INTO A FRAGRANT SPICY SALT AND HAND THEM AROUND WITH DRINKS. SZECHUAN PEPPERCORNS CAN BE BOUGHT AT ASIAN FOOD STORES.

SERVES FOUR TO SIX

INGREDIENTS

    12 quails' eggs
    2½ cups strong Lapsang souchong tea
    1 tablespoon dark soy sauce
    1 tablespoon dry sherry
    2 star anise pods
    lettuce leaves, to serve
    ground Szechuan red peppercorns
    sea salt, to mix

1 Place the quails' eggs in cold water and bring to the boil. Time them for 2 minutes from when the water boils.

2 Remove the eggs from the pan and run them under cold water to cool. Tap the shells all over so they are crazed, but do not peel yet.

3 In a saucepan, bring the tea to a boil and add the soy sauce, sherry and star anise. Re-boil the eggs for about 15 minutes, partially covered so the liquid does not boil away.

4 Cool the eggs, then peel them and arrange on a small platter lined with lettuce leaves. Mix the ground red peppercorns with equal quantities of salt and place in a small side dish.

BEET ROULADE

THIS ROULADE IS SIMPLE TO MAKE, YET WILL CREATE A STUNNING IMPRESSION. PREPARE IT IN THE AUTUMN WHEN BEETS ARE AT THEIR BEST.

SERVES SIX

INGREDIENTS

    8 ounces fresh beets, cooked and
      peeled
    ½ teaspoon ground cumin
    2 tablespoons butter
    2 teaspoons grated onion
    4 eggs, separated
    salt and freshly ground black pepper
For the filling
    ⅔ cup crème fraîche or sour cream
    2 teaspoons white wine vinegar
    generous pinch of dry mustard powder
    1 teaspoon sugar
    3 tablespoons chopped fresh parsley
    2 tablespoons chopped fresh dill
    3 tablespoons horseradish relish

1 Line and grease a jelly roll pan and then preheat the oven to 375°F.

2 Roughly chop the beets, then blend to a purée in a food processor and beat in the cumin, butter, onion, egg yolks and seasoning. Turn the beet purée into a large bowl.

3 In another bowl that is spotlessly clean, whisk the egg whites until they form soft peaks. Fold them carefully into the beet mixture.

4 Spoon the mixture into the jelly roll pan, level and bake for about 15 minutes, until just firm to the touch.

5 Have ready a clean dish towel laid over a wire rack. Turn the beet mixture out onto the towel and remove the paper carefully in strips.

6 Beat the crème fraîche or sour cream until lightly stiff, then fold in the remaining ingredients. Spread this mixture onto the beet mixture. Roll up the roulade in the towel and allow it to cool.

PAN BAGNA

YOU NEED THREE ELEMENTS FOR THIS FRENCH PICNIC CLASSIC: A REALLY FRESH FRENCH BAGUETTE, RIPE JUICY TOMATOES AND GOOD, EXTRA-VIRGIN OLIVE OIL.

SERVES THREE TO FOUR

INGREDIENTS

   1 long French baguette, split in half
   1 garlic clove, halved
   4–6 tablespoons extra-virgin olive oil
   3–4 ripe tomatoes, thinly sliced
   salt and freshly ground black pepper
   1 small green bell pepper, thinly sliced
   2 ounces Gruyère cheese, thinly sliced
   a few pitted black olives, sliced
   6 fresh basil leaves

1 Rub the cut surface of the bread with the garlic and discard the clove. Brush half of the olive oil on both halves of the bread.

2 Lay the tomato slices on top, season well and top with the pepper. Drizzle with the remaining oil.

3 Top the tomatoes with the cheese slices, olives and basil leaves. Sandwich the loaf together firmly and wrap it in plastic wrap for an hour or more. Serve cut diagonally into thick slices.

SANDWICHES, ROLLS <u>AND</u> FILLINGS

THERE IS AN INCREASING VARIETY OF WONDERFUL BREADS AND ROLLS NOW FOR THE PICNIC PACKER TO CHOOSE FROM — NOT ONLY VARIATIONS ON WHITE AND WHOLE-WHEAT BREADS, BUT ALSO FLAVORED BREADS SUCH AS ONION, WALNUT, TOMATO SWIRL AND BLACK OLIVE. MAKE SURE THE BREADS ARE FRESH AND SPREAD THEM RIGHT UP TO THE EDGES. ONCE FILLED, WRAP IN PLASTIC WRAP AND CHILL UNTIL YOU NEED THEM. REMEMBER TO ALLOW TO RETURN TO ROOM TEMPERATURE BEFORE EATING.

FILLING IDEAS
Unless specified, keep the fillings in separate layers rather than mixing the ingredients together.

• De-rinded Brie or Camembert, mixed with chopped walnuts or pecans and served with frisee or curly endive lettuce.

• Yeast extract, scrambled egg (made without milk) and bean sprout (especially good with alfalfa sprouts). Spread the bread or roll with yeast extract rather than mixing it into the egg.

• Fry onions in olive oil until crisp and brown. Cool. Layer with shredded young raw spinach leaves and grated cheese mixed with a little mayonnaise.

• Real English cucumber sandwiches. Peel strips from a whole cucumber to leave it stripey, then slice thinly on a mandoline or a food processor slicer. Sprinkle lightly with salt and leave to drain for 30 minutes in a colander. Pat dry. Sprinkle lightly with a little vinegar and black pepper. Sandwich in very fresh bread and cut off the crusts.

SESAME EGG ROLL

*A JAPANESE-INSPIRED IDEA. AN
EGG PANCAKE IS ROLLED UP WITH
A CREAMY WATERCRESS FILLING
AND SERVED IN THICK SLICES.*

SERVES THREE TO FOUR

INGREDIENTS

  3 eggs
  1 tablespoon soy sauce
  1 tablespoon sesame seeds
  1 teaspoon sesame seed oil
  salt and freshly ground black pepper
  1 tablespoon sunflower oil
  3 ounces cream cheese with garlic
  1 bunch watercress, chopped

1 Beat the eggs with the soy sauce,
sesame seeds, sesame seed oil and
seasoning.

2 Heat the sunflower oil in a large frying
pan until quite hot, then pour in the egg
mixture, tilting the pan so it covers the
bottom. Cook until firm.

3 Allow the pancake to stand in the pan
for a few minutes, then turn out onto a
chopping board and cool completely.

4 Beat the cream cheese until soft,
season well, then mix in the chopped
watercress. Spread this over the egg
pancake, then roll it up firmly. Wrap in
plastic wrap and chill.

HOMEMADE COLESLAW

*FORGET STORE-BOUGHT COLESLAW! MAKING YOUR OWN AT HOME IS QUICK AND EASY TO DO — AND IT
TASTES FRESH, CRUNCHY AND WONDERFUL.*

SERVES FOUR TO SIX

INGREDIENTS

  ¼ firm white cabbage
  1 small onion, finely chopped
  2 celery stalks, thinly sliced
  2 carrots, coarsely grated
  1–2 teaspoons caraway seeds (optional)
  1 dessert apple, cored and chopped
    (optional)
  ½ cup walnuts, chopped (optional)
  salt and freshly ground black pepper
For the dressing
  3 tablespoons mayonnaise
  2 tablespoons light cream, half-and-
    half or plain yogurt
  1 teaspoon grated lemon rind
  salt and ground black pepper

1 Cut and discard the core from the
cabbage quarter, then shred the leaves
finely. Place in a large bowl.

2 Into the cabbage, toss the onion, celery
and carrot, plus the caraway seeds, apple
and walnuts, if using. Season well.

3 Mix the dressing ingredients together
and stir into the vegetables. Cover and
allow to stand for 2 hours, stirring
occasionally, then chill the coleslaw lightly
before serving.

MALFATTI WITH RED SAUCE

IF YOU EVER FELT DUMPLINGS
WERE A LITTLE HEAVY, TRY
MAKING THESE LIGHT ITALIAN
SPINACH AND RICOTTA MALFATTI
INSTEAD. SERVE THEM WITH A
SIMPLE TOMATO AND RED BELL
PEPPER SAUCE.

SERVES FOUR TO SIX

INGREDIENTS
   1 pound fresh leaf spinach, stems
     trimmed
   1 small onion, chopped
   1 garlic clove, crushed
   1 tablespoon olive oil
   2 cups ricotta cheese
   ⅔ cup dried bread crumbs
   ½ cup all-purpose flour
   1 teaspoon salt
   ¼ cup freshly grated Parmesan cheese
   fresh nutmeg, grated, to taste
   3 eggs, beaten
   2 tablespoons butter, melted
For the sauce
   1 large red bell pepper, chopped
   1 small red onion, chopped
   2 tablespoons olive oil
   1 can (14 ounces) tomatoes, chopped
   ⅔ cup water
   generous pinch dried oregano
   salt and freshly ground black pepper
   2 tablespoons light cream or
     half-and-half

1 Blanch the spinach in the tiniest
amount of water until it is limp, then drain
well, pressing it through a sieve with the
back of a ladle or spoon. Chop very finely.

COOK'S TIP
Quenelles are oval-shaped dumplings. To
shape the malfatti into quenelles, you
need two teaspoons. Scoop up the
mixture with one spoon, making sure it is
mounded up, then, using the other
spoon, scoop the mixture off the first
spoon, twisting the top spoon into the
bowl of the second.
   Repeat this action two or three times
until the quenelle is smooth, and then
gently knock it off onto a plate, ready
to cook.

2 Lightly fry the onion and garlic in the
oil for 5 minutes, then mix with the
spinach together with the ricotta, bread
crumbs, flour, salt, most of the Parmesan
and nutmeg.

3 Let the mixture cool, add the eggs
and melted butter, then mold into 12
small sausage shapes.

4 Meanwhile, make the sauce by lightly
sautéing the pepper and onion in the oil
for 5 minutes. Add the tomatoes, water,
oregano and seasoning. Bring to a boil,
then simmer for 5 minutes.

5 When cooked, remove from the heat
and blend to a purée in a food processor.
Return to the pan, then stir in the cream.
Check the seasoning.

6 Bring a shallow pan of salted water to a
gentle boil, drop the malfatti into it a few
at a time and poach them for about
5 minutes. Drain them well and keep
them warm.

7 Arrange the malfatti on warm plates
and drizzle with the sauce. Serve topped
with the remaining Parmesan.

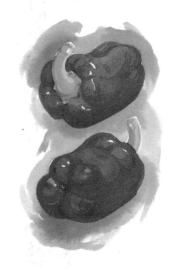

CURRIED MANGO CHUTNEY DIP

A QUICKLY MADE, TANGY AND
SPICY DIP OR DRESSING, IDEAL AS
A DIP FOR STRIPS OF PITA BREAD,
GRISSINI OR STICKS OF FRESH
CHOPPED VEGETABLES.

SERVES FOUR TO SIX

INGREDIENTS

   1 onion, chopped
   1 garlic clove, crushed
   2 tablespoons sunflower oil
   2 teaspoons mild curry powder
   8 ounces plain yogurt
   2 tablespoons mango chutney
   salt and freshly ground black pepper
   2 tablespoons chopped fresh parsley

1 Gently fry the onion and garlic in the oil for 5 minutes until they are soft. Add the curry powder and cook for another minute, then allow the mixture to cool.

2 Spoon into a food processor with the yogurt, chutney and seasoning and blend until smooth.

3 Stir in the parsley and chill before serving with a variety of vegetable crudités and strips of bread.

NUTTY MUSHROOM PÂTÉ

SPREAD THIS DELICIOUS,
MEDIUM-TEXTURED PÂTÉ ON
CHUNKS OF CRUSTY FRENCH
BREAD AND EAT WITH CRISP
LEAVES OF LETTUCE AND SWEET
LITTLE CHERRY TOMATOES.

SERVES FOUR TO SIX

INGREDIENTS

   1 onion, chopped
   1 garlic clove, crushed
   1 tablespoon sunflower oil
   2 tablespoons water
   1 tablespoon dry sherry
   1 cup chopped white mushrooms
   salt and freshly ground black pepper
   ¾ cup cashews or walnuts, chopped
   5 ounces low-fat cream cheese
   1 tablespoon soy sauce
   few dashes Worcestershire sauce
   fresh parsley, chopped, and a little
     paprika, to serve

1 Gently fry the onion and garlic in the oil for 3 minutes, then add the water, sherry and mushrooms. Cook, stirring, for about 5 minutes. Season to taste and allow to cool a little.

2 Put the mixture into a food processor with the nuts, cheese and sauces. Blend to a rough purée – do not let it become too smooth.

3 Check the seasoning, then spoon into a serving dish. Swirl the top and serve lightly chilled, sprinkled with parsley and paprika.

ANTIPASTI WITH AIOLI

FOR A SIMPLE APPETIZER MAKE A BOWL OF THE CLASSIC FRENCH/SPANISH AIOLI SERVED WITH A SELECTION OF VEGETABLES AND BREADS.

SERVES FOUR TO SIX

INGREDIENTS
  4 garlic cloves
  2 egg yolks
  ½ teaspoon salt
  freshly ground black pepper
  1¼ cups extra virgin olive oil
To serve
  red or yellow bell pepper, cut into thick
    strips
  fennel, cut into slivers
  radishes, halved if large
  white mushrooms
  broccoli florets
  grissini sticks
  French bread, thinly sliced

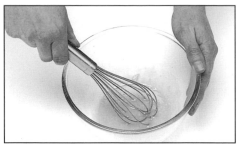

1 Crush the garlic into a bowl, then beat in the egg yolks, salt and some ground black pepper.

2 Stand the bowl on a damp cloth and slowly trickle in the oil, drop by drop, whisking with a balloon whisk until you have a thick, creamy sauce. As the sauce thickens, you can add the oil in slightly larger amounts.

3 Spoon the aioli into a bowl. Arrange the dipping food around the bowl and serve lightly chilled.

CAMEMBERT FRITTERS

THESE DEEP-FRIED CHEESES ARE QUITE SIMPLE TO DO. THEY ARE SERVED WITH A RED ONION MARMALADE, WHICH CAN BE MADE IN ADVANCE AND STORED IN THE REFRIGERATOR.

SERVES FOUR

INGREDIENTS
For the marmalade
  2 pounds red onions, sliced
  3 tablespoons sunflower oil
  3 tablespoons olive oil
  1 tablespoon coriander berries, crushed
  2 large bay leaves
  3 tablespoons granulated sugar
  6 tablespoons red wine vinegar
  2 teaspoons salt
For the cheese
  8 individual portions of Camembert
  1 egg, beaten
  1 cup dried bread crumbs, to coat
  oil, for deep-frying

1 Make the marmalade first. In a large saucepan, gently fry the onions in the oil, covered, for about 20 minutes, or until they are soft.

2 Add the remaining marmalade ingredients, stir well and cook uncovered for another 10–15 minutes, until most of the liquid has been absorbed. Cool and then set aside.

3 Prepare the cheese by first scratching the rind lightly with a fork. Dip first in egg, then in bread crumbs to coat well. Dip and coat a second time if necessary. Set on a plate.

4 Pour oil into a deep-fryer to one-third full; heat to 375°F.

5 Carefully lower the coated cheeses into the hot oil, three or four at a time, and fry until golden and crisp, about 2 minutes or less.

6 Drain well on paper towels and fry the rest, reheating the oil in between. Serve hot with some of the marmalade.

VIRTUALLY VEGETARIAN

For all those demi-vegetarians who just cannot resist fish and seafood, here is a selection of appetizers and main-course dishes that combine unusual vegetables and herbs with fish in nutritious and flavorsome ways.

WATERCRESS SOUP

SERVES FOUR

INGREDIENTS
 1 tablespoon sunflower oil
 1 tablespoon butter
 1 medium onion, finely chopped
 1 medium potato, diced
 6 ounces watercress
 1⅔ cups fish
   or vegetable stock
 1⅔ cups milk
 lemon juice
 salt and freshly ground black pepper
 sour cream, to serve (optional)

1 Heat the oil and butter in a large saucepan and fry the onion over low heat until soft but not browned. Add the potato, fry gently for 2–3 minutes and then cover and sweat for 5 minutes over low heat, stirring occasionally.

2 Strip the watercress leaves from the stalks and roughly chop the stalks.

3 Add the stock and milk to the pan, stir in the chopped stalks and season with salt and pepper. Bring to a boil and then simmer gently, partially covered, for 10–12 minutes, until the potatoes are tender. Add all but a few of the watercress leaves and simmer for 2 minutes.

4 Process the soup in a food processor or blender, and then pour into a clean saucepan and heat gently with the reserved watercress leaves. Taste when hot, add a little lemon juice and adjust the seasoning.

5 Pour the soup into warmed soup bowls and swirl in a little sour cream, if using, just before serving.

COOK'S TIP
If you leave out the sour cream, this is a low-calorie but nutritious soup, which, served with crusty bread, makes a satisfying meal.

WATERCRESS AND THREE-FISH TERRINE

THIS IS A PRETTY, DELICATE DISH, IDEAL FOR A SUMMER BUFFET PARTY OR PICNIC. SERVE WITH LEMON MAYONNAISE OR SOUR CREAM AND A WATERCRESS AND GREEN SALAD.

SERVES SIX TO EIGHT

INGREDIENTS
 1 pound monkfish, filleted
 6 ounces lemon sole, filleted
 1 egg plus 1 egg white
 3–4 tablespoons lemon juice
 4 tablespoons white bread crumbs
 1¼ cups heavy cream
 3 ounces smoked salmon
 ¾ cup roughly chopped watercress
 salt and freshly ground black pepper

1 Preheat the oven to 350°F and line a 6-cup loaf pan with parchment paper.

2 Cut the white fish into rough chunks, discarding the skin and any bones. Put the fish into a food processor. Season.

3 Process briefly and add the egg and egg white, lemon juice, bread crumbs and cream. Process to a paste. Put the mixture in a bowl. Process 5 tablespoons of the mixture with the smoked salmon. Transfer to a separate bowl. Process 5 tablespoons of the white fish mixture with the watercress.

4 Spoon half of the white fish mixture into the base of the prepared loaf pan and smooth the surface with a spatula.

5 Layer the watercress mixture, then the smoked salmon mixture and top with the remaining white fish mixture and smooth the top.

6 Lay a piece of buttered waxed paper on top of the mixture and then cover with foil. Place the loaf pan in a roasting pan half-filled with boiling water, and cook in the oven for 1¼–1½ hours. Toward the end of the cooking time the terrine will begin to rise, which indicates that it is ready.

7 Allow to cool in the pan and then turn onto a serving plate and peel away the parchment paper. Chill for 1–2 hours.

GNOCCHI WITH OYSTER MUSHROOMS

GNOCCHI MAKES AN UNUSUAL AND PLEASANT ALTERNATIVE TO PASTA. IT IS BLAND ON ITS OWN BUT BRINGS OUT THE OYSTER MUSHROOM FLAVOR IN THIS DISH AND ITS SOFT TEXTURE CONTRASTS WITH THE FIRMNESS OF THE MUSHROOMS.

SERVES FOUR (as a snack)

INGREDIENTS
   8 ounces oyster mushrooms
   1 tablespoon olive oil
   1 ounce butter, plus extra to serve
   1 medium onion, finely chopped
   1 garlic clove, crushed
   4 plum tomatoes, peeled and chopped
   3–4 tablespoons vegetable stock or
      water
   11-ounce packet plain potato gnocchi
   2 teaspoons chopped fresh parsley
   Parmesan cheese, cut in shavings,
      to serve

1 Trim the mushrooms and cut into halves or quarters, if they are large. Heat the oil in a large frying pan and fry the onion and garlic over low heat for about 4–5 minutes until softened but not browned, stirring frequently.

2 Increase the heat, add the mushrooms to the pan and sauté for about 3–4 minutes, stirring constantly.

3 Stir in the chopped tomatoes, stock or water and seasoning and then cover and simmer for about 8 minutes until the tomatoes are very soft and reduced to a pulp. Stir occasionally.

4 Cook the gnocchi in a large pan of salted boiling water for 2–3 minutes (or according to the instructions on the packet) and then drain well. Place in a large warmed serving bowl and stir in the butter and chopped parsley.

5 Pour the mushroom and tomato mixture over the top, stir briefly and sprinkle with the Parmesan cheese.

COOK'S TIP
If the mushrooms are very large, the stalks are likely to be tough, therefore they should be discarded. Always tear rather than cut oyster mushrooms.

SEAFOOD AND OYSTER MUSHROOM STARTER

THIS DISH IS A REMARKABLY QUICK TO PREPARE. IT CAN BE MADE INTO A MORE SUBSTANTIAL DISH BY STIRRING 10–12 OUNCES OF COOKED PASTA SHELLS INTO THE SAUCE AT THE END.

SERVES FOUR

INGREDIENTS
   1 tablespoon olive oil
   ½ ounce butter
   1 garlic clove, crushed
   6 ounces oyster mushrooms,
      halved or quartered
   4–6 ounces peeled shrimp
   4 ounces cooked mussels, optional
   juice of ½ lemon
   1 tablespoon medium dry sherry
   ⅔ cup heavy cream
   salt and freshly ground black pepper

1 Heat the oil and butter in a frying pan and sauté the garlic for a few minutes, then add the mushrooms. Cook over moderate heat for 4–5 minutes until soft, stirring from time to time.

2 Reduce the heat and stir in the shrimp, mussels and lemon juice. Cook for 1 minute, stirring continuously. Stir in the sherry and cook for 1 minute.

3 Add the cream and cook gently until heated through but not boiling. Taste and adjust the seasoning and then spoon into warmed serving dishes. Serve immediately with chunks of Italian bread.

CUCUMBER AND TROUT MOUSSE

THIS IS A VERY LIGHT, REFRESHING MOUSSE, MAKING THE MOST OF THE CLEAN TASTE OF CUCUMBER. SERVE IT AS AN APPETIZER OR FOR A LIGHT LUNCH WITH A GREEN SALAD. YOU COULD ALSO GARNISH WITH A CHERVIL LEAF OR A VERY THIN LEMON SLICE.

SERVES SIX

INGREDIENTS
    1 small cucumber
    2–3 smoked trout fillets,
      about 6 ounces total weight
    ½ cup sour cream
    1 tablespoon powdered gelatin
    ⅔ cup vegetable stock
    12–14 pimiento-stuffed olives, sliced
    2 tablespoons lemon juice
    1 teaspoon finely chopped fresh
      tarragon
    salt and freshly ground black pepper
    ⅔ cup heavy cream
    2 egg whites
    peeled shrimp and lemon wedges,
      to garnish
For the topping
    1 tablespoon powdered gelatin
    6 tablespoons vegetable stock

1 Lightly oil six ramekins. To prepare the topping, take one quarter of the cucumber and slice thinly. Sprinkle the gelatin over the stock, leave to soak for a few minutes and then place over a saucepan of simmering water and stir until completely dissolved.

2 Spoon a little of the gelatin mixture into each dish and arrange two or three cucumber slices on top. Put in the fridge to set. Add the remaining gelatin mixture and return to the fridge to set.

3 To make the mousse, peel and very finely dice the remaining cucumber and put in a bowl. Flake the fish, discarding the skin and any bones, and add to the cucumber. Beat in the sour cream.

4 Sprinkle the gelatin over 2 tablespoons of water in a bowl and let soak for a few minutes. Place over a pan of simmering water and stir until dissolved.

5 Heat the stock. Stir in the dissolved gelatin and let sit until cool but not set. Pour over the trout and stir in the olives, lemon juice, tarragon and seasoning.

6 Lightly whip the cream and whisk the egg whites until stiff. Fold the cream into the trout mixture, followed by the egg whites. Spoon the mousse into the ramekins, leveling the surface. Cover and chill for 1–2 hours and then unmold onto serving plates.

7 Garnish with any remaining cucumber slices together with a few peeled shrimp and some lemon wedges.

CORN <u>AND</u> SCALLOP CHOWDER

FRESH HOMEGROWN CORN IS IDEAL FOR THIS CHOWDER, ALTHOUGH CANNED OR FROZEN CORN ALSO WORKS WELL. THIS SOUP IS ALMOST A MEAL IN ITSELF AND MAKES A PERFECT LUNCH DISH.

SERVES FOUR TO SIX

INGREDIENTS
2 ears corn or 7 ounces frozen or
   canned corn
2½ cups milk
1 tablespoon butter or margarine
1 small leek or onion, chopped
2 strips bacon, finely
   chopped
1 small garlic clove, crushed
1 small green bell pepper, seeded
   and diced
1 celery stalk, chopped
1 medium potato, diced
1 tablespoon all-purpose flour
1¼ cups vegetable stock
4 scallops
4 ounces cooked fresh mussels
pinch of paprika
⅔ cup light cream or half-and-half
salt and freshly ground black pepper

1 Using a sharp knife, slice down the ears of the corn to remove the kernels. Place half of the kernels in a food processor or blender and process with a little of the milk.

2 Melt the butter or margarine in a large saucepan and gently fry the leek or onion, bacon and garlic for 4–5 minutes, until the leek is soft but not browned. Add the bell pepper, celery and potato and sweat over low heat for another 3–4 minutes, stirring frequently.

3 Stir in the flour and cook for about 1–2 minutes, until the mixture is golden and frothy. Gradually stir in the milk and corn mixture, stock, the remaining milk and corn kernels and seasoning.

4 Bring to a boil, reduce the heat to a gentle simmer and cook, partially covered, for 15–20 minutes, until the vegetables are tender.

5 Pull the corals away from the scallops and slice the white flesh into ¼-inch slices. Stir the scallops into the soup, cook for 4 minutes and then stir in the corals, mussels and paprika. Allow to heat through for a few minutes and then stir in the cream, if using. Adjust the seasoning to taste and serve.

STIR-FRIED CHINESE LEAVES <u>WITH</u> SCALLOPS

A SPEEDY STIR-FRY MADE USING SALAD VEGETABLES AND SCALLOPS. BOTH THE CHINESE RADISH AND CHINESE LEAVES HAVE A PLEASANT CRUNCHY "BITE," AND THE CHINESE LEAVES CARRY THE SAUCE.

SERVES FOUR

INGREDIENTS

10 prepared scallops
4–5 tablespoons vegetable oil
3 garlic cloves, finely chopped
½-inch piece fresh ginger, finely sliced
4–5 scallions, cut lengthwise into
   1-inch pieces
2 tablespoons medium dry sherry
½ Chinese radish (daikon), cut into
   ½-inch slices
1 Chinese cabbage, chopped
   lengthwise into thin strips
For the marinade
1 teaspoon cornstarch
1 egg white, lightly beaten
pinch of white pepper
For the sauce
1 teaspoon cornstarch
3 tablespoons oyster sauce

6 Heat another 2 tablespoons of oil in the wok, add the remaining garlic, ginger and scallions and stir-fry for 1 minute. Add the corals, stir-fry briefly and transfer to a dish.

1 Rinse the scallops and separate the corals from the white meat. Cut each scallop into 2–3 pieces and slice the corals. Place them on two dishes.

2 For the marinade, blend together the cornstarch, egg white and white pepper. Pour half over the scallops and the rest over the corals. Leave for 10 minutes.

3 To make the sauce, blend the cornstarch with 4 tablespoons of water and the oyster sauce and set aside.

4 Heat about 2 tablespoons of the oil in a wok, add half of the garlic and let it sizzle, and then add half the ginger and half of the scallions. Stir-fry for about 30 seconds and then stir in the scallops (not the corals).

5 Stir-fry for ½–1 minute until the scallops start to become opaque and then reduce the heat and add 1 tablespoon of the sherry. Cook briefly and then spoon the scallops and the cooking liquid into a bowl and set aside.

7 Heat the remaining oil and add the daikon. Stir-fry for about 30 seconds and then stir in the cabbage. Stir-fry for about 30 seconds and then add the oyster sauce mixture and about 4 tablespoons of water. Allow the cabbage to simmer briefly and then stir in the scallops and corals, together with all their liquid and cook briefly to heat through.

CAULIFLOWER, SHRIMP AND BROCCOLI TEMPURA

ALL SORTS OF VEGETABLES ARE DELICIOUS DEEP-FRIED JAPANESE-STYLE (TEMPURA). FIRM VEGETABLES, SUCH AS CAULIFLOWER AND BROCCOLI, ARE BEST BLANCHED BEFORE FRYING BUT SNOW PEAS, RED AND GREEN BELL PEPPER SLICES, AND MUSHROOMS CAN SIMPLY BE DIPPED IN THE BATTER AND FRIED.

SERVES FOUR

INGREDIENTS
½ cauliflower
10 ounces broccoli
8 raw shrimp
8 white mushrooms (optional)
sunflower or vegetable oil, for
  deep frying
lemon wedges and sprigs of cilantro,
  to garnish
soy sauce, to serve
For the batter
4 ounces all-purpose flour
pinch of salt
2 eggs, separated
¾ cup ice water
2 tablespoons sunflower or vegetable
  oil

1 Cut the cauliflower and broccoli into medium-size florets. Blanch all the florets for 1–2 minutes. Drain. Refresh under cold running water. Set aside. Peel the shrimp, but leave their tails intact. Set aside.

2 To make the batter, place the flour and salt in a bowl, blend together the egg yolks and water and stir into the flour, beating well to make a smooth batter.

3 Beat in the oil and then whisk the egg whites until stiff and fold into the batter.

4 Heat the oil for deep frying to 375°F. Coat a few of the vegetables and prawns in the batter and then fry for 2–3 minutes until lightly golden and puffy. Transfer to a plate lined with paper towels and keep warm while frying the remaining tempura.

5 Arrange the tempura on individual plates, garnish with lemon and cilantro and serve with little bowls of soy sauce.

COOK'S TIP
Try cooking other vegetables in this way, such as eggplant and zucchini, or even the young delicate leaves of cauliflower, or celery leaves.

FENNEL AND MUSSEL PROVENÇAL

INGREDIENTS
  2 large fennel bulbs
  4–4½ pounds fresh mussels in their
    shells, well scrubbed under cold
    water and beards removed
  ¾ cup water
  sprig of thyme
  1 ounce butter
  4 shallots, finely chopped
  1 garlic clove, crushed
  1 cup white wine
  2 teaspoons all-purpose flour
  ¾ cup light cream
  1 tablespoon chopped fresh parsley
  salt and freshly ground black pepper
  sprig of dill, to garnish

1 Trim the fennel and cut into slices ¼ inch thick and then cut into ½-inch sticks. Cook in a little salted water until just tender and drain.

2 Discard any mussels that are damaged or do not close. Put in a large saucepan, add the water and thyme, cover tightly, bring to the boil and cook for about 5 minutes until the mussels open, shaking occasionally.

3 Transfer the mussels to a plate and discard any that are unopened. When cool enough to handle, remove them from their shells, reserving a few in their shells for a garnish.

4 Melt the butter in a saucepan and fry the shallots and garlic for 3–4 minutes until softened but not browned. Add the fennel, fry briefly for 30–60 seconds and then stir in the wine and simmer gently until the liquid is reduced by half.

5 Blend the flour with a little extra wine or water. Add the cream, parsley and seasoning to the saucepan and heat gently. Stir in the blended flour and the mussels. Cook over low heat until the sauce thickens. Season to taste and pour into a warmed serving dish. Garnish with dill and reserved mussels in their shells.

BRAISED FENNEL WITH TOMATOES

INGREDIENTS
  3 small fennel bulbs
  2–3 tablespoons olive oil
  5–6 shallots, sliced
  2 garlic cloves, crushed
  4 tomatoes, peeled and chopped
  about ¾ cup dry white wine
  1 tablespoon chopped fresh basil or
    ½ teaspoon dried
  1½–2 ounces fresh white bread
    crumbs
  salt and freshly ground black pepper

1 Preheat the oven to 300°F. Trim the fennel bulbs and cut into slices about ½ inch thick.

2 Heat the olive oil in a large saucepan and fry the shallots and garlic for about 4–5 minutes over moderate heat until the shallots are slightly softened. Add the tomatoes, stir-fry briefly and then stir in ⅔ cup of the wine, the basil and seasoning. Bring to a boil, add the fennel, then cover and cook for 5 minutes.

3 Arrange the fennel in layers in an ovenproof dish. Pour the tomato mixture over and sprinkle the top with half the bread crumbs. Bake in the oven for about 1 hour. From time to time, press down on the crumb crust with the back of a spoon and sprinkle over another layer of bread crumbs and a little more of the wine. The crust slowly becomes golden brown and very crunchy.

Sweet Pepper Choux <u>with</u> Anchovies

The ratatouille vegetables in this dish are roasted instead of stewed, and have a wonderful aromatic flavor. Any combination of red, green or yellow bell peppers can be used. For vegetarians, omit the anchovies.

SERVES SIX

INGREDIENTS
  1¼ cups water
  4 ounces butter or margarine
  5 ounces all-purpose flour
  4 eggs
  4 ounces Gruyère or Cheddar cheese,
    finely diced
  1 teaspoon Dijon mustard
  salt
For the filling
  3 bell peppers; red, yellow and green
  1 large onion, cut into eighths
    or sixteenths
  3 tomatoes, peeled and quartered
  1 zucchini, sliced
  6 basil leaves, torn in strips
  1 garlic clove, crushed
  2 tablespoons olive oil
  about 18 black olives, pitted
  3 tablespoons red wine
  ¾ cup passata or puréed canned
    tomatoes
  2-ounce can anchovy fillets, drained
  salt and freshly ground black pepper

1 Preheat the oven to 475°F and grease six individual ovenproof dishes. To prepare the filling, halve the peppers, discard the seeds and core and cut into 1-inch chunks.

2 Place the peppers, onion, tomatoes and zucchini in a roasting pan. Add the basil, garlic and olive oil, stirring so the vegetables are well coated. Sprinkle with salt and pepper and then roast for about 25–30 minutes until the vegetables are just beginning to blacken at the edges.

3 Reduce the oven temperature to 400°F. To make the choux pastry, put the water and butter or margarine together in a large saucepan, heat until the butter melts. Remove from the heat and add all the flour immediately. Beat well with a wooden spoon for about 30 seconds until smooth. Allow to cool slightly.

4 Beat in the eggs, one at a time, and then continue beating until the mixture is thick and glossy. Stir in the cheese and mustard, then season with salt and pepper. Spoon the mixture around the sides of the prepared dishes.

5 Spoon the vegetables into a large mixing bowl, together with any juices or scrapings from the bottom of the pan. Add the olives and stir in the wine and passata or puréed tomatoes. (Or, you can stir these into the roasting pan but allow the pan to cool slightly otherwise the liquid will boil and evaporate.)

6 Divide the pepper mixture between the six dishes and arrange the drained anchovy fillets on top. Bake in the oven for about 25–35 minutes until the choux pastry is puffy and golden. Serve hot with a fresh green salad.

SAMPHIRE WITH CHILLED FISH CURRY

EVEN IF YOU'RE A BIG CURRY FAN, DON'T BE TEMPTED TO ADD TOO MUCH CURRY PASTE TO THIS DISH. YOU NEED ONLY THE MEREST HINT OF MILD CURRY PASTE SO THAT THE FLAVOR OF THE SAMPHIRE AND FISH CAN STILL BE APPRECIATED.

SERVES FOUR

INGREDIENTS

6 ounces samphire
12 ounces fresh salmon steak or fillet
12 ounces sole fillet
fish stock or water
4 ounces large peeled shrimp
1 ounce butter
1 small onion, very finely chopped
2 teaspoons mild curry paste
1–2 teaspoons apricot jam
⅔ cup sour cream
sprig of mint, to garnish (optional)

1 Trim the samphire and blanch in boiling water for about 5 minutes until tender. Drain and set aside.

2 Place the salmon and sole in a large frying pan, cover with fish stock or water and bring to the boil. Reduce the heat, cover and cook for 6–8 minutes until the fish is tender.

COOK'S TIP
As the samphire has a fresh salty tang of the sea, there is not really any need to add extra salt to this recipe.

3 Transfer the fish to a plate and when cool enough to handle, break the salmon and sole into bite-size pieces, removing any skin and bones. Place in a mixing bowl with the shrimp.

4 Melt the butter in a saucepan and gently fry the onion for 3–4 minutes until soft but not brown. Add the curry paste, cook for 30 seconds, then remove from the heat. Stir in the jam. Allow to cool and then stir in the sour cream.

5 Pour the curry cream over the fish. Arrange the samphire around the edge of a serving plate and spoon the fish into the center. Garnish with a sprig of mint.

LEEK AND MONKFISH WITH THYME SAUCE

MONKFISH IS A POPULAR FISH, THANKS TO ITS EXCELLENT FLAVOR AND FIRM TEXTURE.

SERVES FOUR

INGREDIENTS
 2 pounds monkfish, cubed
 salt and pepper
 generous ⅓ cup butter
 4 leeks, sliced
 1 tablespoon flour
 ⅔ cup fish or vegetable stock
 2 teaspoons finely chopped fresh
  thyme, plus more to garnish
 juice of 1 lemon
 ⅔ cup light cream or half-and-half
 radicchio, to garnish

1 Season the fish to taste. Melt about a third of the butter in a pan and fry the fish for a short time. Set aside. Fry the leeks in the pan with another third of the butter, until they have softened. Set aside with the fish.

2 In a saucepan, melt the rest of the butter, add the remaining butter from the pan, stir in the flour and add the stock. As the sauce begins to thicken, add the thyme and lemon juice.

3 Return the leeks and monkfish to the pan and cook gently for a few minutes. Add the cream and season to taste. Do not let the mixture boil again, or the cream will separate. Serve immediately, garnished with thyme and radicchio leaves.

FISH STEW WITH CALVADOS, PARSLEY AND DILL

THIS RUSTIC STEW HARBORS ALL SORTS OF INTERESTING FLAVORS AND WILL PLEASE AND INTRIGUE. MANY VARIETIES OF FISH CAN BE USED—JUST CHOOSE THE FRESHEST AND BEST.

SERVES FOUR

INGREDIENTS

2 pounds assorted white fish
1 tablespoon chopped parsley, plus a
  few leaves to garnish
8 ounces mushrooms
1 can (8 ounces) tomatoes
salt and pepper
2 teaspoons flour
1 tablespoon butter
2 cups cider
3 tablespoons Calvados
1 large bunch fresh dill sprigs,
  reserving 4 fronds to garnish

1 Chop the fish roughly and place it in a casserole or stewing pot with the parsley, mushrooms, tomatoes and salt and pepper to taste.

2 Preheat the oven to 350°F. Work the flour into the butter. Heat the cider and stir in the flour and butter mixture a little at a time. Cook, stirring, until liquid has thickened slightly.

3 Add the cider mixture and the remaining ingredients to the fish and mix gently. Cover and bake for about 30 minutes. Serve with garnish.

SMOKED SALMON AND DILL PASTA

THIS HAS BEEN TRIED AND TESTED AS BOTH A MAIN-DISH SALAD AND AN APPETIZER, AND THE ONLY PREFERENCE STATED WAS THAT AS A MAIN DISH YOU GOT A LARGER PORTION, SO THAT MADE IT BETTER.

SERVES TWO (as a main course)

INGREDIENTS
 salt
 3 cups pasta twists
 6 large sprigs fresh dill, chopped, plus
   more sprigs to garnish
 2 tablespoons extra virgin olive oil
 1 tablespoon white wine vinegar
 1¼ cups heavy cream
 pepper
 6 ounces smoked salmon

1 Boil the pasta in salted water until it is just cooked. Drain and run under cold water until completely cooled.

2 Make the dressing by combining all the remaining ingredients, except for the smoked salmon and reserved dill in the bowl of a food processor, and blend well. Season to taste.

3 Slice the salmon into small strips. Placed the cooled pasta and the smoked salmon in a mixing bowl. Pour the dressing on top and toss carefully. Transfer to a serving bowl and garnish with the dill sprigs.

AVOCADO AND PASTA SALAD WITH CILANTRO

SERVED AS ONE OF A VARIETY OF SALADS OR ALONE, THIS TASTY COMBINATION IS SURE TO PLEASE. THE DRESSING IS FAIRLY SHARP, YET TASTES WONDERFULLY FRESH.

SERVES FOUR

INGREDIENTS
 3¾ cups fish or vegetable stock
 1¼ cups pasta shells or bows
 4 stalks celery, finely chopped
 2 avocados, chopped
 1 clove garlic, peeled and chopped
 1 tablespoon finely chopped fresh
   cilantro, plus some whole leaves to
   garnish
 1 cup grated mature Cheddar cheese
For the dressing
 ⅔ cup extra virgin olive oil
 1 tablespoon cider vinegar
 2 tablespoons lemon juice
 grated rind of 1 lemon
 1 teaspoon French mustard
 1 tablespoon chopped fresh cilantro
 salt and pepper

1 Bring the stock to a boil, add the pasta and simmer for about 10 minutes until just cooked. Drain and cool under cold running water.

2 Mix the celery, avocados, garlic and chopped cilantro in a bowl and add the cooled pasta. Sprinkle with the grated Cheddar.

3 To make the dressing, place all the ingredients in a food processor and process until the cilantro is finely chopped. Pour over the salad and toss before serving. Garnish with cilantro.

DESSERTS AND BREADS

Here is a variety of mouthwatering sweet treats, from delicate summer fools to Christmas pudding — as well as great recipes for freshly baked cakes and crusty homemade breads.

SUMMER FRUIT GÂTEAU WITH HEARTSEASE

NO ONE COULD RESIST THE APPEAL OF LITTLE HEARTSEASE PANSIES. THIS CAKE WOULD BE LOVELY FOR A SENTIMENTAL SUMMER OCCASION IN THE GARDEN.

SERVES SIX TO EIGHT

INGREDIENTS
    16 heartsease pansy flowers
    superfine sugar, to crystallize
    2 eggs, plus white of one more for
      crystallizing
    scant ½ cup soft margarine,
      plus more to grease mold
    scant ½ cup sugar
    2 teaspoons honey
    1¼ cups self-rising flour
    ½ teaspoons baking powder
    2 tablespoons milk
    1 tablespoon rosewater
    1 tablespoon Cointreau
    confectioners' sugar, to decorate
    1 pound strawberries
    strawberry leaves, to decorate

1 Crystallize the heartsease pansies by painting them with lightly beaten egg white and sprinkling with superfine sugar. Let dry.

2 Preheat the oven to 375°F. Grease and lightly flour a ring mold. Place the soft margarine, sugar, honey, flour, baking powder, milk and 2 eggs in a large mixing bowl and beat well for 1 minute. Add the rosewater and the Cointreau and mix well.

3 Pour the mixture into the prepared pan and bake for 40 minutes. Let stand for a few minutes and then turn out onto a serving plate.

4 Sift confectioners' sugar over the cake. Fill the center of the ring with strawberries. Decorate with crystallized heartsease flowers and some strawberry leaves.

BORAGE, MINT AND LEMON BALM SORBET

BORAGE HAS SUCH A PRETTY FLOWER HEAD THAT IT IS WORTH GROWING JUST TO MAKE THIS RECIPE, AND TO FLOAT THE FLOWERS IN SUMMER DRINKS. THE SORBET ITSELF HAS A VERY REFRESHING, DELICATE TASTE, PERFECT FOR A HOT AFTERNOON.

SERVES SIX TO EIGHT

INGREDIENTS
    2 cups sugar
    2 cups water
    6 sprigs mint, plus more to decorate
    6 lemon balm leaves
    1 cup white wine
    2 tablespoons lemon juice
    borage sprigs, to decorate

1 Place the sugar and water in a saucepan with the washed herbs. Bring to a boil. Remove from the heat and add the wine. Cover and cool. Chill for several hours, then add the lemon juice. Freeze in a suitable container. As soon as the mixture begins to freeze, stir it briskly and return to the freezer. Repeat every 15 minutes for at least 3 hours, or until ready to serve.

2 To make small ice bowls, pour about ½ inch cold boiled water into small freezer-proof bowls about 2 cups in capacity, and arrange some herbs in the water. Place in the freezer. Once this has frozen, add a little more water to cover the herbs and freeze.

3 Place a small freezer-proof bowl inside each larger bowl and put a heavy weight inside, such as a metal weight from some scales. Fill with more cooled boiled water, float more herbs in this and freeze.

4 To release the ice bowls, warm the inner bowl with a small amount of very hot water and twist it out. Warm the outer bowl by standing it in very hot water for a few seconds, then tip out the ice bowl. Spoon the sorbet into the ice bowls, decorate with sprigs of mint and borage and serve.

LEMON MERINGUE BOMBE WITH MINT CHOCOLATE

THIS EASY ICE CREAM WILL CAUSE A SENSATION AT A DINNER PARTY. IT IS UNUSUAL, BUT THE MOST DELICIOUS COMBINATION OF TASTES THAT YOU CAN IMAGINE.

SERVES SIX TO EIGHT

INGREDIENTS

2 large lemons
⅔ cup granulated sugar
3 small sprigs fresh mint
⅔ cup heavy cream
2½ cups plain yogurt
2 large meringues
8 ounces good-quality mint chocolate, grated

1 Pare the rind off the lemons with a potato peeler, then squeeze them for juice. Place the lemon rind and sugar in a food processor and blend finely. Add the cream, yogurt and lemon juice and process thoroughly. Pour the mixture into a mixing bowl and add the meringues, roughly crushed.

2 Reserve one of the mint sprigs and finely chop the rest. Add to the mixture. Pour into a 1-quart glass bowl and freeze for 4 hours.

3 When the ice cream has frozen, scoop out the middle and pour in the grated mint chocolate. Replace the ice cream to cover the chocolate and refreeze.

4 To turn out, dip the bowl in very hot water for a few seconds to loosen the ice cream, then turn it upside down over the serving plate. Decorate with grated chocolate and a sprig of mint.

MINT <u>AND</u> PINK GRAPEFRUIT FOOL

MINT CAN EASILY RUN WILD IN THE HERB GARDEN; THIS IS AN EXCELLENT WAY OF USING UP AN ABUNDANT CROP.

<u>SERVES FOUR TO SIX</u>

INGREDIENTS

1 pound tart apples, peeled, cored and sliced
1 cup pink grapefruit segments
3 tablespoons honey
2 tablespoons water
6 large sprigs mint, plus more to garnish
⅔ cup heavy cream
1¼ cups custard

1 Place the apples, grapefruit, honey, water and mint in a pan, cover and simmer for 10 minutes, until soft. Leave in the pan to cool, then discard the mint. Purée the mixture in a food processor.

2 Whip the heavy cream until it forms soft peaks and fold into the custard, reserving 2 tablespoons to decorate. Carefully fold the cream into the apple and grapefruit mixture. Serve in individual glasses, chilled and decorated with swirls of cream and small sprigs of mint.

PASSION FRUIT AND ANGELICA SYLLABUB

PASSION FRUIT'S UNIQUE FRAGRANCE AND FLAVOR MAKE THIS SYLLABUB QUITE IRRESISTIBLE.

SERVES SIX

INGREDIENTS
   6 passion fruit
   1 tablespoon chopped crystallized
     angelica, plus more to decorate
   grated rind and juice of 2 limes
   ½ cup white wine
   ⅓ cup confectioners' sugar
   1¼ cups heavy cream
   ⅔ cup plain yogurt

1 Scoop out the flesh, seeds and juice of the passion fruit and divide among 6 serving dishes. Place the crystallized angelica in a food processor with the lime rind and juice and blend to a purée.

2 In a large bowl, mix the lime purée with the wine and sugar. Stir until the sugar is dissolved.

3 Whip the cream until it begins to form soft peaks and then gradually beat in the wine mixture – the cream should thicken slightly. Whisk in the yogurt.

4 Spoon the cream mixture over the passion fruit and refrigerate until ready to serve. Decorate with more crystallized angelica before serving.

JAPANESE FRUIT SALAD <u>WITH</u> MINT AND COFFEE

THIS DESSERT WAS SERVED IN A JAPANESE DEPARTMENT STORE. ALTHOUGH IT SOUNDS A LITTLE STRANGE, IT WORKS VERY WELL — THE COFFEE FLAVOUR IS EXCELLENT WITH THE FRUIT.

<u>SERVES SIX</u>

INGREDIENTS

- 12 canned lychees and the juice from the can
- 1 small fresh pineapple
- 2 large ripe pears
- 2 fresh peaches
- 12 strawberries
- 6 small sprigs of mint plus 12 extra sprigs to decorate
- 15ml/1 tbsp instant coffee granules
- 30ml/2 tbsp boiling water
- 150ml/¼ pint/⅔ cup double cream

1 Peel the fruit as necessary and chop into equal-sized pieces. Place all the fruit in a large glass bowl and pour on the lychee juice.

2 Put the mint, coffee granules and boiling water in a food processor. Blend until smooth. Add the cream and process again briefly.

3 Serve the fruit salad drained and chilled, with sprigs of mint, and the coffee sauce separately.

CLEMENTINES IN BEAUMES DE VENISE WITH GERANIUM

THE FANTASTIC BONUS OF USING THIS RECIPE IS THAT YOU HAVE HALF A BOTTLE OF BEAUMES DE VENISE LEFT OVER, WHICH SIMPLY HAS TO BE DRUNK AS A DIGESTIF.

SERVES SIX

INGREDIENTS
   10 whole clementines
   12 scented geranium leaves
   ½ bottle Muscat de Beaumes de Venise
      or other dessert wine
   orange leaves, to decorate

1 Peel the clementines and remove the pit. Place the clementines in a glass dish and pour the wine on top.

2 Add the scented geranium leaves and refrigerate overnight. Discard the leaves, then serve chilled and decorated with orange leaves. Any leftover juice can be served as a digestif.

CHOCOLATE MINT TRUFFLE FILO PARCELS

THESE EXQUISITE LITTLE PARCELS ARE UTTERLY IRRESISTIBLE. THERE WILL BE NO LEFTOVERS.

EIGHTEEN PARCELS

INGREDIENTS

1 tablespoon very finely chopped mint
¾ cup ground almonds
2 ounces semi-sweet chocolate, grated
2 dessert apples, peeled and grated
4 ounces créme fraîche or ricotta cheese
9 large sheets filo pastry
⅓ cup melted butter
1 tablespoon confectioners' sugar
1 tablespoon cocoa powder, to dust

1 Preheat the oven to 375°F. Mix the mint, almonds, chocolate, créme fraîche or ricotta cheese and grated apple in a bowl. Cut the filo pastry sheets into 3-inch squares and cover with a cloth to stop them from drying out.

2 Brush a square of filo pastry with melted butter, lay a second sheet on top, brush again, and place a spoonful of filling in the middle of the top sheet. Bring in all four corners and twist to form a purse shape. Repeat to make 18 parcels.

3 Place the filo parcels on a baking sheet, well brushed with melted butter. Bake for approximately 10 minutes. Let cool and dust with the confectioners' sugar and then with the cocoa powder.

YOGURT <u>WITH</u> APRICOTS <u>AND</u> PISTACHIOS

IF YOU ALLOW A THICK YOGURT TO DRAIN OVERNIGHT, IT BECOMES EVEN THICKER AND MORE LUSCIOUS. ADD HONEYED APRICOTS AND NUTS, AND YOU HAVE AN EXOTIC YET SIMPLE DESSERT.

SERVES FOUR

INGREDIENTS
  1 pint plain yogurt
  ⅔ cup dried apricots, snipped
  1 tablespoon honey
  orange rind, grated
  2 tablespoons unsalted pistachios,
    coarsely chopped
  ground cinnamon

VARIATION
For a simple dessert, strain the fruit, cover with yogurt and sprinkle with light brown sugar and a little mixed spice or cinnamon.

1 Place the yogurt·in a fine sieve and let it drain overnight in the fridge over a bowl.

2 Discard the whey from the yogurt. Place the apricots in a saucepan, barely cover them with water and simmer for just 3 minutes, to soften. Drain and cool, then mix with the honey.

3 Mix the yogurt with the apricots, orange rind and nuts. Spoon into sundae dishes, sprinkle with a little cinnamon and chill.

FRESH PINEAPPLE SALAD

THIS REFRESHING SALAD CAN BE PREPARED AHEAD. ORANGE FLOWER WATER IS AVAILABLE AT MIDDLE EASTERN FOOD STORES OR GOOD SUPERMARKETS.

SERVES FOUR

INGREDIENTS
  1 small ripe pineapple
  confectioners' sugar, to taste
  1 tablespoon orange flower water, or
    more if desired
  generous ½ cup fresh dates, pitted and
    quartered
  1 cup sliced fresh strawberries
  few fresh mint sprigs, to decorate

1 Cut the skin from the pineapple and, using the tip of a vegetable peeler, remove as many eyes as possible. Quarter lengthwise, remove the core, then slice.

2 Lay the pineapple in a shallow, pretty, glass bowl. Sprinkle with sugar and orange flower water.

3 Add the dates and strawberries to the pineapple, cover and chill for at least 2 hours, stirring once or twice. Serve lightly chilled, decorated with a few mint sprigs.

WALNUT AND RASPBERRY MERINGUE

MAKE SURE YOU BEAT THE EGG WHITES UNTIL STIFF TO FORM A GOOD FIRM FOAM FOR THE MERINGUE.
WHEN YOU FOLD IN THE NUTS, THE MERINGUE WILL HOLD ITS SHAPE.

SERVES FOUR TO SIX

INGREDIENTS
  3 egg whites
  few drops of fresh lemon juice
  1 cup superfine sugar
  ¾ cup walnuts, finely chopped
  ¾ cup créme fraîche or heavy cream
  few drops vanilla extract
  confectioners' sugar, to taste
  1 pound fresh raspberries

2 Whisk the egg whites in a spotlessly clean and grease-free bowl with the few drops of lemon juice. (This gives a more stable foam.)

3 When the whites are softly stiff, gradually whisk in the sugar until thick and glossy. Quickly and carefully fold in the nuts.

6 Whip the crème fraîche with the vanilla and sugar until the mixture is quite stiff.

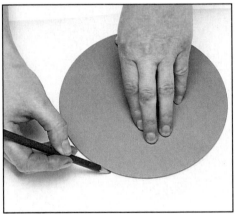

1 Preheat the oven to 325°F. Draw three 8-inch circles on non-stick parchment paper. Place the circles on baking sheets.

4 Spread or pipe the mixture onto the three paper circles. Bake for 40–50 minutes, until firm and crisp on top. This may have to be done in batches.

5 Cool on a wire rack and peel off the paper. Store in an airtight container until ready to serve.

7 Reserving a few raspberries for decoration, crush the rest and mix into the cream mixture.

8 Spread the fruit cream on the three meringues. Sandwich them together and decorate the top layer with the reserved raspberries.

COOK'S TIP
Don't waste egg whites if you have recipes that call for yolks only. They freeze very well and can be stored in batches of 3 or 4 whites at a time. In fact, when thawed, frozen egg whites make a much better foam.

RUM-BAKED BANANAS

THIS IS A QUICK, HOT DESSERT THAT BAKES IN JUST MINUTES. WHEN COOKED, BANANAS HAVE A VERY FULL FLAVOR THAT IS ENHANCED BY RUM AND ORANGE. SERVE THIS DISH WITH A DRIZZLE OF CREAM.

SERVES FOUR

INGREDIENTS

4 bananas
grated rind and juice of 1 orange
2 tablespoons dark rum
¼ cup brown sugar (optional)
generous pinch of ground ginger
fresh nutmeg, grated
3 tablespoons butter

1 Preheat the oven to 350°F. Peel the bananas and slice them into four large ramekins.

2 Spoon the orange juice and rum over the sliced bananas. Sprinkle with the sugar, if using, orange rind and spices. Dot with butter.

3 Cover the ramekins with small pieces of foil or buttered parchment paper and bake for 15 minutes. Allow to cool slightly before serving with cream or plain yogurt.

MUESLI BARS

INSTEAD OF BUYING EXPENSIVE CRUNCHY OAT BARS, BAKE YOUR OWN. THEY ARE MUCH TASTIER AND QUITE EASY TO MAKE. USE MUESLI WITH NO ADDED SUGAR FOR THE BARS.

MAKES 12-16

INGREDIENTS

4 cups muesli
5 tablespoons sunflower oil
5 tablespoons honey
1 teaspoon pumpkin pie spice
1 egg, beaten
3 tablespoons dark brown sugar
(optional)

COOK'S TIP
To make your own muesli, buy bags of flaked grains and oats at your local health food store. As these will make a large amount, you need to make sure you eat a lot of muesli! Choose jumbo oatmeal, barley flakes and wheat flakes, then add seeds, dried fruits and nuts of your choice.

1 Preheat the oven to 325°F. Grease and line a shallow baking pan about 7 × 11 inches.

2 Combine all the ingredients and spoon into the pan, patting the mixture until it is level.

3 Bake for 30–35 minutes, until light brown around the edges. Remove, cool slightly then mark into 12–16 pieces.

4 Cool completely, turn out onto a wire rack and break into the marked pieces. Store in an airtight container.

CHOCOLATE AND LEMON FROMAGE BLANC

WHAT BETTER WAY TO ADD IRON TO YOUR DIET THAN BY EATING SOME GOOD DARK CHOCOLATE? CONTRAST THE RICHNESS WITH TANGY FROMAGE BLANC.

SERVES FOUR

INGREDIENTS
   5 ounces dark chocolate
   3 tablespoons water
   1 tablespoon rum, brandy or whisky
     (optional)
   grated rind of 1 lemon
   1 cup low-fat fromage blanc
To decorate
   kumquats, sliced
   sprigs of mint

1 Break up the chocolate into a heatproof bowl. Add the water and either melt very slowly over a pan of gently simmering water or in a microwave on full power for 2–2½ minutes.

2 Stir well until smooth, then let the chocolate cool for 10 minutes. Stir in the alcohol, if using, and the lemon rind and fromage blanc.

3 Spoon into four elegant wineglasses and chill until set. Decorate with kumquats and sprigs of mint.

ORANGE, HONEY AND MINT TERRINE

VERY REFRESHING AND EASY TO MAKE, THIS IS AN IDEAL DESSERT TO SERVE AFTER A RICH MEAL, AS IT IS A GOOD PALATE CLEANSER.

SERVES SIX

INGREDIENTS
   8–10 oranges
   2½ cups fresh orange juice
   2 tablespoons honey
   4 teaspoons agar
   3 tablespoons chopped fresh mint
   mint leaves to decorate (optional)

1 Grate the rind from two oranges and set aside. Cut the peel and membrane from the oranges, then slice each one thinly, removing any seeds and saving any juice.

2 Heat the orange juice (plus any saved) with the honey, reserved rind and agar. Stir the mixture until it dissolves.

3 Pack the orange slices into a 2 pound loaf pan, sprinkling the mint in between. Slowly pour the hot orange juice on top. Tap the pan lightly so all the juice settles.

4 Chill the terrine overnight, if possible, until it is quite firm. When ready to serve, dip the pan briefly into very hot water and turn the terrine out onto a wet platter. Decorate with more mint leaves, if you wish. Serve cut into thick slices.

HALVA

The Greeks love homemade halva, which they cook in a saucepan with semolina, olive oil, sugar, honey and almonds. You can either eat it warm or let it set and cut it into slices or squares.

MAKES 12-16 PIECES

INGREDIENTS

2 cups granulated sugar
4½ cups water
2 cinnamon sticks
1 cup olive oil
3 cups semolina
¾ cup blanched almonds, 6–8 halved,
   the rest chopped
½ cup honey
ground cinnamon, to serve

1 Reserve 4 tablespoons sugar and dissolve the rest in the water over low heat, stirring occasionally.

2 Add the cinnamon sticks, bring to a boil, then simmer for 5 minutes. Cool and remove the cinnamon sticks.

3 Heat the olive oil in a large heavy-bottomed saucepan and, when it is quite hot, stir in the semolina. Cook, stirring occasionally, until the semolina turns a golden brown, then add the chopped almonds and cook for another minute or so.

4 Keep the heat low and carefully stir in the syrup. Bring the mixture to a boil, stirring constantly. When it is just smooth, remove the pan from the heat and stir in the honey.

5 Cool slightly and mix in the reserved sugar. Pour the halva into a greased and lined shallow pan, pat it down and mark into squares.

6 Sprinkle the halva lightly with ground cinnamon and place one almond half on each square. When set, cut up and serve.

RICE CONDÉ SUNDAE

*COOK A RICE PUDDING ON
TOP OF THE STOVE FOR A LIGHT,
CREAMY TEXTURE. THIS IS
PARTICULARLY GOOD SERVED
COLD AND TOPPED WITH FRUIT.*

SERVES FOUR

INGREDIENTS
⅓ cup rice
2½ cups milk
1 teaspoon vanilla extract
½ teaspoon ground cinnamon
3 tablespoons granulated sugar
To serve
Choose from: strawberries, raspberries
or blueberries
chocolate sauce
slivered toasted almonds

1 Put the rice, milk, vanilla extract,
cinnamon and sugar in a medium
saucepan. Bring to a boil, stirring
constantly, and then turn down the heat to
a gentle simmer.

2 Cook the rice for 30–40 minutes,
stirring occasionally. Add extra milk if it
reduces too quickly.

3 Make sure the grains are soft, then
remove the pan from the heat and allow
the rice to cool, stirring it occasionally.
When cool, chill the rice in the
refrigerator.

4 Just before serving, stir the rice and
spoon into four sundae dishes. Top with
fruit, chocolate sauce and almonds.

VARIATION
Milk puddings are at last enjoying a
comeback in popularity. Instead of simple
pudding rice try using a Thai fragrant or
jasmine rice for a delicious natural flavor.
For a firmer texture, an Italian Arborio rice
makes a good pudding, too.

There's no need to use a lot of high-fat
milk or cream either. A pudding made
with low-fat or even skim milk can be just
as good and is much more healthy.

PEAR AND HAZELNUT TART

IF YOU HAVE DIFFICULTY
FINDING GROUND HAZELNUTS,
GRIND YOUR OWN OR USE
GROUND ALMONDS.

SERVES SIX TO EIGHT

INGREDIENTS
   1 cup all-purpose flour
   ¾ cup whole-wheat flour
   8 tablespoons sunflower margarine
   about 3 tablespoons cold water
For the filling
   ½ cup self-rising flour
   1 cup ground hazelnuts
   1 teaspoon vanilla extract
   4 tablespoons superfine sugar
   4 tablespoons butter, softened
   2 eggs, beaten
   3 tablespoons raspberry jam
   1 can (14 ounces) pears in juice
   a few chopped hazelnuts, to decorate

1 Stir the flours together in a large mixing bowl, then rub in the margarine until the mixture resembles fine crumbs. Mix to a firm dough with the water.

2 Roll out the pastry and use it to line a 9-inch tart pan, pressing it firmly up the sides after trimming, so the pastry sits above the pan a little. Prick the base, line with waxed paper and fill with dried beans. Chill for 30 minutes.

3 Preheat the oven to 400°F. Place the pan on a baking sheet and bake blind for 20 minutes, removing the paper and beans for the last 5 minutes.

4 Meanwhile, beat all the filling ingredients together except for the jam and pears. If the mixture is a little thick, stir in some of the pear juice.

5 Reduce the oven temperature to 350°F. Spread the jam on the pastry base and spoon the filling on top.

6 Drain the pears well and arrange them cut side down in the filling. Scatter the nuts on top and bake for 30 minutes, until risen, firm and golden brown.

VARIATION
This is also good made with ground almonds and canned apricots or pineapple pieces. For chocoholics, add 2 tablespoons cocoa powder to the flour in the filling (and even to the pastry if you want to make it richer and more chocolatey), plus a little grated lemon rind. Instead of raspberry jam, you could use chocolate spread and top with the pears.

THREE-FRUITS COMPOTE

MIXING DRIED FRUITS WITH FRESH ONES MAKES A GOOD COMBINATION, ESPECIALLY IF DELICATELY FLAVORED WITH A LITTLE ORANGE FLOWER WATER.

SERVES SIX

INGREDIENTS
    1 cup dried apricots
    1 small ripe pineapple
    1 small ripe melon
    1 tablespoon orange flower water

1 Put the apricots in a saucepan with a cup water. Bring to a boil, then simmer for 5 minutes. Let cool.

2 Peel and quarter the pineapple, then cut the core from each quarter and discard. Cut the flesh into chunks.

3 Seed the melon and scoop balls from the flesh. Save any juices that fall from the fruits and add them to the apricots.

4 Stir in the orange flower water and mix all the fruits together. Pour into an attractive serving dish and chill lightly before serving.

VARIATION
A good fruit salad needn't be a boring mixture of multicolored fruits swimming in sweet syrup. Instead of the usual apple, orange and grape type of salad, give it a theme, such as red berries: Even a dish of just one fruit nicely prepared and sprinkled lightly with some sugar and fresh lemon juice can look beautiful and taste delicious. Do not use more than three fruits in a salad, so that the flavors remain distinct.

RED BERRY TART WITH LEMON CREAM FILLING

JUST RIGHT FOR WARM SUMMER DAYS, THIS TART IS BEST FILLED JUST BEFORE SERVING SO THE PASTRY REMAINS MOUTH-WATERINGLY CRISP. SELECT RED BERRIES SUCH AS STRAWBERRIES, RASPBERRIES OR RED CURRANTS.

SERVES SIX TO EIGHT

INGREDIENTS
1¼ cups all-purpose flour
¼ cup cornstarch
3 tablespoons confectioners' sugar
8 tablespoons butter
1 teaspoon vanilla extract
2 egg yolks, beaten
For the filling
8 ounces cream cheese, softened
3 tablespoons lemon curd
grated rind and juice of 1 lemon
confectioners' sugar, to sweeten (optional)
1 cup mixed red berries
3 tablespoons red currant jelly

1 Sift the flour, cornstarch and sugar together, then rub in the butter until the mixture resembles bread crumbs. This can be done in a food processor.

2 Beat the vanilla into the egg yolks, then mix into the crumbs to make a firm dough, adding cold water if necessary.

3 Roll out dough and use to line a 9-inch round tart pan, pressing the dough well up the sides after trimming. Prick the base of the pastry with a fork and allow it to rest in the refrigerator for 30 minutes.

VARIATION
There are all sorts of delightful variations to this recipe. For instance, leave out the red currant jelly and sprinkle lightly with confectioners' sugar or decorate with fresh mint leaves. Alternatively, top with sliced kiwi fruits or bananas.

4 Preheat the oven to 400°F. Line the pastry with waxed paper and weight down with dried beans. Place the pan on a baking sheet and bake for 20 minutes, removing the paper and beans for the last 5 minutes. When cooked, cool and remove the pastry shell from the pan.

5 Cream the cheese, lemon curd and lemon rind and juice, adding confectioners' sugar to sweeten, if you wish. Spread the mixture over the pastry.

6 Top the tart with the fruits. Warm the red currant jelly and drizzle it over the fruits just before serving.

AVOCADO AND LIME ICE CREAM

*THEIR RICH TEXTURE MAKES
AVOCADOS PERFECT FOR A
SMOOTH, CREAMY AND DELICIOUS
ICE CREAM.*

SERVES FOUR TO SIX

INGREDIENTS
 4 egg yolks
 1¼ cups heavy cream
 ½ cup granulated sugar
 2 ripe avocados
 grated rind of 2 limes
 juice of 1 lime
 2 egg whites
 few unsalted pistachio nuts, to serve

2 As the cream rises to the top of the pan at the point of boiling, remove it from the heat.

4 Peel and mash the avocados until they are smooth, then beat them into the custard with the lime rind and juice. Check for sweetness. Ice cream should be quite sweet before freezing, as it loses flavor when ice-cold. Add extra sugar now if you think it is needed.

5 Pour the mixture into a shallow container and freeze it until it is slushy. Beat it well once or twice as it freezes to prevent large ice crystals from forming.

1 Beat the yolks in a heatproof bowl. In a saucepan, heat the cream with the sugar, stirring it well until it dissolves.

3 Gently pour the beaten egg yolks into the scalded cream, adding them in small amounts from a height above the saucepan. This prevents the mixture from curdling. Allow the mixture to cool, stirring it occasionally, then chill.

COOK'S TIP
If you have an ice cream machine, then simply pour the mixture into the basin and switch on. There is no need to add the egg whites as air is already beaten in with the paddle.

6 Whisk the egg whites until softly stiff and fold into the ice cream. Return the mixture to the freezer and freeze until firm. Cover and label. Use within four weeks, decorated with pistachio nuts.

HONEY AND LEMON SPICY MINCEMEAT

LIKE CHRISTMAS PUDDING, MINCEMEAT IS BEST MADE A FEW WEEKS AHEAD TO ALLOW THE FLAVORS TO MATURE. THIS MIXTURE IS LIGHTER THAN MOST TRADITIONAL RECIPES.

MAKES 3 POUNDS

INGREDIENTS

1 cup shredded vegetarian suet
1½ cups currants
1 large cooking apple, coarsely grated
grated rind of 2 lemons
grated rind and juice of 1 orange
¾ cup chopped prunes
¾ cup pitted dates, chopped
1 cup raisins
1¼ cups golden raisins
1 cup flaked almonds
6 tablespoons honey
4 tablespoons brandy or rum
1 teaspoon pumpkin pie spice
½ teaspoon ground cloves or allspice

1 Mix all the ingredients together in a large mixing bowl. Cover and store in a cool place for two days, stirring the mixture occasionally.

2 Sterilize clean jam jars by placing them in a warm oven for 30 minutes. Cool, then fill with mincemeat, and seal with wax and screw tops. Label and store until required.

CINNAMON AND MOLASSES COOKIES

THE SMELL OF HOMEMADE COOKIES BAKING IS SURPASSED ONLY BY THEIR WONDERFUL TASTE! THESE COOKIES ARE SLIGHTLY STICKY, SPICY AND NUTTY.

MAKES 24

INGREDIENTS

2 tablespoons black molasses
4 tablespoons butter or margarine
1 cup all-purpose flour
¼ teaspoon baking soda
½ teaspoon ground ginger
1 teaspoon ground cinnamon
¼ cup light brown sugar
1 tablespoon ground almonds or
  hazelnuts
1 egg yolk
1 cup confectioners' sugar, sifted

1 Heat the molasses with the butter until it just begins to melt.

2 Sift the flour into a large bowl with the baking soda and spices, then stir in the sugar and almonds or hazelnuts.

3 Beat the molasses mixture briskly into the bowl together with the egg yolk and draw the ingredients together to form a firm but soft dough.

4 Roll out the dough on a lightly floured surface to a ¼-inch thickness and stamp out shapes, such as stars, hearts or circles. Re-roll the trimmings for more shapes. Place on a very lightly greased baking sheet and chill for 15 minutes.

5 Meanwhile, preheat the oven to 375°F. Prick the cookies lightly with a fork and bake them for 12–15 minutes, until just firm. Cool on wire racks to crisp up.

6 To decorate, mix the confectioners' sugar with a little lukewarm water to make it slightly runny, then drizzle it over the cookies on the wire rack.

MINCE PIES WITH ORANGE CINNAMON PASTRY

MAKES 18

INGREDIENTS

2 cups all-purpose flour
3 tablespoons confectioners' sugar
2 teaspoons ground cinnamon
10 tablespoons butter
grated rind of 1 orange
¼ cup ice-cold water
1½ cups vegetarian mincemeat
1 beaten egg, to glaze
confectioners' sugar, to dust

1 Sift together the flour, confectioners' sugar and cinnamon, then rub in the butter until it forms crumbs. (This can be done in a food processor.) Stir in the grated orange rind.

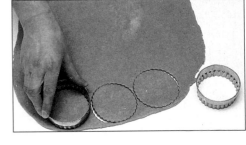

2 Mix to a firm dough with the ice-cold water. Knead lightly, then roll out to a ¼-inch thickness.

3 Using a 2½-inch round cutter, cut out 18 circles, re-rolling as necessary. Then cut out 18 smaller 2-inch circles. If desired, cut out little shapes from the center of the smaller circles.

4 Line two muffin tins with the 18 larger circles – they will fill one and a half pans. Spoon a small spoonful of mincemeat into each pastry shell and top with the smaller pastry circles, pressing the edges together lightly to seal.

5 Glaze the tops of the pies with beaten egg and leave to rest in the refrigerator for 30 minutes. Preheat the oven to 400°F.

6 Bake the pies for 15–20 minutes, until they are golden brown. Remove them to wire racks to cool. Serve just warm and dusted with confectioners' sugar.

CHRISTMAS PUDDING

DRIED PRUNES AND APRICOTS ADD AN UNUSUAL TEXTURE AND DELICIOUS FLAVOR TO THIS RECIPE.

MAKES TWO 1-QUART PUDDINGS

INGREDIENTS

5 cups fresh white bread crumbs
2 cups shredded vegetarian suet or ice-cold butter, coarsely grated
1 cup flour
1 cup brown sugar
2 teaspoons pumpkin pie spice
2½ cups currants
2½ cups raisins
1¾ cups golden raisins
1 cup pitted prunes, chopped
¾ cup dried apricots, chopped
¾ cup candied peel, chopped
¾ cup glacé cherries, washed and chopped
rind of 1 large lemon, grated
4 eggs, beaten
2 tablespoons black molasses
⅔ cup beer or milk
4 tablespoons brandy or rum

1 Grease two 1-quart pudding bowls and line the bottoms with small rounds of waxed paper.

2 Mix all the ingredients together well. If you intend to put lucky coins or tokens in the mixture, boil them first to ensure they are clean and wrap them in foil.

3 Pack the mixture into the two bowls, pushing it down lightly.

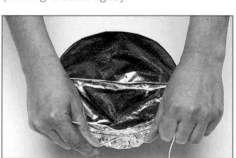

4 Cover each pudding with greased waxed paper and a double thickness of foil. Secure it around the rim with kitchen string.

5 Place two old china saucers in the base of two large saucepans. Stand the bowls on the saucers, pour boiling water to come two-thirds of the way up and boil gently for about 6 hours, checking the water level regularly and topping it up with more boiling water.

6 When cooked, cool the puddings, remove the foil and paper, then cover again to store. On Christmas Day, boil for about 2 hours and serve with brandy butter and cream or custard.

RICH CHOCOLATE CAKE

AN ATTRACTIVE ALL-IN-ONE CAKE SANDWICHED WITH A SIMPLE BUT DELICIOUS GANACHE ICING.

SERVES SIX TO EIGHT

INGREDIENTS

- 1 cup self-rising flour
- 3 tablespoons cocoa
- 1 teaspoon baking powder
- 10 tablespoons butter, softened, or sunflower margarine
- ¾ cup superfine sugar
- 3 eggs, beaten
- 2 tablespoons water

For the icing

- 1 bar (5 ounces) dark chocolate
- ⅔ cup heavy cream
- 1 teaspoon vanilla extract
- 2 tablespoons apricot or raspberry jam

1 Grease and line a deep 8-inch round cake pan. Preheat the oven to 325°F.

2 Put all the cake ingredients in a large bowl or food processor. Beat well with a wooden spoon or blend in the food processor until the mixture is smooth and creamy.

3 Spoon into the cake pan and bake for about 40–45 minutes or until risen and springy to the touch. Cool upside down on a wire rack for 15 minutes, then turn out and set aside to cool completely.

4 To make the icing, break the chocolate into a heatproof bowl and pour in the cream and vanilla extract. Melt in a microwave on full power for 2–3 minutes, or over a pan of simmering water.

5 Cool the icing, stirring it occasionally, and chill lightly until it thickens. Split the cake in half. Spread the jam on one half and half the icing on top of that.

6 Sandwich the two halves together and spread the rest of the icing on top, swirling it attractively or marking it with the tip of a table knife. Decorate as desired with candies or candles—even edible flowers can add a nice touch.

PASSION CAKE

THIS CAKE IS ASSOCIATED WITH PALM SUNDAY. THE CARROT AND BANANA GIVE IT A RICH, MOIST TEXTURE.

SERVES SIX TO EIGHT

INGREDIENTS

    1¾ cups self-rising flour
    2 teaspoons baking powder
    1 teaspoon cinnamon
    ½ teaspoon grated fresh nutmeg
    10 tablespoons butter, softened, or
      sunflower margarine
    ¾ cup brown sugar
    grated rind of 1 lemon
    2 eggs, beaten
    2 carrots, coarsely grated
    1 ripe banana, mashed
    ¾ cup raisins
    ½ cup walnuts or pecans, chopped
    2 tablespoons milk
For the frosting
    7 ounces cream cheese, softened
    3 tablespoons confectioners' sugar
    juice of 1 lemon
    grated rind of 1 orange
    6–8 walnuts, halved
    raw or brown sugar, to sprinkle

1 Line and grease a deep 8-inch cake pan. Preheat the oven to 350°F. Sift the flour, baking powder and spices into a bowl.

2 Using an electric mixer, cream the butter and sugar with the lemon rind until it is light and fluffy, then beat in the eggs. Fold in the flour mixture, then the carrots, banana, raisins, nuts and milk.

3 Spoon the mixture into the prepared pan, level the top and bake for about 1 hour, until the cake has risen and the top is springy to touch. Turn the pan upside down and let the cake cool in the pan for 30 minutes. Turn onto a wire rack.

4 When cool, split the cake in half. Cream the cheese with the confectioners' sugar, lemon juice and orange rind, then sandwich the two halves together with half of the frosting.

5 Spread the rest of the frosting on top, swirling it attractively. Decorate with the walnut halves and sprinkle with the raw or brown sugar.

CHOCOLATE AND MINT FUDGE CAKE

CHOCOLATE AND MINT ARE POPULAR PARTNERS, AND THEY BLEND WELL IN THIS UNUSUAL RECIPE. THE FRENCH HAVE BEEN USING POTATO FLOUR IN CAKES FOR YEARS. MASHED POTATOES WORK JUST AS WELL.

ONE CAKE

INGREDIENTS
  6–10 fresh mint leaves
  ¾ cup superfine sugar
  ½ cup butter, plus extra to
    grease pan
  ½ cup freshly made mashed
    potatoes
  2 ounces semisweet chocolate, melted
  1½ cups self-rising flour
  pinch of salt
  2 eggs, beaten
For the filling
  4 fresh mint leaves
  ½ cup butter
  1 cup confectioners' sugar
  2 tablespoons chocolate mint liqueur
For the topping
  1 cup butter
  ¼ cup granulated sugar
  2 tablespoons chocolate mint liqueur
  2 tablespoons water
  1½ cups confectioners' sugar
  ¼ cup cocoa powder
  pecan halves, to decorate

1 Tear the mint leaves into small pieces and mix with the superfine sugar. Leave overnight. When you use the flavored sugar, remove the leaves and discard them.

2 Preheat the oven to 400°F. Cream the butter and flavored sugar with the mashed potatoes, then add the melted chocolate. Sift in half the flour with a pinch of salt and add half the beaten eggs. Mix well, then add the remaining flour and the eggs.

3 Grease and line an 8-inch pan and add the batter. Bake for 25–30 minutes, until a skewer or pointed knife stuck into the center comes away clean.

4 Turn out onto a wire rack to cool. When cool, split into two layers.

5 Chop the mint leaves in a food processor, then add the butter and sugar. Once the cake is cool, sprinkle the chocolate mint liqueur over both halves and sandwich together with the filling.

6 Put the butter, granulated sugar, liqueur and water in a small pan. Melt the butter and sugar, then boil for 5 minutes. Sift the confectioners' sugar and cocoa and add to the butter and liqueur mixture. Beat until cool and thick. Cover the cake with this mixture, and decorate with the pecan halves.

STRAWBERRY MINT SPONGE

THIS COMBINATION OF FRUIT, MINT AND ICE CREAM IS A REAL WINNER.

ONE CAKE

INGREDIENTS
  6–10 fresh mint leaves, plus more to
    decorate
  ¾ cup superfine sugar
  ¾ cup butter, plus extra to grease pan
  1½ cups self-rising flour
  3 eggs
For the topping
  2 pints strawberry ice cream
  2½ cups heavy cream
  2 tablespoons mint liqueur
  2 cups fresh strawberries, to decorate

1 Tear the mint into pieces and mix with the sugar. Leave overnight.

2 Grease and line a deep springform cake pan. Preheat the oven to 375°F. Remove the mint from the sugar. Mix the butter and sugar together and add the flour, then the eggs. Turn the mixture into the pan.

3 Bake for 20–25 minutes, until a skewer or pointed knife inserted in the center comes away clean. Turn out onto a wire rack to cool. When cool, carefully split horizontally into two equal halves.

4 Clean the cake pan and line it with plastic wrap. Put the bottom half of the cake back in the pan. Spread on the ice cream mixture and level the top. Put on the top half of the cake and freeze for 3–4 hours.

5 Whip the cream with the mint liqueur. Remove the cake from the freezer and quickly spread a layer of whipped cream all over it, leaving a rough finish. Put the cake back into the freezer until about 10 minutes before serving. Decorate the cake with the strawberries and place fresh mint leaves on the plate around the cake.

CARROT CAKE AND GERANIUM CHEESE

AT A PINCH YOU CAN JUSTIFY CARROT CAKE AS BEING GOOD FOR YOU — AT LEAST THIS IS AN EXCUSE FOR TAKING A GOOD MANY CALORIES ON BOARD. BUT THE FLAVOR IS DEFINITELY WORTH IT.

ONE CAKE

INGREDIENTS
  2–3 scented geranium leaves
    (preferably with a lemon scent)
  2 cups confectioners' sugar
  1 cup self-rising flour
  1 teaspoon baking soda
  ½ teaspoon ground cinnamon
  ½ teaspoon ground cloves
  1 cup brown sugar
  1½ cups grated carrot
  ½ cup golden raisins
  ½ cup finely chopped preserved ginger
  ½ cup pecans
  ⅔ cup sunflower oil
  2 eggs, lightly beaten
  butter to grease tin
For the cream cheese topping
  generous ¼ cup cream cheese
  2 tablespoons softened butter
  1 teaspoon grated lemon rind

1 Put the geranium leaves, torn into medium-sized pieces, in a small bowl and mix with the confectioners' sugar. Leave in a warm place overnight for the sugar to absorb the scent of the leaves.

2 Sift the flour, baking soda and spices together. Add the brown sugar, carrots, raisins, ginger and pecans. Stir well, then add the oil and beaten eggs. Mix with an electric beater for about 5 minutes, or 10–15 minutes longer by hand.

3 Preheat the oven to 350°F. Grease a 5 x 9-inch loaf pan, line the bottom with waxed paper, and then grease the paper. Pour the batter into the pan and bake for about 1 hour. Remove the cake from the oven, let stand for a few minutes, and then turn it out onto a wire rack and let stand until cool.

4 While the cake is cooling, make the cream cheese topping. Remove the pieces of geranium leaf from the confectioners' sugar and discard them. Place the cream cheese, butter and lemon rind in a bowl. Using an electric beater or a wire whisk, gradually add the confectioners' sugar, beating well until smooth.

5 Once the cake has cooled, cover the top with the cream cheese mixture.

LAVENDER COOKIES

INSTEAD OF LAVENDER YOU CAN USE ANY OTHER FLAVORING, SUCH AS CINNAMON, LEMON, ORANGE OR MINT.

ABOUT THIRTY

INGREDIENTS
  ¾ cup butter, plus more to grease
    baking sheets
  ½ cup granulated sugar
  1 egg, beaten
  1 tablespoon dried lavender flowers
  1½ cups self-rising flour
  assorted leaves and flowers to decorate

1 Preheat the oven to 350°F. Cream the butter and sugar together, then stir in the egg. Mix in the lavender flowers and the flour.

2 Grease two baking sheets and drop spoonfuls of the mixture onto them. Bake for about 15–20 minutes, until the cookies are golden.

OATMEAL AND DATE BROWNIES

THESE BROWNIES ARE MARVELOUS FOR SPECIAL BRUNCHES OR AS A SNACK-TIME TREAT. THE SECRET OF CHEWY, MOIST BROWNIES IS NOT TO OVERCOOK THEM.

MAKES 16

INGREDIENTS

   5 ounces dark chocolate
   ¼ cup butter
   ¾ cup quick-cook oatmeal
   3 tablespoons wheat germ
   ⅓ cup milk powder
   ½ teaspoon baking powder
   ½ teaspoon salt
   ½ cup chopped walnuts
   ⅓ cup chopped dates
   ¼ cup dark brown sugar
   1 teaspoon vanilla extract
   2 eggs, beaten

1 Break the chocolate into a heatproof bowl and add the butter. Melt them either in a microwave on full power for 2 minutes, stirring once, or in a pan over very gently simmering water.

2 Cool the chocolate, stirring it occasionally. Grease and line an 8-inch square cake pan. Preheat the oven to 350°F.

3 Combine all the dry ingredients in a bowl, then beat in the melted chocolate, vanilla and eggs.

4 Pour the mixture into the prepared cake pan, level the top and bake for 20–25 minutes, until it is firm around the edges yet still soft in the center.

5 Cool the brownies in the pan, then chill them. When they are more solid, turn them out of the pan and cut into 16 squares. Store in an airtight container.

COOK'S TIP
These make a marvelous lunch box or picnic snack, and if you store them for a day or two before eating they will become even more moist and chewy.

CUT-AND-COME-AGAIN FRUITCAKE

*A RICH FRUITCAKE KEEPS
WELL FOR QUITE SOME TIME, SO
KEEP ONE ON HAND FOR WHEN
YOU FEEL LIKE A SLICE OF
SOMETHING SWEET OR GUESTS
DROP IN.*

SERVES EIGHT TO TEN

INGREDIENTS

   1 cup butter, softened, or sunflower
     margarine
   1 cup light brown sugar
   4 eggs, beaten
   1 tablespoon black molasses
   3 cups all-purpose flour
   1 teaspoon pumpkin pie spice
   3 tablespoons milk
   2 pounds mixed dried fruit (such as
     raisins, currants and cherries)
   ½ cup flaked almonds
   grated rind of 1 lemon
   a few blanched almond halves
     (optional)
   a little milk, to glaze (optional)
   2 tablespoons brandy or rum (optional)

1 Preheat the oven to 275°F. Grease and line a deep 8-inch cake pan with doubled waxed paper.

2 Cream the butter and sugar until light and fluffy. Beat the eggs with the molasses and stir into the creamed mixture.

3 Sift the flour with the spice and fold into the butter mixture, alternating it with the milk. Stir in the dried fruit, almonds and lemon rind. Spoon the mixture into the prepared pan. Dip the almond halves in a little milk and arrange them on top.

4 Bake in the lower third of the oven for about 3 hours. When cooked, the top of the cake will feel quite firm and a skewer inserted into the center will come out clean.

5 Let the cake cool for 10 minutes, then, if using the brandy or rum, make small holes in the top with a thin skewer. Slowly pour the alcohol over the cake.

6 Let the cake cool completely in the pan, then turn it out and remove the paper. Wrap it in clean waxed paper and foil or store in an airtight container for one week before cutting.

THAI RICE CAKE

*A CELEBRATION GÂTEAU MADE
FROM FRAGRANT THAI RICE
COVERED WITH A TANGY CREAM
ICING.*

SERVES EIGHT TO TEN

INGREDIENTS
    1¼ cups Thai fragrant or jasmine rice
    4½ cups milk
    ¾ cup superfine sugar
    6 cardamom pods, crushed open
    2 bay leaves
    1¼ cups heavy cream
    6 eggs, separated
For the topping
    1¼ cups heavy cream
    scant 1 cup sour cream
    1 teaspoon vanilla extract
    grated rind of 1 lemon
    3 tablespoons superfine sugar
    fresh berries and sliced star or kiwi
      fruits, to decorate

2 Return the rice to the pan with the milk, sugar, cardamom and bay leaves. Bring to a boil, then lower the heat and simmer the mixture for 20 minutes, stirring occasionally.

3 Let the mixture cool, then remove the bay leaves and any cardamom husks. Turn into a bowl. Beat in the cream and then the egg yolks. Preheat the oven to 350°F.

COOK'S TIP
This is a good cake to serve to those with a gluten allergy, as it is flour free.

4 Whisk the egg whites until they are softly stiff and fold into the rice mixture. Spoon into the prepared pan and bake for 45–50 minutes, until risen and golden brown. The center should be slightly wobbly – it will firm up as it cools.

5 Chill overnight in the pan. Turn out onto a large serving plate. Whip the heavy cream until stiff, then stir in the sour cream, vanilla extract, lemon rind and sugar.

6 Cover the top and sides of the cake with the whipped cream, swirling it attractively. Decorate with berries and sliced star or kiwi fruits.

1 Grease and line a deep 10-inch round cake pan. Boil the rice in unsalted water for 3 minutes, then drain.

APPLE AND APRICOT CRISP

LIGHTLY COOK THE FRUIT BASE FIRST FOR THE BEST RESULTS.

<u>SERVES FOUR TO SIX</u>

INGREDIENTS

   1 can (15 ounces) apricot halves in
     natural juice
   1 pound cooking apples, peeled and
     sliced
   granulated sugar, to taste (optional)
   grated rind of 1 orange
   fresh nutmeg, grated
For the topping
   1¾ cups all-purpose flour
   ½ cup oatmeal
   10 tablespoons butter or sunflower
     margarine
   ¼ cup light brown sugar
   light brown sugar, to sprinkle

1 Preheat the oven to 375°F.
Drain the apricots, reserving a little
of the juice.

2 Put the apples in a saucepan with a
little of the reserved apricot juice and
sugar to taste. Simmer for just 5 minutes
to cook the fruit lightly.

3 Transfer the apples to an ovenproof pie
dish and stir in the apricots, orange rind
and nutmeg to taste.

4 Rub the flour, oats and butter or
margarine together until they form fine
crumbs. (You can use a food processor if
you prefer.) Stir in the brown sugar.

5 Scatter the topping over the fruit,
spreading it evenly. Sprinkle with a little
light brown sugar. Bake for about
30 minutes, until golden and crisp on
top. Let cool slightly before serving.

FRENCH APPLE CAKE

WITH ITS MOIST TEXTURE AND FRUITY FLAVOR, THIS CAKE IS IDEAL AS A DESSERT ACCOMPANIED BY A LITTLE WHIPPED CREAM OR CRÈME FRAÎCHE.

SERVES SIX TO EIGHT

INGREDIENTS
    1 pound cooking apples or tart dessert
        apples, cored and chopped
    1 cup self-rising flour
    1 teaspoon baking powder
    ⅔ cup superfine sugar
    6 tablespoons milk
    ½ cup butter, melted
    3 eggs
    1 teaspoon fresh nutmeg, grated
For the topping
    6 tablespoons butter, softened, or
        sunflower margarine
    ½ cup superfine sugar
    1 teaspoon vanilla extract
    sifted confectioners' sugar, to dust

1 Preheat the oven to 325°F. Grease and line the base of a deep 9-inch round cake pan.

2 Put the apples in the prepared pan.

3 Put all the remaining cake ingredients, except 1 egg, in a bowl or food processor. Beat to a smooth batter.

4 Pour the batter over the apples in the pan, level the top, then bake for 40–45 minutes, until lightly golden.

5 Meanwhile, cream the topping ingredients together with the remaining egg. Remove the cake from the oven and spoon the topping over it.

6 Return the cake to the oven for another 20–25 minutes until it is golden brown. Cool the cake in the pan, then turn it out and finish with a light dusting of confectioners' sugar.

ZUCCHINI CROWN BREAD

ADDING GRATED ZUCCHINI AND CHEESE TO A LOAF MIXTURE WILL KEEP IT TASTING FRESHER FOR LONGER. THIS IS A GOOD LOAF TO SERVE WITH A BOWL OF SPECIAL SOUP.

SERVES EIGHT

INGREDIENTS

  1 pound zucchini, coarsely grated
  salt
  5 cups all-purpose flour
  2 packages active dry yeast
  ¼ cup freshly grated Parmesan cheese
  freshly ground black pepper
  2 tablespoons olive oil
  lukewarm water, to mix
  milk, to glaze
  sesame seeds, to garnish

1 Place the zucchini in a colander and sprinkle it lightly with salt. Let drain for 30 minutes, then pat dry.

2 Mix the flour, yeast and Parmesan together and season with black pepper.

3 Stir in the oil and zucchini and add enough lukewarm water to give you a good firm dough.

4 Knead the dough on a lightly floured surface until it is smooth, then return it to the mixing bowl, cover it with oiled plastic wrap and let rise in a warm place.

5 Meanwhile, grease and line a 9-inch round baking pan. Preheat the oven to 400°F. When the dough has doubled in size, turn it out of the bowl, punch it down and knead it lightly. Break into eight balls, rolling each one and placing it in the tin as shown. Brush the tops with milk and sprinkle with the sesame seeds.

6 Let rise again, then bake for 25 minutes or until golden brown. Cool slightly in the pan, then turn out the bread to cool more.

ROSEMARY FOCACCIA

ITALIAN FLAT BREAD IS BECOMING INCREASINGLY POPULAR AND IS VERY EASY TO MAKE USING PACKAGED BREAD MIX. ADD TRADITIONAL INGREDIENTS LIKE OLIVES AND SUN-DRIED TOMATOES.

SERVES FOUR

INGREDIENTS

  1 pound packaged white bread mix
  ¼ cup extra-virgin olive oil
  2 teaspoons dried rosemary, crushed
  8 sun-dried tomatoes, snipped
  12 black olives, pitted and chopped
  ¾ cup lukewarm water
  sea salt flakes

1 Mix the bread mix with half the oil, the rosemary, tomatoes, olives and water until it forms a firm dough.

2 Turn out the dough onto a lightly floured surface and knead thoroughly for 5 minutes. Return the dough to the mixing bowl and cover with a piece of oiled plastic wrap.

3 Let the dough rise in a warm place until it has doubled in size. Meanwhile, lightly grease two baking sheets and preheat the oven to 425°F.

4 Turn out the risen dough, punch down and knead again. Divide in two and shape into rounds. Place on the baking sheet, and punch hollows in the dough. Drizzle the remaining olive oil on top and sprinkle with salt.

5 Bake the focaccia for 12–15 minutes, until golden brown and cooked. Slide off onto wire racks to cool. Eat slightly warm.

BROWN SODA BREAD

THIS IS VERY EASY TO MAKE —
SIMPLY MIX AND BAKE — AND AN
EXCELLENT RECIPE FOR THOSE
NEW TO BREAD MAKING.

MAKES ONE 2 POUND LOAF

INGREDIENTS

   4 cups all-purpose flour
   3 cups whole-wheat flour
   2 teaspoons salt
   1 tablespoon baking soda
   4 teaspoons cream of tartar
   2 teaspoons superfine sugar
   ¼ cup butter
   3¾ cups buttermilk or skim milk
   extra whole-wheat flour, to sprinkle

1 Lightly grease a baking sheet. Preheat the oven to 375°F.

2 Sift all the dry ingredients into a large bowl, adding any bran left in the sifter back to the bowl.

3 Rub the butter into the flour mixture, then add enough buttermilk to make a soft dough. You may not need all of it, so add it cautiously.

4 Knead lightly until smooth, then transfer to the baking sheet and shape into a large round about 2 inches thick.

5 Using the floured handle of a wooden spoon, form a large cross on top of the dough. Sprinkle with a little extra whole-wheat flour.

6 Bake for 40–50 minutes, until risen and firm. Cool for 5 minutes before transferring to a wire rack to cool more.

CARDAMOM AND SAFFRON TEA LOAF

AN AROMATIC SWEET BREAD IDEAL FOR AFTERNOON TEA, OR LIGHTLY TOASTED FOR BREAKFAST.

<u>MAKES ONE 2 POUND LOAF</u>

INGREDIENTS
generous pinch of saffron strands
3 cups lukewarm milk
2 tablespoons butter
8 cups all-purpose flour
2 packages dry active yeast
3 tablespoons superfine sugar
6 cardamom pods, seeds extracted
⅔ cup raisins
2 tablespoons honey
1 egg, beaten

1 Crush the saffron into a cup containing a little of the warm milk and let soak for 5 minutes.

2 Rub the butter into the flour, then mix in the yeast, sugar and cardamom seeds (these may need rubbing to separate them). Stir in the raisins.

3 Beat the remaining milk with the honey and egg, then mix into the flour along with the saffron milk and strands, stirring well until a firm dough is formed. You may not need all the milk: it depends on the flour.

4 Turn out the dough and knead it on a lightly floured board for about 5 minutes, until smooth.

5 Return the dough to the mixing bowl, cover with oiled plastic wrap and leave in a warm place until doubled in size. This could take 1–3 hours.

VARIATION
For simplicity, leave out the saffron and cardamom and add 2 teaspoons ground cinnamon.

6 Turn the dough out onto a floured board again, punch it down, knead for 3 minutes, then shape it into a fat roll and fit it into a greased loaf pan.

7 Cover with a sheet of lightly oiled plastic wrap and let stand in a warm place until the dough begins to rise again. Preheat the oven to 400°F.

8 Bake the loaf for 25 minutes, until golden brown and firm on top. Turn out of the pan, and as the loaf cools, brush the top with honey. Slice when cool and spread with butter. The bread is also good lightly toasted.

DINNER MILK ROLLS

MAKING BREAD ESPECIALLY FOR YOUR DINNER GUESTS IS NOT ONLY A WONDERFUL GESTURE, IT IS ALSO QUITE EASY TO DO. YOU CAN VARY THE SHAPES OF THE ROLLS TOO.

MAKES 12–16

INGREDIENTS
    4 cups all-purpose flour
    2 teaspoons salt
    2 tablespoons butter
    1 package active dry yeast
    scant 2 cups lukewarm milk,
      plus cold milk, to glaze
    poppy, sesame and sunflower
      seeds or sea-salt flakes,
      to garnish

1 Sift the flour and salt into a large bowl or food processor. Rub in the butter, then mix in the yeast.

2 Mix to a firm dough with the milk, adding it cautiously if the dough is a little dry, in case you don't need it all.

3 Knead for at least 5 minutes by hand, or for 2 minutes in a food processor. Place in a bowl, cover with oiled plastic wrap and let rise until doubled in size.

4 Turn out of the bowl, punch down and knead again, then break off into 12–16 pieces and either roll each one into a round or make into fun shapes.

5 Place on a greased baking sheet, glaze the tops with extra milk and sprinkle with seeds or sea-salt flakes.

6 Let rise again while you preheat the oven to 450°F. Bake the rolls for 12 minutes or until golden brown and cooked. Cool on a wire rack. Eat the same day, as homemade bread goes stale quickly.

INDIAN PAN-FRIED BREAD

INSTEAD OF YEAST, THIS DOUGH USES BAKING SODA AS A RISING AGENT. TRADITIONAL INDIAN SPICES ADD A TASTY BITE.

MAKES ABOUT 24

INGREDIENTS
    2 cups whole-wheat flour
    2 cups all-purpose flour
    1 teaspoon salt
    1 teaspoon sugar
    2 teaspoons baking soda
    2 teaspoons cumin seeds
    2 teaspoons black mustard seeds
    1 teaspoon fennel seeds
    1 pint plain yogurt
    6 tablespoons vegetable ghee or
      clarified butter
    5 tablespoons sunflower oil

1 Mix the flours with the salt, sugar, baking soda and spices. Mix to a firm dough with the yogurt. Be sure to add the yogurt gradually, as you may not need it all.

2 If the dough is too dry, add cold water slowly until you achieve the correct consistency. Cover and chill for 2 hours.

3 Divide the dough into 24 pieces and roll each piece out to a thin round. Stack the rounds under a clean dish towel as you roll out the rest.

4 Fry the breads in the hot ghee or butter and oil, starting with one-quarter and adding more ghee or butter and oil each time you fry. Drain the breads well on paper towels and store under the dish towel. Serve with curries and raitas.

INDEX

508   *Index*

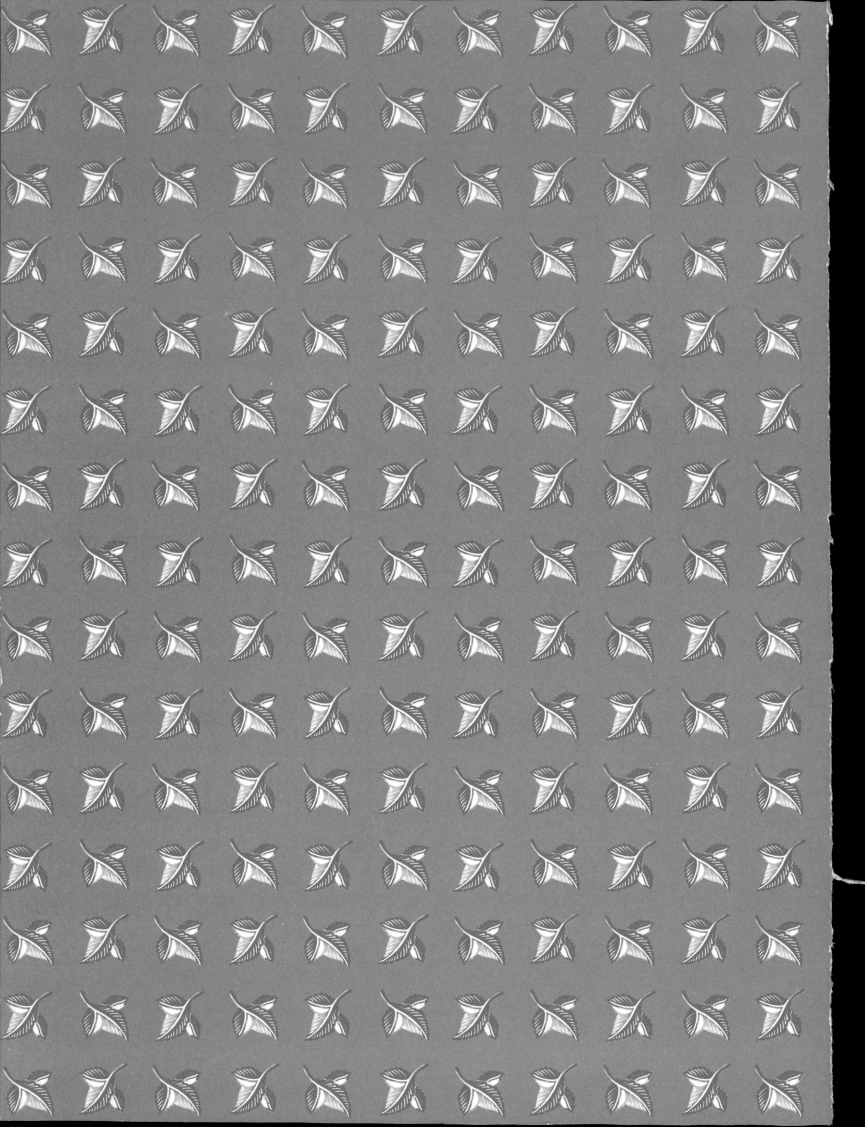